D0719302

RESEARCH IN
ACCOUNTING IN
EMERGING ECONOMIES

olume 4

Research in Accounting in Emerging Economies

R.S. Olusegun Wallace, Managing and Joint Editor
John M. Samuels, Richard J. Briston, and Shahrokh M. Saudagaran, Joint Editors

Volume 1: published as *Research in Third World Accounting* in 1991, edited by R. S. Olusegun Wallace

Volume 2: published as *Research in Third World Accounting* in 1993, edited by R. S. Olusegun Wallace

Volume 3: published in 1995, edited by R. S. Olusegun Wallace

Supplement 1: *Accounting and Development: A Special Case for Africa,* published in 1999, edited by R. S. Olusegun Wallace and Shabani Ndzinge (as guest editor)

RESEARCH IN ACCOUNTING IN EMERGING ECONOMIES

Edited by

R. S. OLUSEGUN WALLACE
Department of Accounting and MIS
College of Industrial Management
King Fahd University of Petroleum & Minerals
Dhahran, Saudi Arabia

JOHN M. SAMUELS
Department of Accounting and Finance
University of Birmingham, England

RICHARD J. BRISTON
Department of Accounting and Finance
University of Hull, England

SHAHROKH M. SAUDAGARAN
Leavey School of Business and Administration
Santa Clara University

VOLUME 4

JAI PRESS INC.
Stamford, Connecticut

100 Prospect Street
Stamford, Connecticut 06901-1640

ISBN: 1-55938-995-8

Manufactured in the United States of America

CONTENTS

INVITED REFEREES

LIST OF CONTRIBUTORS

Mohammad Abu-Nassar	Department of Accounting University of Jordan Irbid, Jordan
Kamran Ahmed	Department of Accounting and Management La Trobe University Australia
Hasan Al-Basteki	Department of Accounting University of Bahrain Bahrain
Jassim S. Al-Rumaihi	Department of Accounting and Business Finance King Fahd University of Petroleum and Minerals
David Alexander	Centre for International Accounting Research Department of Accounting and Finance University of Hull, England
Richard Briston	Centre for International Accounting Research Department of Accounting and Finance University of Hull, England
Roger Buckland	Department of Accountancy University of Aberdeen Aberdeen, Scotland

Terence E. Cooke — Department of Accounting
University of Exeter
Devon, Exeter

Turgut Çürük — University of Nigde Turkey

Joselito G. Diga — Department of Commerce
Australian National University
Canberra, Australia

Chen Feng — School of Business
University of Hong Kong
Hong Kong

Moshe Hagigi — School of Management
Boston University
Boston, MA

Graeme L. Harrison — School of Economic and Financial Studies
Macquarie University, Australia

John L. Hutagaol — Multilateral Tax Affairs Directoriate
General of Taxation Indonesia

Ranko Jelic — Centre for International Accounting Research
Department of Accounting and Finance
University of Hull, England

P. L. Joshi — Department of Accounting
College of Business Administration
University of Bahrain
Bahrain

Z. Jun Lin — Department of Accountancy and Law
Hong Kong Baptist University
Hong Kong

Jill L. McKinnon — School of Economic and Financial Studies
Macquarie University Australia

Stephen Owusu-Ansah	Department of Accounting & MIS King Fahd University of Petroleum and Minerals Dhahran, Saudi Arabia
David M. Power	Department of Accounting and Business Finance University of Dundee Dundee, Scotland
Derek Purdy	Department of Economics Faculty of Letters and Social Science
Brian A. Rutherford	Canterbury Business School The University of Kent at Canterbury Canterbury, Kent
Shahrokh M. Saudagaran	Santa Clara University Santa Clara, California
C. Donald Sinclair	Department of Accounting and Business Finance University of Dundee Dundee, Scotland
Mishiel Suwaidan	Department of Accounting Yarmouk University, Jordan
Jia Tan	Institute of Accounting Research and Education School of Management Boston University Boston, Massachussetts
Lydia Thomson	Department of Accountancy University of Aberdeen Aberdeen, Scotland
R. S. Olusegun Wallace	Department of Accounting & MIS King Fahd University of Petroleum and Minerals Dhahran, Saudi Arabia

Eng C. Wu — School of Management, Boston University, Boston, Massachussetts

Habib M. Zafarullah — School of Social Science, University of New England, Australia

PREFACE

In line with the practice of drawing attention to the accounting (broadly defined) needs, problems, and solutions in the heterogeneous group of countries often described as emerging economies, this issue of the annual brings together a collection of 14 chapters devoted to 13 of such countries. The chapters deal with accounting development, financial reporting and management accounting issues from five separate (though interrelated) regions: Pacific Rim (China); South Asia (Bangladesh, Pakistan, and India); Europe (Turkey and Czech Republic); Middle East (Bahrain, Jordan, and Saudi Arabia); and Southern Africa (Tanzania and Zimbabwe). The topics in this issue include: accounting education and certification; recent improvements in financial reporting regulation; compliance with international accounting standards in countries that have adopted them as local standards; perceptions of user needs for corporate reporting; accounting education systems; the distribution of financial ratios and budgetary control systems.

This volume, like the previous ones, presents a case for the continuing differences in the level of sophistication between accounting in emerging economies and accounting in developed countries. The recurrent theme is the nexus between accounting and culture. The first of the five-part volume is devoted to China. It contains two chapters. The first chapter by Lin and Feng examines how China is seeking to improve its accounting regulation through the adoption of internationally accepted accounting practices, especially those developed by the International Accounting Standards Committee (IASC). They suggest the change process is evolutionary and not revolutionary, and is in line with the parallel progress toward market-oriented economic reforms. The ultimate goal is to bring accounting regulation under one umbrella, instead of the present system which allows many ministerial and provincial authorities to formulate accounting regulations. The second chapter in this part is by Hagigi, Tan, and Wu. They examine how international accounting practices and factors affect Chinese accounting practices. They specifically focus on accounting for state-owned enterprises, joint ventures, and public corporations. They also explain how the financial ratios of the three types of enterprises differ among themselves and from those in the United States. The two chapters in this part are complementary and should be read together to understand the reforms underway in China.

Part II contains three chapters on accounting and financial control in South Asia. The first by Diga and Saudagaran discusses the pre-1998 reforms in financial reporting in Indonesia arising from the impact of developments in capital market. This chapter was accepted in 1997 prior to the economic crisis that Indonesia went through in 1998. As a result, this chapter has to be read in the context of pre-1998 Indonesia. Many changes have taken place since June 1998 that are not recorded in this chapter. However, the changes are not so many as to make the contents of this chapter irrelevant to Indonesia. There are several lessons to be learned by many countries that are running too fast with economic reorganization. The next chapter by Hutagaol, Harrison, and McKinnon is in a similar mold and is likely to be affected by the events of mid-1998. It was also accepted in 1997. However, this chapter is concerned with the machinery for statutory control in accounting and regulation, showcasing the Development and Financial Supervisory Board of Indonesia. This case study provides a good example of how accounting can be influenced by its historical and cultural contexts. The next chapter by Ahmed and Zaffarullah reports the results of a comparative evaluation of accounting education and certification in India, Pakistan, and Bangladesh. It looks at both university and professional education and training of accountants in the three countries, highlighting the major problems and suggesting remedial measures.

There are two chapters on Europe in Part III. The first by Çürük and Cooke considers the acceptability in Turkey of international accounting standards on the treatment of lease contracts. The authors conclude that the principles contained in IAS 17 *Accounting for Leases* are acceptable to accountants in Turkey who were respondents to the questionnaire used to elicit opinions on the acceptability of IAS 17. The second chapter by Jelic, Alexander, and Briston dwells on how a transitional economy such as the Czech Republic is coping with the regulation of accounting practices, using consolidation accounting as a case study. They argue that accounting needs to not only respond to economic changes, it also needs to play a more active role by affecting the reforms.

The five chapters in Part IV focus on the future of accounting education, budgetary control, the use of financial ratios, and financial reporting in the Middle

East. The first chapter reports on the results of a survey of the opinions of accounting experts on the strategies for enhancing accounting profession and practices in Bahrain. In chapter 9, Joshi examines the relationships among budget participation, information asymmetry, budget emphasis, budget attitude and budgetary slack, using opinions elicited from 43 managers in a large-sized company located in Bahrain. He concludes that when information asymmetry, budget participation and budget emphasis are high and budget attitude is positive, budgetary slack is low and vice versa. The implication to be drawn from the similarity of finding in this chapter with those from previous studies located in other countries is that human nature is unchanging across time and space. Chapter 10, by Al-Rumaihi, Power, and Sinclair, focuses on the cross-sectional distribution of financial ratios in Saudi Arabia and concludes that the distribution of financial ratios in Saudi Arabia exhibit major departures from normality. In chapter 11, Abu-Nassar and Rutherford report the results of a study of the differences between the information needs of some user groups (e.g., individual and institutional shareholders, bank loan officers, stockbrokers and academics) and the information provided by 96 of the 112 firms that are listed on the Amman Financial Market. Essentially, this study examines the adequacy of financial reporting from the points of view of users and preparers in Jordan. The last chapter in this part compares the voluntary disclosure behavior of two groups of companies that are differentiated by entry into the capital market for funds and concludes that companies raising capital from the equity market tend to disclose more information than those that do not raise capital from the equity market. However, the chapter concludes that free market pressures are unlikely to work as a vehicle for promoting an efficient and effective corporate financial reporting system if they are not supported by a strong regulatory framework to ensure full and consistent disclosure. It is not enough to let the companies report what they think the users want. They need to be told what are essential for them to disclose to the users.

The last part of this issue consists of two chapters. The first by Alexander, Briston, and Wallace provides a report of the process by which accounting education was changed in Tanzania. The second chapter by Owusu-Ansah looks at the degree of noncompliance with corporate disclosure requirements in Zimbabwe.

Much of the information in this issue points to the inadequacies of accounting in the countries studied from the point of view of the countries themselves and when compared with what exists in developed economies. As a result, the inadequacies of accounting in these countries provide a critical point of departure from considering whether these countries are prepared to take part in the march toward harmonization of accounting that is being propagated by the standard-setters from the developed world, the global organizations for harmonization of reporting practices (International Accounting Standards Committee and International Organization of Securities Commissions) and accounting and auditing practices (the International Federation of Accountants).

In Volume 3 of this annual, I pointed out that the task of providing an annual which carries quality chapters evaluated and accepted after a double-blind review is not easy. It is the more difficult in a world in which standards of research are rising and several specialist journals are emerging. These two trends make it difficult to have sufficient articles for the annual publication of this series; as a result, some papers accepted several months ago have had to wait for sufficient articles to be accepted before publication.

I like to acknowledge the generous sponsorship of the RAEE editorial office by King Fahd University of Petroleum and Minerals, Dhahran, Saudi Arabia.

R. S. Olusegun Wallace
Managing Editor

INTRODUCTION TO THE SERIES

This annual arose out of the belief that the international accounting literature should devote more attention to the study of the accounting problems and issues of emerging economies (developing and newly industrialized countries). The annual continues to serve as a forum for new research into accounting in developing countries as well as to publish traditional work relevant to this area.

The task of the joint editors is to continue to justify a series of publications on accounting in emerging economies. Many readers might ask why the subject of accounting in emerging economies needs to be differentiated from accounting in developed countries. Why cannot, or should not, emerging economies just adopt the same practices, the same accounting concepts and techniques as those economies that have already industrialized with either market economies or planned economies?

Some readers might point to the growing literature on international accounting, suggesting that a certain amount of this is concerned with emerging economies. This is undoubtedly true. *The International Journal of Accounting* has over the last quarter of a century published numerous articles on the accounting practices in individual countries that populate the group describable as emerging economies. Most of the international accounting literature is not, however, concerned with the particular problems of accounting in these countries, and when it is, it is not always sensitive to their special needs. Often, the normative type articles tend to imply that all that emerging economies need to do is adopt the accounting techniques of, say, either the United States or the United Kingdom and this will satisfy their needs. Such literature assumes that capital markets in emerging economies are based predominantly on a stock exchange and that this stock exchange is efficient. The accounting techniques suggested for emerging economies are those that are believed will improve the efficient allocation of scarce resources through such capital markets. This is of course desirable, but often this "international" literature ignores the particular problems of emerging economies, because the main objective of the accounting reports based on the U.K./U.S. model is to satisfy the needs of shareholders, whereas in many emerging economies few enterprises have private shareholders. Investment decisions are often not made on financial grounds, and the market for information is imperfect.

The annual concerns itself with theoretical, empirical and applied research into the macro and micro accounting issues of emerging economies. It is concerned with the relevance of international accounting standards to emerging economies.

Undoubtedly, there is a need for such international accounting standards. With global capital markets, there is a need for a company quoted on more than one stock exchange to produce accounts that are similar in substance from one country to the next. Such harmonized accounting standards are needed by users, and are also helpful to preparers of accounts. But, the current overemphasis on external reporting means that scant attention is paid to the areas of accounting which are considerably more important to emerging economies.

Further problems that many emerging economies face include:

the need to increase the number of trained accountants

the question of the level of training required: technician level or full professional level

the organization of a profession: should it cover public as well as private sector accounting?

the lack of accountability: does anybody take any notice of the accounting and audit reports produced?

inadequate management accounting: too little attention is paid to the development of effective managerial accounting systems

inadequate internal and external reporting/auditing

Some of the accounting needs in emerging economies are the same as those in industrialized countries and some are different. The annual encourages debates on such issues and assists in the development of accounting as a subject in emerging economies.

The desire of the annual is to raise the level of interest in the specific problems of accounting in emerging economies and raise the awareness of the real issues, so that accounting in these countries will not just be seen as a matter of copying what is done in industrialized countries. Through an increasing awareness of the real issues and the accounting practices advocated in it, the annual has become relevant to actual needs, and is making a real contribution to the accounting development process of emerging economies.

The editorial policy is to publish in the annual articles that comply with the foregoing.

R. S. Olusegun Wallace,
Richard J. Briston,
John M. Samuels, and
Shahrokh Saudagaran

EDITORIAL POLICY AND MANUSCRIPT SUBMISSION GUIDELINES

1. All manuscripts should be submitted to the Managing Editor, typewritten and double-spaced on A4 or 8½" by 11" white paper. Only one side of a page should be used. Margins should be set to facilitate editing, duplication and reviewer's annotation except as noted:
   a. Tables, figures and exhibits should appear on a separate page and should be reasonably interpreted without reference to the text. Each should be numbered and have a title. The author should indicate where each should be inserted in the text.
   b. Footnotes should be numbered consecutively throughout the manuscript with superscript numerals, and placed either at the foot of the relevant page or at the end of the text. Footnotes should not be used for literature citations. Instead, such citations of author's names and year of publication should be shown in parentheses in the body of the text, for example, (Atiase, 1985), (Samuels and Oliga, 1982).
2. Manuscripts should include a cover page with the author's name and affiliation.
3. Manuscripts should include on a separate lead page, a nonmathematical 150-250 word abstract of research question(s), method(s) and major

conclusions. The author's name and affiliation should not appear in the abstract.

4. In order to be assured of an anonymous review, authors should not identify themselves directly or indirectly. Reference to unpublished working papers and dissertations (or theses) should be avoided. If necessary, authors may indicate that the reference is being withheld for the reasons cited above. Authors should submit four copies of any and all research instruments which would assist the evaluation of manuscripts but are not expected to be published along with the text.
5. Topical headings and subheadings should be used. Main headings in the manuscript should be centered and secondary headings should be flush with the left-hand margin. For a helpful guide to usage and style, refer to *The Elements of Style* by William Strunk, Jr. and E. B. White.
6. Manuscripts must include a list of references which contain only those works actually cited, giving all the data necessary for unambiguous identification. For a guide to the preparation of references, see *A Manual for Writers of Term Papers, Theses and Dissertations* by Kate L. Turabian.
7. Manuscripts under review by other publications should not be submitted just as manuscripts submitted to us for consideration will be assumed to be firmly submitted on a "first refusal" basis. Complete reports of research presented at a national or regional conference of a professional association (e.g., African Accounting Council, British and American Accounting Associations, and so on) and "State of the Art" papers are acceptable.
8. Each manuscript submitted is subject to the following review process:
   a. The paper is reviewed by the Managing Editor for general suitability for this publication.
   b. For those that are judged suitable, at least two reviewers are selected and a double blind review process takes place.
   c. Using the recommendations of the reviewers, the Managing Editor will decide whether the particular manuscript should be accepted as it is, revised, or rejected for publication.

Deviations may occur from the general process outlined above in specific cases. Where revision is recommended, the revised manuscript may have to undergo another round of the review process.

9. Although initial submission should be on paper, the authors of accepted articles will be expected to submit the final version of their manuscripts both on paper and on a double (low) density or high density (preferably high density) diskette. Authors will receive more detailed instructions for electronic submission upon notification of acceptance for publication.
10. Each author will be provided with one complete volume of the publication in which their article appears and each leading author will receive twenty-five (25) offprints of the article.

11. Four copies of each manuscript should be submitted to R.S. Olusegun Wallace, Managing Editor, *Research in Accounting in Emerging Economies*, King Fahd University of Petroleum and Minerals, KFUPM Box 1995, Dhahran 31261, Saudi Arabia, with a submission fee of 30 pounds sterling drawn on a UK bank.

PART I

ACCOUNTING IN THE FAR EAST: CHINA

TOWARD INTERNATIONALLY ACCEPTED ACCOUNTING PRACTICES: IMPROVEMENT OF CHINESE ACCOUNTING REGULATIONS

Z. Jun Lin and Chen Feng

ABSTRACT

This chapter reports on the developments of Chinese accounting regulations with a focus on most recent efforts in revamping the Chinese accounting regulations since 1993. Significant changes in Chinese accounting regulations and accounting practices have taken place. These changes have stemmed from China's economic reforms to shift the original centrally planned economy to a market-oriented economy. Reform of accounting regulations took a lead in the internationalization drive of Chinese accounting. Remarkable progress has been made in redesigning accounting regulations to enhance the understandability and comparability of Chinese accounting information with respect to the internationally accepted accounting practices. Respectively, the systematic structure, the recent changes and improvements, as well as the prospect of future development of the Chinese accounting regulations are examined in this chapter.

Research in Accounting in Emerging Economies, Volume 4, pages 3-15.

ISBN: 1-55938-995-8

INTRODUCTION

In recent years, China has experienced the most rapid economic development in the world. The booming Chinese economy is very attractive for international investors due to its great potential and its huge domestic market. But many international investors are hesitant to move into the Chinese market at the moment. One of the major hurdles deterring the move is the very different nature of Chinese accounting systems which few foreigners can understand and effectively utilize. Since accounting is an important business language that facilitates capital flows, the poor Chinese accounting systems have tended to hamper the growth of economic and business exchanges between China and the rest of the world. However, there was a fundamental change in Chinese accounting in early 1990s. New accounting regulations and accounting systems were introduced into the country which have remarkably reduced the differences between Chinese accounting and internationally accepted accounting practices (Ge and Lin 1993). Such changes should be of great interest to the international business community.

Comparable and useful accounting information is vital for various economic decisions. The promotion of uniformity and comparability of accounting practices through a standardization of accounting policy has long been a common practice in most countries (May and Sundem 1976; Byington and Sutton 1991). Most research agrees that the development of standardizing accounting policy will contribute to the improvement of accounting practices in any given country (Bromwich and Hopwood 1983; Puxty et al., 1987; Gray and Roberts 1991; Warnock 1992).

In China, standardized accounting policy is in the form of government accounting regulations. After the founding of the People's Republic in 1949, Chinese government continuously stipulated mandatory accounting regulations to accommodate the needs of the government's economic and financial policies. Governments exercised a rigid administration in formulating accounting regulations and controlling accounting treatments in all economic entities. Apparently, Chinese accounting practices have long been quite different from those of most other countries (industrial countries in particular) in the world.

Significant changes have taken place in Chinese accounting as China moved toward a market-oriented economy in the past decade. Particularly, Chinese accounting regulations have changed dramatically resulting from the ambitious economic reforms in the country. The recent development of the accounting regulations has not only facilitated the economic changes in China, but has also improved the understandability and comparability of Chinese accounting with respect to the internationally accepted accounting practices (Lin 1988a; Lefebvre and Lin 1990; Fang and Tang 1991). Particularly, Chinese government revamped the accounting systems through the introduction and implementation of a set of new national accounting regulations in late 1993. This experimentation is definitely a significant step forward in moving Chinese accounting towards the accounting practices prevailing in most of the industrialized countries.

This study will highlight the evolution of Chinese accounting regulations. It commences with a description of the existing framework of the accounting regulations in China. The recent developments of Chinese accounting regulations are delineated with an emphasis upon their impact on the changes in Chinese accounting. Some remaining problems in Chinese accounting regulations and the prospective solutions are discussed. Finally, a brief conclusion ends the chapter.

STRUCTURE OF CHINESE ACCOUNTING REGULATIONS

China adopted a formal-Soviet style, highly centralized economic system when the communist party came to power in 1949. The state maintained strict economic planning and administrative control over all segments of the economy. In conjunction with a centrally planned economic system, accounting practices were rigidly administered by the central authorities. The primary objective of accounting regulations was to direct accounting work to carry out a bookkeeping function for the state's treasury and supply necessary accounting and other economic data for formulation, supervision, extraction and analysis of various state planning and controls. Centrally regulated and detailed accounting policies and rules served those needs.

Many government authorities have been involved in setting detailed and mandatory accounting regulations in the early period of China's socialist economy. Thus Chinese accounting regulations were originally developed separately by varied business ownerships and by different types of industry or operation pattern. However, as authorized by the Accounting Act of the People's Republic of China of 1985, the State Ministry of Finance is responsible for establishing national accounting regulations for all businesses, governments, and other nonprofit organizations across the country. In particular, the Administration Bureau of Accounting Affairs (called the Bureau of Accounting Regulations before 1981), a division of the Ministry of Finance, is the leading accounting policymaking body in China. It has the authority to formulate and enforce national accounting regulations and to interpret or amend the existing accounting regulations.

The backbone of Chinese accounting regulations was the so-called *Uniform Accounting System for the State-owned Industrial Enterprises* (UAS). The regulation stipulates: (1) the uniform Chart of Ledger Accounts (specifying the general ledger and sub-ledger accounts to be used by all state-owned industrial enterprises); (2) the basic types or formats of financial reports (including specification of all line items of the financial statements); (3) the rudimentary procedures of bookkeeping and financial reporting; (4) the guidelines for application of designated ledger accounts for the accumulation of transaction data; and (5) other requirements regarding the administration of accounting affairs (such as the organizational structure, staffing, documentation of the accounting process, the legal responsibility of accountants, and so on). The UAS is highly uniform and extremely detailed in most technical aspects.

Besides the UAS, there concurrently exist numerous sets of supplementary accounting regulations for specific industry and business ownership. Some supplementary regulations are set by the State Ministry of Finance, while most of the others are set by various central authorities. For example, several ministerial authorities in the central government were authorized to formulate the accounting regulations for industries such as commerce, railways, post and telecommunications, manufacturing of heavy equipment, light industrial goods, transportation, textile, chemistry, capital construction, banking and financial institutions, etc. These subsets of accounting regulations, being as detailed as the UAS, are more industry-specified aiming at facilitating the economic planning and control by the related ministerial authorities. In addition, owing to an imbalance in economic and social developments, the provincial governments (through the Bureau of Finance in each province) are allowed to formulate certain supplementary regulations on accounting and financial reporting applicable to enterprises under their jurisdictions. Those supplementary accounting regulations incorporate the specific economic and financial policies in individual provincial jurisdictions. They are usually mandatory as well. In theory, all of the sub- and supplementary regulations should be consistent with the UAS.

Hence, Chinese accounting regulations form a complex system. This system consists of the Accounting Act, the UAS, the industry/business-ownership specified sub-regulations, and the supplementations set by the provincial authorities. Figure 1 demonstrates the structure of accounting regulations in China.

ACCOUNTING REGULATIONS FOR FOREIGN-AFFILIATED BUSINESSES

Changes were initiated in Chinese accounting regulations in the course of China's economic reforms with the goal of moving toward a harmonization with the internationally accepted accounting practices. However, such changes are from an evolutionary rather than a revolutionary process. The motive forces of the changes stem from the development of a market-oriented economy in the country.

At the beginning of the 1980s, economic reforms aimed at decentralization of economic planning and administration resulted in a diversified economy in China. Various ministerial and provincial authorities gained substantial autonomy in economic planning and control. However, the state intended to retain the then planned economic system and was not ready to relinquish the administration of accounting regulations. In addition, as the economy became significantly diversified, a need to enhance the state's economic supervision or control was emphasized. Thus, Chinese government introduced the Accounting Act in 1985

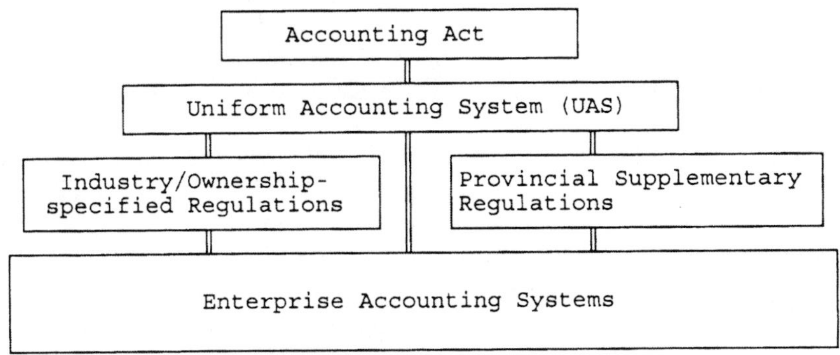

Figure 1. Structure of Chinese Accounting Regulations

as an effort to strengthen the accounting controls at the macroeconomic level. The new Accounting Act not only legalized the state's control of accounting processes but also reinforced the need for a centralized administration of accounting work. It delegates a legal endorsement of the authority of the UAS. The Accounting Act explicitly states that the State Ministry of Finance is the ultimate authority for the establishment of the national accounting regulations, and that other ministerial or provincial authorities, with the consent of the Ministry of Finance, may formulate certain industry-specified or supplementary accounting regulations for their own jurisdiction (Article 25, The Accounting Act 1985). Obviously, accounting regulations at that time were leaning more toward a centralized rather than a decentralized administration. Such an attempt was a deviation from the designated goals of the economic reforms.

The first turning point in the significant changes of Chinese accounting regulations was related to the inflows of foreign capital. Resulting from the "open-to-outside-world" policy adopted by the Chinese government, foreign investments mainly in the form of joint ventures with Chinese and foreign capital mushroomed in the country in the early 1980s. However, the UAS, being designed for the state-owned enterprises, was difficult to apply to the new business pattern. The State Ministry of Finance had to formulate a draft of *Accounting Regulation for the Joint Ventures with Chinese and Foreign Investments* (ARFJV) in 1983 which was officially issued and implemented in 1985 as a part of Chinese government's efforts to create a favorable investment environment to attract foreign capital.

Technically, the ARFJV intends to follow the internationally accepted accounting practices in terms of the Chinese economic conditions. The ARFJV laid out requirements on basic types or formats of accounting records and statements as well as accounting procedures on transactions relating to the joint venture with foreign investments. Those requirements were substantially different from the provisions in the UAS. Especially, the ARFJV has incorporated most of the internationally accepted accounting principles with a major exception of the "Conservatism" (Prudence) accounting convention and certain specific provisions for asset valuation or operating expense accounts (Lefebvre and Lin 1990). Subject to an artificially stabilized price system and a restrictive adoption of the actual (historical) cost accounting principle, no allowances or reservations were permitted for any possible loss in Chinese business (such as provision for bad debts, inventory write-off, exchange fluctuations or contingent operating losses, and so forth). All losses could only be recognized when they actually occur. Nevertheless, the ARFJV, overall, is fairly close to the internationally accepted accounting practices (International Accounting Standards in particular). It has made a considerable contribution to the internationalization process of Chinese accounting in the past years.

According to the Law of People's Republic of China on the Joint Ventures Using Chinese and Foreign Investments and the Income Tax Law of People's Republic of China for the Joint Ventures with Chinese and Foreign Investments, all joint ventures within Chinese territory must comply with the ARFJV. However, the joint ventures are allowed to prepare a secondary set of financial statements in terms of foreign GAAP for particular users abroad so long as the foreign partners solely bear the costs. The application of the ARFJV in the country, however, is relatively limited because the vast majority of the state-owned enterprises have to comply with the UAS instead of the ARFJV.

Since the mid 1980s, economic reforms have made remarkable progress with more liberal economic policies being adopted by Chinese government. For example, various forms of cooperation or business association with foreign capital other than the joint ventures emerged. The government also withdrew the original requirement of a majority holding of equity by Chinese partners in the foreign-capital affiliated businesses. Foreign investors were encouraged to increase their equity-holding in business. As a result, foreign-capital dominated or exclusive foreign-capital businesses increased dramatically. Yet, their accounting work and financial statements were significantly diversified due to a lack of specified accounting regulations or standards. In order to ensure that the taxation and other administrative authorities can obtain comparable accounting information and to update the ARFJV with needed solutions for emerging new accounting issues in practice, the State Ministry of Finance stipulated a new set of Accounting Regulations for Business Enterprises with Foreign Investments (ARFFI) to replace the ARFJV in early 1992. The new set of accounting regulations is an attempt to provide minimum uniform guidelines for harmonizing the diverse accounting practices adopted by various types of foreign-capital affiliated business in China. The ARFFI, technically similar to the ARFJV in most aspects, has made certain significant changes. A series of new provisions for bad-debt allowance or contingent liabilities (which must be consented to by related government authorities), currency exchange adjustments, and consolidation requirements are introduced. In addition, the information requirements for the state's economic planning and control have been relatively reduced. As a result, the ARFFI not only has a broader applicability to all types of foreign-capital-affiliated businesses operating in China, but it also takes a further step forward in improving the conformity with the internationally accepted accounting practices.

In June 1992, another set of regulations, Accounting Regulations for Enterprises Experimenting the Share-capital System (ARFSCE), was jointly issued by the State Ministry of Finance and the State Commission on Economic Structure Reforms. This set of accounting regulations is designed to accommodate the recent experimentation of the share-capital (stock company) system in China. As the experiment has become a most favorable endeavor in the new wave of Chinese economic reforms, many state-owned enterprises have adopted (or intend to adopt) the share-capital system with shareholders consisting of the state, other entities, individuals (including employees and public investors), and/or foreign investors. Hence, accounting systems of the share-capital companies had to be restructured as the UAS was no longer applicable or relevant to the newly introduced capitalist-style business pattern. Apparently, the ARFSCE (amended in 1998) is a close duplication of the ARFJV (now the ARFFI). It incorporates many provisions on accounting transactions dealing with stock equity, capital assessment, asset valuation, liability recognition, and income determination and dividend distribution. Most of them are modelled after the internationally accepted practices. Although this regulation is on an experimental basis, its implication is significant since it represents an official extension of the internationally accepted accounting practices to the state-owned stock companies in China.

NEW NATIONAL ACCOUNTING REGULATIONS

Despite the issuance of those newly developed accounting regulations, the UAS remains the official accounting regulation to be followed by the majority of state-owned enterprises, although the State Ministry of Finance has made some amendments or supplementary provisions to accommodate economic changes on a piecemeal basis. However, there has been a mounting demand for a reform of the UAS since the late 1980s. Criticisms against the UAS have been voiced by an increasing number of accounting academics and practitioners. They argued that the UAS was over-emphasized on the state's economic planning and control at the expense of the information needs of the enterprises' other internal and external users (e.g., management, investors, creditors, and other stakeholders). The authoritativeness of the UAS has long been overstated and many provisions or rules in the UAS were exposed to unnecessary fluctuations associated with frequent changes in the government's specific economic and financial policies. In addition, there were considerable inconsistencies in the provisions or rules in the UAS and a variety of other sets of industry-specified or supplementary accounting regulations. All of the deficiencies mentioned above have inevitably resulted in inconsistent accounting information over different time periods and incomparability among varied economic entities (Yian 1992).

In pace with the progress of economic reforms, Chinese accountants have further realized that a thorough revamp of the accounting systems for the state-owned business is badly needed. Many have contended that the state should produce certain general accounting guidelines or standards in response to the needs of the economy instead of the all-inclusive and detailed set of rules for enterprises, because the rigorous provisions for charts of ledger accounts, itemized formats of financial statements, and highly restrictive accounting treatments have become inapplicable in today's diversified economic reality in China. Others argued that the procedure for setting accounting regulations deserves a serious overhaul, such that: (1) a more independent and widely represented accounting policymaking (standard-setting) body, instead of the state's ministerial authorities, should be created to ensure accounting regulations would reflect the information needs of all interested parties; and (2) a conceptual framework should be developed for setting accounting regulations in order to reduce or eliminate inconsistency in the regulations (Ge 1992).

Despite serious resistance at the beginning, those proposals were gradually recognized and accepted by the Chinese accounting profession and the government authority in charge of accounting affairs. In the late 1980s, the redesign of the UAS became a high priority on the agenda of accounting reforms. In addition, the Accounting Society of China (ASC), the leading national accounting association comprising accounting administrators, practitioners, and educators, has initiated concrete efforts to study the conceptual issues relating to setting accounting regulations. In 1989, the Study Group on Accounting Principles and Standards was created by the ASC with a mandate to study and issue the non-binding Recommendations on Financial Accounting Standards for Business Enterprises. The first six recommendation projects have been planned for 1991-1995, and they are:

(1) The Qualitative Requirements of Accounting Information;
(2) The Truthfulness of Accounting Information;
(3) Depreciation Accounting for Fixed Assets;
(4) Accounting for Currency Transaction;
(5) Off-Financial-Statements Disclosure of Supplementary Information on Price Changes; and
(6) Accounting Issues under the Share-capital System.

These study projects, similar to the conceptual framework studies in many western countries, would identify and recommend a series of basic accounting principles or guidelines for setting accounting regulations in China in the future.

In addition, the demand for replacing the UAS with less restrictive accounting standards (similar to that in the west) has also been accepted by the Administration Bureau of Accounting Affairs in the State Ministry of Finance. Since the end of the 1980s, substantial efforts have been devoted to developing a set of general accounting standards applicable to all economic entities across the country (Jiang 1992). After several years of discussion and preparation, the State Ministry of Finance officially issued the Accounting Standards for Business Enterprises on December 3, 1992, which became effective on July 1, 1993.

The issuance of new accounting standards indicates significant changes in Chinese accounting. It represents an official effort to revamp, in terms of the internationally accepted practices, the accounting systems for the state-owned enterprises. In addition, as a uniform set of national accounting standards applicable to all economic entities, it is a substantial effort to harmonize the accounting regulations for all industries and business patterns including state-owned and other business ownership in the country. The newly stipulated guidelines for both accounting measurement and disclosure (including the formats of financial statements) are remarkably similar to the prevailing practices in the western world. As well, the newest set of national accounting standards provides a better balance for the information needs of enterprises' varied stakeholders and incorporates the International Accounting Standards to a maximum extent. In addition, 13 new industrial accounting regulations have been issued by the State Ministry of Finance as the supplements to the Accounting Standards for Business Enterprises.[1] As a result, all of the state-owned enterprises have started to switch their accounting systems to the new models stimulated by the Accounting Standards and related accounting regulations since the latter part of 1993. It is believed that, after the implementation, the new accounting standards and regulations have dramatically enhanced the understandability and comparability of Chinese accounting practices, domestically and internationally.

REMAINING PROBLEMS AND PROSPECTIVE SOLUTIONS

There have been dramatic improvements in Chinese accounting regulations in recent years. However, a noticeable gap remains between the Chinese practices and the internationally accepted practices. The Chinese government authorities and accounting profession have contemplated additional changes to improve the accounting regulations and practices in the country in the near future.

For instance, a more specific effort will be made to harmonize the accounting regulations within the country. As mentioned earlier, there concurrently exist various sets of national accounting regulations and sub-regulations for different business ownerships or industries in the country, and inconsistency among them is substantial.[2] Even among those newly introduced and implemented accounting regulations (i.e, ARFFI, ARFSCE, and so forth), as well as the 13 new industrial accounting regulations, noticeable variances remain. Such a great variety of accounting regulations and their varied contents may/have result(ed) in considerable inconsistency and diversified accounting practices across the country. Due to the existence of so many supplementary regulations or provisions, even the uniform national accounting regulations have frequently been overridden. Hence, many Chinese accountants have argued that the current state of coexistence of numerous national accounting regulations and other industry-specified or provincial supplementary regulations should be terminated (Ge 1992).

A goal of developing only one set of nation-wide accounting regulations has been initiated by the Chinese accounting authority. The justification of allowing other ministerial or provincial authorities to formulate accounting regulations is under reexamination. At present, substantial efforts are being devoted to reconcile or reduce the inconsistency or discrepancy among the various sets of accounting regulations. More recently, the Administration Bureau of Accounting Affairs under the State Ministry of Finance started a new project since 1997 to establish about 30 specific accounting standards dealing with major accounting transactions as an attempt to replace all other existing industry-specified accounting regulations (Lin et al. 1998).[3] This move dramatically promotes the consistency and comparability of accounting information across the country.

In addition, improvement of the technical process in setting accounting regulations or standards receives further attention. A series of possible changes in the format and content of accounting regulations or standards are under consideration. It is recognized that the traditional format of Chinese accounting regulations (i.e., focusing mainly on disclosure and presentation aspects such as specifying the chart of ledger accounts and the stringently itemized formats of financial statements) is not an effective way to direct accounting work to provide useful information for external users other than government authorities. A uniform chart of ledger accounts and accounting reports could not be applicable to all entities in varied industries with diversified business conditions. The changing economic environments will frequently make the pre-determined chart of ledger accounts or itemized formats of financial statements irrelevant or obsolete. Thus, the future Chinese accounting regulations or standards should be based on major transactions or practical issues. In particular, the measurement and recognition issues will be emphasized to warrant a consistent treatment for all business entities. Such types of regulations or standards will place an emphasis on consistent and comparable accounting treatments in substance over form and enhance the comparability of accounting information in all segments of the economy.

Another direction of future development is toward the increasing study of the conceptual framework for setting accounting standards or regulations. As indicated by past experience, the lack of theoretical justification has resulted not only in inconsistency among individual provisions or rules in Chinese accounting regulations but also in some unnecessary misinterpretation or misapplication in practice.[4] To overcome this problem, Chinese accounting regulatory authority has decided that the necessary theoretical reasoning will be incorporated for the recommended procedures in each new accounting standard in the future. This is similar to the format of the International Accounting Standards. In addition, the Chinese accounting profession has realized the need for a coherent conceptual framework for setting accounting regulations or standards. Although the actual progress of developing the framework is unsatisfactory so far, substantial achievement in this area will be made to facilitate the setting of standards along with the progress of reforms in economic and accounting administrative systems in the country.

Finally, reconciling Chinese accounting regulations and the internationally accepted accounting standards will be a continuous effort in Chinese accounting reforms. Although there is remarkable progress in the internationalization drive, much must be done to narrow the differences between Chinese accounting and the internationally accepted practices. Especially, many new standards will be developed based on the prevailing international conventions, to provide guidelines for accounting treatments of the emerging new transactions in the process of the market-oriented economy. These new standards will definitely reduce or narrow the differences between Chinese accounting and the practices prevailing in the industrial world.

CONCLUSION

There have been remarkable developments in Chinese accounting regulations during the last decade with a move toward internationally accepted practices. The process, resulting from rapid changes in Chinese economy, is evolutionary rather than revolutionary. To date, a set of new accounting regulations fairly similar to the prevailing practices in the western world has been installed for all entities within the country. Many changes are underway. It is believed that Chinese accounting regulations will be improved continuously in pace with the progress of economic reforms. As the Chinese economy is heading toward a market-oriented economy, its accounting regulations and accounting practices will certainly become internationalized, and a better understanding and comparability of Chinese accounting is attainable in the near future.

ACKNOWLEDGMENT

The authors are grateful to two anonymous reviewers and the editor for their comments and suggestions on the early draft of this chapter.

NOTES

1. These new supplementary industrial accounting regulations include: Accounting System for Industrial Enterprises—Chart of Accounts and Accounting Statements; Accounting System for Commerce and Trade Enterprises—Chart of Accounts and Accounting Statements; Accounting System for Transportation Enterprises—Chart of Accounts and Accounting Statements; Accounting System for Nonbanking Financial Institutions—Chart of Accounts and Accounting Statements; Accounting System for Tourist and Service Enterprises—Chart of Accounts and Accounting Statements; Accounting System for Capital Construction Enterprises—Chart of Accounts and Accounting Statements; Accounting System for Real Estate and Land Development Enterprises—Chart of Accounts and Accounting Statements; Accounting System for Aviation and Space Astronautic industries—Chart of Accounts and Accounting Statements; Accounting System for Broadcasting and Television Enterprises—Chart of Accounts and Accounting Statements; and Accounting System for Enterprises Operating Abroad—Chart of Accounts and Accounting Statements.

2. There are over 100 various industry-specified accounting regulations in existence and over one-third of their contents are inconsistent up to 1994.

3. The project is financially supported by the World Bank, with technical assistance from Deloitte & Touche International. The Exposure drafts of first five standards (including Inventories, Account Receivable, Depreciation, Account Payable, and Accounting Policies) were released for publics comments in late 1994. Officially, release of those new accounting standards started in 1997.

4. In all existing Chinese accounting regulations, most provisions are stated in terse-clause format without theoretical justifications. Thus misinterpretation and misapplication are not rare in practice.

REFERENCES

Bromwich, M., and A. G. Hopwood. 1983. *Accounting Standard Setting: An International Perspective*. London: Pitman.

Byington, J. R., and S. G. Sutton. 1991. The self-regulating profession: An analysis of the political monopoly tendencies of the audit profession. *Critical Perspectives on Accounting* 2(4): 315-330.

Fang, Z. L., and Y. W. Tang. 1991. Recent accounting development in China: An increased internationalization. *The International Journal of Accounting* 26(2): 88-103.

Ge, J. 1992. How to use the international experience in setting Chinese accounting standards. *Accounting Research* (Beijing, in Chinese) 2: 16-19.

Ge, J., and Z. J. Lin. 1993. Economic reforms and the accounting internationalization in the People's Republic of China. *Journal of International Accounting Auditing and Taxation* 2(2): 129-143.

Gray, S. J., and C. B. Roberts. 1991. East-west accounting issues: A new agenda. *Accounting Horizons* 5(1): 42-50.

Jiang, G. 1992. Initial experiment of setting accounting standards in China. *Accounting Research* (Beijing, in Chinese) 2: 26-30.

Lefebvre, C. and L. Q. Lin. 1990. Internationalization of financial accounting standards in the People's Republic of China. *The International Journal of Accounting* 25(4): 170-183.

Lin, Z. J. 1988a. A survey of current accounting development in the People's Republic of China. In *Advances in International Accounting*, Vol. 2, ed. K. Most, 99-110.

Lin, Z. J. 1988b. *Accounting Assumptions, Principles, and Standards*. Beijing: Economic Sciences Publishing Co.

Lin, Z. J., D. C. Yang, and L. Wang. 1998. *Accounting and Auditing in China*. Hants: Ashgate Publishing (UK) Ltd.

May, R. G., and G. L. Sundem. 1976. Research for accounting policy: An overview. *The Accounting Review* (October): 747-463.

Most, K. S. 1986. *Accounting Theory* (2nd ed.). Toronto: Holt, Rinehart and Winston.

Puxty, A. G., H. C. Wilmott, D. J. Cooper, and T. Lowe. 1987. Modes of regulation in advanced capitalism: Locating accounting in five countries. *Accounting, Organization and Society*: 273-291.

Tinker, A. 1984. Theory of the state and state accounting: Economic regulation and political voluntarism in accounting regulatory theory. *Journal of Accounting and Public Policy* (Spring): 55-74.

Warnock, K. 1992. Structure and argument in accounting standards. *Accounting and Business Research* 86(1): 179-187.

Yian, D. 1992. On study of the model and structure of Chinese accounting standards. *Accounting Research* (Beijing, in Chinese) 2: 20-25.

FINANCIAL REPORTING IN THE EMERGING CHINESE ECONOMY: STATE OWNED ENTERPRISES, JOINT VENTURES, AND PUBLIC CORPORATIONS

Moshe Hagigi, Jia Tan, and Eng C. Wu

ABSTRACT

The Chinese market offers great opportunities for foreign investors. At the same time, however, these opportunities are risky. The Chinese economy is vulnerable to political uncertainty, regulatory restrictions, government intervention, and other potentially disturbing economic conditions, such as high inflation. China is in the early stages of developing an appropriate economic infrastructure to attract increased foreign investments to its capital market, which is growing at a rapid rate. The investment opportunities in China will, no doubt, increase immensely due to the 1997 unification with Hong Kong, increasing the need to understand the financial reporting issues of the enterprises in this emerging economy. The aim of this chapter is to contribute to a better understanding of the mechanisms through which accounting practices are developed internationally by tracing factors affecting Chinese accounting practices and identifying their impact on Chinese financial reporting.

Research in Accounting in Emerging Economies, Volume 4, pages 17-28.

ISBN: 1-55938-995-8

INTRODUCTION

As China's economy becomes more market-oriented and industrialized, foreign investors increasingly require the ability to analyze and interpret the financial statements of Chinese companies. China's large population creates a promising market for foreign goods and services, and low-cost labor and government policies encourage foreign investment in Chinese ventures. Furthermore, as a growing number of Chinese companies compete in the international market, the necessity to be familiar with the financial statements of these companies is becoming widely recognized.

China, however, lacks an established infrastructure for financial reporting. In addition, while the most common business formation in China is currently the state-owned enterprise, as China moves away from a "Soviet Union model" of accounting toward a "free economy model," businesses are changing to joint ventures or public companies. The differences between the three types of ownership structures add to the complexity of analyzing Chinese financial reports. This study will explore the primary factors shaping accounting practices in China and examine the impact of various environmental factors on key financial ratios. The effects of these factors are illustrated by contrasting Chinese ratios to U.S. industry averages. Empirical illustrations are performed for each of the three Chinese enterprise forms separately, as well as for Chinese enterprises as a whole.

THE ECONOMIC BACKGROUND AND ACCOUNTING SETTINGS

Recent Changes in the Chinese Economy

China's economic environment has undergone drastic change since 1978, when the "economic reform" period began and the "open policy" was instituted. The Chinese government has attempted to industrialize the country's agricultural-based economy and create a market-oriented economy. It has also recognized the need for foreign capital and advanced technology imports. As a result, the Chinese government developed a series of policies, laws, and regulations to encourage and stimulate foreign investment. It eliminated restrictions previously placed on foreign companies, and granted them preferential tax treatment. It also reduced customs barriers in several large cities (e.g., Shanghai, Tianjing, Guangdong, and Shenzhen) and established several free trade zones. At the same time, Chinese financial markets and stock exchanges were quickly emerging.

Many multinational corporations responded favorably to these changes. General Electric, Motorola, Johnson & Johnson, Phillips, and others set up joint ventures in China. Foreign investors actively purchased "B" shares of Chinese companies listed in the Shanghai and Shenzen Stock Exchanges.[1] These activities resulted in a massive influx of capital, advanced technologies, and modern management techniques, all of which have helped to improve the economic infrastructure of the country.

The Accounting Settings in the Pre-Reform Period

Between 1949 and 1979, China's accounting system was primarily based on the model of the former Soviet Union. The basic premise of this model can be found in the equation: "fund applications equal fund sources," which not only reflects an accounting procedure, but also demonstrates the essence of socialist economies. As a socialist, centrally planned economy, state-owned firms in China had no authority to make independent decisions on purchases, sales, or funds allocation. The above equation could be further broken down into three parts, illustrating the limited movement of resources and use of funds:

1. Fixed assets = Fixed funds;
2. Current assets = Current funds;
3. Specific assets = Specific funds.

The size of each fund was determined by government appropriation or by state-owned lending bank, and the funds could be used only for a specific, pre-determined purpose, authorized by the government. Under such a system, accounting systems were very limited in scope and focused mainly on collecting and recording data for government use.

The Accounting Settings in the Post-Reform Period

Since the institution of the "open policy" in 1979, foreign companies operating in China have been permitted to use accounting procedures which are more compatible with international accounting practices. As of January 1993, China's basic accounting equation has changed to the conventional equation:

Assets = Liabilities + Shareholders Equity.

The new Chinese accounting standard reflects the combined influence of the International Accounting Standards and the FASB's conceptual framework. Consistent with these standards, the main Chinese accounting principles are: materiality, consistency, comparability, objectivity, conservatism, and full disclosure. The newly legislated standards include[2]:

1. Accounting for state-owned property, depreciation, intangible assets, inventory, translation of foreign currency statements, accounts receivable and uncollectibles accounts, long-term investments, interest expense,

revenue recognition and revenue distribution, measurement and reporting of securities, the effects of price changes, and liquidation issues;
2. Balance sheets and profit and loss statements;
3. Statements of changes in financial position;
4. Consolidations;
5. Accounting for adjustments related to previous events.

China's accounting reform has extended the role of accounting beyond that of a passive recording tool for managerial control. It is now also aimed at addressing the needs of local and foreign investors. As a result, independent public accounting firms were established[3] to carry out the new tasks. The "Big-6" accounting firms also expanded their operations in China. They have been actively involved in projects including the valuation of initial public offerings of state-owned enterprises in the Hong Kong and New York Stock Exchanges, and auditing for companies issuing "B" shares in Chinese stock markets. The sociological attributes of the Chinese bureaucracy are still reflected in the nation's accounting system. Despite the recent reforms aimed at meeting international accounting standards, past practices have not been completely eliminated. For example, the industry-specific accounting rules of the Soviet model are binding until new standards are fully developed and enforced.

The bureaucratic nature of the Chinese government is reflected in the details required by accounting regulations. There are currently three levels of financial accounting regulations. The Accounting Law, enacted in 1985 and revised at the end of 1995, is at the top of the hierarchy. The Accounting Standards, applicable to all enterprises operating in China, constitutes the second level. The Company Law, which relates only to limited liability companies, comprises the third level. The Company Law requires the following detailed disclosures[4]:

- Statements of Assets and Liabilities;
- Statements of Profit and Loss;
- Statements of Changes in Financial Position;
- Explanations of Financial Conditions;
- Statements of Profit Distribution.

Due to the centralized nature of the Chinese economy, financial reporting practices strictly follow tax regulations. For example, obsolete inventory or uncollected accounts receivable are not deductible for tax purposes, and therefore are not recognized as expenses for financial reporting. Similarly, in an effort to require companies to report more income and pay more taxes, the Chinese government rarely permits the use of accelerated depreciation for tax purposes. Therefore, the use of accelerated depreciation in financial reporting is rare as well.

THE IMPACT OF ENVIRONMENTAL FACTORS ON CHINESE FINANCIAL RATIOS: AN EMPIRICAL ILLUSTRATION

Any attempt to meaningfully compare financial ratios of two countries must make adjustments for the differences in environmental factors such as accounting practices, economic situations, government and tax structures, and cultural settings. This section illustrates the impact of environmental factors on financial reporting by contrasting the financial ratios of Chinese enterprises to United States' norms in similar industries.

The scope of this empirical section is merely illustrative due to difficulties in obtaining data (particularly data related to Chinese joint-ventures).[5] The sample includes four joint ventures, 10 public corporations, and one state-owned enterprise in China. The main industries represented are textiles, real estate, fast food, and hotels, although the sample spans the manufacturing, wholesaling, retailing, and service sectors. For this section, common-size balance sheets, income statements, and selected financial ratios were calculated for the three-year period of 1993-1995. Each of these ratios was then compared, in a standardized form, to U.S. industry averages for companies of comparable size, using figures from the *Annual Statement Studies* of Robert Morris Associates. The ratio differences between the Chinese enterprises and their U.S. counterparts were divided by the U.S. ratios to provide insight into the relative magnitude of the differences. The ratios of the individual Chinese enterprises are occasionally irregular (i.e., negative numbers); as a result, the U.S. ratios were placed in the denominators.

Characteristics of Chinese Financial Ratios

Asset Composition

Chinese enterprises cannot rely on the availability of external sources of funds in adverse times because the Chinese capital market is only in its early stages of development. Therefore, as Table 1 reveals, these enterprises keep a larger portion of their assets in the form of Cash and Equivalents than their American counterparts. For Chinese enterprises most of these assets are in "short-term investments" rather than "cash." China's high inflation rate allows enterprises that keep their assets in short-term investments to benefit from a high rate of return in the securities market. The return on these short-term investments comprises a significant part of their "non-operating income."

China's economic reform has encouraged many enterprises to "go public." Frequently, especially in the case of joint ventures, most of the proceeds from the stock issuance are used for capital expenditure. This explains the relatively large amount of "construction work in progress" and "investments in other business

Table 1. Comparison Between Chinese and U.S. Common-Size Financial Statements Based on the Years 1993–1995 (In percentage) as: Chinese Item-U.S. Item

	Type of Enterprises			
Item	*Joint Venture*	*State-Owned Enterprise*	*Public Corporation*	*Overall Enterprise*
BALANCE SHEET				
Cash and Equivalents	91.52	63.25	158.22	107.69
Trade Receivables (net)	–84.02	20.77	–54.56	–58.84
Inventory	66.07	–28.75	–62.57	25.45
Other Current Assets	106.49	588.15	51.92	184.14
Total Current Assets	–27.83	23.84	0.64	–4.63
Fixed Assets	26.99	–36.95	–9.95	–2.90
Intangibles (net)	59.88	–94.71	–9.73	2.03
Other Noncurrent Assets	129.26	–56.86	153.51	148.36
Total Assets	0.00	0.00	0.00	0.00
Current Liabilities	–6.89	48.56	–13.83	–7.85
Long Term Debt	–36.20	–91.06	-49.01	–48.82
Deferred Taxes	–100.00	–5.00	–100.00	–85.38
Other Noncurrent Liabilities	–68.07	–88.75	–15.84	–55.18
Equity	5.33	–12.07	44.02	30.81
Equity and Liabilities	0.00	0.00	0.00	0.00
INCOME STATEMENT				
Net Sales	0.00	0.00	0.00	0.00
Gross Profit	–37.00	–38.06	–12.26	–27.26
Operating Expenses	27.00	–18.11	–64.67	–7.32
Operating Income	–316.60	–137.78	291.71	124.30
All Other Expenses (net)	–86.96	–142.00	–178.23	–154.12
Net Income Before Taxes	–456.78	–136.15	779.74	437.90

lines," on Chinese financial statements. As compared to U.S. companies, the item "other non-current assets" in Table 1 is substantially higher for Chinese public corporations and joint ventures. It is lower for state-owned enterprises, which do not have proceeds from stock issuance.

Financial Leverage

Chinese enterprises are more likely to finance expansion by issuing equity than debt securities. State-owned enterprises frequently use treasury bonds, which are issued by the government in large quantities. The other enterprises have had difficulty making effective use of the developing Chinese credit market. Chinese banks are tightly controlled by the government and limited in their ability to lend to the public. Also, the monetary authorities use the money supply as a tool to control the inflation rate and fine tune the pace of economic growth. These government interests do not always coincide with the interests of commercial banks and public enterprises. Thus, in Table 1, except for the current liabilities of state-owned enterprises, the financial leverage of Chinese enterprises is lower relative to the U.S. norm. As a result, the relative "equity" of Chinese enterprises, other than state-owned enterprises, is higher than that of their U.S. counterparts.

The items "deferred tax liability/assets" and "income tax payable" have been combined into the "deferred tax" line for purposes of this analysis. On this item, Table 1 reveals a substantial difference between the United States and China due to the Chinese taxation system. Chinese enterprises pay taxes each quarter, in advance, based on their taxable income of the previous year. They do not receive refunds if and when it is discovered that their "true" taxable income was less than the "expected" taxable income. Instead, an overpayment is considered an advance payment for the following quarter. In contrast, if the enterprise's current taxable income is greater than that of the previous year and the enterprise has underpaid, they are required to pay the taxes immediately and are penalized. As a result, Chinese public corporations and joint ventures owe virtually no tax. Table 1 shows a difference of 100 percent between China and the United States.

Inventory Turnover

The development and effectiveness of Chinese inventory management is still lagging behind that of other advanced countries and methods such as "just-in-time" have not yet been adopted there. The transportation infrastructure has not fully developed to accommodate business needs. Therefore, many Chinese companies keep higher levels of inventories than companies in other countries. Prior to the economic reform, managers were not concerned by large inventories because they did not need to market the goods. The central administration made all production and distribution decisions. The current Chinese enterprises, however, are concerned about this inefficiency because in a free market economy they can no longer rely on the government as an outlet for their sales.

The excess inventory has also resulted from the Chinese decision-makers' lack of experience in estimating the market demand for their goods. Frequently, they over-produce in an attempt to take advantage of great market demand for some fashionable item, without regard to the risks of changing consumers' tastes. Additional explanation for the excess of reported inventory relates to an accounting practice, common to Chinese enterprises, of delaying the write-off of obsolete inventories. The low Chinese inventory turnover ratio in Table 2 reflects the above discussion.

Profitability

The norms of the Chinese profitability ratios generally vary from one form of ownership to another as we shall detail in the separate analysis of each individual type of enterprise. On the item "other expenses," however, all forms of Chinese

***Table* 2.** Comparison Between Chinese and U.S. Selected Financial Ratios Based on the Years 1993–1995 (In percentage) as: Chinese Item–U.S. Item U.S. Item

	Type of Enterprises			
Ratio	*Joint Venture*	*State-Owned Enterprise*	*Public Corporation*	*Overall Enterprise*
Current Ratio	27.56	−19.75	21.58	20.17
Receivables Turnover	−20.15	−88.71	11.05	−14.52
Inventory Turnover	−77.75	−79.61	−34.34	−69.26
Liquidity Ratio	91.42	63.25	158.22	107.64
Sales Turnover	−78.12	−87.64	−78.62	−78.82
Debt Ratio	−21.89	−0.35	−29.52	−25.62
Return on Assets (ROA)	−113.56	−102.61	−15.01	−42.78
Return on Sales (ROS)	−455.76	−160.00	779.74	437.30
Return on Equity (ROE)	−70.86	−102.58	9.35	14.70

Where: Current Ratio = Current Assets/Current Liabilities
Receivables Turnover = Sales/Receivables
Inventory Turnover = Cost of Goods Sold/Inventory
Liquidity Ratio = Cash and Marketable Securities/Total Assets
Sales Turnover = Sales/Total Assets
Debt Ratio = Total Liabilities/Total Assets
Return on Assets (ROA) = Operating Income/Total Assets
Return on Sales (ROS) = Net Income (before tax)/Sales
Return on Equity (ROE) = Net Income (before tax)/Equity

enterprises are similar. The Chinese accounting system defines "other expenses" as "*net* nonoperating expenses" (i.e., nonoperating expenses minus nonoperating revenue). Many Chinese companies derive revenue from their long term investments in other business lines to make up for their loss on operations. Revenues from long-term investments are viewed as nonoperating income, and therefore deducted from "nonoperating expenses" to arrive at the "net nonoperating expense." Hence, the Chinese enterprises, typically, report substantially lower "other expenses" than their U.S. counterpart companies.

Characteristics of Chinese Joint Ventures' Financial Ratios

The profitability ratios of Chinese joint ventures are substantially lower than those of their U.S. counterpart enterprises. In most cases, these ratios are even lower than those of the other Chinese enterprises. These lower reported earnings do not, however, reflect the true picture of profitability. This situation stems from the tendency of foreign investors to report lower earnings in order to benefit from a preferential tax treatment. Joint ventures use several ways to reduce reported sales and to inflate reported expenses[6]. For example, they inflate the reported depreciation expenses by transferring the completed portion of "construction work in progress" to the "fixed assets" section and starting to depreciate it before the completion of the whole project. Clearly, such a procedure is not permitted, but it is difficult for auditors to detect.

Another example relates to utilizing government tax return policy on exports to escape tax. Since 1994, China has imposed a value-added tax, at a rate of 17 percent, on every purchase or sale. For exported goods, however, the tax is refunded. Furthermore, tariffs on raw materials, imported for subsequent export, are also refunded. As a result, some joint ventures, which were affiliated with other foreign companies, have imported and exported to themselves through their affiliated companies to receive refunds from the government. While this procedure is illegal and risky some enterprises cannot resist the strong temptation.

Finally, joint ventures are able to "manage earnings" because they typically have substantial intangible assets. In most cases, both the foreign investors and the Chinese contribute such assets. The foreign partners supply patents, royalty, and technological know-how, while the Chinese provide land occupancy rights. The valuation of such intangible assets, as well as their amortization, are extremely complicated and subjective. This may enable the joint venture's management flexibility for determining desired accounting figures.

Distinguishing Features of Chinese State-owned Enterprises' Ratios

Higher Receivables and Payables

State-owned enterprises typically have higher receivables and payables than U.S. companies and other Chinese enterprises. In China, the collection of receivables and payables between state-owned enterprises is difficult and inefficient because each enterprise is owned by the same entity: the state. There is no internal regulation or procedure to offset or enforce collection of accounts owed by one state enterprise to another state enterprise. For example, if Party A owes to Party B, Party B owes the same amount to Party C, and Party C owes the same amount to Party A, Party A might be reluctant to pay to Party B, claiming that it has not received its debt from Party C. The serious difficulties experienced by state-owned enterprises as a result of this "debt triangle" is much less noticeable in other Chinese enterprises. The existence of such a phenomenon might justify allowing state-owned enterprises to recognize bad debt expenses.

Additional Items in the "Current Assets" Section

The financial reporting of Chinese state-owned enterprises has been regulated more rigorously by the government than the reporting of other enterprises. State-owned enterprises are required to report their statements in greater detail. This applies, in particular, to current assets. As a result, in financial statements of Chinese state-owned enterprises there are more items in "other current assets" than in the financial statements of U.S. companies. For example, items such as "unauthorized loss on current assets and untransferred expenses" exist only on the statements of Chinese state-owned enterprises.

Lower Profitability

Prior to the economic reform, state-owned enterprises provided a large amount of income to the Chinese government. The state-owned enterprises retained from their revenue only enough funds to maintain "normal operations." The remainder of their revenue was transferred to the government, which, when necessary, appropriated funds for expansion. All funds appropriated to the enterprises were designated for specific uses. This protected economic environment no longer exists. The lack of initiative and flexibility which now characterizes the financial operations of state-owned enterprises results, in many cases, in substantial losses and an increasing number of state-owned enterprises depending on government subsidies. This situation is reflected in the profitability ratios of Table 2.

Chinese Public Corporations' Financial Ratios

The financial ratios of Chinese public corporations are substantially healthier than those of other Chinese enterprises. The managers of public corporations are motivated to project a positive image because they report to shareholders and are affected by public opinion.

Higher Proportion of Equity Financing

Chinese public corporations are financed mainly by equity. Many of these enterprises were formerly state-owned enterprises. The economic reform caused the availability of subsidies to decline, and pushed state-owned enterprises to go public and finance their operations and expansions by issuing equity securities.

The relatively young nation-wide stock-exchange is increasing in popularity in China. As a result of the relatively small number of securities traded and the increasing number of investors, stock prices have consistently risen at sharp rates. The average share price for the companies traded on the Shanghai Exchange in April 1992, was 160 times the earnings per share. At the same time, the corresponding average share price for typical Wall Street companies was only 13 times the earnings per share. To mitigate this situation, the Chinese government issued certificates specifying, and thus, limiting, the number of stocks each individual investor could buy. These certificates, however, soon became tradable themselves through a "black market." Therefore, while public corporations have had difficulties obtaining debt financing, they have been able to take advantage of market enthusiasm and issue large amounts of equity securities.

Healthier Profit Ratios

Many market participants in China are relatively less informed and knowledgeable with respect to securities than investors in developed financial markets. Managers of public corporations still feel some pressure to report acceptable profitability ratios. This applies, in particular, to companies issuing B shares because the shares are issued to foreign investors who generally have many alternative investment opportunities.

Table 1 reveals that the profitability ratios of Chinese public corporations are higher than those of other Chinese enterprises. Although Chinese public corporations typically have lower gross profit ratios than their U.S. counterparts, they have much higher operating profits. We propose several explanations for this phenomenon: lower labor costs, lower interest expenses due to smaller levels of debt financing, and the recognition and reporting of substantial amounts of revenues from currency exchange as a result of the recent devaluation of the Chinese currency.

CONCLUDING REMARKS

The Chinese market offers great opportunities for foreign investors. At the same time, however, these opportunities are risky. The Chinese economy is vulnerable to political uncertainty, regulatory restrictions, government intervention, and other potentially disturbing economic conditions, such as high inflation. China is in the early stages of developing an appropriate economic infrastructure to attract increased foreign investments. The Chinese capital market is growing at a rapid rate. The volume of the Shenzhen Stock Exchange transactions in 1992 was US$ 7.7 billion. While small as compared to other developed markets, this was 12 times greater than the volume of transactions in 1991. In the early 1990s, the State Council granted approval for more than 10 Chinese state-owned enterprises to issue shares in Hong Kong and to be listed in the Hong Kong Stock Exchange. Other Chinese enterprises have been accepted to be listed in the New York Stock Exchange. The investment opportunities in China, no doubt, increased immensely due to the 1997 unification with Hong Kong, increasing the need to understand the financial reporting issues of the enterprises in this emerging economy.

This chapter has sought to contribute a better understanding of the mechanisms through which accounting practices are developed internationally by tracing factors affecting Chinese accounting practices and identifying their impact on Chinese financial reporting.

NOTES

1. The Chinese government enabled overseas investors to trade in a Chinese stock exchange for the first time in February 1992. There are currently two types of shares listed in the Shanghai and Shenzhen Stock Exchange. Only local investors are permitted to trade in "A" shares, while overseas investors may trade in "B" shares.

2. See, for example, Ministry of Finance, the People's Republic of China, "Accounting Standards of Business Enterprises," December 1992.

3. In 1982, the first public accounting firm certified by the Ministry of Finance was established in Shanghai. At the same time, a national standardized test for accountants (CICPA) was introduced.

4. See, for example, Chow, Chau, and Gray (1996).

5. A substantial amount of the information used in this study was obtained on the condition of anonymity.

6. This discussion is based on interviews with some Chinese accountants.

REFERENCES

Adhikari, A., and S. Z. Wang. 1995. Accounting for China. *Management Accounting* 76 (10): 27-32.

Blake, J., and S. Gao (Eds.). 1995. *Perspectives on Accounting and Finance in China*. London: Routledge.

Borensztein, E., and J. D. Ostry. 1996. Accounting for China's growth performance. *American Economic Review* 86 (2): 224-228.

China Financial Department. 1992. *Accounting System and Procedure of Foreign Investment Enterprise*.

China. *Euromoney, 1994 Guide to Developments in World's Bond Markets supplement* (September) 1994: 12-15.

Chow, L. M., G. K. Chau, and S. J. Gray. 1996. Accounting reforms in China: Cultural constraints on implementation and development. *Accounting & Business Research* 26 (1): 29-49.

Davidson, R. A., A. M. G. Gelardi, and F. Li. 1996. Analysis of the conceptual framework of China's new accounting system. *Accounting Horizon* 10 (1): 58-74.

Graham, L. E., and A. H. Carley. 1995. When East meets West. *Financial Executive* 11 (4): 40-45.

Improving the numbers. *Business China* 22 (7) (April 1), 5-6.

Inside Jobs. *Business China* 21 (3) (February 6), 6.

Luo, Y. 1995. Business strategy, market structure, and performance of international joint ventures: The case of joint ventures in China. *Management International Review* 35 (3): 241-264.

Ministry of Finance, People's Republic of China. 1992. *Accounting Standards of Business Enterprises*. December.

Robert Morris Associates. (various issues). *Annual Statement Studies*.

Rudnick, D. 1994. China connections. *Euromoney* (May): 105-128.

Shanghai University of Finance and Economics. 1987. *Accounting and Auditing in the People's Republic of China—A Review of Its Practices, Systems, Education and Developments*. Joint research study by Shanghai University of Finance & Economics, PRC, and Center for International Accounting Development, University of Texas. August.

Tang Y. W., L. Chow, and B. J. Cooper. 1994. *Accounting and Finance in China: A Review of Current Practice*. Hong Kong: Longman.

Winkle, G. M., H. F. Huss, and C. Xi-Zhu. 1994. Accounting standards in the People's Republic of China: Responding to economic reforms. *Accounting Horizons* 8 (3): 48-57.

Worth fad? *Business China* 21 (2) (January 23), 7.

PART II

ACCOUNTING AND FINANCIAL CONTROL IN SOUTH ASIA

PRE-1998 REFORMS IN FINANCIAL REPORTING IN INDONESIA:

THE IMPACT OF CAPITAL MARKET DEVELOPMENTS

Joselito G. Diga and Shahrokh M. Saudagaran

ABSTRACT

For a country with a population approaching 200 million and a gross domestic product in excess of US $200 billion, relatively little has been written about financial reporting in Indonesia. Perhaps one factor contributing to the scarcity of accounting research on Indonesia was the perception of serious economic underdevelopment associated with the country in the past. However, the economic performance of Indonesia since the 1980s belies this image. Another factor may have been the difficulty of obtaining English-language material, particularly on accounting-related matters. This chapter discusses how Indonesia's financial reporting system has attempted to keep abreast with rapid changes occurring in the country's capital market. It demonstrates the level of importance attached by government and private sector policymakers in an emerging economy to ensuring an adequate basis for financial reporting. Evidence is provided on how changes in the financial reporting regulatory structure have meshed with the Indonesian government's aim to strengthen the domestic capital market. The analysis here provides insights to the changes deemed necessary to

Research in Accounting in Emerging Economies, Volume 4, pages 31-49.

ISBN: 1-55938-995-8

attain a mature capital market, one of the key imperatives of development for emerging and transitional economies. It suggests how an appropriate set of financial reporting policies can contribute towards a more efficient domestic capital market that can harness the funds flowing in from overseas. Finally, the discussion of Indonesia provides evidence on how an emerging economy can improve its financial reporting system in a relatively short period of time, considering its limited financial and technical resources. It also helps to address the dearth of accounting research on one of the more important emerging economies in Asia.

INTRODUCTION

The purpose of this chapter is to analyze recent developments in Indonesian financial reporting in the context of changes in the country's capital market. During the last 25 years, Indonesia has undergone a profound transformation economically and politically. These changes in the country's political and socio-economic landscape have been engendered by Indonesia's increasing links to the international market economy and the imperatives of attaining sustained economic growth in a country of about 200 million (Robison 1993).

This chapter discusses how Indonesia's financial reporting system has attempted to keep pace with rapid changes occurring in the country's capital market. It demonstrates the level of importance attached by government and private sector policymakers in an emerging economy to ensuring an adequate basis for financial reporting. Evidence is provided on how changes in the financial reporting regulatory structure have meshed with the Indonesian government's aim to strengthen the domestic capital market. It also addresses the dearth of accounting research on one of the more important emerging economies in Asia.

Surprisingly, for a country of its size and economic importance, relatively little has been written about financial reporting in Indonesia. Perhaps one reason was the perception of serious economic underdevelopment associated with the country in the past. However, the economic performance of Indonesia since the 1980s belies this image. An average growth rate of 5.5 percent in the 1980s accelerating to growth of 7 percent per annum in the 1990s has firmly placed Indonesia in an upward trajectory economically (ADB 1995). Another probable reason for the scarcity of accounting research on Indonesia was the difficulty of obtaining English-language material, particularly on accounting-related matters. Fortunately, this too is changing as Indonesia increasingly becomes a dynamic economic player in Southeast Asia and as more multinational firms establish a base of operations there, seeking to tap its abundant human and natural resources.

The analysis here provides insights to the changes deemed necessary to attain a mature capital market, one of the key imperatives of development for emerging and transitional economies. It suggests how an appropriate set of financial reporting policies can contribute towards a more efficient domestic capital market that can harness the funds flowing in from overseas (Walter 1993). Finally, the discussion of Indonesia provides evidence on how an emerging economy can improve its financial reporting system in a relatively short period of time, considering its limited financial and technical resources.

The remainder of this chapter will address the following issues. Section 2 provides an overview of the current state of accounting in Indonesia. It introduces the concept of an "accounting infrastructure" developed in prior research and applies this concept to Indonesia. In section 3, we analyze the growth of Indonesia's capital market, considered one of the best performing emerging markets worldwide (IFC 1994). We trace the historical development of the country's capital market and the evolution of its underlying institutional structures. The growth of Indonesia's capital market is linked to increased demands for adequate and reliable financial information on listed companies. The fourth section then proceeds to discuss the reforms in financial reporting implemented in Indonesia. These reforms are in terms of developing an appropriate legal infrastructure for financial reporting and upgrading the number of skilled accounting personnel. The final section summarizes the discussion and presents the policy implications of financial reporting reforms carried out in Indonesia.

CURRENT STATE OF ACCOUNTING INFRASTRUCTURE IN INDONESIA

In general, assessments about the state of financial reporting in emerging economies have been somewhat unflattering. In an evaluation of the accounting infrastructure in developing countries, the World Bank (1990) concluded that, "in developing countries, accounting and auditing practices are sometimes weak, and financial laws and regulations do not demand accurate and timely financial reports." The report then emphasized that "developing an effective accounting and auditing profession is essential for building efficient financial markets" (p. 90). This broad recommendation has been reiterated by the Asian Development Bank (ADB 1995), a multilateral developing agency that is quite visible in Indonesian economic affairs: "accounting information is an essential element of infrastructure for a financial system.... Though many [developing countries] have made improvements in their securities market, further disclosure and reporting improvements in most [developing countries] are warranted" (p. 229).

In his Ford Foundation sponsored study of the Indonesian accounting system, Enthoven (1975) was rather circumspect although his conclusions were clear: "The [enterprise] accounting systems, procedures and information at most medium and small—but also many large—establishments is considered not to be in good shape.... As a matter of fact, neither the area of financial accounting nor management or cost accounting, can be said to have developed in most enterprises to such a degree that they portray relevant and useful information for analysis, policy, planning and control of enterprise activities; nor are they effectively used for aggregative purposes, including the national accounts" (p. 11).

Twenty years later, the ADB (1995) described the legal and accounting framework in Indonesia as being "weak" with "limited recent attempts at improvement." It also added that "present corporate and tax laws in Indonesia require that adequate financial records be kept, but do not impose accounting requirements and standards to ensure financial disclosure" (p. 227).

Several centuries of foreign occupation in Indonesia, particularly under the Dutch, engendered a receptiveness towards Western accounting practices (Sukoharsono and Gaffikin 1993). The popularity of foreign-based accounting practices has been reinforced by Indonesia's adoption of U.S.-based accounting practices, beginning in the 1970s (Yunus 1988). Amalgamation of these two foreign accounting systems resulted in a "dualistic accounting system" in Indonesia where the training and certification still reflected Dutch methods but where accounting standards and practices were patterned clearly on U.S. methods. Briston (1990) was particularly critical of the transplantation of foreign accounting methods and concepts into the country. He asserted that "Indonesia's system reflects the problems encountered by most developing countries, and demonstrates how the implanting of foreign systems into an incompatible environment can cause wastage and stifle relevant development" (p. 208).

These evaluations of the state of accounting in Indonesia create the impression that the country has failed to consolidate improvements, if any, attained in corporate financial reporting. In comparison, our assessment here provides evidence that significant strides have been made to improve the quality of accounting in the country.

A particularly useful framework for understanding the nature of financial reporting reforms carried out in Indonesia has been suggested by Wallace and Briston (1993). The accounting infrastructure framework which they recommend comprises: (1) the *supply function* which refers to the training and education of accountants and auditors who are the information producers; (2) the *demand function* consisting of the information users, including information intermediaries, information screening mechanisms such as inter-firm comparisons, and stock exchanges and banks; and (3) *quality control systems* which include the laws and regulations that govern the production, transmission and usage of information, the legal entities that monitor and implement the laws and regulations and the personnel that validate the information produced.

In this chapter, the demand function is discussed in the next section in the context of developments in Indonesia's capital market. Specifically, we find that the rapid growth of the domestic capital market creates constructive pressure to improve the quality of financial reporting in the country. The supply function is discussed in the context of attempts to improve the basis of academic and professional accounting education in the country. Finally, the quality control systems are analyzed in terms of recent reforms implemented in Indonesia's financial reporting regulatory system. The last two dimensions of the accounting infrastructure are discussed in the fourth section of the chapter.

GROWTH OF INDONESIA'S CAPITAL MARKET

This section provides an overview of the growth of Indonesia's capital market, particularly its banking sector and securities markets. It provides the context for understanding reforms carried out in Indonesia's financial reporting system, particularly with respect to privately owned entities. It also highlights the important role played by accounting within a developing country's capital market.

Banking Sector

Indonesia's banking sector has traditionally played a dominant role as a source of long-term finance for corporate activities in the country. Since its independence, Indonesia's financial sector was dominated, apart from Bank Indonesia (the country's central bank), by five state-owned banks which owned about 70 percent of banking sector assets in 1985 (Andersen 1993). Under this environment, credit for industrial and commercial activities was controlled tightly by the government and went into state-preferred areas of investments. Economic activities were controlled largely by state-owned enterprises and a handful of large business conglomerates (Suseno and Tarihoran 1989; Robison 1993).

The weakening of oil prices in 1982-1983, Indonesia's principal source of government revenues, resulted in the government pushing for reform of its financial sector in order to stimulate private sector savings and reduce the dependence on financing from government-owned banks (Andersen 1993; Financial Times 1993). The first phase of deregulation took the form of removing restrictions on deposit rates, elimination of credit ceilings and reducing the availability of refinancing schemes available to state-owned banks. The second phase of the banking sector deregulation which began in 1988 (and is known locally as "Pakto 88") included the easing of restrictions on the entry of new banks and setting up of new branches. The number of new banks entering the market, including foreign joint venture banks, was 66 over a two-year period between 1988 and 1990. Statistics showing the growth of the banking system and the number of banks are provided in Table 1. Reserve requirements were also reduced from 15 percent to 2 percent, thus allowing a greater amount of credit to be available for private sector undertakings. While these deregulation measures resulted in much greater efficiency in the banking sector and improvement in the country's GDP growth and balance of payments (particularly with the diversification of the non-oil based economic activities), they also had negative effects on the Indonesian financial system. The reform measures generated

Table 1. Indonesia's Banking Sector

	1985	*1990*	*1995*
Number of Commercial Banks†	75	155	240
Total assets controlled (in US$ billions)	30	70.4	111

Note: †Includes the five major state-owned commercial banks, private national commercial banks and foreign banks/joint ventures.

Sources: SEACEN (1991); Financial Times (1993); FEER (1995); Financial Times (1996).

unsustainable levels of credit growth as a greater number of banks competed for clients. When Bank Indonesia eventually tightened credit policies, the low quality of banks' loans was exposed. Weaknesses in the supervision over bank lending activities led to a crisis of confidence in the banking sector, particularly after the near collapse of a major commercial bank in the early 1990s.[1]

Against this backdrop, the Indonesian government increasingly sought to improve the quality of supervision over the banking sector. In particular, the government announced a policy to implement the capital adequacy requirements defined in the Basle Accord of 1988 on all banks operating domestically.[2] The decision to adhere to the capital adequacy standards in the Basle Accord was a turning point in terms of highlighting the importance of accounting practices of banks in Indonesia. As specified by the ADB (1995, p. 213), "the measurement of a bank's capital, and thus the effectiveness of minimum capital requirements as a prudential regulatory tool, is wholly dependent on the accounting framework and accounting conventions used by banks and their regulators." The subsequent disclosure of poor quality loan assets carried by some Indonesian commercial banks increased pressure on the Central Bank to impose regulations aimed at improving the quality of financial reporting of Indonesian financial institutions.

Securities Markets

As early as 1912, the Association of Securities Traders of Indonesia, considered the precursor of the present day Jakarta Stock Exchange, was established by Dutch merchants in Jakarta. In 1924, similar associations were established in Surabaya and Semarang, two other large Indonesian cities. These informal stock exchanges catered to the Dutch business community and investors who dominated the industrial, commercial and agricultural sectors in the country at that time. These exchanges were closed during the Second World War and the years immediately following. They reopened in 1952, principally to raise capital needed to rebuild the Indonesian economy and continued to operate until 1958. The nationalization of foreign-owned enterprises and the political and economic instability that followed had a detrimental effect on the stock markets and they remained moribund until the 1970s when government reforms facilitated the revival of the stock markets.

The stock market reforms introduced in the 1970s were aimed at addressing two important goals. First, the stock market was seen as a means of facilitating the mobilization of domestic savings and reducing the country's reliance on foreign-sourced funds. Second, the stock market also provided a mechanism for foreign partners in joint ventures in Indonesia (known by their local designation of *Penanaman Modal Asing* or simply PMAs) to divest part of their equity holdings to Indonesian nationals and legal entities in compliance with government regulations.[3] The reforms included tax breaks designed to encourage listings on the Jakarta Stock Exchange (JSE). More importantly, two influential government agencies were created to assist the development of the domestic capital markets. The first, referred to as *Bapepam* (short for *Badan Pelaknana Pasar Modal*) or "Capital Market Executive Agency" was established to regulate the JSE. A second agency, PT (*Persero*) Danareksa, was a national investment trust company whose purpose was to promote the equitable distribution of income by purchasing securities from the market and then selling these as small denomination fund certificates to Indonesians.[4]

The first public listing of a domestic entity occurred in August 1977 when PT Semen Cibinong was listed on the revitalized JSE. By 1983, 23 companies had listed their shares on the JSE. Most of the listed companies were foreign joint venture companies in the industrial sector complying with government regulations regarding foreign ownership ceilings. Between 1983 and 1987, however, the JSE was rather dormant as a result of unfavorable macroeconomic conditions in the country and discriminatory regulations. In particular, tax on gains on equity securities and bonds were much higher compared to interest on bank deposits leading investors to prefer the latter.

In 1987, the government implemented major deregulation measures to further enhance the operations of the stock market. These measures included eliminating daily price limits on the movement of listed securities, relaxation of listing and issuance requirements, and clarification and expansion of foreign ownership in listed domestic entities. A 15 percent withholding tax imposed on bank deposits also significantly improved the comparative returns from securities investments relative to bank deposits. Licenses were also granted to additional securities brokers and investment houses and foreign intermediaries were allowed to operate in the country.

Apart from the main exchange, a smaller Surabaya Stock Exchange (SSE) was reopened in June 1989. Securities in the SSE are cross-listed on the JSE. An over-the-counter market (OTC or *Bursa Parallel)* was also established in 1988 to encourage smaller companies which could not meet the profit history requirements of the JSE to raise capital.

Further regulatory reforms were carried out in 1990 when the old Bapepam was replaced by a new agency (also known as "Bapepam"), the *Badan Penga-*

Table 2. Indonesia's Securities Markets

	1984	*1990*	*1993*
Number of listed domestic companies†	23	125	174
Total Market Capitalization (US$ millions)	85	8,081	32,953
Total Value Traded (US$ millions)	2	3,992	9,158

Note: †Jakarta Stock Exchange
Sources: JSE (1993); IFC (1994).

was Pasar Modal or the "Capital Market Supervisory Agency." The principal difference was that the new agency focused on overall supervision of the country's securities markets rather than managing the day-to-day operations of the JSE. The latter function was taken over by a private entity in 1992, the PT Bursa Efek Jakarta, a limited liability company owned and operated by licensed stock brokers and underwriters who are members of the JSE. The investment fund business, which was previously the monopoly of PT Danareksa, was also opened to the private sector to encourage the growth of mutual funds. The result of these changes was reflected in the tremendous growth of Indonesia's capital markets over a relatively short 10 year period ending in 1993.

The changes in the structure of the capital markets created broad demand for quality and timely financial information on listed Indonesian entities. As demand for Indonesian securities increased, a greater number of domestic and foreign information intermediaries (i.e., stock brokers and investment houses) established operations in the country. The presence of these information intermediaries and the greater number of small investors entering the market were instrumental in pressuring the government to implement wide ranging reforms in Indonesia's financial reporting system.[5]

REFORMS IN FINANCIAL REPORTING

Increased demand for adequate financial and other information on companies was a principal catalyst for reforms in Indonesia's financial reporting regulation. The reforms had two important dimensions. One aspect of the reform process was aimed at improving the quality of accounting standards governing Indonesian companies. The second component of the reform focused on redressing the severe shortage of skilled accounting personnel in the country.

Accounting Standards and Regulations

Since the introduction of double-entry bookkeeping techniques in Indonesia by Dutch traders and administrators in the seventeenth century, financial reporting in Indonesia has always been influenced strongly by Dutch accounting thought and practices (Sukoharsono and Gaffikin 1993). One of the most enduring pieces of legislation governing financial reporting in Indonesia was the Indonesian Code of Business Law. This law was introduced in 1848 and was patterned after the early Dutch Commercial Code (*Wetboek van Koophandel*) which, in turn, was influenced heavily by the Napoleonic Code in France. Until 1995, when the law was replaced, the Code of Business Law provided the broad framework for financial reporting in Indonesia.

Similar to early Continental European commercial legislation, the Code of Business Law did not provide specific guidelines on what companies ought to report. It required that anyone carrying on a business must keep sufficient records to enable the rights (presumably assets) and obligations (liabilities) of the person to be determined (Samidjo 1985). The law, however, did not specify the accounting records nor the procedures that each business ought to follow to carry out the provisions of the law. In this environment, the majority of the companies did not consider proper financial reporting an important aspect of corporate accountability. Indeed, until 1995 most companies were not required under law to prepare financial statements and undergo an independent audit of their accounts. There were a few exceptions, however. Several types of companies were required to prepare financial statements and have these audited by a registered auditor: foreign joint venture companies (PMAs), branches of foreign companies, companies under contract with the government and/or those obtaining loans from state-owned banks. Comments by Briston (1990) aptly summarize the state of legislation affecting financial reporting in Indonesia until the mid-1990s: "Indonesia is operating an out-of-date Commercial Code adopted in the nineteenth century that is incompatible with today's commercial environment.... Reform of the Indonesian Commercial Code is also long overdue. Well-developed companies legislation might enhance the growth of the private sector, as investors are more willing to invest if their interests are recognized and protected by law" (p. 205).

The cornerstone of this reform was finally established with the enactment of the *Limited Liability Company Law* (Law No. 1/1995) in March 1995 by the Indonesian Parliament. The law provides a firm legal basis for establishing a limited liability company and clarifies the rights and responsibilities of various parties involved in the company. The most significant provisions of the new law, from the perspective of Indonesian financial reporting, are found in Chapter 4 ("Annual Report and Use of Profits"). The Company Law (Art. 56) stipulates that all limited liability companies prepare a set of financial and other reports within five months after the fiscal year end. The required reports include:

- a balance sheet, profit and loss statement and notes to financial statements of the parent company
- consolidated financial statements of the corporate group
- an operating report including forecasts of likely developments
- a management report discussing the principal activities of the company, as well as changes and problems impacting on these activities
- names of members of boards of executives and directors and details of their salaries and other remuneration

The new Company Law also requires the financial statements to be audited by a licensed auditor if the company is involved in mobilizing private funds, issues securities to the public or is a limited liability company (Art. 59). Furthermore, it requires that financial statements be prepared in accordance with Indonesian Financial Accounting Standards as approved by the Indonesian Institute of Accountants and other relevant state agencies. Any departures from required standards must be explained and justified by company management (Art. 58). Finally, the law imposes strict responsibility on the company's executives and board of directors for information contained in the reports (Arts. 57/60). Executives and board members are jointly liable for false or misleading information in the reports.

The legislative infrastructure over financial reporting has been reinforced further by the promulgation of Indonesia's new *Capital Market Law* (Law No. 8/1995) which replaced the rather dated Emergency Law on Stock Exchange (Law No. 67/1952). The Capital Market Law defines, among others, the broad framework for financial reporting for public companies. Public companies are defined as those:

- whose shares are already owned by not less than 300 shareholders; and
- with paid-up capital of not less than Rupiah 3 billion or some other amount defined by government regulations (Art. 1).

The new Capital Market Law stipulates clearly the need for adequate and timely disclosure of material information on public companies. Material information is defined as any information that can influence the decisions of investors with respect to corporate securities (Art. 1). Several provisions in the new Capital Market Law directly impact on financial reporting in the country. Chapter 8 of the law identifies accountants as one group of professionals supporting the development of capital markets (Art. 64). The law requires accountants to be licensed by an appropriate government agency and to register with Bapepam. Registered accountants are also required to comply with the ethical code and professional standards of the Institute of Indonesian Accountants (Art. 66). Moreover, the law places an onus on accountants to expeditiously report to Bapepam violations of the Capital Market Law and matters that can jeopardize the financial status of

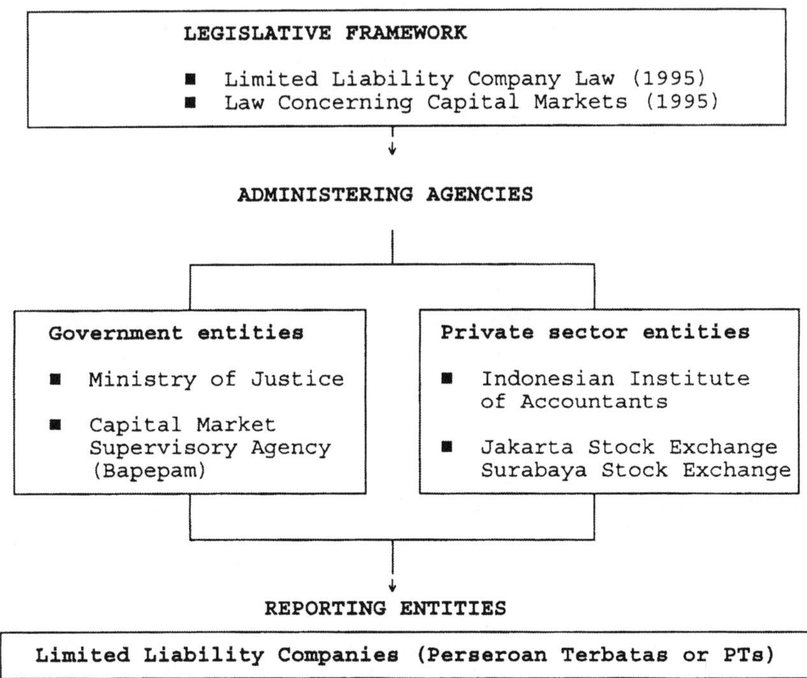

Figure 1. Regulatory Framework for Financial Reporting in Indonesia

companies and institutions involved in the capital market (Art. 68). Finally, public companies are required to ensure that financial reports submitted to Bapepam are prepared on the basis of "generally prevailing accounting principles," defined as those principles prescribed by the Indonesian Institute of Accountants (IAI) and other accounting practices commonly used in capital markets. Even after recognizing the prominent role of the IAI in defining domestic accounting rules, the law gives Bapepam an overriding power to stipulate financial reporting requirements for public companies in Indonesia.

Enactment of the two laws has radically changed the regulatory framework governing financial reporting of Indonesian companies. The new framework is described in Figure 1.

As shown in Figure 1, Indonesia has adopted a mixed regulatory approach which harnesses the contributions of both government and private sector agencies. As the agencies tasked with implementing the new laws, the Ministry of Justice and Bapepam will continue to play an influential role in defining the scope of financial reporting in Indonesia. In particular, Bapepam has assumed an increasingly active role in prescribing disclosure requirements for listed companies. Bapepam's Circular SE-24/PM/1987 "Directives Regarding the Form and Contents of Financial Statements of Indonesian Listed Companies" prescribes, in broad terms, the format and disclosures of companies listed in Indonesia's stock exchanges (Bapepam 1987).[6] Bapepam has also become more activist in implementing the disclosure rules on listed companies, imposing fines and penalties on companies violating extant rules (Subardiyoto 1993).

The role of private sector agencies in strengthening Indonesian financial reporting reforms has also increased substantially. Privatization of the Jakarta Stock Exchange in 1992 ensured a larger voice for the private sector in defining the listing and disclosure requirements for listed companies in Indonesia. The current listing requirements at the JSE are based heavily on accounting information requiring, among others, that:

- the applicant's financial reports be audited by a registered accountant/auditor and have received an unqualified audit opinion for the latest fiscal year;
- the company be in operation for at least three years as shown in its accounting reports;
- the company have made operational and net profits in the latest two fiscal years; and
- the company own at least Rupiah 20 billion in assets; Rupiah 7.5 billion in shareholders' equity of which Rupiah 2 billion is paid-up capital (JSE 1994).

Moreover, listed companies are required to submit accounting reports regularly to the JSE administering body including:

- annual financial statements audited by an accountant registered with Bapepam;
- semi-annual reports audited by a registered accountant;
- unaudited quarterly reports; and
- weekly net asset values reports for investment fund issuers (JSE 1994).

The listing and ongoing requirements indicate the importance attached by the JSE to adequate financial reporting, without which confidence in Indonesia's stock markets would diminish.

The Indonesian Institute of Accountants (known by its local designation IAI for "Ikatan Akuntan Indonesia") has also played an increasingly active role in shaping the country's financial reporting regulations. The IAI was called upon by the government to formulate accounting rules necessary to support reforms in Indonesia's capital markets in the 1970s. The result was a set of Indonesian Accounting Principles (*Prinsip Akuntansi Indonesia* or PAI) prepared by the IAI in 1973 which became the cornerstone of generally accepted accounting principles in the country. The IAI promulgated a revised set of accounting principles in 1984 in order to recognize the increasing deregulation of the Indonesian economy which saw a greater role being played by the private sector (IAI 1984). It was therefore appropriate that the revised set of accounting principles was linked closely with making investment and other decisions in the private sector, as expressed in revised PAI (Article 1): "In principle, the purpose of Financial Accounting and Financial Statements is to make available financial information regarding a company that will be used by interested parties as material for consideration in making economic decisions" (IAI 1984). Notably, the revised set of accounting principles increasingly reflected U.S. accounting concepts and practices.[7]

The possible reasons for this shift have been explored elsewhere (Yunus 1988; Briston 1990; Diga and Yunus 1997). However, the ascendancy of U.S.-based accounting practices in Indonesia has been accompanied by a corresponding decline in the influence of Dutch accounting thought, based largely on the principles of business economics, on Indonesian accounting practice. On a practical level, with one significant exception, there does not appear to be much conflict between U.S. and Dutch accounting principles. The main exception is current cost accounting where Dutch emphasis on "sound business practice" recognizes the acceptability and serviceability of current replacement cost as a valuation method. In contrast, historical cost is the preferred valuation method in the U.S. and in Indonesia. In particular, revaluation of fixed assets is prohibited in Indonesia except when sanctioned specifically by government decree following an official devaluation of the Indonesian currency (IAI 1984).

In its 1994 annual congress, the IAI has recommended another significant shift in Indonesian financial reporting by supporting International Accounting Standards (IAS) as the basis for domestic accounting rules. In total, 21 IAS have been adopted as Indonesian Financial Accounting Standards (FAS) to replace the Indonesian Accounting Principles (PAI) last revised in 1984. The 21 IAS currently adopted are shown in Table 3 below. In addition, the IAI has adopted the IASC's "Framework for the Preparation and Presentation of Financial Statements" as a basis for setting future accounting standards (IASC 1994).

The move towards IAS has received strong support from Bapepam (1987) and the JSE who view these rules as essential in modernizing and internationalizing Indonesia's capital market. Significantly, the promulgation of the new Limited Liability Company Law and Capital Market Law in 1995 now provide a statutory basis for Indonesian accounting standards, something that was ostensibly absent in the past.

Human Resources Development[8]

The second aspect of Indonesia's financial reporting reforms focuses on upgrading the number of skilled Indonesian accountants. The shortage of qualified accountants in Indonesia has been recognized as a severe handicap in

Table 3. IAS Adopted as Indonesian Financial Accounting Standards

IAS 1 -	Disclosure of Accounting Policies
IAS 3 -	Depreciation Accounting
IAS 7 -	Cash Flow Statements
IAS 8 -	Net Profit or Loss for the Period, Fundamental Errors and Changes in Accounting Policies
IAS 9 -	Research and Development Costs
IAS 10 -	Contingencies and Events After the Balance Sheet Date
IAS 11 -	Construction Contracts
IAS 13 -	Presentation of Current Assets and Current Liabilities
IAS 14 -	Reporting Financial Information by Segment
IAS 15 -	Information Reflecting the Effects of Changing Prices
IAS 16 -	Property, Plant and Equipment
IAS 17 -	Accounting for Leases
IAS 18 -	Revenue
IAS 21 -	The Effects of Changes in Foreign Exchange Rates
IAS 22 -	Business Combinations
IAS 24 -	Related Party Disclosures
IAS 25 -	Accounting for Investments
IAS 27 -	Consolidated Financial Statements and Accounting for Investments in Subsidiaries
IAS 28 -	Accounting for Investments in Associations
IAS 30 -	Disclosures in the Financial Statements of Banks and Similar Financial Institutions
IAS 31 -	Financial Reporting of Interests in Joint Ventures

improving the quality of Indonesian financial reporting practices (Briston 1990). As of 1992, there were an estimated 11,500 accredited accountants in Indonesia out of a population of 185 million (Price Waterhouse 1992). The expanding economy and lack of adequate educational resources meant fierce competition for the available accountants. The situation has been exacerbated by the requirement until the early 1990s that all graduates of the university *sarjana* course (including those in accounting) had to serve for at least three years in government service.[9] A number of institutions are involved in attempting to redress these problems.

The Indonesian Accountancy Development Foundation (*Yayasan Pengenbangan Ilmu Akuntansi Indonesia*) was established in 1974, under the auspices of the IAI. The aim of this foundation is to orient the development of the accounting profession toward the needs of private businesses and the Indonesian community in general. It provides training programs and research related to Indonesian accounting.

A concerted effort to upgrade the scope and standards of accounting education began in 1985 with the establishment of the *Coordinating Agency for Accounting Development* (CAAD) also known by its Indonesian name, *Tim Koordinasi Pengembangan Akuntansi* (TKPA). The agency was created under the auspices of Indonesia's Ministry of Finance and Ministry of Education and Culture, which both exercised oversight responsibility. The mandate of the CAAD/TPKA was broad and encompassed the improvement of accounting standards, practices, and education in both the private and government sectors. During the period from 1985-1988 the agency focused on planning the areas that will be covered by the Accountancy Development Project. From 1988-1994, after obtaining substantial funding from the World Bank and the Indonesian government, the first phase of the Accountancy Development Project was implemented. The project had two principal components: (a) education and (b) professional practice. Within this framework, the CAAD acted as "a think tank and change agent as well as providing a coordination and information role" (Abdoelkadir and Yunus 1994, 68). With respect to educational development, the first component, the agency oversaw the development of new Indonesian language textbooks and training materials and implemented programs to train teachers at the post-secondary level. In this regard, the government-run State School of Government Accounting (known by its local name *Sekolah Tinggi Akuntansi Negara* or STAN) as well as the eight state universities provide the bulk of training for accountants in both the private and government sectors.

With respect to accountancy development at the level of practice, a report issued by a group of experts titled "A Strategy for Accounting Development 1994-2000" outlined a strategy for development. The recommended strategy was to develop further accounting in the private sector as a means of dovetailing with the Indonesian government's shift toward private-sector led development. Surprisingly, however, the report also suggested that funding for activities to improve Indonesian accounting be refocused from the private sector to the government sector. The view was that accountancy development in the private sector required only modest investments to achieve substantial improvements. Instead, the requirement was to implement reforms in the legislative and institutional infrastructure governing private sector accounting.

The promulgation of the *Limited Liability Company Law* and *Capital Market Law* has already resulted in significant headway towards creating the necessary legal and institutional infrastructure. Moreover, the government has agreed to establish a Directorate for Public Accounting and Directorate for Appraisal Company Development within the Ministry of Finance. The Directorate for Public Accounting will be tasked with establishing rules and procedures for certifying various grades and specializations in accounting. It is expected, however, that the certifying exams will be conducted by the IAI. The Directorate for Appraisal Company Development is tasked with overseeing the activities of domestic appraisal companies and securities rating agencies in order to improve practices in this area. In addition, a detailed and long-term study of accounting personnel needs in business and government is currently being undertaken to identify required accounting specializations and training grades in the future.

POLICY IMPLICATIONS AND FUTURE DEVELOPMENTS

In recent years, the Indonesian government has recognized the crucial role of financial reporting reform in the overall framework of improving the domestic capital markets, consistent with policy recommendations provided by the ADB and the World Bank. The decision to place financial reporting firmly in the policy agenda resulted in a two pronged approach toward reform. First, significant changes were made in the legal infrastructure governing corporate financial reporting. Moreover, specific government agencies and private sector organizations have been given clear mandates to ensure that the laws were implemented. Second, a program for raising the quality of skilled accountants was organized. This latter aspect of the reform process is decidedly of a long-term nature and it will probably take several years before tangible improvements are realized. Both aspects of reform underscore the importance of government commitment, without which little could be accomplished.

The success of Indonesia's institutional reforms in the area of corporate financial reporting can be assessed in part by the robust growth of its capital market. Without the regulatory infrastructure provided by an adequate system of financial reporting, it will be increasingly difficult, if not impossible, to sustain the development of Indonesia's capital market. This chapter has provided evidence on how policymakers in an emerging market have attempted to pursue quality financial reporting against the backdrop of domestic constraints and limited resources.

From a policy viewpoint, however, doubts have been expressed regarding the appropriateness and serviceability of "borrowed" accounting methods and concepts in the Indonesian environment. For instance, despite the pro-IAS stance of influential agencies such as the World Bank, several authors have warned against the detrimental effects of wholesale adoption of foreign accounting standards (Samuels and Piper 1985; Hove 1986; Briston 1990). In this regard, Indonesia appears to have taken a pragmatic route toward accounting development. On the one hand, the significant resources required to formulate domestic accounting standards in relation to the limited financial and human resources of a developing country such as Indonesia preclude a strictly "bottoms up" approach to developing standards. Moreover, the tremendous growth of Indonesia's capital markets has relied to a large extent on the steady inflow of foreign funds into the country (World Bank 1989; ADB 1995). Under such an environment, it was perceived by Indonesian policy makers that adoption of internationally acceptable accounting standards (and IAS do reflect accounting standards in the most prominent stock markets, i.e., London and New York) would enhance the level of confidence of foreign portfolio investors in the Indonesian capital market.

Given extant realities, and the route that Indonesian policymakers have decisively adopted, further consideration should be given to "customizing" IAS to reflect Indonesian financial reporting requirements. This route has been followed by other ASEAN countries, particularly Malaysia and Singapore, which have also adopted IAS. This approach requires domestic accounting standard setters to consider possible incompatibilities between the IAS prescription and domestic conditions and alter IAS appropriately. For example, the recommendations of IAS 31 Financial Reporting of Interests in Joint Ventures, which was adopted by the IAI in 1994, needs to be interpreted in the context of domestic regulations covering foreign joint ventures (PMAs). Indonesia has increasingly relaxed the entry requirements for PMAs but still imposes foreign equity ceilings and other requirements for companies engaged in certain activities. Also, the IAS have not addressed accounting issues of particular interest to developing countries. These include accounting for enterprises engaged in agricultural and natural resource extraction activities. Accounting for these enterprises is particularly important given Indonesia's large natural resources base and the need to ensure sustainable development of these resources. These gaps in IAS create opportunities for Indonesian accounting policymakers to work with other developing countries in formulating accounting standards that are appropriate for their needs.

Overall, Indonesia's recent experience in financial reporting reform demonstrates what can be accomplished through a concerted effort by government and the private sector to raise the quality of domestic corporate accounting practices. The coalescing of requisite elements of the accounting infrastructure, that is, supply conditions, demand conditions and adequate regulatory systems provided an opportunity to make substantial progress in a relatively short span of time. In this respect, the experience of Indonesia provides important lessons for other emerging economies aiming to improve their domestic capital markets at the soonest possible time.

NOTES

1. This was Bank Summa, owned and controlled by one of Indonesia's prominent business families. The bank experienced a run when the extent of its liabilities, particularly to financially troubled companies in the same corporate group, became known.

2. The Basle Accord of 1988 refers to the agreement of bank regulators of industrial countries meeting in Basle, Switzerland. In this agreement, sponsored by the Bank for International Settlements, countries agreed to impose a common set of minimum capital requirements on their banks. The agreement called for a bank's capital to be at or above a level that is equal to 8 percent of the bank's assets, with the assets being measured on a risk-weighted basis. Bank regulators in a number of emerging markets, including Indonesia, have announced their intention to adhere to the standard specified in the Basle Accord.

3. PMAs are the only legal mode of entry for foreign companies in Indonesia. Their operations are governed by the Foreign Capital Investment Law (Law No. 1/1967) which is enforced by the Foreign Investment Board.

4. A Persero is a limited liability company in Indonesia. The names of such entities are usually preceded by "PT."

5. Occurrences of perceived financial reporting lapses which were widely publicized also increased the pressure brought to bear on the government. In one case, a listed company, Argo Pantes,

reported a significant earnings figure prior to its listing only to disclose six weeks later that the true figure was 65 percent lower than the earlier reported figure (Financial Times 1993).

6. Bapepam's (1987) circular on the form and contents of financial statements has been patterned after the U.S. Securities and Exchange Commission Regulation S-X.

7. The 1984 Accounting Principles (PAI) promulgated by the IAI was patterned after the American Institute of Certified Public Accountants' (AICPA's) Accounting Research Study No. 7 *Inventory of Generally Accepted Accounting Principles for Business Enterprises* (AICPA 1965).

8. The contribution to this section by Dr. Hadori Yunus, Partner of Hadori & Rekan and Lecturer in Gadjah Maja University, is gratefully acknowledged.

9. The university *sarjana* was the basic undergraduate program offered in accounting and was typically completed in 4-7 years.

MANAGING EDITOR'S NOTE

The original title of this chapter was changed by the Managing Editor from "*Recent* Reforms in Financial Reporting in Indonesia: The Impact ..." to "*Pre-1998* Reforms in Financial Reporting in Indonesia: The Impact ..." to take cognizance of the financial crises in Indonesia after the chapter had been accepted for publication.

REFERENCES

Abdoelkadir, K., and H. Yunus. 1994. Developments in Indonesian accountancy. In *Conference Proceedings—Seventh International Conference on Accounting Education,* 59-72. New York: International Association for Accounting Education and Research.

American Institute of Certified Public Accountants (AICPA). 1965. Inventory of generally accepted accounting principles for business enterprises. *Accounting Research Study No. 7.* New York: AICPA.

Andersen, P. S. 1993. Economic growth and financial markets: The experience of four Asian countries. In *Finance and the International Economy*, Vol. 7, ed. R. O'Brien. New York: Oxford University Press for the Amex Bank Review.

Asian Development Bank (ADB). 1995. *Asian Development Outlook 1995 and 1996.* New York: Oxford University Press for the ADB.

Badan Pelaknana Pasar Modal (Bapepam). 1987. *Directives Regarding the Form & Content of Financial Statements of Indonesian Listed Companies.* Jakarta: Bapepam.

Briston, R.J. 1990. Accounting in developing countries: Indonesia and the Solomon Islands as case studies for regional cooperation. *Research in Third World Accounting* 1: 195-216.

Diga, J., and H. Yunus. 1997. Accounting in Indonesia. In *Accounting in the Asia-Pacific Region*, eds. N. Baydoun, K. Nishimura and R. Willett. Sydney: John Wiley.

Enthoven, A.J.H. 1975. *An Evaluation of Accountancy Systems, Developments and Requirements in Asia.* North Carolina: Graduate School of Business Administration, University of North Carolina.

Far East Economic Review (FEER). 1995. Focus on Asian capital markets. July 27:37-59.

Financial Times. 1993. *Banking in the Far East 1993: Structures and Sources of Finance.* London: Financial Times Business Information.

Financial Times. 1996. *Financial Times Survey: Indonesia.* June 25, pp. 1-6.

Hove, M. R. 1986. Accounting practices in developing countries: Colonialism's legacy of inappropriate technologies. *International Journal of Accounting Education and Research* 22 (1): 81-100.

Indonesian Institute of Accountants (IAI). 1984. *Indonesian Accounting Principles.* Jakarta: IAI.

International Accounting Standards Committee (IASC). 1994. *International Accounting Standards Numbers 1-31*. London: IASC.

International Finance Corporation (IFC). 1994. *Emerging Stock Markets Factbook 1994*. Washington, DC: IFC.

Jakarta Stock Exchange (JSE). 1993. *Fact Book 1993*. Jakarta: JSE.

Jakarta Stock Exchange (JSE). 1994. *Jakarta Stock Exchange Regulations*. Jakarta: JSE.

Price Waterhouse. 1992. *Doing Business in Indonesia*. Jakarta: Drs. Hadi Sutanto & Rekan.

Republic of Indonesia. 1995. *Law of the Republic of Indonesia Concerning Capital Markets—Law No. 8/1995*. Jakarta: Government of the Republic of Indonesia.

Republic of Indonesia. 1995. *The Limited Liability Company—Law No. 1/1995*. Jakarta: Government of the Republic of Indonesia.

Robison, R. 1993. Indonesia: Tensions in state and regime. In *Southeast Asia in the 1990s: Authoritarianism, Democracy and Capitalism,* eds. K. Hewison, R. Robison, and G. Rodan. New South Wales: Allen & Unwin.

Samidjo. 1985. *Pengantar Hukum Indonesia (Introduction to Indonesian Law)*. Bandung: C. V. Arminco.

Samuels, J.M., and A. G. Piper. 1985. *International Accounting: A Survey*. London: Croom Helm.

South East Asian Central Banks (SEACEN). 1991. *SEACEN Financial Statistics: Money and Banking*. SFS Series No. 1, July. Kuala Lumpur: SEACEN Research and Training Center.

Subardiyoto. 1993. Capitalizing on the stocks boom. *Economic & Business Review Indonesia* 84 (November 20): 6-8.

Sukoharsono, E. G., and M.J.R. Gaffikin. 1993. The genesis of accounting in Indonesia: The Dutch colonialism in the early 17th century. *Indonesian Journal of Accounting and Business Society*: 4-26.

Suseno, S., and S. A. Tarihoran. 1989. Development of the capital market in Indonesia. In *The Development of Capital Markets in the SEACEN Countries*, ed. N.B.K. Kuala. Lumpur: SEACEN.

Wallace, R.S.O., and R. J. Briston. 1993. Improving the accounting infrastructure in developing countries. *Research in Third World Accounting* 2: 201-224.

Walter, I. 1993. Emerging equity markets: Tapping into global investment flows. *ASEAN Economic Bulletin* 1: 1-19.

World Bank. 1990. *Financial Systems and Development*. Washington, DC: International Bank for Reconstruction and Development.

Yunus, H. 1988. *History of Accounting in Developing Nations: The Case of Indonesia*. Birmingham, UK: University of Birmingham.

STATUTORY CONTROL IN ACCOUNTING AND REGULATION: A CASE STUDY OF THE DEVELOPMENT AND FINANCIAL SUPERVISORY BOARD (BPKP) OF INDONESIA

John Liberty Hutagaol, Graeme L. Harrison, and Jill L. McKinnon

ABSTRACT

This study examines the role of government, through the role of the *Badan Pengawasan Keuangan dan Pembangunan* (BPKP—Development and Financial Supervisory Board) in the development of accounting and regulation in Indonesia. Indonesia and BPKP are used as a case study to examine Gray's (1988) proposition relating the "accounting value" of statutory control to Hofstede's national cultural dimensions. The study uses qualitative analysis of primary and secondary data in documentation and literature, and data from interviews with key respondents, to demonstrate how the historical and cultural contexts of Indonesia give rise to a substantial degree of statutory control and government influence and involvement in

Research in Accounting in Emerging Economies, Volume 4, pages 51-72.

ISBN: 1-55938-995-8

accounting and regulation in Indonesia contemporarily. That influence and involvement is described through the relationship between BPKP and the accounting profession and professional accounting firms in Indonesia. The case study provides support for Gray's (1988) proposition.

INTRODUCTION

This study examines the role of government, through the role of the *Badan Pengawasan Keuangan dan Pembangunan* (the Development and Financial Supervisory Board, hereafter abbreviated to BPKP) in the development of accounting and regulation in Indonesia. As the largest and highest ranking internal government audit board in Indonesia, the study focuses on BPKP's location in the supervisory apparatus of government, and its regulatory relationship with the state companies, the accounting profession, and public accounting firms.

There are two motivations for the study. The first is to add to the existing literature on accounting and regulation in Indonesia as an emerging nation assuming increasing political and economic importance in the Asia-Pacific region. The second is to use Indonesia as a case study to examine Gray's (1988) proposition relating the "accounting value" of professionalism (versus statutory control) to Hofstede's (1980) national cultural dimensions of power distance, individualism, and uncertainty avoidance.

With respect to the latter, Gray (1988) proposed that a country characterized as high power distance, collectivist (low individualist) and uncertainty avoiding, would also be characterized by a high degree of statutory control, one aspect of which is state or government involvement in accounting and professional regulation. In their multi-country test of this (and other of Gray's propositions), however, Salter and Niswander (1995) did not find support for association between statutory control and the cultural dimensions of high power distance and collectivism.[1] Salter and Niswander (1995) also noted the relatively low power of the cultural variable in statistical explanation of the cross-sectional variation in statutory control among the 29 countries in their sample. In light of this, they argued for the importance of other factors, including historical factors and level of economic development in explaining the contemporary level of statutory control in specific countries and, hence, in explaining variation in levels across countries.

This argument is consistent with that of other researchers into the determinants of accounting generally in specific countries. Cooke and Wallace (1990) and Wallace (1987), for example, convey the diversity of factors which influence and form a country's "accounting profile." And, with respect to historical factors, Previts and colleagues (1990) and McKinnon (1986, 25) point to their importance in understanding present day conventions and systems of accounting and regulation in specific countries.

Another potential reason for the absence of support for the linkage between the level of statutory control and the cultural dimensions of power distance and collectivism in the Salter and Niswander (1995) study may lie in the use of a cross-sectional methodology. While a strength of such a methodology is that it allows the examination of a number of variables across a range of countries, a corresponding limitation is that it is not able to examine the depth or subtlety of the relation between culture and the "accounting value." To capture this relation, an alternative approach using a more in-depth analysis within a country-specific, case-based methodology may be warranted.

Based on the foregoing, this study uses Indonesia as a case nation, and relies on qualitative analysis to examine Gray's proposition of the relation between culture and statutory control in the context of that country. Indonesia was chosen because it is a high power distance, collectivist society (Hofstede 1983, 82) and, hence, exhibits the aggregate cultural characteristics which Salter and Niswander (1995, 383) argue are most likely to be associated with statutory control. Cognizant of the arguments above, however, the study: (i) draws on the dimensions of power distance and collectivism as they manifest themselves in Indonesian culture; and (ii) includes examination of Indonesia's history of colonization since the early sixteenth century, and the associated implications for its economic development, to add historical and economic factors as potential explanators of the contemporary level of statutory control in accounting in Indonesia.

A further reason for choosing Indonesia (and constituting the second motivation for the study) is that while there is literature on accounting in Indonesia, including publications from the international professional firms covering technical detail on accounting practices (see, for example, Spicer and Oppenheim 1989; Coopers and Lybrand 1992; and Price Waterhouse 1996), and academic literature and research covering accounting generally and accounting education and training (see, for example, Hadibroto 1975; Enthoven 1977; Abdoelkadir 1982; Arya 1990; Briston 1990; Briston and Hadori 1993), that literature and research is still relatively sparse compared with the literature in the international accounting domain dealing with Anglo-American and major European countries.

Additionally, little of the existing literature focuses on the role of government and the state in accounting in Indonesia, despite the perceived importance of examining such a role in international accounting studies (Choi and Mueller 1992, 40; McKinnon 1986, 316-321).[2] Consequently, the second motivation and contribution of the study is to provide additional knowledge and understanding of accounting regulation and the role of government in regulatory relationships in Indonesia.

The study is based on qualitative analysis of primary and secondary data in documentation and literature, and on interviews with key respondents using personally administered, structured questionnaires. To provide a blending of "insider" and "outsider" perspectives, both English and Indonesian language literature were drawn on where possible. In some instances, however, only Indonesian language material was available. A contribution of the study, in this respect, is to bring this latter information into the English language literature.

The interview respondents were selected for their knowledge and experience in the areas at issue in the study. Interviews were conducted with respondents in four categories: (i) expert authorities on Indonesian culture and history, (ii) key officials (both past and present) of BPKP, (iii) senior representatives and office-holders of *Ikatan Akuntan Indonesia* (the Indonesian Accountants Association as the accounting professional body), and (iv) representatives of Indonesian state companies. Nineteen respondents were interviewed over a one-month period in 1994, with interviews lasting one to two hours. While the interviews were guided by structured questionnaires, open-ended answers and elaborations were sought, and probe questions were used. The list of interviewee respondents is given in the Appendix. The chapter is organized as follows. The next section traces briefly the political and economic history of Indonesia, and discusses key components of Indonesian culture, in order to develop the historical and cultural context in which Indonesian accounting and regulation have developed and operate. Following that, BPKP's role in accounting and regulation is examined, specifically its location within the supervisory apparatus of government, and its relationship with the state companies, the accounting profession, and public accounting firms. Finally, some conclusions are drawn about the role of government in accounting and regulation in Indonesia.

THE HISTORICAL AND CULTURAL CONTEXT

Indonesia has a rich history reaching back thousands of years. From the start of its international economic relations (with Chinese and Indian traders) in the early centuries AD (Lubis 1990, 27), Indonesia maintained extensive trading with a variety of nationals including the Portuguese, Spanish, Dutch, British and Arabs, as well as the Chinese and Indians, through to the late sixteenth century.[3]

Indonesia's recent history has been characterized by continuous colonization from the start of the sixteenth century until its ultimate independence in 1949. Motivation for the colonization was the desire of the foreign traders to monopolize control over the rich natural resources of the Spice Islands; the means were military force and occupation. Initiating colonization were the Portugese in 1511, followed by the Dutch who, to institutionalize their influence and control, established in 1611 the *Verenigde Oostindische Compagnie* (VOC—The United Dutch Traders' Colonial Government, initially the United East India Company) (Zainu'ddin 1980, 79).

With the exception of two intervening periods,[4] the Dutch Colonial Government controlled Indonesia for over three centuries until World War II, when control passed to the Japanese during their wartime occupation of the South East Indies from 1942 to their fall to the Allied Forces in 1945. The subsequent vacuum of power in Indonesia was used by the indigenous people to declare independence on August 17, 1945 (Dahm 1971, 113; Lubis 1990, 175). Despite efforts by the British and Dutch to re-establish Dutch political power, Indonesian military resistance and strong international pressure on the British and Dutch governments repelled these efforts, and led to the recognition of an independent Indonesia at the Round Table Conference in Den Haag on December 27, 1949 (Zain'uddin 1980, 232).

The literature on Indonesian history allows several conclusions relevant to understanding the current state of accounting and regulation. The first is that, since the early sixteenth century, Indonesia has suffered political and economic turmoil and adversity. The brief chronology above, while dispassionate, shows Indonesia's subjugation to continuous intervention by other nations for many centuries. Nor was that intervention beneficent. Rather, the Dutch maintained a disregard for the welfare of the Indonesian people throughout their period of colonization, during which they maintained a regime of heavy taxes and *heerendiensten* (forced labor), and continually exploited Indonesia's economy for their own benefit (Lubis 1990, 165 and 193-199). Zainu'ddin (1980, 137) and Lubis (1990, 147) both refer to the general legacy of economic degradation and hardship caused to the Indonesian people by the Dutch colonization.

A second conclusion from the historical literature is that, until as recently as 1966, political interests and activities dominated and prejudiced economic ones in Indonesia. Even after securing independence from the Dutch in the late 1940s, the new Indonesian government was faced with a number of internal rebellions, as well as continued international confrontations and regular conflicts among, and changes of, political parties in government.[5] In 1959, President Sukarno transferred national power from the parliament to the president, thus creating an era referred to as "guided democracy" under the control of Sukarno as *Bapak Revolusi* (Revolution Father) (Caldwell and Utrecht 1979, 107; Grant 1966, 47). However, this concentration of power failed to redress the emphasis on political relative to economic or social matters (Lubis 1990, 185).

The continued political preoccupations carried high economic and social cost. At the macroeconomic level, programs such as the eight-year plan and the *Deklarasi Ekonomi* (Economic Declaration) were not managed adequately or successfully. Fund allocations were concentrated on areas such as the purchase of military weapons, with the development of social welfare infrastructure being correspondingly neglected (Caldwell and Utrecht 1979).

A further reason for Indonesia's economic deterioration was the absence of a state budget to guide national development. Such absence facilitated the misallocation of funds for unproductive purposes and for corruption, and resulted in hyper-inflation rates of some 500 percent per annum in 1965, which virtually destroyed the Indonesian economic system and inflicted a heavy burden of poverty on the Indonesian people (Caldwell and Utrecht 1979, 116-117; Grant 1966, 97). The consequent large gap between the rich and the poor led to the coup attempt by the Indonesian Communist Party in September 1965. Repelled by the Indonesian people and army led by General Suharto, the coup failed and resulted in the fall of Sukarno and his replacement by President Suharto (Grant 1966, 81; Mackie and MacIntyre 1994, 10). This marked the end of what is known as "the old order" of Indonesia after independence and the start of *zaman orde baru* (the new order).

The advent of "the new order" saw significant national development planned and carried out by the Indonesian people, led by, and with heavy involvement of, government. The government embarked on a program of stabilization and economic rehabilitation policies, including food price stabilization (Grant 1966, 97; Hill 1994, 62), foreign and domestic investment and foreign aid (Dahm 1971, 225), and rationalization of the organizational structures of the state companies (Habir 1990). Additionally, since 1969, regular five-year national plans (*Repelita*) have been implemented covering areas such as education, politics, religion, health care, and economics (Hill 1994, 66).

The final conclusion from the historical literature is that the continual economic degradation of Indonesia prior to "the new order" produced the knowledge that national development required educated Indonesian people, and a government active and versed in economic management. This latter realization resulted in the development, in 1966, of the *Aparat Pengawasan Fungsional Pemerintah* (APFP), the government supervisory apparatus, which characterizes the significant role played by the government in social and economic life in contemporary Indonesia. This is returned to later when the BPKP, as a key part of the government supervisory apparatus, is examined for its role in accounting and regulation. Prior to that, aspects of Indonesian culture are discussed, particularly the concept of *Pancasila*, again with the purpose of subsequently locating the accounting and regulation process within that cultural context.

The Culture of Indonesia

With over 13,000 islands, Indonesia has been said to have about 500 cultures, each with its own language, customs and values (Sumardjan, interview). Overarching this, however, is the concept of *Bhineka Tunggal Ika* (the Unity from Diversity):

> The *Bhineka Tunggal Ika* means the Unity from Diversity. This means that our nation consists of multi ethnics, cultures, languages, customs and habits; however, it is Indonesia. An example: the diversity is beautiful multi colors such as red, white, yellow and green. However, if those colors are mixed with each other, they cause a white color. Thus, one (unity) is in the diversity (Hamid, interview).

Bhineka Tunggal Ika is given expression in *Pancasila*, a formulation of five basic principles embodied in the preamble to the 1945 Constitution, and which pervades all aspects of Indonesian life at national, group, and individual levels

(Bahan Penataran Pegawi Negeri 1981). *Pancasila* is recognized as the foundation of state and the highest source of law in Indonesia through its influence on the Constitution, as well as the embodiment of the national identity, way of life, and the national purpose and soul (Densu, interview; Lakunnu, interview). The principles are: a belief in the one and only God; a just and civilized humanity; the unity of Indonesia, democracy guided by the inner wisdom in the unanimity arising out of deliberations among representatives; and social justice for all the people of Indonesia (Department of Information 1991, 14).

Although the name *Pancasila* was provided by Sukarno at the time of the 1945 Constitution, its principles have a long ancestry in Indonesian values such as *percaya pada Tuhan Maha Esa* (belief in God), *goton royong* (mutual assistance), *mufakat* (consensus), *musyawarah* (deliberation), and harmony in relations among individuals, and between individuals and society, and between nature and God (Densu, interview; Hamid, interview).

Drawing on the historical literature presented earlier and the characteristics of *Pancasila*, Indonesian culture can be located in Hofstede's (1980) taxonomy as low individualism (collectivist) and high power distance.[6]

Describing individualism as the degree to which individuals are integrated into groups, and the extent to which individual interests dominate group interests, Hofstede (1983, 80) rated Indonesia as a low individualism (i.e., collectivist) society. This is corroborated by Reeve (1985, 25) and Kitley (1994), and is consistent with the norms and values inherent in *Pancasila*, which guide the Indonesian people to place the national interest above that of the individual, to emphasize deliberation (*musyawarah*), to achieve group consensus, and to provide mutual help (*gotong royong*) (Dahm 1971, 105). *Pancasila*, and particularly the component value of *gotong royong*, orient Indonesian collectivism to the community as the focal group. This contrasts with Chinese and Japanese forms of collectivism, where the focal group is the family and the organization respectively (Whitley 1991).

Although *Pancasila* comprises principles of democracy, deliberation to attain consensus, and equal respect for human beings, this does not mean that Indonesian culture is low power distance in Hofstede's (1980) taxonomy. Hofstede (1980, 122) describes power distance as the way in which societies handle the problem of human inequality. Low power distance societies are characterized by a norm value that inequalities between people should be minimized and, to the extent that hierarchies exist within society and its organizations, they exist only for administrative convenience (Hofstede 1980, 122). High power distance societies are characterized by the acceptance of inequality and its institutionalization in hierarchies which locate people in their "right places."

In these terms, Indonesia is a high power distance culture. Hierarchical structure has been institutionalized in Indonesian society since the coming of the Hindu-Buddhism religions and kingdoms in the early centuries AD, with their emphasis on hierarchy and the kinship system (Hardjowardojo 1976, 35). These kingdoms created sharp and enduring differences in social statuses between the king and royal associates, and the Indonesian people (Lubis 1990, 23-24). Although the kingdoms were displaced by the Dutch Colonial Government (itself a form of enforced hierarchy), the hierarchical structure of Indonesian society was perpetuated with the creation of the *priyayi* (the traditional aristocracy) (Hill 1994, xvii), a selected group of indigenous Indonesians who were used as mediators between the Colonial Government and the populace (Caldwell and Utrecht 1979, 18). The *priyayi* enjoyed privileges through power, consistent with the structure of a high power distance society. After independence, the Indonesian Government was dominated by the *priyayi*, who fitted into positions of power easily and naturally because they were accustomed to the privileges and benefits of education and authority.

Hofstede (1983, 82), Kitley (1994), and Mackie and MacIntyre (1994) all corroborate the high power distance nature of Indonesian society, with the latter (1994, 28) contending that "open criticism of the ruler or the authorities, or dissent from official doctrine, is a source of acute psychic discomfort to many Indonesians."[7]

The operationalization of *Pancasila*, itself, is a manifestation of Indonesia's high power distance culture. As noted earlier, *Pancasila* is explicitly incorporated into the Constitution of 1945, and is required by law to be adopted as the sole foundation of all social and political organizations in Indonesia (Densu, interview). All Indonesians are taught *Pancasila* formally in courses from elementary school through to senior high school (Lakunnu, interview). Civil servants must attend courses and pass examinations in *Pancasila* to enter the service and are required to take further courses as they progress in the bureaucracy. The commitment of the government to implement *Pancasila* illustrates the extent to which government power reaches into social life in Indonesia (Mackie and MacIntyre 1994, 15).

THE ROLE OF BPKP IN ACCOUNTING AND REGULATION IN INDONESIA

The remainder of the chapter examines the role of government, through the role of BPKP, in accounting and regulation in Indonesia. First, BPKP is located within Indonesia's State Functional Supervisory Apparatus, including its relationship with the state companies, following which BPKP's roles in relation to (i) the accounting profession and (ii) professional accounting firms are examined.

The historical section of the chapter drew the conclusion that the continual economic degradation of Indonesia prior to "the new order" in 1966 brought the knowledge that national development required educated people and a government active and versed in economic management. The cultural section of the chapter reinforced government involvement in economic and social life in Indonesia as consistent with the dictates of a high power distance society. This historical and cultural context found expression in the establishment in contemporary Indonesia of the *Aparat Pengawasan Fungsional Pemerintah* (APFP—the state functional supervisory apparatus).

The state supervisory apparatus comprises five government audit bodies; *Badan Pengawasan Keuangan dan Pembangunan* (BPKP—the Development and Financial Supervisory Board) as the largest internal government audit board operating at national level, and supported by other boards operating at ministerial and departmental (*Irjen*), regional (*Irwilprop*), district (*Irwilkab/kodya*), and State Company (*Satuan Pengendalian Intern—SPI*) levels.

The State Companies (*Badan Usaha Milik Negara*, commonly referred to by the acronym BUMN) are involved in a wide range of industries,[8] and play a central role in the development of the Indonesian economy and the welfare of its people. The vast resources under the control of the BUMN and their strategic importance to the Indonesian economy mean that the government is concerned to ensure that their operations are efficient and consistent with national goals (Sutoyo 1988, 15; Habir 1990, 90). Consequently, the BUMN are a major focus of the State supervisory apparatus, and of BPKP in particular.

BPKP was established in 1983 (*Keppres No. 31/1983*) when it was recognized that its predecessor, the *Direktorat Jenderal Pengawasan Keuangan Negara* (DJPKN—the Directorate General of State Financial Control) was failing to function effectively. DJPKN had been established in 1968 to supervise and audit government agencies including ministries and departments, and the state companies (Sidik 1991, 7-9; Gandhi 1985, 8-9). An essential problem with DJPKN consistently identified in our interviews was its hierarchical location in the bureaucracy, being under and responsible to the Ministry of Finance. Hierarchically, it was on the same level as the government ministries and departments it was responsible for auditing. As such it was not accepted by its auditees as having sufficient power and status to fulfil its role (Gandhi, interview; Sidik, interview; Abdoelkadir, interview).

To overcome this problem, BPKP was established with direct accountability to the president, making it the highest ranking internal audit institution in the government hierarchy (Sutoyo, interview; Gandhi, interview). BPKP thus occupies a privileged position in Indonesia's economic and government structure, with its power stemming from its hierarchical status and knowledge base. BPKP is also extremely large with, currently, some 8,000 officials. It is widely recognized as the pool of state accountants (Hutagaol, interview), and, as its officials were substantially those from the pre-existing DJPKN, that knowledge base carried over directly to the BPKP. The replacement of the DJPKN with the BPKP essentially constituted a change of name with the primary objective being to reposition its hierarchical location. This latter is particularly important from a cultural contextual viewpoint, reinforcing the importance of power derivation from hierarchical status and superiority in high power distance cultures.

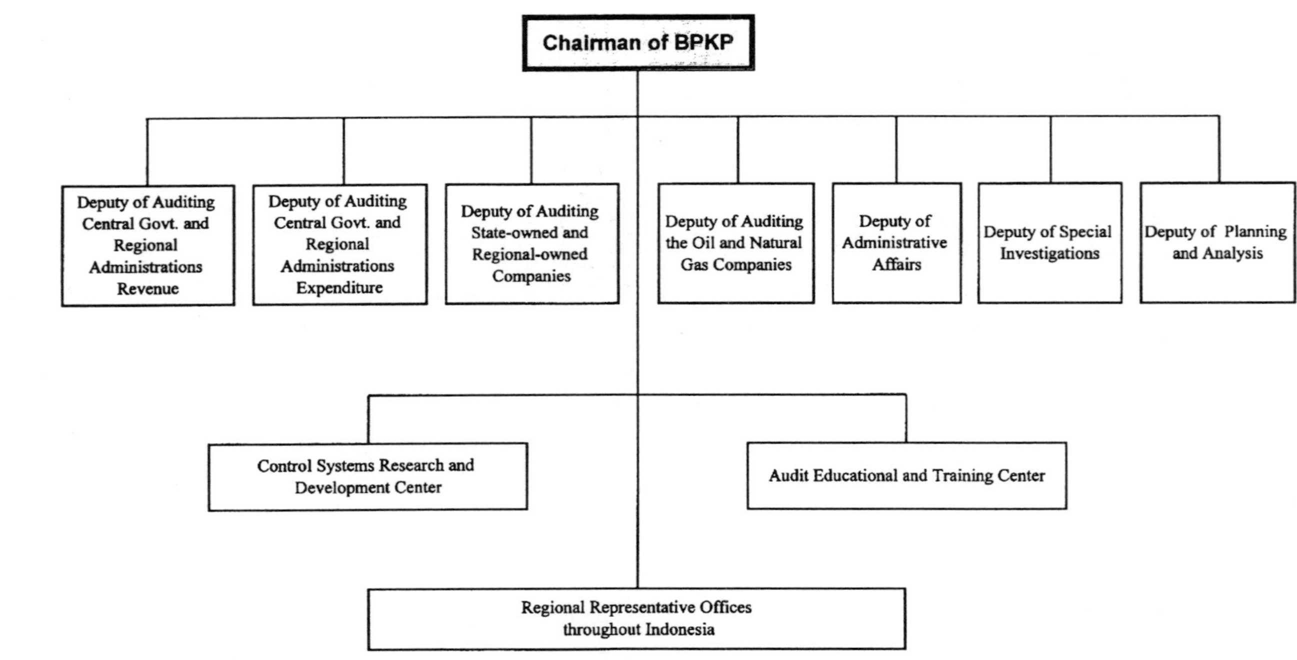

Source: Adapted from the Decree of the Chairman of BPKP: Kepress 188/K/1983, and Kepress No. 31/1983.

Figure 1. The Organizational Structure of BPKP

Under *Kepress No 31/1983*, BPKP has three all-embracing roles: "formulator of the program for development and financial supervisory policy, supervisor of the state financial management, and supervisor of development" (Gandhi 1985, 17). It has broad functions and extensive powers expressed in terms of the rights of its auditors and the scope of their audit supervision. The organizational structure through which BPKP operates is shown in Figure 1, where the functional, institutional and geographical spread of its influence is apparent.

BPKP's audit and supervisory scope extends to all activities of government including the implementation of the national plan and the management of state finances and assets. It also involves supervision of the internal audits of government agencies and the Indonesian state companies. With respect to the state companies (BUMN), *Keppres No 31/1983, Inpres No 15/1983* and *PP No 3/1983* provide BPKP with the responsibility for fulfilling two main roles, acting as (i) external auditor and (ii) guide and supervisor.

As external independent auditor, BPKP's role is to conduct both financial and operational audits of the BUMN (Yuliana, interview; Sumardi, interview) and to identify any instance of management fraud or abuse (Soebyakato, interview).The results of BPKP's audit are reported to the company's Board of Directors (*PP No 3/1983, article 32*), and, while it is the corporate senior executives who are responsible for following up the recommendations of BPKP's audit, Hutagaol (interview) notes that "the follow up of the audit findings is also monitored by BPKP." BPKP's audit report is also used by both the minister to whom the company is accountable, and the Minister of Finance in their evaluation and approval of the financial statements (*PP No 3/1983, article 10*).

In its role as guider and supervisor of the BUMN, BPKP provides a broad range of guidance including monitoring the implementation of the corporate budgets and working plans, providing technical and operational advice to the staff of *Satuan Pengendalian Intern* (SPI as the internal audit unit), providing training courses, and evaluating the management internal control and accounting systems of the companies (Sutoyo, interview; Tamtomo, interview; Sjamsir, interview). In terms of the accounting methods adopted by the state companies, BPKP also has an influential role in developing, together with the Indonesian Accountants Association and the company concerned, accounting standards for the company (Abdoelkadir, interview). (This is returned to in the next section when the relation between BPKP and the accounting profession in Indonesia is discussed.)

The importance and status of BPKP with respect to, and as perceived by, the government agencies and state companies, came through consistently in our interviews. Gandhi (interview) expressed it as follows:

> there is an increase in the will of the top executive of the state institutions to have an unqualified opinion from BPKP. Even the top executive of the state institutions and all their officials hold a special party when they have an unqualified opinion. However, this is linked to their prestige. This is not because of their increased awareness about the importance of BPKP's recommendation for their management.

The last two sentences in Ghandi's statement reflect the impact of a high power distance societal norm in institutional interactions in that they show that what is perceived important by those in lower hierarchical (institutional) statuses is the approval *per se* of those in higher statuses, rather than the specific content of their interactions.

In addition to reporting regularly to the Vice-President of Indonesia on the implementation of BPKP's roles, the Chairman of BPKP also maintains a special relationship with the Attorney General and the National Police. Audit findings that relate to criminal acts such as corruption are reported and discussed with the Attorney General, with those involving falsification or stealing reported to the national police (Gandhi, interview; Sutoyo, interview). While the state functional supervisory apparatus plays a central and major role in internal control in Indonesia, it is interesting to note that, in 1988, this was supplemented by *Pengawasan Masyarakat* (control by the people). Control by the people operates through PO Box 5000 (*tromol 5000*) (*Warta Pengawasan* 1994, 28). Through PO Box 5000, a person can anonymously report criminal acts, such as corruption, to the government. Cases reported are handled directly by the Vice-President of Indonesia. From 1988 to 1993, some 90,000 cases (about 15,000 per year) were reported (Warta Pengawasan 1994, 28). Of these, 39,500 have resulted in criminal acts being proven, with a further 27,500 still under investigation.

Control by the people is seen by the government as an effective device to achieve both sound management of national development and "clean" government (Warta Pengawasan 1994, 28). While the existence and widespread use of a form of control such as this may seem unusual to Anglo-American readers, it may be seen as quite consistent with Indonesian culture. Of particular relevance here are the second, third, and fifth principles of *Pancasila*: a just and civilized humanity, the unity of Indonesia, and social justice for all people of Indonesia. Values associated with these principles include "defend truth and equality," "avoid exploitation of other people," and "devotion to the nation's and state's interests." Corruption typically advantages specific individuals and disadvantages (or exploits) others; additionally, it typically subverts national interests through, for example, avoiding compliance with taxation and other legislation. Thus, it can be seen to have adverse effects on either other people in society or the national interest, and, therefore, to violate the values explicit in *Pancasila*.

The high power distance of Indonesian culture also reinforces the consistency of this behaviour. Hofstede (1980, 119) notes that high power distance societies place a high emphasis on "conformity," and the fact that the person reporting the corrupt or illegal practice remains anonymous is consistent with the "secrecy" characteristic of high power distance (Gray 1988). In fact, the veil of anonymity in "whistle-blowing" may be one of the few ways in which the social values of ensuring truth and justice for all people, and of avoiding exploitation of other people, can be pursued in a high power distance society, where there are constraints on the ability of people at lower social hierarchical levels to bring instances of corrupt or illegal behaviour to the attention of people in higher authority in overt ways.

BPKP and the Accounting Profession

The *Ikatan Akuntan Indonesia* (IAI—the Indonesian Accountants Association) is the country's sole professional accounting body, and the body responsible for accounting standard setting. It has a relatively short history, having been established only in 1957 (Abdoelkadir, interview). Indigenous accounting and accountants themselves have a similarly short history in Indonesia. During the long period of Dutch colonization, the accountants were essentially Dutch or English (Abdoelkadir 1982, 17).[9] Given the repression of education in Indonesia during colonization, this meant that, in 1957 following the Dutch withdrawal, there were only five qualified Indonesian accountants; the first graduates of the first accounting program in an Indonesian university which, itself, had commenced only in 1953 (Hadibroto 1975, 129).

The recent and limited base from which the accounting profession in Indonesia began meant that Indonesia had only 60 qualified accountants in 1962, and still less than 900 by the end of 1973 (Abdoelkadir, interview); the year of issue of Indonesia's first accounting principles, audit standards, and code of ethics.[10] With the development of Indonesia's economy and business sector in the last decade has also come the development of professional accounting, such that there are now some 14,800 registered accountants (Muchtar, interview).

The IAI represents all accountants in Indonesia, whether employed in the public or private sector. Its management consists of three operational levels: *pengurus pusat* (the central management comprising the chairman, secretary and treasurer); *pengurus cabang* (branch management); and *seksi* (chapters). A fourth level is *kongres* (congress), which is held every four years, is attended by representatives of all branches and chapters, and which selects the IAI chairman, who subsequently selects other members of the central management (Tim Pengembangan Akuntansi Indonesia 1993).

IAI has a Board of Advisers (*Dewan Penasehat*), the function of which is to provide advice for IAI management, a Board of Honor (*Dewan Kehormatan*), with the function to maintain the compliance of accountants with the code of ethics (*kode etik akuntan*), and four committees which are subordinate to the chairman: Committee of Accounting Principles (*Prinsip Akuntansi Indonesia—PAI*), Committee of Audit Standards (*Norma Pemeriksaan Akuntan—NPA*), Committee of Code of Ethics (*Kode Etik Indonesia*), and Committee of Taxation (*Perpajakan*). The first two of these are responsible for the setting of accounting and audit standards.

Although there is no regulation governing the relationship between BPKP and the IAI, and although IAI is the sole standard setting body, the interviews conducted in this research carried clear indication of the government's influence, through BPKP, in accounting development and standard setting in Indonesia. This influence is achieved and maintained in several ways. The first is the placement of BPKP officials on IAI committees, and in influential positions in the IAI management structure. Gandhi (interview), Sutoyo (interview) and Sidik (interview) all noted the involvement of BPKP officials in IAI committees, including the standard-setting committees, and Hutagaol (interview) noted that the chairmen of BPKP's regional administrations are invited to be either the adviser to, or the chairman of, the regional IAI branches, while the chairman of BPKP itself is invited to be a member of the prestigious IAI Board of Honor. In addition, all BPKP's accountants are members of IAI.

A second influence is the dependence of IAI on the government for financial support (Suta, interview). Consistently raised by interviewees was the funding limitation of the IAI and its implications for the development of the IAI's professionalism. Kartikahadi (interview) noted the voluntary nature of work for the IAI because of its inability to fund permanent staff; and both Abdoelkardi (interview) and Mira (interview) argued that IAI has lacked, and continues to lack, professional research and operational management staff.

The third way in which the government, through BPKP, maintains its influence in accounting development is via its requests to, and cooperation with, the IAI in establishing accounting standards and policy for industries or areas where BPKP, in its role of audit supervisor, identifies a need. Abdoelkadir (interview) expressed it in the following way: "Due to the different perceptions between BPKP and its auditees concerning particular business transactions, BPKP asks IAI to cooperate to set up new accounting standards where it is considered they are needed."

Abdoelkadir (interview) and Suta (interview) provided examples of such participation by BPKP, and cooperation by the IAI, in the development of accounting standards for the telecommunications, leasing, and real estate industries. Finally, and this is returned to in the next section dealing with the relationship between BPKP and the public accounting firms in Indonesia, it is the government which has the authority to sanction and/or revoke the licenses of public accountants—the IAI does not have this authority (Kartikahadi, interview).

There are a number of potential reasons for the involvement of BPKP in the activities and standard-setting processes of the IAI. One is that such involvement is needed because of the differences in the attained states of the BPKP and IAI, in both financial and personnel terms, at this point in time. While the IAI suffers the lack of its own funding and professional staff, BPKP, with its size of some 8,000 officials and its years of experience clearly provides an important resource and knowledge base for the IAI. It may be argued that the support and involvement of BPKP is needed until the IAI attains the degree of professionalism sufficient to operate without the financial support and knowledge base of the government and BPKP.

However, the interviews, while predicting a necessary increase in the professionalism of the IAI through permanent staff and self-financing (Suta, interview), also predicted an increase, rather than a reduction, in the involvement of BPKP and, hence, the government, in accounting development and standard-setting in Indonesia (Sidik, interview). Irsan Yani, the Deputy Chairman of BPKP, argued that this involvement would maintain and increase because BPKP, in its statutory audit supervisory role of government agencies and the state companies, was the main user of the IAI's products of accounting and auditing standards (Warta Pengawasan 1994, 44). In that role, and with its hierarchical ranking, BPKP has both the responsibility and the power through status that would suggest a maintained and increased involvement in accounting development, particularly in, and consistent with the dictates of, a high power distance society.

While Indonesia's history and high power distance culture point to the appropriateness of government involvement and influence in the standard-setting process, our interviews suggest that there is no evidence of a move to remove the standard-setting process from the IAI. Rather, the interviews generally conveyed the indication that it is considered important that the process itself remain with the IAI.

A conclusion that may be drawn from the interviews in this respect is that the IAI is seen as needed to accommodate the interests of all concerned parties, including the influential governmental regulatory bodies such as BPKP, the Ministry of Finance, and *Bapepam* (the Capital Market Supervisory Board). In the absence of a sole authorized standard-setting body (in the IAI), it was felt that these bodies might seek to establish their own accounting standards for given issues; a situation which would inevitably bring them into open conflict and competition. The existence and use of IAI as the sole authorized body allows a mechanism within which consensus can be achieved among these influential government bodies. This approach reflects, and is consistent with, the values of *mufakat* (consensus) and *musyawarah* (deliberation), and their encapsulation in the fourth principle of *Pancasila*, which emphasizes deliberations among representatives to attain an outcome acceptable to all.

Nonetheless, while, on the surface, the IAI is the sole authorized standard-setting body, and maintains as an entity overtly separate and distinct from BPKP, our interviews disclose that the two entities are operationally closely intertwined, allowing the influence and interests of the latter substantial expression in the activities of the former, and, hence, in accounting and regulation in Indonesia generally.

BPKP and the Public Accounting Firms

As for accountants and the accounting profession, the development of public accounting firms in Indonesia was relatively slow until the middle to late 1970s (Abdoelkadir, interview). The limited number of accountants was itself a factor in this, but another was the nature of the enterprises, many of which were family owned and managed partnerships with no requirements for their accounts to be audited (Hadibroto 1975).

The number of public accounting firms has grown substantially since then,[11] with the major early impetus being the government's move in 1979, driven by the motive of increasing taxation revenues, to provide that financial statements audited by public accounting firms would be accepted for tax purposes (President Instruction No. 6/1979, implemented by Ministry of Finance Decree No. 108/1979).

With the increase in the role and importance of the accounting firms, the government issued, in 1986, regulations to govern their operations and to provide for their guidance and supervision (Ministry of Finance Decree No. 763/KMK.011/1986). The responsibility for guidance was vested in the Ministry of Finance, and the responsibility for monitoring and supervision vested in BPKP. As the main users of the services of public accounting firms are the private sector and the government, itself, including the state companies (Gultom 1991, 2), BPKP is concerned that the independence, integrity, objectivity and competence of public accounting firms in performing audits are maintained (BPKP 1993, 5). To carry out this function, BPKP issued, in 1993, *Pedoman Umum Penelaahan Tata Kerja Kantor Akuntan Publik* (General Guidelines for Supervision of the Public Accounting Firm's Administration).

Under these guidelines, BPKP auditors have scope to evaluate public accounting firms' management in performing audit services for their clients, as well as having involvement in other activities of the firms through consultation, administrative assistance, and review of the firms' financial statements. BPKP also requires that the public accounting firms maintain a system of standard quality known as *Sistem Pengendalian Mutu*, which provides control and evaluation of auditing from planning through to reporting, and is based on the accounting principles, audit standards, the code of ethics and other regulations (BPKP 1993, 5-6).

If the regular BPKP audit evaluation indicates that the accounting firm has breached the audit standards or the code of ethics, a special audit of that firm is conducted. Should this special audit confirm the breach, BPKP reports this directly to the Ministry of Finance together with a proposal for sanction to be imposed on the firm (Kartomo, interview). Having evaluated BPKP's audit finding and called for, and heard, the accounting firm's response, the ministry decides and issues sanctions, including revocation of licenses of practitioners in the firms (Kartomo, interview). In 1993, for example, some 20 licenses were revoked by the Ministry of Finance as a result of this process.

The interviewees consistently stressed the importance of BPKP's monitoring and supervision role because of the circumstances of public accounting firms in Indonesia currently. Gandhi, the first Chairman of BPKP, noted, in this respect, that lack of auditor independence, and malpractice in the form of audit opinions which reflect the interests of clients, were "not uncommon" in Indonesia (Gandhi, interview). Kartikahardi, the current Chairman of the Committee of Accounting

Principles, pointed to other practices being engaged in by some public accountants which stimulated and required government control.

> The requirements to establish a public accounting firm are relatively easy. This situation is used by particular accountants as "gambling." Instead of [working as a] public accountant, they work for management in other companies. Their licenses as public accountants are used by other people. These public accounting firms receive fee of commission without doing any audit jobs (Kartikahardi, interview).

Kartikahardi's reference to "gambling" means that people engaging in this practice hold public accounting licenses, but do not practice as public accountants. Rather, they work in other firms or as civil servants, and allow their public accountant licenses to be used by others. They subsequently put their licensed signatures to the work of others and collect a commission. Kartikahardi (interview) states that "these public accountant firms are liquidated by the Minister of Finance—they have to choose their profession as public accountant or otherwise." Abdoelkadir (interview) attributes this behavior and other instances of malpractice, corruption and collusion, on the part of civil servants to their poor salary conditions:

> Not all people have strong identity, such as integrity, so they easily change their mind due to the insufficient salary. They perform misconduct such as criminal acts to meet their needs. Thus, I recommend that the economy of the civil servants should improve. In addition, this also requires the commitment of superiors. The superiors should provide good conduct so their subordinates will follow them.

Mackie and MacIntyre (1994, 21) also note the fact that civil servant and official salaries in Indonesia "have lagged far behind the cost of living (so that in 1990, for example, they provided for barely one-third of an official's household needs)."

CONCLUSIONS

This chapter has sought to portray the role of government, through the role of BPKP (the Development and Financial Supervisory Board) in the development of accounting and regulation in Indonesia. The chapter drew on both history and culture, with the former providing: (i) the unique circumstances of Indonesia's long period of colonization to explain the fact that indigenous accounting and regulation are quite recent phenomena in Indonesia; and (ii) the background of institutionalized hierarchy and societal repression as partial explanators of the government's influential and active role in contemporary economic and social matters generally. Culture was drawn on to reinforce societal acceptance of government influence as being consistent with the general dictates of high power distance, collectivist cultures, and with the specific principles of *Pancasila*.

The interviews carried out for the research clearly demonstrate the influence of government in accounting development and regulation in contemporary Indonesia. Those interviews described and emphasized the ways in which BPKP maintains hands-on influence over the activities of the state companies, the accounting profession, and public accounting firms, as part of the *Aparat Pengawasan Fungsional Pemerintah* (the state functional supervisory apparatus). The interviews also demonstrated the extent of government influence in accounting development and standard-setting relative to that of the professional accounting body. An historical explanation alone might suggest that this relativity could be transitional arising from the late development of the accounting profession and its currently weak financial and personnel resource base. Certainly, the interviews predict an increase in the professionalism of the accounting body in Indonesia as it develops.

However, when the cultural context is also taken into account, the prediction from the interviews that the future will see an increase rather than a reduction in government involvement is consistent with an on-going preference for, and acceptance of, government influence, relative to that of the professional accounting bodies, in accounting development and standard-setting in a high power distance, collectivist society. This Indonesian case study, therefore, provides support for Gray's (1988) and Salter and Niswander's (1995) hypothesized association between statutory control and the cultural dimensions of high power distance and collectivism. As such, the contemporary and expected future position in Indonesia is similar to other high power distance, collectivist countries, such as Japan (McKinnon 1986), and stands in contrast to the greater extent of professional body influence in Anglo-American nations.

APPENDIX

Interviewees

Abdoelkadir, Drs. K. K.	Chairman and member of the Board of Honor of the Indonesian Accountants Association (IAI) and Executive Secretary of the Coordination Team for the Development of Accountancy.
Densu, Drs. H. D.	Chairman of the Board of Educational Guidance for Implementation of the Guidance for Understanding and Implementation of *Pancasila* (BP-7), for the District Administration of Ujung Pandang of the Regional Administration of South Sulawesi.
Gandhi, Drs.	Former Chairman of BPKP, currently senior official of the Audit Supreme Board of Indonesia, and member of the Advisory Board of the Indonesian Accountants Association.

Hamid, Mr A. M.	Head of Art of the Regional Administration of South Sulawesi.
Hutagaol, Drs. V.	Head of BPKP's Regional Administration of South Sulawesi.
Kartikahardi, Drs. H.	Chairman of the Committee of Accounting Principles and Standards, and Managing Partner of the public accounting firm *Hans Tuanakotta Mustofa*, an associate of Deloitte Touche Tohmatsu International.
Kartomo, Drs. W.	Director of Accountant and Appraisal (Ministry of Finance), former director of BPKP, former Head of BPKP's Regional Administration of South Sumatra, and former Head of BPKP's representative office in Bonn, Germany.
Lakunnu, Drs. H. U.	Chairman of the Board of Educational Guidance for Implementation of the Guidance for Understanding and Implementation of *Pancasila* (BP-7) for Regional Administration of South Sulawesi.
Mira, Dra.	Senior official of BPKP and member of the Committee of Accounting Principles of the Indonesian Accountants Association.
Muchtar, Mr. M.	Member of Directorate of Accountant and Appraisal, Ministry of Finance.
Sidik, Drs. S.	Chairman of the Center of Research and Development Systems of BPKP, and a former Director of BPKP.
Sjamsir, Ir. H.	President Director of PT *(Persero) Perkebunan XXXII* (a state plantation company).
Soebyakato, Ir.	President Director of PT *(Persero) Tonasa* (a state cement industrial company).
Sumardi, Ir.	President Director of PT *(Persero) Pelabuhan Indonesia IV* (a state company).
Sumardjan, Prof. S.	Senior Lecturer in Sociology at the State University of Indonesia.
Suta, I. G. P. A.	Member of the Committees of Accounting Principles and Audit Standards (IAI), and Head of the Financial Corporation II Bureau of the Capital Market Supervisory Board.
Sutoyo, Drs. M.	Chairman of the Board of Honor of the Indonesian Accountants Association, member of the public

	accounting firm *SGV Utomo*, an associate of Arthur Andersen, and a former Deputy Chairman of BPKP.
Tamtomo	Chairman of the Unit of Internal Control of PT*(Persero) Pelabuhan Indonesia IV* (a state company).
Yuliana, Dra. M. W.	Deputy Chairman of the Unit of Internal Control of PT*(Persero) Reasuransi Umum Indonesia* (a state insurance company).

NOTES

1. Salter and Niswander (1995) did find support for the association between statutory control/professionalism and uncertainty avoidance.

2. Both Hadibroto (1975) and Arya (1990), in their studies of accounting and disclosure practices in Indonesia note, but do not explore, the importance of the role of the Indonesian government.

3. Good descriptions of Indonesian history during this period are provided in Grant (1966), McKay (1976), Caldwell and Utrecht (1979), Zainu'ddin (1980), Lubis (1990), and Ricklefs (1993), and with respect to commercial development, Briston (1990). Together with other references, these form the basis for the historical section of this paper.

4. From 1794 to 1810 when the French assumed control as a consequence of their occupation of Holland itself (National Development Information Office 1992, 11), and from 1811 to 1816 when the British took control as a result of military confrontation with the French and Dutch over the Indonesian island of Java (Zainu'ddin 1980, 116; Lubis 1990, 131-136).

5. Internal rebellions included the *Darum Islam* in 1947 which sought to establish an Indonesian Moslem State, and the *Madiun* rebellion which sought to create a Communist regime, while international confrontations included the take-over of West Irian from the Dutch by military force in 1962, and the confrontation with the British over the formation of the Federation of Malaya in 1963 (Grant 1966; Caldwell and Utrecht 1979).

6. In terms of Hofstede's dimensions, Indonesia also displays moderate uncertainty avoidance. However, since Gray's (1988) hypothesized association was between statutory control and high power distance, low individualism and high uncertainty avoidance, this study focuses on the first two dimensions which are directly applicable to Indonesia. Additionally, Salter and Niswander (1995, 383) suggest that high power distance and low individualism are the two dimensions that are most likely to be associated with statutory control.

7. See Kitley (1994) for a discussion of the differences between Indonesia and Anglo-American nations on the dimensions of individualism and power distance, and of the practical implications of these differences for doing business in Indonesia.

8. The industries include transport, telecommunications, tourism, steel, cement, building and construction, electrical equipment, automobile assembly, sugar and rubber plantations, textiles, and import-export (Habir 1990, 104-107).

9. For a discussion of Dutch accounting in Indonesia during the period of colonization, see Sukoharson and Gaffikin (1993). Additionally, an insightful analysis of the post-colonial Dutch and American influences on the development of accounting education in Indonesia is provided by Briston and Hadori (1993).

10. The *Prinsip Akuntansi Indonesia* (PAI), *Norma Pemeriksaan Akuntan* (NPA), and the *Kode Etik Indonesia*, being the accounting principles, audit standards and code of ethics, respectively.

11. From 12 in 1986 to 382 by the end of 1989 (Gultom 1991, 2) and to 454 currently (Muchtar, interview).

REFERENCES

Abdoelkadir, K.K. 1982. The perceptions of accountants and accounting students on the accounting profession in Indonesia. *Accountancy Development in Indonesia*, Publication No. 12, Coordination Team for the Development of Accountancy.

Arya, N.P.S. 1990. Corporate financial reporting in Indonesia: An analysis of corporate characteristics and information disclosure practices. Unpublished Master of Commerce (Honors) thesis, Department of Accountancy, University of Wollongong.

Bahan Penataran Pegawi Negeri. 1981. *Tim Pembinaan Penatar dan Bahan Penataran Pegawai Republik Indonesia* [Material Course for Civil Servants, The Team of Training Counsellor and Material Course for Civil Servants].

BPKP. 1993. *Badan Pengawasan Keuangan dan Pembangunan*, Surat Kepala BPKP No. S-29/K/1993 tanggal 29 Januari 1993 perihal Pemeriksaan Pajak oleh Tim Gabungan DJP-BPKP tahun 1993/94 [Letter of Head of BPKP Number No. S-29/K/1993 dated 29 January 1993 concerning Tax Audit conducted by the Coordinated Team of BPKP and Directorate General of Taxation].

Briston, R.J. 1990. Accounting in developing countries: Indonesia and the Solomon Islands as case studies for regional cooperation. *Research in Third World Accounting* 1: 195-216.

Briston, R.J., and Y. Hadori. 1993. Role and training of accounting technicians: IFAC's IEG No. 7 and its relevance for Southeast Asia. *Research in Third World Accounting* 2: 245-258.

Caldwell, M., and E. Utrecht. 1979. *Indonesia: An Alternative History*. Sydney: Alternative Publishing Cooperative Limited.

Choi, F.D.S., and G. G. Mueller. 1992. *International Accounting*. Englewood Cliffs, NJ: Prentice-Hall International.

Cooke, T.E., and R. S. O. Wallace. 1990. Financial disclosure regulation and its environment: A review and further analysis. *Journal of Accounting and Public Policy* 9 (2): 79-110.

Coopers and Lybrand. 1992. *International Accounting Summaries: A Guide for Interpretation and Comparison 1992 Supplement*. New York: John Wiley & Sons, Inc.

Dahm, B. 1971. *History of Indonesia in the Twentieth Century*. London: Pall Mall Press.

Department of Information of the Republic of Indonesia. 1991. *The Process and Progress of Pancasila Democracy*.

Enthoven, A.J.H. 1977. Accounting Systems in Third World Economies. Amsterdam: North Holland Publishing Company.

Gandhi. 1985. Pengawasan Keuangan dan Pembangunan. Paper untuk Dies Natalis Universitas Padjajaran ke XXVIII di Bandung, 19 September [Financial Supervision and Development. Paper presented at Inauguration of the State University of Padjajaran XXVIII in Bandung, September 19].

Grant, B. 1966. *Indonesia*. Melbourne: Melbourne University Press.

Gray, S.J. 1988. Towards a theory of cultural influence on the development of accounting systems internationally. *Abacus* 24 (March): 1-15.

Gultom, C. 1991. Bergagai Masalah Dalam Pengawasan Dan Pengendalian Mutu Akuntan Publik [Some Problems in Supervision and Quality Control of Public Accountants]. Paper presented at State University of Airlangga, Surabaya, December 21.

Habir, A.D. 1990. State enterprises. In *Indonesia Assessment*, eds. H. Hill and T. Hull. Canberra: Department of Political and Social Change Research, School of Political Studies, Australian National University.

Hadibroto, S. 1975. A comparative study of American and Dutch accounting and their impact on the profession in Indonesia. *Accountancy Development in Indonesia*, Publication No. 13. Tim Koordinasi Pengembangan Akuntansi.

Hardjowardojo, N. 1976. Basic cultural influences. In *Studies in Indonesian History*, ed. E. McKay, 1-38. Melbourne: Pitman Publishing Pty Ltd.

Hill, H. 1994. *Indonesia's New Order: The Dynamics of Socio-Economic Transformation*. St. Leonards, Australia: Allen & Unwin Pty Ltd.

Hofstede, G.H. 1980. *Culture's Consequences: International Differences in Work Related Values.* Beverly Hills, CA: Sage Publications.

Hofstede, G.H. 1983. The cultural relativity of organisational practices and theories. *Journal of International Business Studies* 14 (Fall): 75-89.

Kitley, P. 1994. The cultural context of doing business in Indonesia. *Asian Review of Accounting*: 139-150.

Lubis, M. 1990. *Indonesia: Land under the Rainbow.* Singapore: Oxford University Press.

Mackie, J., and A. MacIntyre. 1994. Politics. In *Indonesia's New Order: The Dynamics of Socio-Economic Transformation*, ed. H. Hill, 1-53. St. Leonards, Australia: Allen & Unwin Pty Ltd.

McKay, E. 1976. Sixteenth to eighteenth centuries: The significance of the coming of the Europeans. In *Studies in Indonesian History,* ed. E. McKay, 98-123. Melbourne: Pitman Publishing Pty Ltd.

McKinnon, J.L. 1986. *The Historical Development and Operational Form of Corporate Reporting Regulation in Japan.* New York: Garland Publishing Inc.

National Development Information Office. 1992. *Indonesia Source Book.* Jakarta: National Development Information Office.

Previts, G. J., L. D. Parker, and E. N. Coffman. 1990. Accounting history: Definition and relevance. *Abacus* 27 (March): 1-13.

Price Waterhouse. 1996. *Doing Business in Indonesia.* Jakarta: Price Waterhouse World Firm Services BV.

Reeve, D. 1985. *Golkar of Indonesia: An Alternative to the Party System.* Singapore: Oxford University Press.

Ricklefs, M.C. 1993. *A History of Modern Indonesia Since c.1300* (2nd ed.). Basingstoke, Hants: The Macmillan Press Ltd.

Salter, S.B., and F. Niswander. 1995. Cultural influence on the development of accounting systems internationally. *Journal of International Business Studies*, 26 (Second Quarter): 379-397.

Sidik, S. 1991. Perkembangan Pengawasan di Lingkungan Pemerintahan Republik Indonesia. Paper untuk Seminar Sehari Akuntansi dan Auditing di sektor Pemerintahan, 25 Februari, Ikatan Akuntan Indonesia. [The Development of Supervision in the Government Environment. Paper presented at the Workshop concerning Accounting and auditing in the Public Sector, February 25, Indonesian Accountant Association].

Spicer and Oppenheim International. 1989. *Guide to Financial Statements Around the World.* New York: John Wiley & Sons, Inc.

Sukoharsono, E.G., and M. J. R. Gaffikin. 1993. The genesis of accounting in Indonesia: The Dutch colonialism in the early 17th century. *The Indonesian Journal of Accounting and Business Society*: 4-26.

Sutoyo, M. (1988), Sisten Pengawasan BUMN. Paper untuk ceramah pada Seminar Sehari Pengawasan Melekat di Universitas Sam Ratulangi di Manado, 28 November [The Supervisory System of the State Companies BUMN. Paper presented at the Workshop concerning Built-In Control at the State University of Sam Ratulangi in Manado, November 28].

Tim Pengembangan Akuntansi Indonesia (Team for the Development of Accounting in Indonesia). 1993. *Institute of Accountants of Indonesia: Implementation of a Strategy for Development*, amended draft. Jakarta: Indonesia Accountant Association.

Wallace, R.S.O. 1987. Disclosure of accounting information in developing countries: A case study of Nigeria. PhD Dissertation, University of Exeter, England.

Warta Pengawasan. 1994. Positif, Dampak Pengawasan Selama Ini (Positive Impact of the Recent Supervision), No. 10, Thn III, 27-30.

Whitley, R.D. 1991. The social construction of business systems in East Asia. *Organization Studies*: 1-28.

Zainu'ddin, A.G.T. 1980. *A Short History of Indonesia* (2nd ed.). Stanmore, NSW: Cassell Australia.

A COMPARATIVE STUDY OF ACCOUNTING EDUCATION AND CERTIFICATION IN SOUTH ASIA

Kamran Ahmed and Habib M. Zafarullah

ABSTRACT

This chapter provides a comparative evaluation of accounting education and certification in India, Pakistan, and Bangladesh. While the three countries share a common history in the development of accounting education and practices in British India, each has devised its own accounting education and training systems (AETS) suited to its peculiar needs. After independence, certification rules and procedures were redefined and the curricula at the universities were modified to incorporate new concepts and practices. New professional institutes were created or existing ones revitalized to help create a body of professional accountants and auditors. The structure of accounting education is broadly similar in the three countries; subtle variations exist in the way teaching is imparted. The programs of chartered and cost and management institutes, basically variants of overseas models, are geared more to the practicalities of accounting than to pure theoretical concerns. Major problems of accounting education and training at the university and professional organisational levels have been outlined and some remedial measures have been suggested.

Research in Accounting in Emerging Economies, Volume 4, pages 73-95.

ISBN: 1-55938-995-8

INTRODUCTION

Over the past decade, accounting education and training systems (AETS) have received considerable attention from academics and professional accounting around the world (Anyane-Ntow 1992; Osiegbu 1987; Tan et al., 1994; UNCTC 1991). The intensifying international accounting harmonization efforts, increased globalization of trade and industry, and concern for a lack of relevance of accounting stimulated the need for critically understanding the role of AETS and for making accounting education socially and economically more germane.

In a more practical sense, a clear understanding of a country's AETS is important because it helps in assessing its applicability and working in the context of its social and economic environment. To this end, comparative studies are more useful since they give policymakers the ability to easily comprehend the effectiveness and limitations of AETS in their own countries and to equip national planning organizations with the skills to develop appropriate systems matching the needs of their countries. However, the existing literature on AETS mainly focuses on single countries largely in the developed world. Thus, research on comparative accounting education and the professional certification process in developing countries has been limited, thereby leaving a gap in our awareness of the constraints and inadequacies faced by them in building effective AETS. This study, to a limited extent, attempts to fill this void. It explores, from a broad comparative perspective, the accounting education system in South Asia, the countries of which share a common historical legacy. It traces the recent developments in AETS in India, Bangladesh, and Pakistan and the efforts made and the constraints faced by each country's professional bodies and universities to advance accounting education.

India, Pakistan, and Bangladesh, together known as the Indian subcontinent, were under British rule for about 200 years until 1947 when India and Pakistan became independent countries. Bangladesh, formerly a province of Pakistan (known as East Pakistan), became an independent country 24 years later. All three countries occupy important positions in the Asian region in terms of geographical location, population, and economic potential.

The manufacturing sector in the three countries is relatively large compared to other emerging economies, contributing about 30 percent to each country's gross national product with the exception of Bangladesh, where its relative contribution is still below 20 percent (ESCAP, 1997). The stock markets in all three countries have been in existence for more than 80 years and have experienced rapid growth in recent times. At the end of 1996, the total market capitalization of the stock exchanges in India, Pakistan, and Bangladesh were about US$122,605 million, US$10,639 million and US$4,551 million, respectively (IFC, 1998), with each achieving a positive growth rate in the last decade (see Table 1).

There have been important initiatives, in recent years, to attract overseas investment, facilitate joint ventures in the industrial sector, streamline the public sector,

Table 1. Some Socioeconomic and Demographic Indicators of India, Pakistan, and Bangladesh to 1996

Indicators	*India*	*Pakistan*	*Bangladesh*
Area (sq km)	3,287,263.00	796,095.00	147,570.00
Population (million)	939.42	134.25	111.45
Adult literacy rate (%)	52.11	36.00	42.00
Number of universities	228.00	38.00	12.00
GDP (in million US $)	356,027.00	64,846.00	31,827.00
GNP per capita (US$)	350.00	380.00	260.00
Growth rate (1990-1996)	3.80	4.80	2.70
Agricultural Production to GDP (%)	25.00	23.50	28.70
Market capitalization (US$)	122,605.00	10,639.00	4,551.00
Number of listed companies	5,999.00	782.00	186.00
World rankings (# of listed companies)	2.00	8.00	39.00

Sources: International Finance Corporation (IFC) (1998), *Emerging Stock Markets Fact Book*, Washington, DC. Economic and Social Commission for Asia and Pacific (1997) *Statistics Yearbook*. Bangkok, Thailand.

revitalize the stock market and provide incentives to develop private entrepreneurship. The recent economic liberalization programs leading to the development of the private sector, together with the reform of the state enterprises to operate in a more competitive environment, have underscored the significance of a professional and efficient accounting system not only to consolidate the gains of economic growth but also to sustain development. Consequently, AETS, as a vital input to economic growth, has attained greater significance.

In section two of this chapter, we provide a brief background of the development of accounting education and training since the British colonial days. This is followed by a comparative discussion of the structure of accounting education at the higher secondary and tertiary levels in section three and the training systems of professional organizations in section four, respectively. Conclusions are drawn in the final section.

DEVELOPMENT OF ACCOUNTING EDUCATION IN COLONIAL AND POST-COLONIAL SOUTH ASIA

The roots of accounting in the Indian subcontinent dates back to pre-colonial period. Some indigenous forms of accounting, namely "Bhahi-Khata"[1] have been in existence for many centuries. Many small entrepreneurs in Bangladesh, India, Pakistan and Sri Lanka (Lall Nigam 1986) still use these indigenous forms of accounting, in different versions and languages. The British East India Company and early European merchants introduced the present double-entry system of accounting in the Indian subcontinent during the colonial period. Consequently, accounting regulations and education system were modelled on the British system.

Statutory obligations since 1850 required a limited liability company to provide audited balance sheets and profit and loss accounts. However, the qualifications of the auditors were not defined until 1913 when a new Companies Act was enforced. This legislation persuaded the provincial government of Bombay[2] to set up a college in 1918 to educate and train people to acquire the Government Diploma in Accountancy (GDA). Later several colleges were set up in major cities including Madras, Lahore, and Calcutta. Apart from such regional initiatives, accounting education and training, in general, became centralized after the promulgation of the Auditors' Certificate Rules (ACR) in 1932 following a major amendment to the 1913 Act. The Indian Accountancy Board (IAB) was established soon after under the aegis of the Indian Commerce Ministry. It functioned to monitor registration, examination and control of auditors and the accounting profession in British India (Sayeed 1992).

Under the ACR, a two-tier examination system—the first examination and the final examination—was introduced. A pass in 12 subjects[3] accredited by the IAB and a minimum of four years' training qualified a person to register himself/herself as a public accountant and entitled him/her to use the identification "Registered Accountant" (RA) after his name. Those with overseas qualifications from such bodies as the Institute of Chartered Accountants in England and Wales (ICAEW) retained their own institutional title "Chartered Accountant" (CA). The creation of this nomenclatorial difference caused the locally trained RAs to mount pressure on the government to authorize them to use the other more attractive title. Their persistent demand, however, remained unheeded until the independence of India and Pakistan in 1947. In the meantime, the IAB acted in an advisory capacity and made significant contribution to the development of professional accounting training in undivided India (Banerjee 1992, 173).

Development of Professional Organizations

After independence, both India and Pakistan (Bangladesh being a part of Pakistan) continued with the same organizational and training structures and adopted the existing ACR and the Companies Act. India took the lead in establishing a professional body, the Institute of Chartered Accountants of India (ICAI), an autonomous body to oversee AETS in the country. The 1949 Chartered Accountants Act paved the way for all RAs to become its members and to convert their title to "CA." India again took the initiative to discard the colonial Companies Act by promulgating a new one in 1956, which still remains the legislative basis of corporate financial reporting and AETS in that country. In the meantime, an organization, limited by guarantee of its members and known as the "Institute of Cost and Works Accountants" (CWA), was set up with the objective of developing and promoting cost accounting in Indian manufacturing industries. It received statutory recognition in 1959.

In Pakistan, the ACR was amended in 1950 but the government was hesitant to forego its hold over professional AETS for over a decade. Following the Indian model, the Pakistan government granted autonomous status to the Institute of Chartered Accountants in 1961 and five years later to the Pakistan Institute of Industrial Accountants (PIIA) (Sayeed 1992). The 1913 Companies Act was repealed by a new Companies Act in 1984, which significantly increased the disclosure requirements of both listed and unlisted companies, introduced cost audit for manufacturing enterprises, made compliance with international accounting standards mandatory, and prescribed a standard format for audit reports (Sayeed 1992).

Bangladesh, after its own independence, inherited the Pakistani model and immediately established two professional bodies: The Institute of Chartered Accountants of Bangladesh (ICAB) and the Institute of Cost and Management Accountants of Bangladesh (ICMAB). Both institutes adopted all the rules and by-laws of their Pakistani counterparts, primarily to maintain continuity (Azizuddin 1984). Until 1994 when a new Companies Act was enacted, amended versions of the 1913 Companies Act were used as guiding principles of professional AETS. The 1994 Act contained many provisions, which are similar to those of the Indian and Pakistani statutes.

STRUCTURE OF ACCOUNTING EDUCATION AT THE HIGHER SECONDARY AND TERTIARY LEVELS

The structure of education is broadly similar in India, Pakistan, and Bangladesh (Figure 1). Upon successful completion of post-secondary public examination, a student has two options (depending upon his/her performance at the higher secondary/intermediate examination) to choose from. One option is to undertake a further two years of tertiary study at a college (not a university) and the second option is a three- or four-year honors level study at a university. Both the two and three year programs in commerce lead to the Bachelor of Commerce (B.Com) or Bachelor of Business Administration (BBA) degree. But while the former provides only a nominal pass (i.e., B.Com. (Pass)), the latter confers a student with an Honors (i.e., B.Com. (Honors)) degree. The latter which is academically more rigorous allows the student to concentrate on any one business subject, such as accounting, management, marketing, finance, or other cognate area of study. Upon obtaining a tertiary first degree (pass or honors), a student may pursue higher studies at the masters level, the length of study depending on the level of the degree obtained. For those with an honors degree, a further study of one year is required to obtain the Master of Commerce (M.Com.) degree, while students with a pass qualification need two years to complete the same program.[4]

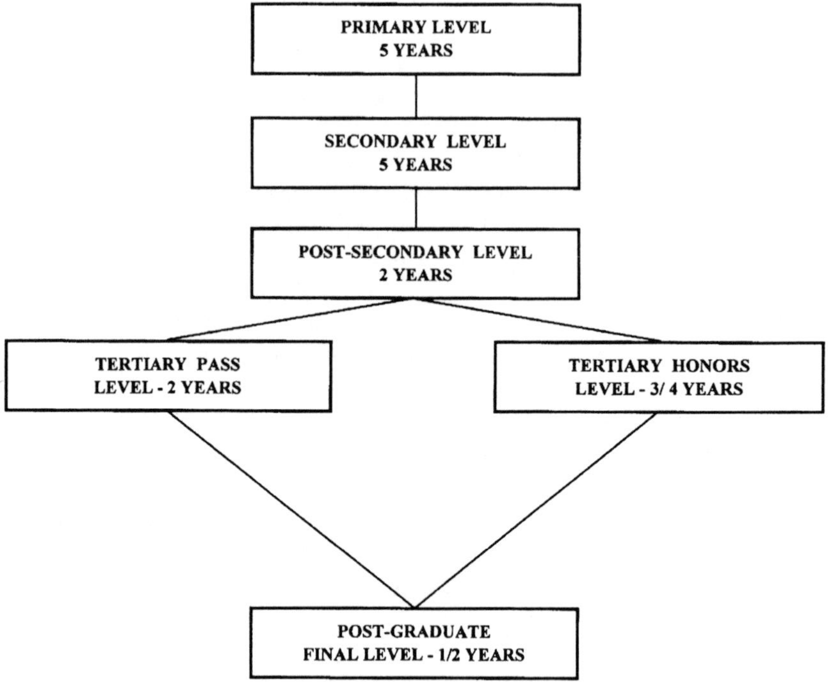

Figure 1. The Structure of Accounting Education in India, Pakistan, and Bangladesh

The availability of an honors course is not uniform across the three countries. While the honors course is only offered at universities and some selected colleges in India and Bangladesh, it is not available for commerce students in Pakistan who have to study for a B.Com. (Pass) either at a university or a college.

In Bangladesh until 1992, colleges offering the B.Com. (Pass) course were affiliates of one of the general universities in the country. With the establishment of the National University to administer, conduct examinations, and confer degrees, all public and private colleges (including university colleges) were brought under its academic control. By contrast in Pakistan and India, all colleges offering both the pass and honors programs in commerce/accounting are not linked to one single nation-wide affiliating university, rather they are clustered along state/provincial lines with general universities. In 1997, there were 228 universities in India, 25 in Pakistan and nine in Bangladesh (Association of Commonwealth Universities 1997). About two-thirds of these universities offer graduate courses in accounting. However, basic accounting is also taught at some of the specialized engineering and agricultural universities.

Tables 2 and 3 show the course contents of B.Com. (Pass) and B.Com. (Honors) in the three countries. There is a broad similarity in the course contents of the two-year (pass) program in all three countries. As far as accounting is concerned, the difference lies in the number of core and elective units. There is only one compulsory accounting unit in India, two in Pakistan and three in Bangladesh, and two elective units in India and Pakistan and none in Bangladesh. The other compulsory units in the program cover areas such as business management (including aspects of finance and banking), mathematics and statistics, business communication and reporting, economics, marketing, and taxation. Each course is one year long and the examination is held under the supervision of the affiliating university. But there is considerable variation in the way each of these fields is covered and in the scale to assess student performance in the three countries. For instance, in India and Bangladesh, students are assessed in 10 units, while the number of units is 13 in the case of Pakistan (ICAP 1997a). Another difference is in the emphasis on cognate fields. As an illustration, economics is highly emphasized in both India and Bangladesh, while the weight is nominal in Pakistan.

Table 2. A Typical Syllabus for the B. Com (Pass) Degree (2-year course) in India, Pakistan, and Bangladesh

India	*Pakistan*	*Bangladesh*
Compulsory	**Part I**	1. Business Communications and Office Practice
1. Business Mgmt. (3 papers)	1. Accounting	2. Management (3 papers)
2. Economics and Others (4 papers)	2. Banking, Currency and Finance	3. Accounting (3 papers)
3. Principles and Practice of Accounting (1 paper)	3. Business Communications and Report Writing	4. One subject from the following:
	4. Business Mathematics and Statistics	Economics (3 papers)
Plus 2 papers from four groups:	5. Economics	Finance (3 papers)
Accountancy Group	6. Introduction to Business	Marketing (3 papers)
1. Adv. Accounting and Costing	7. Islamic Studies or Ethical Behavior	(Total Marks 1,000)
2. Auditing and Taxation (Total Marks 1,000)	**Part II**	
	8. Business Taxation	
	9. Business Law	
	10. Economics of Pakistan	
	11. Fundamental of Cost Accounting	
	Plus 2 special courses of 100 each from any one of four separate groups comprising: Accounting, Insurance, Marketing and Transport (Total Marks 1,300)	

For a long time, the honors program in all three countries has spanned a three-year period, comprising either year-long or semester units. However, in recent years there has been a move in some universities in Bangladesh to extend the length by one year in line with undergraduate accounting programs in the United States. Currently four universities, including the University of Dhaka, have introduced a four-year honors program (eight semesters) in accounting in order to broaden the scope of subject contents without disrupting the thrust on major or core courses.

Initially, as a continuation of the British tradition, economics dominated the accounting curriculum in these countries (Ghosh 1990). Later, commerce as a distinctive discipline gradually gained prominence but while most universities have followed the traditional pattern of providing students the opportunity to attain some proficiency over commerce as a general subject, some have also adopted a more focused plan for specialization in accounting. For example, for the Honors program in accounting, instruction in both accounting and auditing is intensive but other cognate areas (e.g., business law, economics, public finance, marketing management, taxation, and statistics) are also taught.

With respect to the tertiary accounting education structure, major universities in Bangladesh moved away from the traditional British system and adopted the semester system for commerce students from 1978-79. The three-year duration was retained in order to maintain a balance with the overall government education policy. The three-year semester system has now been discarded in favor of a four-year program. The Faculty of Management Studies at the University of Delhi in India has also moved to a semester system in recent years for its Master of Business Administration (MBA) program, but the Commerce Faculty has retained the year-long system. In Pakistan, the year-long two-year B.Com. is still the only option available to commerce students. While, most Indian or Pakistani universities have modified the contents of their several accounting courses, any major fundamental restructuring in the university accounting education is yet to be undertaken (Banerjee 1992; Sayeed 1992). In this respect, Bangladesh, despite being the most economically weak country among the three, has taken the lead in university accounting education by increasing the depth and breath of subject coverage (see Table 3).

Along with the honors program in accounting, major universities in India, Pakistan and Bangladesh offer Masters of Business Administration (MBA) and doctorates with specialization in accounting. The course curricula of the MBA program are more oriented toward the development of financial management and marketing skills than accounting skills. While the MBA program in its varying format (full-time, part-time, executive) has become very popular and demanding, the program with major in accounting is yet to gain popularity compared with other business areas such as finance and marketing. This is mainly because the job prospects for professionally qualified accountants is much better than that of MBAs with a major in accounting as well as the lack of recognition of holders of MBA as qualified accountants.

Table 3. A Typical Syllabus for the B. Com (Honors) Degree (3-year course)* in India and Bangladesh

India (University of Delhi)	*Bangladesh (University of Dhaka)*
First Year	**First Year (1st Semester)**
Modern Business Organization	Basic Accounting
Financial Accounting	Introduction to Business
Micro Economics - Theory and Practice	Mathematics for Business Decision - I
Business Statistics	Business Communications
Business Law	**First Year (2nd Semester)**
Plus two additional papers from other related areas	Intermediate Accounting
	Micro Economics
	Mathematics for Business Decision - II
Second Year	Principles of Management
Management Concepts and Practices	**Second Year (1st Semester)**
Corporate Accounting	Advanced Accounting - I
Micro Economics - Theory and Practice	Business and Labor Laws
Business Mathematics	Macro Economics
Company Law	Financial Management - I
Income Tax	Basic Business Statistics
Plus one paper from other related areas	**Second Year (2nd Semester)**
	Advanced Accounting - II
Third Year	Laws and Practice of Taxation - I
Macro Economics	Principles of Marketing
Problems of Indian Economy	Applied Business Statistics
Cost Accounting Principles and Methods	Company Laws and Secretarial Practice
Cost Analysis and Control	**Third Year (1st Semester)**
Auditing	Laws and Practice of Taxation - II
Plus two additional papers from five optional groups	Financial Management - II
	Auditing - I
	Third Year (2nd Semester)
(Total Marks 1250)	Advanced Accounting - III
	Laws and Theory of Insurance
	Cost Accounting - II
	Introduction to Computer
	Business Environment and Entrepreneurship Development
	Fourth Year (1st Semester)
	Computer Application
	Introduction to Management Accounting
	Working Capital Management
	Organizational Behavior
	Auditing - II
	Fourth Year (2nd Semester)
	Development Theory and Bangladesh Economy
	Introduction to Operation Research
	Security Analysis and Portfolio Management
	Accounting Theory
	Introduction to Government Accounting
	Plus Viva of 100 (25 each year) marks over 4 years
	(Total Marks 1900)

Note: *Universities in Pakistan do not offer the three-year B.Com (Honors) program in accounting.

PROFESSIONAL ACCOUNTING EDUCATION AND TRAINING

Since professional education and training systems in accounting in South Asia were adopted during the British period, they share the same colonial legacy. It is, therefore, not surprising that all three countries have almost similar training and education methods and procedures. As mentioned in the preceding section, there

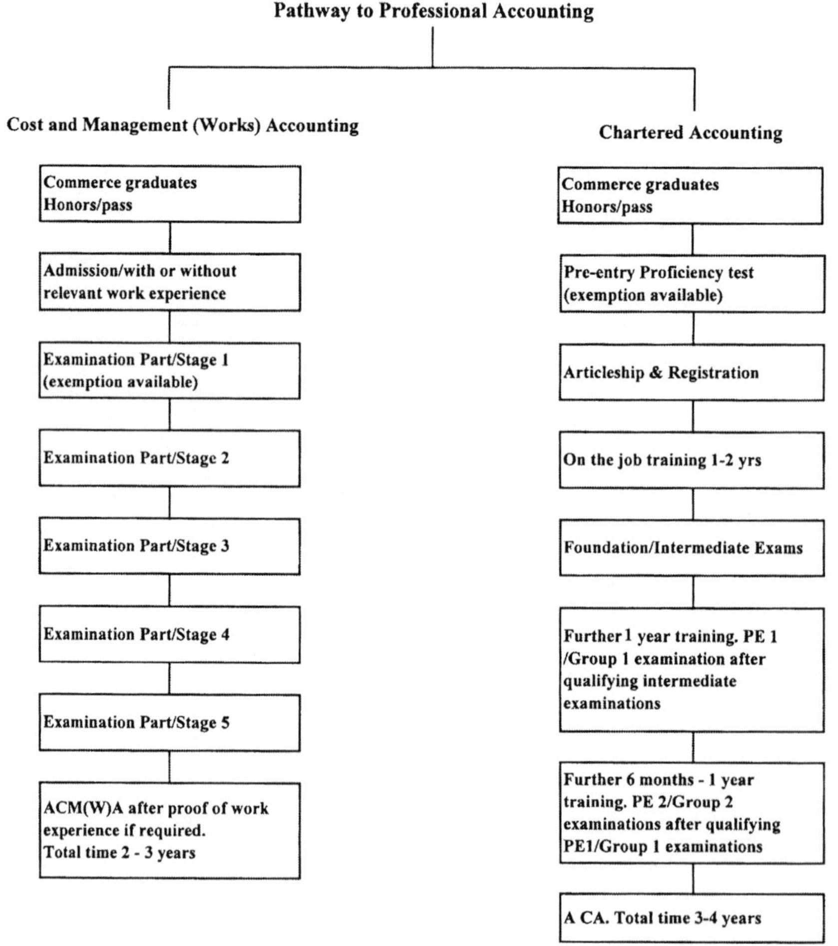

Figure 2. Typical Structure of Professional Accounting Education Pathway to Professional Accounting

are two main types of institutes in each of the three countries: (1) Institute of Chartered Accountants and (2) Institute of Cost and Management (Works) Accountants. The pathways to professional membership of each of two bodies are summarized in Figure 2. Since the two types have different emphasis on course contents, employment and training procedures, we examine them separately.

Institutes of Chartered Accountants

Candidates wishing to become chartered accountants in their respective countries are required to serve as articled students with accredited practicing accounting firms for a minimum period of either three or five years, depending on their qualifications. They are also required to pass all examinations given by the institutes of chartered accountants. Presently, depending on their background and qualifications, students may need to complete a foundation course, in addition to sitting for an entrance examination. This system is claimed to have the potential to raise the quality of professional education but has increased the length of the training period—up to two years, in Pakistan.

The duration of the total training (articleship) period also depends on candidates' qualifications. For a candidate with a Masters degree in commerce, the minimum training period is three years, while for other graduates (including commerce graduates) the articleship period is normally four years. The purpose of the articleship is to impart practical training to a student during the course under the guidance and supervision of a principal while he/she prepares for the examinations. A student cannot take the professional examination unless the minimum training period (normally 18 months) has been completed. This system claims to have a major advantage over the purely academic method. Universities with a higher student-teacher ratio preclude students from obtaining more direct individual attention from their instructors. On the other hand, the system has been criticized for being too parochial because of its greater focus on the technical aspects of accounting, thereby failing to balance theory and practice.

Since their inception, the three institutes have made several changes to their curricula to keep up with the times. For example, in India the ICAI has amended the syllabus at least six times since 1949 (Banerjee 1992). In Pakistan, a new syllabus was introduced in 1995 and a new training scheme is scheduled to become effective from June 1999. The ICAB has also revised the syllabus several times, the most recent being in 1990.

The structure of the examination and the subjects covered are similar for the three institutes but the sequence of offerings differs (See Table 4). What is taught at the foundation level in Pakistan may be offered at other levels in India or Bangladesh. However, it is noted that none of the syllabi includes any course on accounting theory or international accounting. There is little emphasis on the financial reporting practices prevalent in developed and emerging countries.

Table 4. Professional Examination Syllabi of the Institute of Chartered Accountants of India (ICAI), Pakistan (ICAP), and Bangladesh (ICAB)

ICAI (1996)	*ICAP (1997)*	*ICAB (1995)*
Foundation Examination	**Foundation: 1**	**Intermediate: Group A**
(Exemption allowed for certain graduates)	1. Communication and Behavioral Skills	1.1 Financial Accounting -I
1. Fundamentals of Accounting	2. Business Mathematics*	1.2 Auditing - 1
2. Mercantile Law	3. Business Statistics*	1.3 Economics and Statistics
3. Mathematics and Statistics	4. Mercantile Law*	
4. Economics	5. Economics*	**Intermediate: Group B**
	6. Financial Accounting - 1	1.4 Taxation - I
Intermediate Examination: Group I		1.5 Business and Commercial Law
	Foundation: 2	
1. Advanced Accounting	7. Information Technology	1.6 Cost Accounting
2. Auditing	8. Cost Accounting	
3. Corporate and Other Laws	9. Company Law*	**Final: Group I**
	10. Taxation*	2.1 Financial Accounting -II
	11. Auditing	2.2 Management Accounting
Intermediate Examination: Group II	12. Financial Accounting - 2	2.3 Taxation - II
		2.4 Law - II (Company Law)
4. Cost Accounting	**Professional Examination: 1**	2.5 Business Communication
5. Income and Sales Tax	1. Advanced Auditing	
6. Organization and Management and Electronic Data Processing	2. Advanced Financial Accounting	**Final: Group II**
	3. Financial Reporting	3.1 Financial Accounting -III
	4. Corporate Laws and Practice	3.2 Auditing - II
		3.3 Management and Data
		3.4 Financial Management
Final Examination		
7. Advanced Cost Accounting	**Professional Examination: 2**	
	1. Management Accounting	
8. System Analysis, Data Processing and Quantitative Techniques	2. Strategic Financial Management	
	3. Advanced Taxation	
9. Direct Taxes	4. Case Studies	
10. Indirect Taxes		

Note: *50 Marks

Candidates, upon completion of both foundation and professional examinations, are initially admitted to the institute as associate members and are allowed to write "Associate of the Institute of Chartered Accountants" (ACA) after their names. After five years of continuous membership and acquisition of experience prescribed by the institute, an associate member is entitled to become a Fellow Chartered Accountant (FCA). In June 1995, there were 700 CAs in Bangladesh with about 25 percent in practice, the rest serving in various private and public sectors firms. In India, the number of registered CAs was 74,352 as on April 1996 (ICAI 1996). The total membership of the Institute in Pakistan was 2,097 in March 1997 of which 445 were in public practice (ICAP 1997b).

Table 5. Professional Examination Syllabi of the Institute of Cost and Management (Works) Accountants of India (ICWAI), Pakistan (ICMAP), and Bangladesh (ICMAB)

ICAI (1996)	*ICAP (1997)*	*ICAB (1995)*
Foundation (Optional)	**Part I**	**Intermediate: Level - I**
1. Basic Business Knowledge	1. Accounting - 1	101 Financial Accounting - I
2. Basic Economics	2. Accounting - II	102 Fundamentals of
3. Basic Mathematics	3. Economics	Management & Production
4. Basic Accountancy	4. Industrial and Commercial	Technology
	Law	103 Business Mathematics and
Intermediate: Stage - I		Statistics
1. Management and	**Part II**	104 Business Communications
Organization	1. Cost Accounting - I	and Report Writing
2. Business and Economic	2. Cost Accounting - II	
Legislation	3. Communication and Report	**Intermediate: Level -II**
3. Quantitative Methods	Writing	201 Financial Accounting - II
4. Cost Accounting	4. Business Mathematics and	202 Cost Accounting - I
	Statistics	203 Managerial Economics
Intermediate: Stage - II		204 Information Technology
1. Management Economics	**Part III**	Management - I
2. Advanced Financial	1. Advanced Accounting - I	
Accounting	2. Advanced Accounting - II	**Intermediate: Level -III**
3. Business Taxation	3. Production Technology and	301 Business Laws
4. Cost and Management	Management	302 Cost Accounting - II
Accounting	4. Taxation	303 Management Accounting
		304 Information Technology
Final: Stage III	**Part IV**	Management
1. Information Technology	1. Advanced Cost and	
and Computer Application	Management Accounting - I	**Final: Level IV**
2. Operations Management	2. Advanced Cost and	401 Corporate Laws and
and Control	Management Accounting - II	Secretarial Practice
3. Project Management	3. MIS Data Processing	402 Advanced Accounting
and Control	4. Corporate Law and	403 Management
4. Cost Audit	Secretaries Practice	Accounting - II
		404 Taxation
Final: Stage IV	**Part V**	
(Advanced Management	1. Financial Management - I	**Final: Level V**
Accounting)	2. Financial Management - II	501 Accounting for Managerial
1. Techniques and Control	3. Auditing	Control
2. Financial Management	4. Org. Management and	502 Financial Management
3. Strategic Management	Marketing	503 Advanced Management
4. Internal and Management		and Marketing Theories
Audit	(Total 20 papers)	504 Auditing
(Total 16 papers)		
		(Total 20 papers)

The Institute of Cost and Management (Works) Accountants

In accord with changing circumstances, the cost and management accountants (CMA) institutes have also revised their course curricula. Since 1961 in India, for example, at least four revisions have been made, each time reducing the emphasis on accounting and broadening other areas such as management information systems and operations management. The Institute in Pakistan has also made several changes in line with the Chartered Institute of Management Accountants in the United Kingdom (CIMA). In Bangladesh, ICMAB has revised the syllabus four times since its inception, the most recent being in 1992 which was in accordance with the suggestions of the United Nations Development Program (UNDP).

Table 5 shows the syllabi of the institutes. In total, there are five stages: three in the intermediate and two in the final. While the maximum number of units to pass in Bangladesh and Pakistan is 20, the number of units is 16 in India. The institutes in the three countries give exemptions to candidates depending on their qualifications. However, unlike the Institute of Chartered Accountants, students of the CMAs are not required to pass all subjects at the same time in a particular examination session; they can complete parts by passing subjects at different times.

The entry requirement is normally a tertiary first degree from a local university, but exemptions are allowed in certain circumstances. After obtaining a pass in the final examinations, a student is admitted as an associate member of the institute, and is entitled to use the initials "ACMA" in Pakistan and Bangladesh and "ACWA" in India. After five years of continuous membership, an associate member is admitted as a fellow of the respective institutes.

Although audit of financial statements are still the sole right of the chartered accountants, cost and management (works) accountants are now entitled to practice as cost auditors in accordance with each country's Companies Acts. However, unlike the institutes of chartered accountants, the cost and management institutes do not have any system of articleship, where experience substitutes for practical training. Experience can be gained before and during training or after taking the examinations. This system of self-training is perceived to be convenient from the students' point of view because they study while earning their livelihood. However, from the standpoint of employers, it is perceived to be very ineffective and narrow since no supervised training is provided and the firm where an employee works may have very little or no formal accounting systems in existence.

PROFESSIONAL AND UNIVERSITY TRAINING AND EXAMINATION SYSTEMS: EVALUATION AND SUGGESTIONS

An evaluation of the structure and entry requirements suggests that the approach of the professional institutes to training in India, Pakistan, and Bangladesh is still steeped in tradition. The entry requirements for non-commerce graduates are still very inflexible as they are required to sit for the entrance examination and then follow it by the foundation examination. Although the institutes have reduced the maximum period of articleship from seven to five years to attract academically sound students from non-commerce disciplines, the time taken to complete the professional examination remains drawn out. While in recent years the Bangladesh and Indian institutes have enlarged the exemption criteria for noncommerce students, the ICAP has introduced new entry requirements, which apparently work against students with a different background. For some students in Pakistan, completion of the training period may take up to six years because many courses taken at the college level will not receive exemptions.

Ansari and Aziz (1981), Chattopadhaya (1981) and Parry and Nag (1984) observe that the primary focus of the professional bodies in the subcontinent is the obtainment of technical proficiency in applying the current concepts, techniques, and methods by their students. An analysis[5] of the contents of current syllabi and past examination papers of these institutes suggests that an understanding of company law and taxation principles by their students and their ability to solve complex accounting problems are the principal criteria to assess their competence. Several authors have argued over the past two decades that professional accountants with only technical skills are inadequately prepared for entry into the profession. Today, accounting practice, whether in government, public enterprises or industry is more dynamic and complex and needs to address a variety of issues than it did even a few years ago (Sundem 1992). Therefore, a combination of both theoretical postulates and practical methodology is essential for accounting practitioners to have any positive impact on financial management systems. To be successful in the profession, a multi-disciplinary approach to accounting education is imperative to meet challenges and complexities in a developing country with its multifarious developmental problems.

In the United States between 1967 and 1989, at least 17 accounting educational models were proposed at the initiative of seven professional bodies. These models are unvarying in many respects regarding skills and knowledge essential for entry into the accounting profession. For instance, a report by several international accounting firms has identified, in addition to technical skills and knowledge, communication, intellectual and interpersonal skills, general knowledge and organizational and business knowledge as key requirements (Arthur Andersen et al., 1989). Hilmy (1989) stresses the importance of strengthening the liberal arts knowledge base while integrating accounting with other business disciplines in the accounting curriculum. Like the United States, many other developed countries, such as New Zealand, have already implemented programs requiring students to do at least 40 percent liberal arts subjects before being eligible for the professional examinations. In India, Pakistan, and Bangladesh, technically oriented subjects outweigh non-technical ones in the current syllabi. This reflects poorly on the quality of overall student performance. For example, a comparative study of the educational skills of chartered accountancy students in Bangladesh and the United Kingdom found that students in the former scored higher points in technical aspects, but scored lower points in conceptual understanding and writing ability compared with their British counterparts (Parry and Nag 1984).

The institutes in the subcontinent rely mainly on practical training obtained during the articleship period. The underlying assumption is that practical training facilitates a student's preparation for his/her professional examinations and, possibly, reduces dependence on formal studies. The assumption does not appear to have validity in the real world. The very low pass rate (for example, in Bangladesh it has never exceeded 14 percent since the formation of the ICAB) is indicative of the weakness of the institutes' academic policies. Parry and Nag (1984), Banerjee (1992), and Sayeed (1992) have also highlighted this problem. Several factors are attributable to the low pass rate: intake of low quality students, infrequent contact between students and teachers, inadequate time for preparation, and high attrition rate of competent students (Ansari and Aziz 1981; Ghosh 1990). The low pass rate could also be ascribed to the conservative examination policy pursued by the accounting profession. The institutes themselves have emphasized this concern for low success rate and have adopted measures to improve the success rate by requiring students to attend formal coaching classes, submit regular assignments, and do take-home examinations on weekends.

The low pass rate is not helpful in improving the quality of accounting education as it not only reduces the motivation of existing students but also discourages bright potential students from being attracted to the accounting profession. Traditionally, the more brilliant students in these countries are interested in medicine or engineering. However, the recent changes to the entry requirements and the decreased employment opportunities for doctors and engineers within the country and overseas (in particular, the oil rich Middle-East countries) are expected to persuade brighter students to choose accounting as a career.

The institutes permit students a minimum leave period (normally about six weeks) to prepare for examination. However, many practicing firms, particularly the smaller ones, do not allow their students sufficient time for pre-exam preparation. There is another problem. Many trainee students who are able to forge good rapport with their firms and obtain full-time employment there before or after completion of their articleship period, either take the examinations in a half-hearted manner or, because of work pressure, decide not to take the professional examinations at all and prefer to remain as "CCs" (course complete). This is not unexpected considering the pitiably low trainee allowance (about US$50, in most cases) given by the practicing firms which is less than one-third of an equivalent full-time job. Then there are doubts about limited job opportunities and the uncertainty of passing examinations.

Historically, however, qualified professional accountants in South Asia have enjoyed a high place in society in terms of higher salary, prestige, and being members of an elite profession. One way to perpetuate their standing is to restrict access to the profession for the sake of maintaining high quality and consistency with the entry policies of previous years. Although "high quality" has never been defined, one approach traditionally followed by these institutes is to conform to the standards prescribed by the Institute of Chartered Accountants in England and Wales (ICAEW), one of the acknowledged leaders in the accounting profession, and basically continuing to maintain its recognition. While not deprecating this disposition, which is attuned by historical reasons, the professional bodies in these countries have been loath to take any lessons from the experience of the professional bodies in Australia, New Zealand, and Singapore, where the pass rate in professional examinations has been maintained at a high level without compromising on quality or standard.[6]

The institutes in the subcontinent do not have full-time teaching staff to give instruction and conduct examinations. They rely totally on part-timers from the profession and the universities. This way, the quality of education is affected with the institutes unable to exercise their control over part-time academic staff and make them accountable for their performance. In Pakistan, for instance, examination questions in auditing, financial accounting and management accounting have been either repeatedly reused from past examination papers or adopted verbatim from those set by overseas institutes, mainly the ICAEW (Shah 1991). Several reasons for adopting such gratuitous practice can be identified. First, senior members of professional bodies, who normally are preferred over their junior colleagues to set examination papers, are preoccupied with other non-academic pursuits and therefore have limited time to develop new questions. Secondly, it is convenient for examiners to look up suggested solutions,[7] which have been in circulation for a long time, rather than making extra efforts to design their own solutions to new questions every year. Finally, there is very limited financial incentive for question setters, although this should be a normal part of their job.

Parry and Nag (1984) have identified some further limitations that restrict the adequate training of articled students in Bangladesh although the same may be true for the other two countries. First, accessibility to practical training is limited since there are very few practicing firms that can take articled students. For example, in Bangladesh, during 1994-1995 there were about 150 CA firms that provided practical training. Secondly, many of the principals of small accounting firms offer only limited practical experience. Chartered accountancy in these countries is still practiced by small accounting firms although the "Big-five" international firms do have a presence in India and Pakistan (Marston and Robson 1997; Sayeed 1992). In India, for example, it is common for large corporations to employ many small firms of auditors than one large auditing company. This reduces opportunities for trainees to come across a variety of accounts and issues. Consequently, when a large number of qualified accountants begin their career in industry and commerce, they are restricted from applying many of the concepts, techniques, and methods they learned in the institutes.

Banerjee (1992) notes that the growth rate of qualified chartered accountants in India has lagged behind the growth rate of joint stock companies where they can be employed. Indeed, the short supply of qualified CAs in the three countries has engendered a kind of elitism in the accounting profession. Small firms are financially handicapped to pay for the services of experienced and competent CAs and hence are unable to have their accounts prepared and audited by them. Further, while qualified accountants prefer to be employed by local or overseas manufacturing or retailing industries, the agricultural sector has traditionally been neglected. Enthoven (1981) suggests, after assessing the accounting needs of South Asian countries, that accounting issues, such as farm accounting, construction engineering, and functional accounting (banks, insurance) be incorporated in the professional accounting curricula. Though accounting for bank, insurance and construction companies has been incorporated in financial and cost accounting courses, farm accounting is yet to be covered by the universities or professional institutes in either of the South Asian countries. This deficiency is, however, not limited to the Indian subcontinent. It is a function of the academic institutions' lack of interest and response, in general, to the problems of small businesses. Farms in the subcontinent are small and are not significant employers of accounting graduates. Currently, the governments depend entirely on the estimates provided by local councils, which are based on past experience and recollection of the farmers. It is regrettable that a proper system of recording inputs and outputs for individual farming unit (cooperatives are exceptions) is yet to be implemented in these countries where their economies are substantially dependent on agriculture.

It is widely recognized that governments and universities have played an important role in the development of accounting education and training in these countries. During the 1960s, the governments of India and Pakistan set up several specialized commerce colleges/institutes and major universities that began offering accounting courses to improve commerce education in their countries. Although this development has been significant considering the lack of resources and infrastructure, it has never been coordinated properly. Professional bodies and universities have had different needs and priorities and developed curricula to fulfil their specific objectives without effective cooperation between them. The professional bodies have a limited role in designing and revising the university accounting courses. Similarly, university academics have a limited say in the development of the curricula in the professional institutes. Although professional institutions incorporate representatives from finance and commerce ministries, the academic decision making committees in accounting departments within universities and colleges are entirely composed of their own staff members and without any outside representatives on them. There is a lack of cooperation and the sharing of ideas and information between academia and the professional community. The institutes have set up their own training structure without any input from the academic community. This has resulted in duplication of the curricula of universities and repetition of many of the things already learned by their students. This has led to a waste of scarce resources. Universities should also establish formal systems of cooperation with the professional bodies incorporating representative from the accounting profession in academic committees either at the faculty or departmental level. However, the universities should not be considered as providers of students for the accounting profession, rather the courses should be broad based with emphasis on conceptual and theoretical understanding.

The scenario is different, in varying degrees, in the United States, Australia, New Zealand, and Singapore, where professional bodies and universities maintain mutually beneficial relationships and consult one another in designing the structure and system of education and training. Professional bodies accredit commerce degrees conferred by an approved academic institution. The universities, on their part, respond to the dynamic and challenging needs of the profession by constantly changing their syllabi and contents. While students may take courses according to personal preferences and goals, some core courses must be taken before the professional bodies can accredit the program. However, in India, Pakistan, and Bangladesh, this alternative option has never been considered partly due to an apprehension that this might dilute the quality of the accounting profession. Wijewardena and Yapa (1998), explain how the Institute of Certified Public Accountants of Singapore has moved away from the traditional British model and successfully improved the quality of accounting education by building synergy with the accounting departments in universities. To improve cooperation between the universities and the professional bodies, the governments in these countries should take the initiative by forming a national council for accounting education and inducting in them distinguished members from industry, commerce, academia, professional community and the general public. Such a council should review, apart from ensuring cooperation between the various agencies involved in accounting education, the existing structure of the profession and the extent to which it is relevant to the needs of the economy.

Teaching methods need reorientation and refocusing since at present there is an overemphasis on lectures at the universities and professional institutions. Lecturers, in general, do not go beyond using the now obsolete blackboard. The use of overhead and slide projectors and electronic boards is yet to find its way in most places. In line with developments in accounting instruction overseas, case studies, seminar presentations, role playing and group discussions should complement lectures. The need for such reorientation has already been recognized and some attempts have been made in recent years by developing case studies on management and financial accounting. In Bangladesh, with the sponsorship of the World Bank, several case studies have been developed but steps have not been taken to publish them, let alone use them as teaching materials. Bangladesh should follow India and Pakistan where several business case studies have already been published and utilized as instructional resources (Banerjee 1992; Sayeed 1992). Across most universities in all three countries, there is a huge scarcity of books and research and resource materials and the exposure to international financial reporting practices has been very limited. In addition, computer technology has very limited application in the syllabi of the universities, mainly because of the lack of computer laboratories for accounting students.[8] In this regard, the government in each country needs to play an important role by encouraging publicly funded universities to generate external funding from industry and business to equip themselves with books, journals and reports as well as hardware and software for accounting analyses.

At present, several partly qualified students, known as CCs, work in several private and public sector organizations where their skills are not recognized and salary and job status are not commensurate with their qualifications and experience. Either the proposed council or the existing institutes of chartered accountants should consider establishing a system to accord formal status to CCs by designating them "Certified Accountants," actually being subordinate to "Chartered Accountants," depending upon their performance in the professional examinations. Such a system will recognize their professional skills, introduce flexibility in options and reduce attrition from the accounting profession.

The graduate program at the universities in the three countries should provide more emphasis on research and publication. In the past, the World Bank and other international organizations offered several post-graduate scholarships to university staff to study in the United States and Britain to improve accounting education in these countries. However, such attempts to improve accounting education have had limited success since the majority of the awardees did not return home. Local long-term and short-term twinning programs with reputed overseas universities in the developed world would be beneficial both for providing exposure to existing academic staff to the current state of accounting in other countries and for helping them build prospective careers in teaching, research, and consultancy in their own countries. The Indian universities have already made some strides in this regard by encouraging junior academics to undertake doctoral studies locally and overseas, engage in research on relevant and topical issues and to publish their findings. The Indian experience can serve as a pointer for Pakistan and Bangladesh.

CONCLUDING COMMENTS

This chapter has attempted a comparative analysis of accounting education and training systems in India, Pakistan, and Bangladesh. The general picture is almost identical in the three countries; differences are noticeable only when specifics are examined. The analysis shows that while accounting systems have evolved over a long period of time, beginning in the pre-colonial days and undergoing some form of modernization during British rule when accounting and auditing methods were imported from Britain to replace traditional practices, accounting education and training as inputs to an efficient accounting system received recognition only in the second half of the twentieth century. Since decolonization the pace of change accelerated to attune accounting systems to the needs of the three independent societies, but, by and large, the

AETS there still carry the vestiges of the colonial past. Thus, the structure of accounting education and training and the policies that regulate them remain entrapped in conservatism and parochialism.

The induction of trainees into professional programs is guided by rigid principles and their training period unduly prolonged. The overemphasis on the technical aspects of accounting breeds so-called specialists devoid of any critical perspective, which can be gained from an understanding of issues in the social sciences and the humanities. Performance evaluation criteria being unjustifiably severe, the number of trainees successfully completing their course is extremely low. This accounts for the low turnout of professional accountants.

Slipshod expansion of accounting education and training systems has been the effect of lack of perspective planning on the long term strategic needs of economic development. In consequence, the systems that have evolved over the years have largely failed to deliver. Higher education policies have been made in a vacuum without appraising both perceived and real needs of the accounting profession, in particular, and the society, in general. The professional institutes are reticent in forging a mutually beneficial relationship with the universities to endow the practice of accounting the professionalism, finesse, and excellence it demands. In a similar vein, the universities are not too keen to collaborate with the professional bodies in improving accounting education.

A sound education policy and elaborate programs for reforms in educational administration and appropriate training policies are imperative in this context. The accounting and business curricula should reflect practical application of concepts and procedures in national development initiatives. The objective of building bridges, that is, linking theory and practice, not only at the universities but also in the professional institutions, must be at the core of accounting education and practice. A concerted effort by the governments in the three countries to raise the standard of AETS with the support of the professional accounting community will improve the accounting infrastructure, which, in turn, will have a positive impact on development planning and implementation. In this regard, continuous interaction between the academic and professional communities will be vital, each complementing the other in refining and rejuvenating accounting and training system.

ACKNOWLEDGMENTS

We would like to thank M.G. Sobhan, G.M. Alam, Y. M. Siddiqi, C.T. Varma and Chowdhury Nazar Ahmad for providing us with relevant information. We also thank John Staunton, M. Milne, a discussant at the 1998 AAANZ Conference in Adelaide, as well as two anonymous reviewers for their comments and suggestions.

NOTES

1. Bhahi means ledger and Khata means accounts. Under the system every account has a "jama" or receipt side and a "Kharcha" or payment side. This system uses only cash, accounts receivable, and accounts payable and is mainly for tax purposes. For further reading, refer to Lall Nigam (1986, 148-161).

2. Presently, Bombay is known as Mumbai and is the capital of the state of Maharashtra.

3. These covered accounting, taxation, economics, mercantile law, and auditing.

4. In a few universities, the M.Com. is a two-year degree program whether one has a B.Com. (Pass) or B.Com. (Honors) degree before joining the program. For example, the University of Delhi, India.

5. The relevant Institutes provided past examination questions and detailed syllabi. These are available upon written request from the authors.

6. For a detailed analysis of accounting education and certification process in these countries readers are advised to see Wells (1992), Newby (1992) and Tan and colleagues (1994).

7. Question-setters are required to submit suggested solutions along with the questions they set.

8. Resources are so scarce in most of the universities that even overhead projectors and transparencies are not available in classrooms.

REFERENCES

Ansari, A.M., and A. Aziz. 1981. Accounting education in Pakistan. In *Accounting Education in Economic Development Management,* ed. A. Enthoven, 243-261. Amsterdam: North Holland.

Anyane-Ntow, K. 1992. *International Handbook of Accounting Education and Certification*, Vol. 1, No. 1. New York: Pergamon Press.

Arthur Andersen and Co., Arthur Young, Coopers and Lybrand, Deloitte Haskins and Sells, Ernst and Whinney, Peat Marwick Main and Co., Price Waterhouse, Touche Ross. 1989. *Perspective on Education: Capabilities for Success in the Accounting Profession*, April.

Association of Commonwealth Universities. 1997. *Year-Book 1997-98*. London.

Azizuddin, A.B.M. 1984. The matching of resources and their availability at regional and international levels—Bangladesh. *Proceedings of the Asia and Pacific Conference on Accounting Education for Development*, Manila, 191-228.

Banerjee, B. 1992. Accounting education in India. In *International Handbook of Accounting Education and Certification*, ed. K. Anyane-Ntow, 167-201. New York: Pergamon Press.

Department of Accounting. 1997. *BBA (Honors) Syllabus*. June, University of Dhaka, Dhaka, Bangladesh.

Chattopadhyay, P. 1981. Accounting education in India. In *Accounting Education in Economic Development Management*, ed. A. Enthoven, 401-431. Amsterdam: North Holland.

Economic and Social Commission for Asia and Pacific (ESCAP). 1997. *Statistical Yearbook, Bangkok*. Thailand.

Enthoven, A. 1981. *Accounting Education in Economic Development Management*. Amsterdam: North Holland.

Ghosh, S. N. 1990. A comparative international study of the education of professional accountants: A case study of Bangladesh. In *Comparative International Accounting Education Standards*, eds. B. E. Needles and V. K. Zimmerman, 97-108. Center for International Education and Research in Accounting, University of Illinois at Urbana, Champaign.

Hilmy, J. 1989. Philosophical foundations of accounting education in the future. *Papers and Proceedings of the Pan-Pacific Conference VI.*

Institute of Chartered Accountants of Bangladesh (ICAB). 1994. *Subjects and Syllabus of the Examinations*. Dhaka, Bangladesh. June.

Institute of Chartered Accountants of Bangladesh (ICAB). 1995. *Annual Report (1994-95)*. Dhaka.

Institute of Chartered Accountants of India (ICAI). 1996. *Education and Training for Chartered Accountants*. New Delhi, India.

Institute of Chartered Accountants of Pakistan (ICAP). 1997a. *Syllabus and Scheme of Education and Training for Foundation and Professional Examination*. Karachi, Pakistan.

Institute of Chartered Accountants of Pakistan (ICAP). 1997b. *Profile June 1997*. Karachi, Pakistan.

Institute of Cost and Management Accountants of Bangladesh (ICMAB). 1996. *Students' Handbook*. Dhaka, Bangladesh.

Institute of Cost and Works Accountants of India (ICWAI). 1994. *Syllabus of Institute of Cost and Works Accountants of India*. Calcutta, India.

Institute of Cost and Management Accountants of Pakistan (ICMAP). 1995. *Syllabus of Institute of Cost and Management Accountants of Pakistan*. Lahore, Pakistan.

International Finance Corporation (IFC). 1998. *Emerging Stock Markets Fact Book*. Washington, DC.

Lall Nigam, B.M. 1986. Bhahi-khata: The pre-pacioli Indian double-entry system of bookkeeping. *Abacus* 22 (2): 148-161.

Marston, C., and P. Robson. 1997. Financial reporting in India: Changes in disclosure over the period 1982 to 1990. *Asia Pacific Journal of Accounting* 4 (1): 109-140.

Osiegbu, P. I. 1987. The state of accounting education in Nigeria. *The International Journal of Accounting* 22 (2): 57-68.

Newby, S. 1992. Accountancy in New Zealand. In *International Handbook of Accounting Education and Certification*, ed. K. Anyane-Ntow, 243-260. New York: Pergamon Press.

Parry, M. J., and A. B. Nag. 1984. *A Study of Accountancy Training in Bangladesh*. The Institute of Chartered Accountants of Bangladesh, Dhaka.

Sayeed, K. A. 1992. A global perspective of accounting education and certification process: Focus on Pakistan. In *International Handbook of Accounting Education and Certification*, ed. K. Anyane-Ntow, 213-232. New York: Pergamon Press.

Sundem, G.L. 1992. Changes in accounting education in the United States: The impact of accounting education change commission. In *International Handbook of Accounting Education and Certification*, ed. K. Anyane-Ntow, 305-318. New York: Pergamon Press.

Shah, A. A. 1991. The education and training of chartered accountants in Pakistan—Present standard and future needs. *Pakistan Accountant* (September): 7-10.

Tan, M. M., P. Y. Hoong, and F. S. Liang. 1994. Accounting education and practice: The Singaporean experience. *The International Journal of Accounting* 29 (2): 161-83.

United Nations Centre for Transnational Corporations (UNCTC). 1991. *Accountancy Development in Africa: Challenge of the 1990s*. New York: United Nations.

University of Delhi. 1999. *Scheme of Examination and Courses of Reading for B.Com (Hons) Courses*. Publication Department, Delhi, India.

Wells, M. 1992. Accounting education in Australia. In *International Handbook of Accounting Education and Certification*, ed. K. Anyane-Ntow, 143-158. New York: Pergamon Press.

Wijewardena, H., and S. Yapa. 1998. Colonialism of accounting education in developing countries: The experience of Singapore and Sri Lanka. *International Journal of Accounting* 33 (2): 269-281.

PART III

ACCOUNTING IN EUROPE

ACCOUNTING FOR LEASE CONTRACTS: THE ACCEPTABILITY OF INTERNATIONAL PRINCIPLES AND PRACTICES IN TURKEY

Turgut Çürük and Terence E. Cooke

ABSTRACT

The transfer of accounting knowledge from developed to developing countries has been criticized by those who see accounting as being environmentally (including culturally) bound. This school of thought argues further that international accounting standards (IASs) may not be universally applicable or acceptable, a view that differs from that of the International Accounting Standards Committee. There has been a considerable rate of growth in leasing in Turkey in recent years, providing an opportunity to assess whether the principles stated in IAS 17, *Accounting for Leases*, are appropriate in developing an accounting standard in Turkey. Turkey is a developing country that is being used here as a case study although it is recognized that developing countries are not homogeneous. Based on responses to a questionnaire sent to accountants in Turkey, the analysis suggests that the principles in IAS 17 are acceptable to accountants in that country. This finding indicates that, on this particular technical issue of accounting for leases, the accounting principles may have some universal appeal.

Research in Accounting in Emerging Economies, Volume 4, pages 99-129.

ISBN: 1-55938-995-8

INTRODUCTION

In 1988, the International Accounting Standards Committee (IASC) agreed to begin an investigation into the accounting needs of developing and newly industrialized countries. As a part of this investigation the Committee decided to make recommendations to the IASC "on the improvement and harmonization of regulations, accounting standards and procedures relating to the presentation of financial statements in such countries.[1] However, the IASC has now designated the project as one of low priority and there is little prospect of it being moved forward in the short-term" (Wallace 1993, 121-122).

Wallace (1993) puts forward a number of possible reasons for the lack of activity by the IASC's Steering Committee on this project. One reason is because the IASC has stated that "International Accounting Standards (IASs) are generally as applicable in developing countries and newly industrialized countries as they are in developed countries" (IASC 1990).

This chapter[2] presents a case study of the possible implementation of the main principles of IAS 17, *Accounting for Leases*, by Turkey in response to changes in its capital markets. Such changes present challenges to accountants as they are obliged to deal with more complex financial transactions including leasing (Bursal 1984).

Turkey serves as an example only, since it is recognized that developing countries are not homogeneous. While the view of the IASC is that IASs are applicable to developing countries, some commentators, such as Samuels and Oliga (1982), have argued that they may do more harm than good. Indeed, Samuels and Oliga (1982) and Samuels (1993) argue that the adoption of IASs by developing countries may be irrelevant to their needs and others suggest that this may lead to resentment. Wallace (1993, 122), for example, reports "that many scholars and indigenous accountants from developing countries are beginning to question and resent the dependence of their countries on rules from outside their own traditions which they perceive to be biased and inimical to their own needs." Samuels (1993) also notes that developing countries may be selective in their adoption of IASs: adopting some IASs in their entirety, adopting others partially, and rejecting the rest. This differential policy toward the adoption of IASs may not be incompatible with the view that accounting standards should be country-specific (Bursal 1984, 93-123).

Because of the variations in opinion about the applicability of IASs to developing countries, a study of the relevance of an IAS in Turkey will add to our understanding of the nature of accounting in developing countries. Wallace (1993, 129)[3] argues that "the identification of the differences between the needs of developing nations and other countries and the challenges which adaptation of modern methods to different environments pose, are exciting stimuli for the study of accounting in developing countries." In this chapter, we respond to that challenge by assessing whether the principles specified in IAS 17 are acceptable to users in

Turkey. The explanation for the relationship between acceptability and relevance needs clarification. Turkish accounting has a history of legal form rather economic substance which contrasts with the approach on leasing adopted by the IASC. If users in Turkey believe that legal form is applicable then finance leases will not be capitalized (Al-Hashim and Arpan 1988, 101). However, if users in Turkey believe that IAS 17 is acceptable then this is recognition of the relevance and importance of economic substance in treating lease contracts.

This chapter considers the growth in leasing in Turkey as one major capital market development and reports on a study of the opinions of accountants in Turkey (as surrogates for the views of preparers/users) about the acceptability in Turkey of principles and practices of accounting for lease contracts.[4]

BACKGROUND

Leasing, as a form of asset financing, has a long history on a global scale,[5] but since the 1950s growth has been very rapid. In some developing countries, such as Turkey, leasing is in its infancy, whereas in many developed countries such as the United States, Great Britain, and Japan, this type of transaction has become an accepted method of capital equipment acquisition. On a worldwide basis, the leasing market is much larger than the medium-term note, Euro-commercial paper, and international equities market (see Table 1).

The development of new financial instruments has led to intense discussions about the methods of accounting for such transactions. Until the 1970s only the United States had an accounting standard on leasing[6] and in general lease contracts were accounted for as rental agreements and presented in the financial statements accordingly. The increased importance of lease arrangements in some developed countries increased the need for consistent accounting and informative reporting on these transactions. Pressure from users and preparers of financial statements including accountants, standard-setting bodies in a number of countries (e.g., the

Table 1. Leasing Relative to Other Capital Market Products in 1993

Capital Market Product	*Volume US $bn*
Loans	799
Eurobonds	409
Leasing	310
Medium-term notes	110
International Equities	40
Euro-commercial paper	28
Euronotes	3

Source: Hornbrook (1995, 2).

United Kingdom, Ireland, Australia, and Canada), led to a review of lease accounting methods and the development of accounting standards on the topic.

Currently, the treatment of lease transactions in financial statements varies widely from country to country. If a broad generalization is to be made, countries that have developed lease accounting standards, such as the United States, Britain, Ireland, Canada, and Australia, have prescribed accounting treatments which place emphasis on the substance of transactions over their legal form (Davies et al., 1992, 805-859). In these countries, the nature of underlying transactions is important and as such, leases are classified into two: operating and finance leases. In contrast, countries that do not have accounting standards or specific provisions relating to accounting for leases (e.g., Germany and France), treat such transactions as operating leases in accordance with their legal form (i.e., as merely rental agreements) in their financial statements (Alexander and Archer 1992, 180, 233-234). In these countries, the operating lease accounting method is the prevailing practice.

In countries where operating leases are distinguished from finance leases, a finance lease is considered to be one in which substantially all the risks and rewards are transferred to the user. All other leases are classified as operating leases. In the case of a finance lease, the leased asset is capitalized by the lessee and depreciated and future lease payments are recognized as a liability by the lessee.[7] The lease payments made by the lessee are apportioned between the finance charge and reduction in the outstanding liability. In the lessor's balance sheet, the leased asset is not recorded as a tangible fixed asset but as a receivable. The lease rentals received by the lessor are apportioned into finance income (interest income) and reduction of the receivable.

Leasing in Turkey is a new form of asset financing having been introduced in its modern form in 1985 (Kurmus 1995, 325). Rapid growth[8] has been seen in this industry (see Table 2) but at present there are a number of problems in this area, such as presentation of lease transactions in the financial statements of lessees and lessors, unfair competition between leasing companies on the one hand and Islamic banks and investment banks on the other hand, and the recent increase in value added tax (VAT) rates on lease transactions,[9] which all need to be solved. In addition, the presentation of lease transactions in the financial statements is one of the most debated subjects within the accounting profession in Turkey. The current position is that there are no accounting rules specific to leasing in tax law with respect to rents (Tekinalp 1992).

According to the rules specified in the Income Tax Law (Arts. 70-79) and Tax Procedural Law (Books 1, 2 and 3), lessors are required to capitalize leased properties and record the depreciation expense on such properties, while lessees are required to record the full amount of rental payments as an expense. Lessees are not allowed to capitalize leased assets and are not obliged to disclose information regarding lease commitments, either in the financial statement themselves or in the notes to the accounts.[10]

Table 2. Volume, Growth and Market Penetration of Leasing—Ranked by Volume in 1993

Rank	*Country*	*Annual Volume (US$bn)*	*% Growth 1989-1993*	*% Market Penetration*
1	United States	125.00	2.1	32.0
2	Japan	59.89	11.0	7.8
3	Great Britain	12.80	(36.8)	19.0
25	Turkey	0.98	308.3	4.4
Top 50 Countries		309.57	n/a	n/a

Source: *World Leasing Yearbook, 1991*, 3 and 1995, 3.

Research Objectives

Accounting problems that need to be addressed in Turkey stem from the lack of suitability of the present tax laws for financial accounting purposes (see Sozbilir 1987; Kazici 1987; Bilginoglu 1985; Uyanik 1990; Sen 1990; Tanis 1991). The problems caused by lack of accounting standards in relation to lease transactions were also highlighted in the unpublished report prepared by the Accounting Standards Working Group of the Organization for Economic Cooperation and Development (OECD 1987) based on responses received from a questionnaire survey. The main argument is that in spite of the fact that the majority of lease contracts are arranged as finance leases in Turkey, not surprisingly, the tax laws say nothing about the disclosure of lease contracts and therefore such transactions are a form of "off balance sheet financing."

The lack of disclosure of leased assets may have serious adverse effects, particularly on the stock market which was formed in 1986 and is at an early stage of development.[11] A survey carried out by Taylor and Turley (1985, 59-66) in the United Kingdom clearly indicated that lease capitalization would improve users' ability to make comparisons between companies. Similarly, Abdel-Khalik (1981) in the United States found that capitalization is somehow useful to users for making comparisons between companies. However, if finance leases are to be capitalized by lessees, the imposition of a lease accounting standard may have economic consequences by providing a disincentive to lease because such contracts do not constitute a form of off-balance sheet financing.

The purpose of this study is to consider lease accounting principles and practices and assess their acceptability in Turkey. This objective is achieved by considering accountants' assessments of acceptability of international accounting principles on leasing to Turkey. Because of the criticism that there is growing resentment of accounting rules that are imported into developing countries (Wallace 1993, 112), it was considered appropriate to consider the accounting principles specified by the IASC rather than those in the United Kingdom or United States as the later are nation-specific[12] and may be less acceptable than IASs.

The question of the needs of expected users is somewhat problematical. The IASC's *Framework for the Preparation and Presentation of Financial Statements* (1989) specified that financial statements should serve the needs of many users including investors, employees, lenders, suppliers and other trade creditors, customers, governments and their agencies, and the public. As a result, information in financial reports should meet the common needs of all users of that report.

In the context of this study, it would be extremely difficult to contact a sample from all the user groups to assess their information needs on accounting for lease transactions. Such an approach would undoubtedly be futile because of cost, the lack of sophistication of the population of users from which opinions can be pooled, and the potential for high nonresponse to questionnaires. Further, because of the complexity of the issues in accounting for leases[13] and the newness of such transactions in Turkey, it is likely that the responses may not be meaningful. An alternative approach that is adopted here is to consult surrogates for user/preparer groups and the two main possibilities are investment analysts and accountants. Investment analysts were excluded for pragmatic reasons, namely that there is no organizational body in Turkey representing their interests and also there is no register or listing of analysts. Instead, accountants were selected because of availability of membership lists and because they were considered to be familiar with the technical issues involved.[14]

Another aspect of the research is to investigate whether the views of accountants in Turkey are homogeneous or whether they vary according to type of accountant. For the purposes of this research, accountants in Turkey were classified into three types, namely: "Yeminli Müsavirler Grubu" (i.e., private sector accountants and auditors similar to Chartered Accountants in England and Wales), "Maliye Bakanligi Denetim Elemanlari" (public sector accountants) and the "academicians."

In February 1994, an Accounting and Auditing Committee was formed with the objective of developing accounting and auditing standards in Turkey (Sigma-Mugan 1995, 151-371). This committee is composed of academicians, government auditors, representatives of the Treasury, the Prime Minister's Audit Board, the CMB, the Ministry of Finance, and Turkish independent accountants, financial advisors and sworn-in financial advisors. In 1995, this committee issued exposure drafts on nine different subjects. A review of these exposure drafts and interviews with members of the committee [15] shows that IASs have had a considerable impact on these Exposure Drafts. As of September 1996, the committee had not issued an Exposure Draft on leasing but the interviews revealed that setting up an accounting standard on leasing was on the agenda of the committee.

Another aspect of this research is that it may be informative not only about accountants' opinions but also about the relationship between accounting and the environment in a developing country. There is a substantial literature surrounding the environmental determinism theory, which suggests that there is association between accounting and its environment (Mueller 1967, 1968; Seidler 1967; Previts 1975; Radebaugh 1975; AAA 1977, 1980; Choi and Mueller 1984; DaCosta et al., 1978; Frank 1979; Nair and Frank 1980; Belkaoui and Masky 1985). One of the early texts on international accounting (Choi and Mueller 1978, 22) recognized that if we "accept the proposition that the environments in which accounting operates are not the same in different countries ... it stands to reason that accounting must necessarily differ from case to case if it is to retain the sharp cutting edge of social utility."

A point worthy of note is that researchers perceive the environment in different ways. Cooke and Wallace (1990), for example, distinguished between internal and external environments in which the former includes the stage of economic development, goals of society, legal rules, political systems, economic systems, level of education, financial press and cultural variables; and the later consists of colonial history, impacts of transnational corporations, regional economic communities, international trade, IASs, and international movements of accounting firms and professionals. In contrast, Belkaoui (1983) differentiated between national environments in terms of only economic and political factors.

In terms of the linkage between accounting standards and national environments, Cooke and Wallace (1990) found that "the level of corporate financial disclosure regulation in many developed countries is likely determined more by internal factors, whereas that of many developing countries is likely determined by external factors." Our research may add to that literature by establishing whether accountants in a developing country such as Turkey consider that a standard on leasing should be tailored specifically to the country's environment (see Bursal 1984) or whether the principles set out in IAS 17 have more general acceptability and therefore are applicable to Turkey. It may be that users consider that the problems of accounting for lease transactions are not of great significance to financial reporting in Turkey because measurement choices may not be crucial where there is adequate disclosure.

RESEARCH METHODOLOGY

Even though IAS 17 provides detailed rules, this research aims only to test fundamental lease accounting concepts, for a number of reasons. First, the acceptability of principles set out in IAS 17, as a basis for a Turkish national standard, was tested with the aid of responses to a questionnaire which was completed by accountants in Turkey. In order to assess acceptability of all the detailed requirements of IAS 17, a more comprehensive questionnaire needed to be prepared. However, it was thought that a more detailed questionnaire may have confused the potential respondents, particularly because lease accounting is a new subject in Turkey and the principles set out in IAS 17 are relatively new to respondents.

Moreover, if the results show that even if the fundamental principles of IAS 17 are not acceptable, there would be no point in understanding further investigation. On the other hand, if the results show that the fundamental principles of IAS 17 are acceptable to Turkey, further work can be undertaken.

Since this research focuses on fundamental concepts and because there may be a lack of understanding of all the issues covered in IAS 17, a contextual delimitation was made at the outset. This delimitation relates to sales type of leases which are excluded from this study because such transactions are prohibited by Turkish leasing law.

RESEARCH DESIGN

Required information in this research was gathered by developing a questionnaire, pre-testing it, modifying it, undertaking the field work and analyzing the data to produce valid and reliable results with the highest possible level of accuracy.

Questionnaire Construction

There are a number of ways by which opinions can be elicited through a questionnaire. We used a combination of suggestible questions that elicited dichotomous (Yes or No) replies and multiple choice answers. However, some of our questions were left open-ended for any unexpected response. An alternative approach to dichotomous answers would be to use a Likert-scale but this was rejected on the grounds that a more sophisticated approach may discourage response and because the issues are relatively new to Turkey and further complications may inhibit replies.

The questionnaire was prepared in English but since respondents were Turkish, it was translated [16] and the Turkish version was sent. At the beginning of the questionnaire, the principles set out in IAS 17 were explained briefly. In order to get a respondent's own opinions s/he was asked to ignore current Turkish tax law.[17]

Questionnaire Development and Pre-Testing

A pilot questionnaire was carried out in Turkey to determine which question(s) needed changing or clarification and to pre-test its structure and context. In addition, the questionnaire was used to estimate the percentage of respondents answering questions in a particular direction.[18]

The pilot survey was directed at a representative sample of the target population and responses received led to some modifications to the research instrument. A summary of the final form of the questionnaire, in English, is shown in Table 3 and the complete questionnaire is available on request.

Table 3. Replies to the Questionnaire

	Yes	No	Other
Q 1* Is it necessary to segregate lease contracts into operating leases or finance leases?	115	33	
Q 2 If your answer is yes (to Q 1), what should be the main criteria for establishing a finance lease?			
(a) * The lease transfers ownership of the asset to the lessee by the end of the lease term	108	6	34
(b) * The lessee has the option to purchase the asset at a price which is expected to be sufficiently lower than the fair value of the asset at the date the option becomes exercisable	94	20	34
(c) * The lease term is for the major part of the useful life of the asset	97	17	34
(d) * The present value at the inception of the lease if the minimum lease payments is greater than or equal to the fair value of the leased asset	96	18	34
Q 3* How should a hire purchase contract be treated for accounting purposes?			
(a) As a lease	101		
(b) As an installment purchase	42		
(c) Other	5		
Q 4* How should a finance lease be recorded in the financial statements of a lessee?			
(a) As a tangible asset and obligation to pay future rentals	105		
(b) As rental expense	36		
(c) Other	7		
Q 5* How should an operating lease be recorded in the financial statements of a lessee?			
(a) As a tangible asset	9		
(b) As rental expense	139		
Q 6⊗ If a lease is capitalized by the lessee, which amount should be recorded as an asset and as a liability?			
(a) Present value of future lease payments	39		
(b) Fair value of the asset	44		
(c) The lower value of (a) or (b)	26		
(d) Total future lease payments	35		
(e) Other	4		
Q 7* How should a finance lease be recorded in the financial statement of a lessor?			
(a) As a tangible asset	36		
(b) As a receivable	108		
(c) Other	4		
Q 8* How should an operating lease be recorded in the financial statement of a lessor?			
(a) As a tangible asset	136		
(b) As a receivable	11		
(c) Other	1		

(continued)

Table 3 Continued

	Yes	No	Other
Q 9⊗ If a lease is recorded as a receivable by a lessor, which amount should be recorded?			
(a) Net investment in the lease (present value of lease payments + unguaranteed residual value)	46		
(b) The cost of the leased asset	82		
(c) Total future lease payments	16		
(d) Other	4		
Q10 Should the accounting treatment of sale and lease-back transactions be carried out in accordance with IAS 17?	91	55	2
Q11⊗ If sale and leaseback transactions result in a finance lease, any excess of sales proceeds over the carrying amount should?			
(a) Be recorded immediately?	63		
(b) Be deferred and amortized over the lease term?	50		
(c) Be both (a) and (b)	34		
(d) Other	1		
Q12* If sale and leaseback transactions result in an operating lease, and the transactions are established at fair value, any profit or less on the sale should:			
(a) Be recorded immediately?	91		
(b) Be deferred and amortized over the lease term?	29		
(c) Be both (a) and (b)?	27		
(d) Other	1		
Q13* Leases of land and building should:			
(a) Be recorded according to IAS 17?	91		
(b) Be accepted as operating leases and capitalized by the lessor?	54		
(c) Other (please specify)?	3		
Q14⊗ If the lease is capitalized by the lessee, should the amount of assets be separately identified from other assets in the lessee's balance sheet?	132	11	5
Q15* If the lease is capitalized by the lessee, should liabilities related to the leased asset be shown separately from other liabilities in the lessee's balance sheet?	132	12	4
Q16*⊗ Should commitments for minimum lease payments with a term of more than one year be disclosed by the lessee in summary form?	130	6	12
Q17 Which of the following should be disclosed in the financial statements of lessees?			
(a)* Renewal or purchase option	122	23	3
(b)⊗ Contingent rentals	84	61	3
(c) Other contingencies arising from the lease	81	64	3

(continued)

Table 3 Continued

	Yes	No	Other
AS 17 requires that the lessor should disclose, in the financial statements or in the footnotes, the following information. In the case of a finance lease, the gross investment in leases, the related unearned finance income and unguaranteed residual value of leased asset (¶ 60); in the case of an operating lease, the amount of the leased asset, by each major class of asset together with the related accumulated depreciation at each balance sheet date (¶ 62).			
Q18* Are the disclosure requirements on finance leases stated in IAS 17 appropriate for Turkey?	89	56	3
Q19* Are the disclosure requirements on operating leases stated in IAS 17 appropriate for Turkey?	122	25	1

Notes: * = Respondents prefer one method to another—statistically significant at the 5 percent level.
⊗ = Differences between and among group responses are statiscally different and therefore, considered in further detail.

Population

The population consisted of three groups of accountants: professional accountants, government accountants, and academic accountants. In selecting the population, two criteria were established in order that the objectives set forth in this study could be met. First, individuals should be reasonably knowledgeable in accounting principles and practice and specifically in Turkish accounting and the area being investigated. Second, they should have sufficient interest in the area such that their responses would reflect serious thought on the matter. The accounting group fitted these criteria best and so were chosen, in effect, as surrogates for preparers/users.

The Relationship Between the Three Groups of Accountants

Each of the three groups included in this survey has a notable effect on the Turkish accounting system. Some members of the survey groups are also members of the Accounting and Auditing Standards Committee which was formed in 1994. Members of each of the three groups were selected because they operate several areas and are employed by different companies or organizations. Therefore, there is the possibility that each group has a different perspective on accounting issues. For instance, government accountants are employed by the Ministry of Finance to audit private and public companies' accounts to ensure compliance with the related tax laws and the Commercial Code with the purpose of protecting the fiscal interest of the government. Therefore, it is possible that this group may consider the situation from a legal and taxation standpoint even though this group was asked to ignore taxation laws.

Professional accountants, in contrast, are engaged in a wide range of activities including working as practicing accountants and as employees in industry. Since they work for private companies, they may be more concerned to protect their clients' interests (lessees and lessors are generally the clients of this group).

As far as the academicians are concerned, they are employed by Turkish universities and their main duties are to undertake research and give lectures. Since they are usually concerned with the theoretical aspects of the subject, it is possible that members of this group would assess situations from a theoretical rather than practical point of view.

While it is the overall results that are crucial, respondents were classified into the three subgroups and the results were analyzed accordingly (see Table 3). The hypotheses to be tested for each question may be expressed in two ways that are formally tested here. First, that over 50 percent of respondents believe one thing rather than another and secondly, whether there are differences in the population among the three groups' responses.

Sampling

Simple random sampling techniques were employed with a confidence level of 95 percent. According to the pilot survey results, the proportion with the particular attribute[19] in the population was estimated to be 80 percent and the desired standard error for this proportion was set at 6 percent.[20] In order to determine the overall required sample size, the following equation was employed (see Moser and Kalton 1979, 147):

$$n = \frac{\pi(1-\pi)}{[\text{S.E. }(p)]^2} \tag{1}$$

where:

- n = required sample size without finite population correction
- π = the proportion with the particular attribute in the population
- $[\text{S.E.}(p)]^2$ = standard error of proportion

For the above mentioned specification, the solution is n = 178, which was the required sample size under the assumption that the population was large enough to ignore the finite population correction. However, the total population in this survey was 805 consisting of 355 professional accountants, 414 government accountants, and 107 academicians and the sample size represented a sizable portion of the population (20.6 percent). Therefore, the initial required sample size calculation was readjusted using the following finite population correction equation (see Moser and Kalton 1979, 147):

$$n' = \frac{n}{1 + (n/N)} \qquad (2)$$

where n' = required sample size with finite population correction

n = required sample size without finite population correction (solution of equation (1), $n = 178$)

N = population size

As a result, the total sample size was found to be 147 with the required sample size for each group[21] being as follows: 53 professional accountants, 54 government accountants, and 40 academicians. To allow for the possibility of unfavorable response rate, 370 questionnaires were sent out on a random basis in proportion to the required sample size for each group (see Table 4).

Response Rate

One hundred and forty-eight replies were received, an effective response rate of 40 percent. A description of the respondents is provided in Table 4.

RESULTS

The results are presented in order of the 19 questions asked; a summary of which is provided in Table 3. A secondary aim is to assess the extent of homogeneity of accountants' views and where differences between the groups are statistically significant the results are reported and discussed. In analyzing responses, the

Table 4. Distribution of the Population, Required Sample Size, Number of Questionnaires Sent, Number and Percentage of Responses Received

Respondent Groups	*Population*	*Required Sample Size*	*Number of Questionnaires Sent*	*Responses* No.	*Responses* %
Professional accountants	335	53	145	59	40.69
Government accountants	414	54	145	50	34.48
Academicians	107	40	80	39	48.75
Total	856	147	370	148	40.00

dichotomous nature of some of the questions led to the selection of nonparametric statistics based on the chi-squared distribution.

The chi-square statistic, like any other statistic, has its limitations. For instance, chi-square does not take sample size into consideration. In addition, if the number of cases in each cell in a cross-tabulation increases, the chi-square statistic also increases (Norusis 1986, 273). Thus, although the results of a chi-square test generally indicate whether there are differences among the groups' responses, there is a problem of interpretation in assessing the strength of those differences. In recognition of this problem, additional statistical tests (such as Cramer's V, contingency coefficient, and phi) were carried out to determine the strength of differences.

Another important limitation in using chi-square analysis is that the probabilities in the table of critical values are based on the assumption that none of the cells of the table has zero or low frequency (Siegel 1956, 178-179). The general rule is that the chi-square statistic should not be used if more than 20 percent of the cells have expected frequency less than five or any expected frequency less than one (Siegel 1956, 178-179). Siegel (1956) suggested that this problem might be overcome by combining adjacent categories into a single pooled category and this suggestion was adopted here.

As might be seen in many of the cross-tabulations, there are some cells in which "missing" was reported. "Missing" represents the number of respondents who did not answer the question and as a result, they were excluded from the statistical tests. The percentage of responses to each question is shown in Table 3 and where there is a significant statistical difference (at the 5 percent level) among the groups' responses, the cross-tabulation is shown.

With respect to Table 3, a chi-square statistic was calculated for each question on the basis that the expected number of cases will be evenly distributed. The results are marked on that table and the text is marked accordingly.

Classification of Leases for Accounting Purposes

According to IAS 17, all leases should be classified as either operating or finance leases. The IASC recommends that if a lease meets at least one of the four criteria listed below (IAS 17, ¶ 5) it should be classified as a finance lease, otherwise it should be classified as an operating lease. These criteria are:

1. the lease transfers ownership of the asset to the lessee by the end of the lease term;
2. the lessee has the option to purchase the asset at a price which is expected to be sufficiently lower than the fair value of the asset at the date the option becomes exercisable;
3. the lease term is for the major part of the useful life of the asset;

4. at the inception of the lease the present value of the minimum lease payments is greater than or equal to the fair value of the leased asset.

In Turkey, there is no distinction between finance and operating leases for accounting purposes. As a consequence, all lease contracts are considered to be rental agreements in the profit and loss account with the lessor capitalizing the leased asset.

Two questions are used to find out whether the above mentioned principles stated in IAS 17 can be adopted as a basis for a national standard in Turkey. In the first question, respondents are asked if it is necessary to segregate lease contracts into operating or finance leases. Those that thought that segregation is important are asked about the main criteria for establishing a finance lease.

Question 1: Is it necessary to segregate lease contracts into operating leases or finance leases?

The response to question 1 (see Table 3) shows that a majority of respondents (over 77 percent of overall respondents, and over 74 percent of each group) found the classification to be important (statistically significant at the 5 percent level). In addition, the statistical tests confirm that there is no significant difference among the groups' responses. While all the group members are strongly in agreement with this classification, academicians are particularly supportive. On the basis of these responses, it may be concluded that accountants would like to change the way in which lease contracts are accounted for in Turkey.

Question 2: If your answer is yes [to Question 1], what should be the main criteria for establishing a finance lease?

The purpose of this question is to assess the acceptability, in Turkey, of criteria recommended in IAS 17 for establishing a finance lease. The responses to this question (see Table 3) reveal that all the criteria recommended by the IASC for determining whether a lease is merely a rental contract or a finance lease for accounting purposes seem acceptable in Turkey since over 63 percent of the overall respondents agreed with all the criteria (see Table 3). This rate of agreement is over 70 percent for the first criterion. Even though more than one half of each group's members found each criterion recommended by the IASC to be acceptable in Turkey, the percentage of academicians who gave positive responses to the first two criteria is relatively higher than that of the other two groups. On the other hand, the professional accountants' support for all the criteria is relatively less than the other two groups. However, the statistical tests show that the differences are not significant.

This question was left open ended so as to give an opportunity for respondents to write down any other appropriate criteria for this classification, but none was mentioned.

Accounting for Hire Purchase Contracts

According to IAS 17 (¶2), the definition of a lease includes contracts for the hire of an asset which contains a provision giving the hirer an option to acquire title to the asset upon the fulfillment of agreed conditions. These contracts are described as hire purchase contracts in certain countries. In some countries, different names are used for agreements which have the characteristics of a lease, for example, bare-boat charters (ICAEW 1987, 185).

As far as Turkish leasing law is concerned, lease contracts may provide a purchase option. However, there is no difference between an ordinary rental agreement and a hire purchase contract from an accounting point of view in Turkey. All hire purchase contracts are treated as operating leases for accounting purposes.

Question 3: How should hire purchase contracts be treated for accounting purposes?

Sixty-eight percent of respondents believe that hire purchase contracts should be treated as leases for accounting purposes in Turkey, while 28 percent thought that they should be treated as installment purchases (statistically significant, see Table 3). Only a few respondents provided a different answer saying that hire purchase contracts should be treated as leases but disclosed under a separate heading.

Among the groups, 64 percent of professional accountants, 66 percent of government accountants, and 76 percent of academicians acknowledged that lease purchase contracts should be treated as stated in IAS 17. In spite of the fact that the majority of professional and government accountants preferred treating hire purchase contracts as leases for accounting purposes, it is apparent that a considerable percentage of them, over 30 percent, wanted to treat them as installment purchases. Although the frequency table (Table 3) indicates that there is a slight difference between academicians and the other two groups' responses on this issue, the statistical tests showed that this was not significant.

The Accounting Treatment of Finance and Operating Leases in the Financial Statements of Lessees

Question 4: How should a finance lease be recorded in the financial statements of a lessee?

The analysis of question 4 shows that, recording a finance lease as a tangible asset with the obligation to pay future rentals was the most frequently mentioned response among all the three groups' members. However, capitalization of finance leases by lessees is contrary to present Turkish lease accounting practice which is based on the tax law. While 24 percent of overall respondents preferred recording finance leases as expense items, the majority of respondents (70.9 percent) preferred such leases to be capitalized by the lessee as stated in IAS 17 (statistically significant, see Table 3). All the three groups' responses to this issue are very similar.

Question 5: *How should an operating lease be recorded in the financial statements of a lessee?*

Ninety-three percent of all respondents stated that an operating lease should be recorded as a rental expense as is currently practiced in Turkey (statistically significant, see Table 3). The response to this question also reinforces the acceptability of the principles set out in IAS 17 as current Turkish lease accounting practice is consistent with international practice. It is somewhat surprising that 6.1 percent of total respondents (12 percent for government accountants) prefer operating leases to be recorded as assets by lessees. Although this question was left open-ended, no alternative treatment was proposed by respondents.

Question 6: *If a lease is capitalized by the lessee, which amount should be recorded as an asset and as a liability?*

The results of question 6 are presented in Table 5 (note that the statistical results shown in Tables 5 to 8 refer to the differences between group responses). It is

Table 5. Asset's Capitalized Value by Lessee

Capitalized Value	*Professional Accountants*		*Academicians*		*Government Accountants*		*Total*	
	No.	*%*	*No.*	*%*	*No.*	*%*	*No.*	*%*
Present value of leased payments	8	13.6	20	51.3	11	22.0	39	26.4
Fair value of leased asset	11	18.6	7	17.9	26	52.0	44	29.7
The lower value of above two	14	23.7	7	17.9	5	10.0	26	17.6
Total future lease payments	23	39.0	5	12.9	7	14.0	35	23.6
Missing	3	5.1	-	-	1	2.0	4	2.7
Total	59	100.0	39	100.0	50	100.0	148	100.0
Chi-square (Pearson)	Significance		Cramer's V		Contingency Coefficient		Phi	
38.32683	0.00000		0.36480		0.45849		0.51591	

noticeable that there is significant variation among groups' preferences. Overall, while a significant percentage of respondents (29.7 percent) favor the fair value of the leased property to be reflected in the lessees' balance sheet, respondents that prefer recording the present value of future lease payments and total lease payments as the asset's capitalized value are 26.4 percent and 23.6 percent respectively. Only 17.6 percent of the respondents support the IAS 17's principle on this issue saying that if a finance lease is capitalized by a lessee, the leased property should be recorded on the lessee's balance sheet at an amount equal to the fair value of the leased asset or, if lower, the present value of the minimum lease payments.

About 51 percent of the academic respondents selected the present value of the leased asset to be recorded as the lessees' capitalized value while 52 percent of responding government accountants supported the fair value of the leased asset. In contrast, 39 percent of responding professional accountants preferred the total lease payments to be recognized as the asset's capitalized value by lessees. Only 13.6 percent and 18.6 percent of responding professional accountants chose the present value of lease payments and the fair value of leased assets respectively. The most significant support (23.7 percent) for IAS 17's principles on this issue came from the Professional Accountants.

Differences in the nature of each group may be the reason for this significant variation among the groups' response on this issue. For instance, government accountants' responses to this question may be strongly related to the requirements stated in Turkish tax accounting legislation even though respondents were asked to ignore taxation. On the other hand, significant support for the acceptability of IAS 17, came from the professional accountants' groups' members who are supposed to take into consideration, not only legal requirements, but also generally accepted (international) accounting principles and standards.

The Accounting Treatment of Finance and Operating Leases in Statement of Lessors

According to IAS 17 (¶ 48-53), a finance lease should be recorded as a receivable at an amount equal to the net investment in the lease, while operating leases should be recorded as property, plant, and equipment in the balance sheets of lessors. In Turkey, all leases are accepted as if they are operating leases and recorded as assets at amounts equal to the purchasing cost of the lease by lessors.

In order to assess whether the required accounting treatment stated in IAS 17 can be adopted in Turkey, as a basis for a national lease standard, three questions (7, 8 and 9) were proposed. The purpose of the first question is to establish the appropriate accounting treatment by lessors, while the aim of the second question is to assess the appropriate accounting by lessors applicable to operating leases. The last question of this section (question 9) asks respondents to determine what amount should be recorded if a lease is treated as a receivable.

Question 7: How should a finance lease be recorded in the financial statements of a lessor?

Responses to question 7 provided interesting results (see Table 3). While lease transactions are recorded as tangible assets by lessors, recording leases as receivables is not practiced in Turkey. However, this survey found that over 73 percent of respondents would like an asset which is subject to a finance lease to be recorded as a receivable by the lessor (statistically significant, see Table 3). The number of respondents who agreed with IAS 17's principle was almost three times more than the respondents who prefer finance leases to be recorded as tangible assets by the lessor, as is currently practiced in Turkey.

As a group, about 74 percent of professional accountants and academicians prefer finance leases to be recorded as a receivable compared with 70 percent of government accountants. The differences are not significantly different.

Question 8: How should an operating lease be recorded in the financial statements of a lessor?

The analysis of question 8, which is designed to assess the appropriate accounting treatment for operating leases, clearly shows that the majority of respondents (91.9 percent) favor them to be recorded as tangible assets by the lessor in the financial statements (statistically significant, Table 3). In contrast, only 7.4 percent prefer recording operating leases as a receivable by the lessor which is contrary to both current Turkish practice and IAS 17's principles. As a group, over 89 percent of each group's members thought that operating leases should be recorded as tangible assets by the lessor.

The considerable support for the acceptability of IAS 17's principles on this issue is not surprising since at present in Turkey all leases (not only operating leases) are capitalized by the lessor.

Question 9: If a lease is recorded as a receivable by a lessor, which amount should be recorded?

As can be seen from Table 6, over 55 percent of overall respondents suggested that, if a leased asset is recorded in the lessor's balance sheet as a receivable, its amount should be equal to the cost of the leased asset. Alternatively, 31 percent of respondents support an amount equal to the net investment in the lease while over 10 percent of them proposed an amount equal to the total rental payments to be recorded as a receivable by the lessor. Only one government accountant respondent provided an alternative, saying that the present value of lease payments should be taken into account.

As a group, the resulting chi-square, Cramer's V, and contingency coefficient from the analysis of responses indicate that there is variation among the groups'

Table 6. Amount of Receivables Recorded by Lessors

Recorded Value	*Professional Accountants*		*Academicians*		*Government Accountants*		*Total*	
	No.	*%*	*No.*	*%*	*No.*	*%*	*No.*	*%*
Net Investment	10	16.9	14	35.9	22	44.0	46	31.1
Cost of leased asset	35	59.3	22	56.4	25	50.0	82	55.4
Total lease payments	12	20.4	3	7.7	1	2.0	16	10.6
Present value of leased rent	-	-	-	-	1	2.0	1	0.9
Missing	2	3.4	-	-	1	2.0	3	2.0
Total	59	100.0	39	100.0	50	100.0	148	100.0

Chi-square (Pearson)	Significance	Cramer's V	Contingency Coefficient	Phi
16.89719	0.00202	0.24138	0.32306	0.34137

responses on this question. This variation is particularly pronounced between the responses from professional accountants and those from government accountants. However, the majority of each group's members (over 50 percent) preferred the cost of a leased asset to be recorded as a receivable by the lessor. As a result, it can be said that the responses received from this question do not conform with the requirements of IAS 17.

Accounting for Sale and Leaseback Transactions

For sale and leaseback transactions, the following accounting treatments are recommended by the IASC in IAS 17 (¶ 54-56). If a sale and leaseback transaction results in a finance lease being capitalized by the lessee, then, any excess of sales proceeds over the carrying amount should not be immediately recognized in income in the financial statements of a seller lessee. If such an excess is recognized, it should be deferred and amortized over the lease term. If sale and leaseback transactions result in an operating lease, it is capitalized by the lessor and if the transaction is established at fair value, any profit or loss should be recorded immediately.

As far as Turkish lease accounting is concerned, all leases (it does not matter whether they are direct lease transactions or sale and leaseback transactions) are capitalized by the lessor and any gain or loss from the original sale is recognized immediately by the seller-lessee.[22] Questions 10, 11, and 12 serve to test the acceptability of IAS 17's principles on this issue to Turkey.

Question 10: Should the accounting treatment of sale and leaseback transactions be carried out in accordance with IAS 17?

The majority of respondents state that the accounting treatment followed by Turkish lessees and lessors for sale and leaseback transactions should be the same as described in IAS 17 (if a sale and leaseback transaction results in a finance lease it should be capitalized by the lessee, otherwise it should be capitalized by the lessor). Even though this principle contrasts with that practiced in Turkey, 61.5 percent of overall respondents support it (statistically significant, see Table 3).

As a group, over 74 percent of academicians, 57 percent of professional accountants, and 56 percent of government accountants agreed with the principles set out in IAS 17 on this subject. It is notable that support for these principles is much greater from responding academic accountants than from responding professional and government accountants. However, the statistical tests show that the differences are not significant.

The responses to question 10 are slightly different to those of questions 4, 5, 7, and 8 which are designed to determine the accounting requirements that lessees and lessors should follow in the case of direct finance leases and operating leases. Over 70 percent of the respondents to questions 4, 5, 7, and 8 state that if the lease contract is a result of a direct finance lease transaction, it should be capitalized by the lessee, otherwise it should be capitalized by the lessor. However, in the case of a sale and leaseback transaction, just over 61 percent of the respondents agreed with these principles.

Questions 11 and 12 are designed to investigate whether or not any profits or losses experienced by seller-lessees from the sale of assets that are leased back under a lease agreement (finance or operating) should be recorded immediately or deferred and amortized over the lease term.

Question 11: If sale and leaseback transactions result in a finance lease, how should any excess of sales proceeds over the carrying amount be treated?

As far as overall response is concerned, 42.6 percent of the respondents preferred that if a sale and leaseback transaction results in a finance lease, any excess of sales proceeds over the carrying amount should be immediately recognized as income in the financial statements of the seller-lessee, as currently practiced in Turkey. This is not consistent with the principles set out in IAS 17. In contrast, 33.8 percent of the respondents preferred that the excess should be deferred and amortized over the lease term and 23 percent wanted an option somewhere between the two (as stated in Table 7).

As far as the groups are concerned, it is apparent from Table 7, and confirmed by the statistical tests, that there is considerable variation in response to this question, especially between academicians and the other two groups. It is interesting

Table 7. Accounting for Excess of Sales Arising from Sale of Leaseback Transactions (Finance Leases)

Accounting Method	*Professional Accountants* No.	%	*Academicians* No.	%	*Government Accountants* No.	%	*Total* No.	%
a) Recorded Immediately	35	59.3	7	18.0	21	42.0	63	42.6
b) Deferred and amortized	14	23.7	22	56.4	14	28.0	50	33.8
c) Option between (a) and (b)	10	17.0	10	25.6	14	28.0	34	23.0
Missing	-	-	-	-	1	2.0	1	0.6
Total	59	100.0	39	100.0	50	100.0	148	100.0

Chi-square (Pearson)	Significance	Cramer's V	Contingency Coefficient	Phi
19.09899	0.00075	0.25488	0.33910	0.36045

to note that even though a sizable proportion of responding professional accountants and government accountants (59 percent and 42 percent respectively) selected recognizing the excess immediately, this option was preferred by only 17.9 percent of academic accountants.

The most popular alternative for responding government accountants was that any excess arising from sale and leaseback should be recorded immediately as required by Turkish tax law. On the other hand, responding academic accountants strongly supported the acceptability of IAS 17 on this issue as they did with many other questions. However, the majority of responding professional accountants, who were assumed to evaluate the situation by taking into consideration the interests of lessees and lessors, would like any excess arising from sale and leaseback transactions to be recorded immediately which is somewhat surprising since this treatment would create a tax disadvantage to the lessee.[23]

Question 12: If sale and leaseback transactions result in an operating lease, and the transaction is established at fair value, should any profit or loss on the sale (a) be recorded immediately; (b) be deferred and amortized; or (c) be somewhere between (a) and (b)?

The purpose of this question is to determine when any profit or loss experienced by the seller-lessee from the sale of assets (if the transaction is established at fair value), that are leased back under an operating lease, should be recognized. Table 3 presents the percentage distribution of respondents' preferences on this question.

The overall response strongly suggests that if sale and leaseback transactions result in an operating lease and the transaction is at fair value, any profit or loss on the sale should be recorded immediately as recommended in IAS 17 (statistically significant, see Table 3). Only 19.6 percent of the respondents prefer deferral with amortization to the profit or loss. Of the total respondents, 18.2 percent favor having an option somewhere between immediate recording and amortization. With respect to individual groups, the statistical tests show that there is no significant variation in responses to this question. More than half of each group members upheld the principles set out in IAS 17 stating that any excess should be recorded immediately.

The Accounting Treatment of Leases of Land and Buildings by Both Lessees and Lessors

According to IAS 17, leases of land and buildings should be capitalized by lessees if the title to the land and buildings is certain to be transferred to the lessee in the future, otherwise they should be capitalized by the lessors. As far as the Turkish case is concerned, tax law requires all leased land and buildings to be capitalized by the lessors only.

Question 13 was designed to establish whether leased land and buildings should be recorded according to IAS 17 or be treated as an operating lease and capitalized by the lessor as is currently practiced in Turkey.

Question 13: Leases of land and buildings should (a) be recorded according to IAS 17; (b) be accepted as operating leases and capitalized by the lessor; (c) other?

Results indicate that leased land and buildings should be capitalized by a lessee if the title of the land and buildings are certain to be transferred to the lessee in the future, otherwise they should be capitalized by the lessor as stated in IAS 17. In contrast, 36.5 percent[24] of respondents prefer leased land and buildings to be capitalized by the lessor, as is currently practiced in Turkey.

The majority of respondents (over 60 percent of each of the groups) chose the principles set out in IAS 17 regarding the accounting treatment appropriate for leased land and buildings (statistically significant, see Table 3). Even though this question was left open-ended, alternative responses were not provided by participants.

The Extent of Disclosure of Leases in the Financial Statements of Lessees

IAS 17 (¶ 57-59) requires the following information to be disclosed in the lessees' financial statements or as a footnote:

- the amount of assets that are the subject of finance leases and related liabilities should be shown separately from other assets and liabilities
- lease commitments with a term of more than one year
- renewal or purchase options
- contingent rentals and other contingencies arising from leases.

Four questions (14, 15, 16, and 17) were used to test whether the disclosure principles set out in IAS 17 should apply to financial statements of lessees in Turkey where there are no mandatory disclosure requirements on leasing. Table 8 presents the responses to the questions in which there is a significant difference between the three groups.

Table 8. Required Disclosure by Lessees

	Required Disclosure		*Professional Accountants*		*Academicians*		*Government Accountants*		*Total*	
			No.	*%*	*No.*	*%*	*No.*	*%*	*No.*	*%*
Q14	Should the amount of assets subject to	Yes	57	96.6	37	94.9	38	76.0	132	89.2
	a finance lease be separately identified	No	-	-	2	5.1	9	18.0	11	7.4
	from other assets?	N.i.	2	3.4	-	-	3	6.0	5	3.4
Q16	Should commitments for minimum lease	Yes	56	94.9	32	82.1	42	84.0	130	87.8
	payments of more than one year be	No	-	-	-	-	6	12.0	6	4.1
	disclosed in summary form?	N.i.	2	3.4	7	17.9	2	4.0	11	7.4
		*	1	1.7	-	-	-	-	1	0.7
Q17b	Should contingent	Yes	30	50.8	32	82.1	22	44.0	84	56.8
	rentals be disclosed	No	27	45.8	7	17.9	27	17.9	61	41.2
	by lessees?	*	2	3.4	-	-	1	2.0	3	2.0

	Chi-square (Pearson)	Significance	Cramer's V	Contingency Coefficient	Phi
Question 14[26]	13.69654	0.00106	0.30421	0.29104	0.30421
Question 16[27]	6.25184	0.04390	0.20623	0.20198	0.20623
Question 17(b)	13.38217	0.00124	0.30379	0.29068	0.30379

Notes: No. = Number; N.i. = Not important; * = Missing

A large majority of the total respondents (89.2 percent) to question 14 preferred that if a lease is capitalized by a lessee, the asset amount and related liability should be identified separately from other assets and liabilities in the lessees' balance sheet in accordance with the requirements of IAS 17 (statistically significant, see Table 3). The analysis of responses to question 14 indicates that 96.6 percent and 94.9 percent of responding professional accountants and responding academic accountants respectively would prefer the amount of an asset subject to a finance lease to be separately identified from the other assets in the lessees' balance sheet. In contrast, the comparable figure for responding government accountants is 76 percent.

Although the statistical tests indicate (see Table 8) differences between groups' responses to this question, it is not particularly important because a significant percentage of each group's members (over 75 percent) support the acceptability of IAS 17's disclosure requirements.

Responses received to question 15 show that (see Table 3) 89.2 percent of total respondents (100 percent of the academicians, 82 percent of the government accountants, and 88 percent of professional accountants) suggest that if a lease is capitalized by a lessee, the related liabilities should be separately identified (statistically significant, see Table 3).

The responses to question 16 support the view that lease payments with a term of more than one year should be disclosed by a lessee in summary form, though at present this is rarely practiced by Turkish companies (statistically significant, see Table 3). Despite this general agreement, the statistical tests indicate that there is variation among the groups' responses. While 94 percent of the responding professional accountants preferred lease payments with a term of more than one year to be disclosed, this was supported by 82 percent and 84 percent of responding academic accountants and responding government accountants, respectively. Even though none of the responding academic accountants disagreed with this view, 17.9 percent of them thought that it was not important.

In addition to the above mentioned disclosure requirement, participants were asked to assess whether or not renewal or purchase options, contingent rentals, and other contingencies arising from leases should be disclosed in the financial statements of lessees in Turkey (question 17). The overall response indicates that renewal or purchase options (see Table 3), contingent rentals (see Table 8), and other contingencies (see Table 3) arising from leases should be disclosed in the lessees' financial statements in Turkey as stated in IAS 17. Although over 50 percent of total respondents agreed with all three disclosure requirements, all the groups agreed with the disclosure of renewal or purchase options. The responses to the other parts of the question were more variable.

The Extent of Disclosure of Leases in the Financial Statements of Lessors

IAS 17 requires that lessors should disclose in the financial statements or in the footnotes the following information:

- In the case of a finance lease, the gross investment, the amount of unearned finance income and the unguaranteed residual value of leased asset (IAS 17, ¶ 60).
- In the case of an operating lease, the amount of the asset by each major class of asset together with the related accumulated depreciation at each balance sheet date (IAS 17, ¶ 62).

Since all leases are considered to be operating leases from an accounting standpoint in Turkey, lessors are only obliged to disclose the value of assets at each balance sheet date. This practice is similar to IAS 17's operating lease disclosure requirement. The only difference is that Turkish companies can disclose either the net book value of the asset (cost of the asset less accumulated depreciation) or the gross value of the asset (cost of the asset together with accumulated depreciation).

Questions 18 and 19 investigated whether the above mentioned principles (set out in IAS 17) can be adopted as a basis for a national standard in Turkey. Responses (see Table 3) indicate that the requirements in IAS 17 for disclosure by the lessor of both finance and operating leases are acceptable to participants as being appropriate to Turkey as a basis for a national standard (statistically significant, see Table 3). Sixty percent of overall respondents acknowledged that the lessors' gross investment in finance leases and the amount of unearned finance income and the residual value of the leased asset should be disclosed by lessors. In addition, 82 percent of respondents acknowledged that the amount of assets by each major class of asset together with related accumulated depreciation arising from operating leases should be disclosed by lessors at each balance sheet date in Turkey as required by IAS 17. The statistical tests show that there is no significant difference in responses between groups.

Summary of Research Findings

Analyses of the responses to the questionnaire revealed that:

1. Even though it is contrary to current practice, the majority of respondents who took part in this survey suggested that the classification of lease contracts into operating or finance leases for accounting purposes, as stated in IAS 17, is applicable to Turkey. The inference from the perceived preferences of respondents is that the four criteria recommended by the IASC are applicable in Turkey.
2. As required by IAS 17, respondents preferred that a lease contract which includes a purchase option be treated as a lease for accounting purposes in Turkey.
3. Consistent with IAS 17, respondents would prefer to see a finance lease in Turkey being recorded as a tangible asset and a liability by the lessee while the charge to income under an operating lease is to be a rental expense.

However, since there is significant variation among respondents' preferences, there was no clear indication as to which value should be recorded as the asset and liability.

4. Respondents would like a finance lease to be recorded as a "receivable" rather than as a tangible asset, while they would like operating leases to be recorded as a tangible asset by the lessor, as stated in IAS 17. However, in contrast to IAS 17 which requires that the receivable value of leased assets should be the net investment in the lease, the majority of respondents preferred a leased asset to be recorded in the lessor's balance sheet as a receivable equal to the cost of the leased asset.
5. Respondents would like lessees to capitalize sales and leaseback transactions that are classified as finance leases, otherwise they would prefer the transaction to be capitalized by the lessor as stated in IAS 17. If sales and leaseback transactions result in an operating lease and the transaction is at fair value, any profit or loss on the sale was suggested to be recognized immediately as recommended in IAS 17. However, in contrast to the principles stated in IAS 17, if sale and leaseback transactions result in a finance lease, respondents would like any excess of sales proceeds over the carrying amount to be recognized immediately as income in the financial statements of the seller lessee.
6. The principles set out in IAS 17 with respect to leased land and buildings are considered to be applicable to Turkey. Respondents would like leased land and buildings to be capitalized by a lessee if the title of the land and buildings are certain to be transferred to the lessee. Otherwise they suggest that leased land and buildings be capitalized by the lessor.
7. Lessees in Turkey are expected by respondents to show assets subject to finance leases and related liabilities separately from other assets in balance sheets. Lessees are also expected by respondents to disclose in the notes to the accounts, their commitments of minimum lease payments in excess of one year and any renewal purchase options. These revealed perceptions of respondents are in agreement with the treatments recommended in IAS 17. However, no clear preference emerged among the respondents as to whether contingent rentals and other contingencies arising from leases are to be disclosed by lessees.
8. In the case of a finance lease, respondents would like lessors to disclose in their financial statements (a) the gross investment; (b) amount of unearned finance income; and (c) residual value of leased asset. In the case of an operating lease, the amount of the asset by each major class together with the related accumulated depreciation at each balance sheet date are expected to be disclosed, which is consistent with the principles stated in IAS 17.

CONCLUSION

The results of this research show that, except for three preferred treatments stated in IAS 17, all the principles set out in IAS 17 are considered applicable and acceptable in Turkey as a basis for a national standard. The three exceptions concern (a) the capitalization value of leased assets which is preferred to be recorded by lessees; (b) the receivable value of finance leases which is preferred to be recorded by lessors; and (c) the recognition of the excess from a sale and leaseback transaction which results in a finance lease. These results (that suggested applicability of IAS 17 to Turkey) are consistent with the recommendations made by individual writers on this issue (see, for example, Bilginoglu 1985; Kazici 1987; Uyanik 1990; Sen 1990; Tanis 1991). In addition, these findings are consistent with work undertaken by Cooke and Wallace (1990) that suggests that external influences are more important than internal factors in developing corporate disclosure regulation in developing countries. However, it can be argued that Turkish internal imperatives with regard to leasing issues coincide with those of IAS 17 and that this may not be the case for other accounting issues.

NOTES

1. The terms of reference of the IASC Steering Committee agreed in October 1989 (see Wallace 1993, 123).
2. This chapter reports in detail the results of a questionnaire that was briefly summarized in Cooke and Çürük (1996).
3. And others such as Perera (1989).
4. For a more detailed consideration of the development of accounting in Turkey, see Cooke and Çürük (1996), and on accounting regulation in Turkey, see Demirag (1993) and Yalkin (1993).
5. For a history of leasing, see Livijn (1990).
6. In the United States, Accounting Principles Board (APB) Opinion No. 5, *Reporting of Leases in Financial Statements of Lessee*, was issued in September 1964 and APB Opinion No. 7, *Accounting for Leases in Financial Statements of Lessors*, followed in December 1966. Statement of Financial Accounting Standards (SFAS) No. 13, *Accounting for Leases*, was issued in November 1976 and superseded the above stated two Opinions.
7. According to IAS 17, a finance lease should be recognized as an asset and a liability in the balance sheet of a lessee at amounts equal at the inception of the lease to the fair value of the leased property, net of grants and tax credits receivable by the lessor or, if lower, at the present value of the minimum lease payments.
8. As a percentage, one of the highest growth rates in the world.
9. For more detail see Kurmus (1995) and Uyanik (1990).
10. This is similar to the position in Germany.
11. In the United Kingdom the lack of disclosure of leased contracts in the financial statements of Court Line led to a Department of Trade inspectors' report to be critical of the accounts at September 30, 1973 in which there were undisclosed leasing obligations of £40 million whereas shareholders' funds were only £18 million (see Davies et al. 1994, 864).
12. And as such are less likely to have neo-colonialist undertones.

13. Calculation of capitalized values and related liabilities of leased assets, allocation of the finance charges to lease periods, determination of depreciation periods and evaluation of depreciation of leased assets require some complicated calculations for both lessees and lessors.

14. A summary of the population is provided in the section on sampling.

15. Interviews were carried out by Turgut Çürük in September 1995 with three of the members of the Accounting and Auditing Standards Committee.

16. The translation was undertaken by Turgut Çürük and reviewed by two Turkish postgraduate students who were studying at the University of Exeter.

17. As of 1997, both the lessee and the lessor must follow the current tax law requirements. Therefore, if respondents did not ignore current tax law, their responses to the questionnaire may have reflected the applicability of IAS 17 to Turkish tax law rather than their own views.

18. Gardner (1978, 112) points out that determination of the required sample size is based on the assumption that something is already known about the variability of the population (the proportion with the particular attribute in the population). He recommends that a pilot survey be carried out to determine the variability in the population in advance. As Vaus (1986, 63-64) points out, "for a population in which most people will answer a question in a particular way or very few answer in a particular way, a smaller sample will do."

19. For more detail see Gardner (1978) and Moser and Kalton (1979).

20. This was considered to be reasonable for a questionnaire of this nature.

21. The required sample size for each group was also calculated by using the same equation explained above.

22. According to the tax law, the only exception to this is when an asset is sold for renewal or modernization purposes. The difference between the sale price of an asset and its book value can be kept on the balance sheet for three years.

23. The lessee is also the seller of the leased assets in sale and leaseback transactions. If any profits from the sale of the leased asset (in terms of differences between the sale price and the book value of the leased asset) is not deferred and amortized over the term of the lease then there should be an immediate adjustment in the income statement. This will have taxation consequences. Since inflation in Turkey is typically in excess of 70 percent per annum any surplus arising from a sale and leaseback transaction would create tax disadvantages to the lessee.

24. Only 31.8 percent of total respondents preferred leased land and buildings to be treated as operating leases and capitalized by lessees. However, 4.7 percent of respondents preferred such assets to be treated as ordinary rent agreements. Since both of the alternative mentioned above give the same results from the accounting point of view they were viewed as the same answer.

25. The chi-square test presented in Table 6 shows that 33.3 percent of the expected frequencies were less than 5. In order to increase the expected frequencies alternative (d) "present value of lease rent" was combined with alternative (a) "net investment." The resulting chi-square, Cramer's V, contingency coefficient, and phi tests were the result of using the adjusted figures.

26. The results of the chi-square test presented in Table 8 show that 66.7 percent of the expected frequencies were less than 5. In order to increase the expected frequencies alternative (b) "No" was combined with alternative (c) "not important." The results of the statistical tests were based on the adjusted figures.

27. The results (see Table 8) of the chi-square test derived from the responses to question 16, show that 66/7 percent of the expected frequencies were less than 5. In order to increase the expected frequencies for some suggestible answers to this question, alternative (b) "No" was combined with alternative (c) "not important" for the chi-square test. The results of the statistical tests were based on the adjusted figures.

REFERENCES

Abdel-Khalik, A. R. 1981. Financial Accounting Standards Board (FASB) Research Report. *The Economic Effects on Leases of FASB Statement No. 13: Accounting for Leases*. Stamford, CT: FASB.

Alexander, D., and S. Archer (Eds.). 1992. *European Accounting Guide*. London: Academic Press.

Al-Hashim, D. D., and J. S. Arpan. 1988. *International Dimensions of Accounting*. Bolton, MA: PWS-Kent Publishing Company.

American Accounting Association (AAA). 1977. Report of the 1975-76 committee on international accounting operations and education 1976-78. *The Accounting Review* 52 (Supplement): 65-132.

American Accounting Association (AAA). 1980. *Accounting education and the third world*. Report of the Committee on International Accounting Operations and Education 1976-78. Sarasota, FL.

Belkaoui, A. 1983. Economic, political, and civil indicators and reporting and disclosure adequacy: An empirical investigation. *Journal of Accounting and Public Policy* 2 (3): 207-219.

Belkaoui, A., and M. Masky. 1985. Welfare of the common man and accounting disclosure adequacy: An empirical investigation. *The International Journal of Accounting Education and Research* 20 (2):81-94.

Bilginoglu, F. 1985. *Muhasebede harmanizasyon: Avrupa ve uluslararasi duzeyde muhasebeye dogru* [Harmonization in accounting: An approach to European and International accounting]. Muhasebe Enstitusu Dergisi (August): 12-24.

Bursal, N. I. 1984. The accounting environment and some recent developments in Turkey. *The International Journal of Accounting* 19 (2): 93-127.

Choi, F. D. S., and G. G. Mueller. 1978. *An Introduction to Multinational Accounting*. Englewood Cliffs, NJ: Prentice-Hall.

Choi, F. D. S., and G. G. Mueller. 1984. *International Accounting*. Englewood Cliffs, NJ: Prentice-Hall.

Cooke, T. E., and T. Çürük. 1996. Accounting in Turkey with reference to the particular problems of lease transactions. *European Accounting Review* 5 (2): 339-359.

Cooke, T. E., and R. S. O. Wallace. 1990. Financial disclosure regulation and its environment: A review and further analysis. *Journal of Accounting and Public Policy* 9 (2): 79-110.

DaCosta, R. C., J. C. Bourgeois, and W. M. Lawson. 1978. A classification of international financial accounting practices. *The International Accounting Education and Research* 13 (2): 73-85.

Davies, M., R. Paterson, and A. Wilson. 1992. *UK GAAP*. Basingstoke: Macmillan Publishers.

Davies, M., R. Paterson, and A. Wilson. 1994. *UK GAAP* (2nd ed.). Basingstoke: Macmillan Publishers.

Demirag, I. S. 1993. Development of Turkish capitalism and accounting regulation in Turkey. *Research in Third World Accounting* 2: 97-120.

Financial Accounting Standards Board. 1977. *Statement of Financial Accounting Standard (SFAS) No. 13: Accounting for Leases*. Stamford, CT: FASB.

Frank, W. G. 1979. An empirical analysis of international accounting principles. *Journal of Accounting Research* 17 (2): 593-605.

Gardner, G. 1978. *Social Surveys for Social Planners*. London: Open University Press.

Hornbrook, A. 1991, 1995. *World Leasing Yearbook*. London: Euromoney Publications.

Institute of Chartered Accountants in England and Wales (ICAEW). 1987. *International Accounting Standards*. London: ICAEW.

International Accounting Standards Committee (IASC). 1989. *Framework for the Preparation and Presentation of Financial Statements*. London: IASC.

International Accounting Standards Committee (IASC). 1990. *IASC News* (October). London: IASC.

Kazici, S. 1987. Leasing. *Vergi Dunyasi*: 22-34.

Leasing Law No. 3326, published in the official newspaper, *Turkey*, No. 18795, June 28, 1985.

Livijn, C. O. 1990. The history of leasing. In *World Leasing Yearbook 1990*, ed. A. Hornbrook, 325-330. London: Euromoney Publications.

Moser, C. A., and G. Kalton. 1971. *Survey Methods in Social Investigation* (2nd ed.). London: Heinemann Educational Books.

Mueller, G. G. 1967. *International Accounting*. New York: Macmillan.

Mueller, G. G. 1968. Accounting principles generally accepted in the United States versus those generally accepted elsewhere. *The International Journal of Accounting Education and Research* 3 (2): 91-103.

Nair, R. D., and W. G. Frank. 1980. The impact of disclosure and measurement practices on international classifications. *The Accounting Review* 55 (3): 426-450.

Norusis, M. J. 1986. *The SPSS Guide to Data Analysis*. Chicago: SPSS.

OECD Committee on International Investment and Multinational Enterprises. 1987. Accounting for leases. Unpublished report prepared for the informal meeting held on May 1987, Paris. DAFFE/IME/NC/87.36.

Perera, M. H. B. 1989. Accounting in developing countries: The case for localised uniformity. *The British Accounting Review* 21 (2): 141-157.

Previts, G. J. 1975. On the subject of methodology and models for international accounting. *The International Journal of Accounting Education and Research* 10 (2): 1-12.

Radebaugh, L. H. 1975. Environmental factors influencing the development of accounting objectives, standards, and practices in Peru. *The International Journal of Accounting Education and Research* 11 (1): 39-56.

Samuels, J. M. 1993. International accounting standards in the third world. *Research in Third World Accounting* 2: 19-43.

Samuels, J. M., and J. C. Oliga. 1982. Accounting standards in developing countries. *The International Journal of Accounting Education and Research* 18 (1): 69-88.

Seidler, L. J. 1967. "International accounting—The ultimate theory course", *The Accounting Review* 42 (4): 775-781.

Sen, M. 1990. *Proje finansmaninda finansal kiralamanin rolu* [Importance of leasing in project finance]. Ankara: Development Bank Ltd. (Turkiye Kalkinma Bankasi).

Siegel, S. 1956. *Nonparametric Statistics for the Behavioral Sciences*. New York: McGraw-Hill.

Sigma-Mugan, C. 1995. Accounting in Turkey. *The European Accounting Review* 4 (2): 351-371.

Sozbilir, H. 1987. Lease accounting for companies. *Mali Sorunlara Cozum*: 29-33.

Vergi Kanunlari (Tax laws). 1995. *Gelir vergisi kanunu, vergi usul kanunu, kurumlar vergisi kanunu* (Income Tax Law, Tax Procedural Law, Corporate Tax Law). Ankara, Turkey: Alkim.

Tanis, V. N. 1991. Finansal kiralamanin muhasebelestirilmesi ve Turkiye uygulamasi (Lease accounting—Turkey case). Unpublished Masters thesis, Cukurova University.

Taylor, P., and S. Turley. 1985. The views of management on accounting for leases. *Accounting and Business Research* (Winter): 59-66.

Tekinalp, U. 1992. Turkey. In *The European Accounting Guide*, eds. D. Alexander and S. Archer, 885-911. London: Academic Press.

Uyanik, S. 1990. *Proje fianansmaninda kiralamanin rolu-Turkiye ornegi* [The importance of leasing in project finance: Turkish case]. Ankara, Turkey: Turkiye Ticaret Sanayi Deniz Ticaret Odlari ve Ticaret Borsalari Birligi Publication.

Vaus, D. A. 1986. *Surveys in Social Research*. London: Allen and Unwin.

Wallace, R. S. O. 1993. Development of accounting standards for developing and newly industrialized countries. *Research in Third World Accounting* 2: 121-165.

Yalkin, Y. K. 1993. Accountancy and capital market regulation in Turkey. *Research in Accounting Regulation* 7: 187-197.

ACCOUNTING IN TRANSITIONAL ECONOMIES:

A CASE STUDY OF CONSOLIDATION REGULATIONS IN THE CZECH REPUBLIC

Ranko Jelic, David Alexander, and Richard Briston

ABSTRACT

The main argument of this chapter is that changes in Czech accounting were initiated by the need for recognition by international investors and signalling of market reforms. We explore the contents of the Consolidation of Accounts regulations issued by the Czech Ministry of Finance in 1993, as a case study of the process of accounting change. However, we argue that in the post-privatization phase of the market reforms it is likely that changes in accounting regulation will be more affected by internal market forces, and that accounting will play a more active functional role.

Research in Accounting in Emerging Economies, Volume 4, pages 131-162.

ISBN: 1-55938-995-8

INTRODUCTION

In the accounting literature regarding developing countries, one of the main themes is how to improve the accounting infrastructure. Briston (1978) focused on what restricts the evolution of accounting in developing countries. Initially, external pressure coming from developed countries prevents "genuine" developments by imposing foreign practices, and later, vested interests create incentives to preserve the new status quo. Lee (1987) defined information production, information diffusion, and monitoring and contract enforcement, as main elements of an accounting infrastructure necessary for economic development. Adopting this definition, Wallace and Briston (1993), proposed alternative strategies and a framework for action to improve the accounting infrastructure in developing countries. These may also be relevant for economies in transition from a command toward a market economy, such as the Central and Eastern European countries (CEEC).

Although the need for "improved" accounting in economies in transition has been urged by both academics and professionals, the process of change, the role of accounting in a transitional economy, and the interrelation of accounting with its social context have only recently been addressed in the accounting literature.[1] We believe that there is a need to analyze accounting change in transitional economies from a different perspective to accounting change in developed, and to some extent, developing countries. The main reason for this is a difference between the process of economic development and that of economic transition. The meaning of economic transition may be explained as follows:

> The process of economic transition from a centralized command economy towards a market economy is not only an intermediate goal contributing to overall economic development, but may also be regarded as an ultimate objective in itself.... The transition from a command to a market economy is the movement towards a new system for the generation and allocation of resources (EBRD 1994).

Indeed, the urgency and scale of the transitional process in Central and Eastern Europe is rare in recent economic history. The changes have dramatically affected the political, economic, and social aspects of these societies. The ingredients of transition are (among others) creation of markets, financial institutions and private enterprises, changes in the legal infrastructure, and creation of a new accounting system. The speed of transition from a command to a market economy is regarded as a priority by policymakers in economies in transition. Slow and partial changes may create a dangerous vacuum, where the old coordination mechanisms and links were abolished and the new ones have still not been put in place. On the other hand, if the changes are too fast, the social costs will be too high, and the reforms would lose public support.[2] However, the actual speed of market reforms would depend on political and economic conditions in a country, public support for and government commitment to the reforms. Any policy recommendations, based on lessons learned from developed countries, must be adjusted for those factors and implemented more quickly in much more elemental conditions.

We believe that notions of accounting development (development of accounting within the existing economic and political environment) and accounting in transition (building of a new accounting infrastructure in an environment without an established legal and regulatory framework, functioning financial markets, well defined property rights, and so on), although strongly interrelated, are distinct. The underlying concept for the former is continuity, whereas for the latter it is discontinuity and speed.[3] Because of this, some contemporary accounting issues in developed countries would probably be analyzed from a different perspective in the transitional economies. Consequently the solutions may be different, and not necessarily best appraised using a developed market economy's criteria. For example, the debate about governmental regulation of financial reporting versus regulation by private sector bodies in transitional economies would probably not be dominated by discussions as to whether there is a market failure in provision of accounting information because a market institutional framework together with reporting entities has yet to be created in transitional countries. Furthermore, speedy and comprehensive changes in accounting (and in any other economic area) in these economies are not possible without a significant governmental involvement. Therefore, changes in accounting regulation ought perhaps to be driven by the government in a transitional economy. It may also be the case that changes in accounting are regarded as an instrument to facilitate realization of some "more important" political and economic objectives during a transitional period. This indicates a possibly different role of accounting in these countries from the role accounting plays in a developed market economy and indeed in some developing countries.

In common with the other "former communist" countries of Eastern Europe, the Czech Republic is actively engaged in the rapid introduction of a capitalist economy. Naturally, this requires that the accounting function is developed both to act as an effective provider of economic information to assist commercial and investor decisions, and to ensure reasonable control through an audit process. More immediately a market institutional framework has to be developed, and privatization facilitated. Thus we hypothesize that changes in accounting regulation were made to facilitate achievement of prioritized government objectives during the privatization phase of the market reforms and postulate that some changes in accounting regulation in the Czech Republic played a signalling role, in order to reduce uncertainty regarding the government's commitment to market reforms, and to gain recognition by EU countries.

This chapter does not claim to provide the wide-ranging longitudinal analysis of the process of accounting change which the situation invites. Its objective is to analyze the process of change in accounting regulation in the Czech Republic in the privatization phase of the market reforms (1989-1994), and to identify some areas for further research. The first section of the chapter provides a brief review of the accounting implications of mass-privatization, and reforms in the financial system in the Czech Republic. The second section focuses on the changes in accounting regulation, in particular on the measure setting out procedures for the consolidation of accounts, ref. no. 281/73570/93, issued by the Czech Ministry of Finance in 1993, in accordance with Section 4 Subsection 2 of the Law No. 563/1991 Collection on Accounting and regulation for disclosure of information on group accounts. We outline some of the requirements in their own right, and relate them both to the situation in the Czech Republic and to European and international norms. In the third section we propose a signalling hypothesis as a theoretical framework for the analysis of the changes in accounting regulation in the Czech Republic. The final section presents conclusions and suggests some areas for further empirical research.

THE ACCOUNTING IMPLICATIONS OF ECONOMIC REFORMS IN THE CZECH REPUBLIC

Within six years, structural reforms and stabilization programs in the Czech Republic have achieved encouraging results. As cited in the *Financial Times Supplement*, June 2, 1995 (Financial Times 1995a), a democratic regime was established as the most important condition for the economic transition; the legal structure and regulatory framework have become similar to those in other market economies; the accessibility and quality of goods and services, together with the price system, have been improved; improvements have been made in controlling inflation (currently just under 10 percent) and the level of international reserves; gross domestic product (GDP) grew by 2.6 percent in 1994; adjustments of foreign trade have been made largely towards the EU area (46 percent); a significant number of the state-owned assets have been privatized and the percentage of GDP generated by the private sector has been drastically increased; the unemployment rate is only 3.6 percent. According to the European Bank for Reconstruction and Development, the Czech Republic is one of the countries that have made most progress in transition towards a market economy (EBRD 1994). While CEEC's countries in transition seem to move towards similar macroeconomic management, there are some important differences when it comes to privatization and emergence of new financial institutions and regulatory frameworks in these countries. Below we outline some of the distinctive Czech characteristics regarding privatization, changes in financial intermediation, and accounting system in general. We believe that these differences are relevant for a better appreciation of the location of accounting in the process of transition to a market economy.

Privatization

Maybe the biggest achievement by the Czech government in the last few years has been the successful mass give-away privatization program. More than 50 percent of state-owned enterprise assets have been privatized, and millions of Czechs have overnight become participants in a shareholder democracy. About 65 percent of the economy is in private hands, compared to about 2 percent before 1989 (measured by private sector share in GDP in mid-1994) (EBRD 1994, 10).

The main methods of privatization in the Czech Republic have been mass privatization via a voucher scheme, direct sales, auctions for small companies, and free transfers to local authorities. The direct sales and the voucher scheme represent, according to the Privatization Law of April 1991, so-called "large" privatization, whereas the other methods comprise "small" privatization. The voucher scheme is a distinctive feature of the Czech privatization process and has attracted the most attention. In the first phase of privatization 1,700 Czech enterprises had to prepare privatization plans. The assets of the enterprises were then transferred to the Czech and Slovak National Property Funds. All Czech citizens over 18 were eligible to buy a booklet of vouchers and subsequently to participate in the bidding process, either directly or indirectly by selling vouchers to privatization intermediaries (investment funds). The latter method proved to be the more popular and investment funds ended up with about 70 percent of vouchers after the first mass privatization round in 1992. The proportion after the second round in February 1994, was slightly lower. The remainder of the vouchers, 30 percent, were owned by other investors. There were on average at least two plans per enterprise, from which the ministries had to choose one (Financial Times 1995a; Bolton and Roland 1992).

The mass privatization program was organized and dominated by the state. Insiders (workers and managers) have played a limited role. For example, the decision as to which privatization project was to be implemented was made by the Ministry of Finance with virtually no involvement of the employees. This is very different from the situation in Poland where workers' representatives have played a significant role in the process of ownership transformation (Friedman and Rapaczynski 1994, 108). Some of the other distinctive features of the program related to implications of privatization for accounting, and the development of mechanisms for corporate control in the Czech Republic.

One of the main problems for privatization in transitional economies has been the valuation of state-owned enterprises. Since these enterprises had operated in an environment with distorted prices, and were following accounting practices of a command economy type, their past performance had little relevance for valuation purposes. Compounding the problem further, many of the enterprises had inherited net deficits from the previous system, and were not viable without restructuring.

The accounting regulations based on the government decree No. 236 of 1989, and the decree of the Federal Ministry of Finance No. 23 of 1990, were still obligatory for the enterprises privatized in 1992. The regulations did not distinguish between the information needed for an impartial evaluation of the enterprise and that required by the government (UN 1993, 122). This made the evaluation of state-owned enterprises even more difficult. For example, the enterprises did not keep records of land and intangible assets, costs of modernization were not included in the actual cost of fixed assets, buildings and machinery were overvalued due to low rates of depreciation, and so forth. Privatization has raised several questions about the accounting practices used and many changes have been implemented. For example, intangible assets have been recorded since 1991. But serious problems remain, and even the leading Western accounting firms have experienced huge difficulties in appraising firms to be privatized.[4]

However, by predominantly relying on the voucher scheme, the Czech Republic has avoided some of the valuation problems arising from informational constraints. For example, the privatization scheme has not required the valuation of privatized companies. Assets were usually recorded according to historical cost, based on net book value, but prices were based on the total number of coupons that the public would be willing to invest in the enterprises. It was only for enterprises seeking foreign capital that a fair market valuation had to be obtained before privatization, and authorized by the Ministry of Finance (UN 1993, 125). It seems that the Czech government realized that getting an objective valuation before privatization was not possible, not only because of the problems involved, but also because of the sheer number of companies to be privatized. The new accounting regulations, which came into force in 1993, were regarded mainly as an integral part of the comprehensive program of economic reforms, rather than as an instrument to help with valuation. This was different from the situation in other countries in the region which favored piecemeal privatization, and where privatization may have influenced changes in accounting regulation to a greater extent.

The privatization investment funds have, without any doubt, facilitated the speed of the privatization process. However, they have created some potential problems for the government. First, the government seems to be a "prisoner" of the funds which possess enormous power, in that they control about 29 percent of all outstanding shares. About 40 percent is in the hands of the National Property Fund and the rest is controlled by other investors. This will further affect development of a regulatory system and the shape of the new financial system. Second, out of the 13 biggest funds which "control" about 56 percent of the voucher privatizations, all but one are owned by the banks. The top 20 funds control 90 percent of the vouchers (Financial Times 1995a). "While the Czech Privatization Law in spirit ruled out such cross-ownership, the government may have responded passively to exploitation of a legal loophole to gain support of the major banks in distributing the voucher books" (Fries 1995, 115). Given that about 40-45 percent of banks are owned by the State Property Agency, a situation has arisen where the state owns banks, banks own investment funds, and investment funds have considerable equity stakes in enterprises. In addition, the state has a significant direct equity stake in enterprises, and some of the investment funds are shareholders in the banks. It is thus unclear who really controls the investment funds and what their role is in enterprise control and restructuring.

According to the law, the maximum stake by an investment fund in any company is 20 percent. In addition, funds are allowed to invest not more than 10 percent of their assets in any single company. Consequently, the funds are not necessarily the single major shareholder in privatized companies. This may prevent them from taking an active role in enterprise restructuring and corporate governance. Furthermore, funds which retained stakes in a large number of companies may find it difficult to monitor all of these companies. For example, the Komercni Fund (controlled by Komercni Banka) has retained stakes in 265 companies (Gray 1995).

Financial Reforms

In the former CEEC, the financial sector was dominated by a state bank which actually played a passive role. Risk was not assessed because uncertainties were "minimized" by the central planning process. Enterprises were aware that their losses would be covered and credit demands accommodated by the state (soft-budget constraint) and therefore did not need to maximize profits. Investments were financed by the credit departments of the central bank. Under this situation, there was no need for financial intermediation and other financial institutions. Since enterprises were accountable only to the state, the state had a monopoly over the financial information provided by enterprises. Except on an aggregate level, information was not publicly available.

The issue whether the state will be able to obtain, process and apply dispersed information, lies at the heart of the debate on "market socialism." Lange (1936/1964) argued that market socialism can always mimic the functioning of a decentralized economy. Therefore, it can perform at least as well as the market economy. Hayek (1945) criticized Lange, and pointed out the importance of decentralization of information. The real problem for socialism, according to Hayek, is not how to obtain information but how to speedily apply the information (Kornai 1992; Dewatripont and Maskin 1990). Since the debate, partial accounting and banking reforms along Lange's lines (particularly during the 1980s) were attempted in socialist countries. However, all of them failed. Looking back, it can be concluded that Hayek was right to argue that socialist systems lack the necessary incentives to obtain and apply information. In this respect financial markets, together with free accountable enterprises, are essential.

Czechoslovakia, like Hungary and Poland, began the reform of the financial sector with banking reforms. In 1990, a two-tier banking system was introduced.

The banking system at that time comprised the following institutions: the Central Bank, two state-owned banks created from the State Bank (one in Czech and the other in Slovak territory), two savings banks, two banks for foreign exchange transactions, and one investment bank. After the dissolution of Czechoslovakia and the establishment of the Czech Republic in 1993, the Czech National Bank, three big commercial banks (Komercni Banka, Investicni Banka, and Czeskoslovenska Obchodni Banka) and one big savings bank (Sporitelna Banka) became the leading banking institutions. A liberal licensing policy has encouraged the presence of about 60 banks which operate in the Czech Republic today. The new banks seem to follow the model of a universal bank, providing for both commercial and investment banking activities (Hrncir 1993, 15). The three commercial banks and the one savings bank dominate the credit market (73 percent of market share) and the market for deposits (78 percent of market share). The reforms in the banking sector have affected corporate accountability and disclosure of financial information. Enterprises are accountable not only to the state, but also to commercial lenders and investors. However, the speed of decentralization has also brought some problems.

As in all transitional economies, new commercial banks hived off from the State Bank have inherited a significant proportion of nonperforming loans. According to national sources, the percentage of bad bank loans in the Czech Republic, Hungary and Poland in 1992, was 19 percent, 29 percent, and 26 percent, respectively (Dittus 1994). However, the Czech approach to bank rehabilitation contrasts sharply with the approaches adopted by Hungary and Poland.[5] The government hived off 20 percent of bad loans into a nonprofit Consolidation Bank (Konsolidacni Banka). About KCs 110 billion of the banks' perpetual loans for inventories given at 6 percent interest have been taken over. The loans were replaced by claims on the Consolidation Bank with eight year maturity and 13 percent interest. Bad debts have remained on the enterprises' balance sheets.

By making Konsolidacni Banka responsible for bad loans restructuring, the government removed the pressure (and probably the incentive) for banks to become actively involved in enterprise restructuring. Experience in bad loans recovery has so far been poor and the lack of incentives for enterprises actually to repay the loans remains a persistent issue.

The overhang of bad loans in the banking sector is a big problem, with an immediate effect on corporate governance and creditors' rights. There is some evidence that banks in the Czech Republic were reluctant to force bankruptcy. Generally, the Czech Republic adopted a very cautious approach towards bankruptcy, in contrast to some other transitional economies (e.g., Hungary). The bankruptcy law was to be put into force in 1991 and, after being twice postponed, it came into effect in 1994.

The Prague Stock Exchange and the over the counter (OTC) market have been in place since 1993. The electronic OTC market is very popular and together with off-market trading, accounts for between 50-80 percent of all daily transactions

(Financial Times 1995a). After a promising start, the Prague Stock Exchange crashed in March 1994.[6] The main obstacle against a larger role for the stock exchange seems to be a lack of transparency. A possible reason may be the previously mentioned special relationship between investment funds (major players at the stock exchange) and leading banks, which possibly precludes the creation of an effective market for corporate information.

CHANGES IN ACCOUNTING REGULATION

From the review of some of the main ingredients of institutional reforms since the Velvet Revolution in 1989, two subperiods in the transition can be identified. The first period (privatization period) was from 1989 to 1994, during which market-oriented reform was initiated, legislation (including accounting) was put in place, a significant number of Czech enterprises were privatized, and the Czech Republic became an independent country. The second period (post-privatization period), started in late 1994 and is characterized by a conflict of old and new, and with initial problems in the functioning of new market institutions, and the application and enforcement of the new legislation.

Like many other transitional CEEC economies, the Czech Republic is a country with a long tradition in accounting. During the late nineteenth and early twentieth century, both accounting practices and legislation in the area of the Czech Republic were strongly influenced by those of Western countries, particularly Germany. After the Communist takeover, the accounting system, like those in other centrally planned economies, was socialized and standardized. A chart of accounts system was in operation, providing a generally uniform accounting approach; and accounting principles, bookkeeping methods, reporting formats, and audit requirements were all stipulated centrally. Audit should not be understood in its normal sense of at least a nominally independent professional appraisal. In essence, it meant merely checking that the boxes had been correctly filled in. Consequently, accounting played a passive role and became a tool for routine monitoring of state enterprises by the government.

Changes in Czech accounting started in 1971 with the law "On Uniform Social-economic Information Systems" and the government decree "On Information Systems of Enterprises." Although general accounts from the Chart of Accounts remained obligatory, selected organizations could have formatted accounts according to their own needs. But this did not alter the basic orientation toward a command economy type of accounting. As a consequence:

- Financial statements were treated as non-public and confidential until 1989;
- Land was the property of the state and was not measured and recorded in accounts;
- There were no accounts for intangibles until 1990;

- Czechoslovakia's state enterprises used to have a number of separate self-balancing parts of the balance sheet: funds for fixed assets, funds for current assets, funds for security and investments and funds for development. Only in 1991 were funds merged into equity for accounting purposes. In addition, reserves have become obligatory and are created from after tax profits;
- Accounting and taxation were not separated.

Only with government decree No. 236/89 in 1989 and the decree of the Federal Ministry of Finance No. 23/90 in 1990, was the process of trying to create an accounting, auditing, and finance-raising infrastructure suitable for a market economy begun. According to decree 23/90, state-owned enterprises, joint-stock companies and joint ventures were to use an identical financial accounting system with double-entry bookkeeping based on generally accepted concepts such as the business entity as a reporting unit, money measurement for transactions, use of historical cost, a going-concern assumption and accrual accounting (UN 1993, 121). The private sector auditing profession was reinstated in the same year, with the establishment of joint ventures. Although important, these changes were still far from meeting the requirements of a market economy. For example, the accounting system at that time did not make a distinction between information needed for an impartial evaluation of the enterprises and that required by the government regulators (UN 1993, 122). It was not until the privatization programs that the traditional approach to accounting changed, with the major changes introduced in 1991 by the new accounting law which applied to all reporting entities. The balance sheet and the profit-and-loss account were identified as the main annual statements and details of the valuation and accounting methods used in the reporting period are to be disclosed. "The law mentions the need for certain disclosures required by a number of international accounting standards, such as a statement of accounting policies, post-balance sheet events, related-party transactions, conflicts of interests, property disputes or potential claims and provisions for third-party claims to assets, pensions, and environmental damage, as appropriate" (UN 1993, 126).

The changes were rapid, and the legal framework for accounting regulation was completed in 1993. The changes have been state-sponsored, and based on legislation, with little public discussion or participation (Seal et al. 1995). The framework consists of three levels: the Commercial Code, the Act on Accounting, and Decrees of the Ministry of Finance. The "true and fair view" principle has been incorporated, together with other key accounting principles, into the new accounting acts which apply to all reporting entities.

The Czech Republic, like other economies in transition, had to decide whether it should try to design a completely new system which might better fit its needs or to imitate one of the systems currently in use. Any attempt at the creation of a new accounting system in the former socialist countries must take into account many constraints, in particular institutional and political realities in those countries, and the lack of any theoretical framework for an accounting system which would best fit their needs.

The imitation alternative needs answers to several questions: Whose model to follow? In particular, either a capital market-oriented or a creditors-oriented system? Should priority be given to IASC or to EU standards? What are the major factors to influence the choice? What is the relationship between accounting changes and institutional changes in a financial system? Even if a conceptual framework had been agreed in Western economies, would it necessarily be an appropriate framework for economies in transition?

It seems that, in general, legislation has been strongly influenced by EU directives, and to some extent by the French accounting system and the international accounting standards (IAS). The most important argument in favor of the French system, as opposed to the Anglo-Saxon accounting system favored by Czech accounting academics, and the historically important German model, was the use of the general chart of accounts (Schroll 1995).

Our objective is to explain why accounting in the Czech Republic continues to be state-dominated, and to examine the process of change in the Czech accounting regulation. Accounting for consolidation is chosen as an example to illustrate the process of change in accounting regulation.

The Proposals for Accounting for Consolidations

The intention regarding consolidated accounts was to move toward international and, particularly, European practice. There are two problems with this process. The first is the fact that new knowledge and skills cannot be acquired overnight. The second is the extent of external diversity in that European and international practices vary significantly.

The Czech consolidation regulations take the form of a decree (Czech Ministry of Finance 1993), under the authority of the 1991 Act on Accounting. Before looking at this material, it is important to be aware of the problems of translation. Advice has been provided to the Czech authorities from a variety of European and international sources in a variety of original languages. The resulting distillation has produced a text in Czech where the key expressions may, or may not, be very close translations of the original English or other European language.

For the purpose of this chapter, we take as our starting point a translation of the Czech Act into English received from Professor Baca of the Prague School of Economics.

First, some definitions, from Article 1.

For the purpose of this Measure, the following two degrees of influence (dependence) of one undertaking over another are distinguished:

a) dominant influence
b) significant influence

Dominant influence

Dominant influence of one accounting entity (parent undertaking) over another one (subsidiary undertaking) is a degree of influence (dependence) ensuing from:

a) direct or indirect holding of more than 50 percent of the subsidiary's equity share capital, unless otherwise provided for by contract or the Articles of Association.
b) a signed "control contract" or provisions in the Articles of Association, if the parent undertaking controls the financial and operating policy of the subsidiary and is simultaneously a shareholder or partner in the undertaking concerned.

Significant influence

Significant influence of one accounting entity (parent undertaking) over another accounting entity (associated undertaking) is a degree of influence (dependence), in which the parent owns directly or indirectly at least 20 percent and at most 50 percent of the associate's equity share capital, unless otherwise provided for by the signed contract or provisions in the Articles of Association.

Parent undertaking

A parent undertaking is an entity exercising, directly or indirectly, a dominant influence over the subsidiary undertakings or a significant influence over the associated undertakings.

Subsidiary undertaking

Subsidiary undertaking is an entity over which another undertaking exercises a dominant influence, either directly or indirectly. Such an entity is considered a subsidiary if the parent undertaking's holding exceeds 50 percent of its equity share capital either directly or indirectly through another subsidiary or other subsidiaries, over which the parent exercises a dominant influence. The size of the parent's participating interest in the equity share capital of that entity should be ascertained by the sum of direct capital interest of another subsidiary or other subsidiaries in the equity share capital of that entity and the direct capital interest of the parent in the equity share capital of that entity.

Associated undertaking

An associated undertaking is an entity over which another undertaking exercises a significant influence directly or indirectly through a subsidiary or subsidiaries.

It is evident from these definitions that a legalistic and precise approach is being attempted. We are given precise percentages and it appears that formal written evidence of control is essential in order to override the message of these simple percentages. The duty to prepare consolidated accounts does not apply to partnerships (including limited partnerships) or unincorporated commercial enterprises, nor to sub-groups, provided that the foreign ultimate holding company produces consolidated accounts consistent with the 7th EC Directive and that the parent of the sub-group does not itself have a Stock

Exchange quotation. These exemptions can be over-ridden at the request of holders of at least 10 percent of the parent's share capital.

Perhaps more interestingly, a parent may choose to exclude from consolidation any subsidiary or associate:

(a) which is a commercial enterprise or a limited partnership,
(b) whose turnover or equity share of the composition of consolidation is insignificant,
(c) over which the parent undertaking is unable to exercise a dominant influence and ownership rights on a long-term basis mainly for political reasons,
(d) which has its registered office in another country and which would incur disproportionately high expenses in obtaining information necessary for the preparation of consolidated accounts,
(e) which uses a different chart of accounts and accounting procedures in its book-keeping than the parent undertaking,
(f) whose securities and deposits were acquired by the parent undertaking exclusively with a view to their subsequent resale,
(g) which is in liquidation or under bankruptcy proceedings under a special regulation, or if it is insolvent.

The most interesting provision here is item (e). Firstly, the wording appears to assume that the enterprises will use a chart of accounts of some sort. Secondly, the likelihood of an overseas subsidiary or associate using a "different chart of accounts and accounting procedures in its bookkeeping" is surely high. Thirdly, the scope is certainly available for an overseas subsidiary or associate to be instructed to make sure that it uses significantly different bookkeeping systems from its parent, if consolidation is likely to be inconvenient. There seems to be a dangerous level of flexibility built into this provision.

Two methods of consolidation are discussed in the regulations, and their usage is precisely delineated.

> Accounts of the parent undertaking and the undertakings over which the parent undertaking exercises a dominant influence are consolidated by the method of full consolidation.
>
> Accounts of the parent undertaking and the undertakings over which the parent undertaking exercises a significant influence are consolidated by the equity method.

Broadly speaking, the requirements for full consolidation follow the general international pattern, but a number of interesting points are discussed here. Firstly there are rules about adjusting the account items to ensure compatibility. These include the following:

> The data from parent and subsidiaries' accounts will be reclassified with regard to the items supplemented in the consolidated balance sheet and consolidated profit-and-loss account and to their content.
>
> The adjustments will be made in accordance with the valuation principles set out in the consolidation rules. Such adjustments will be made only by subsidiary undertakings whose valuation rules differ from the rules set out by the consolidation rules and would significantly affect the picture of asset valuation in the consolidated accounts and the disclosed result.
>
> The depreciation plans determined by the subsidiaries and the resulting depreciation of tangible and intangible fixed assets entered in books of group undertakings are not adjusted for the purpose to draw up consolidated accounts. The inventory accounts' balances are not adjusted, unless otherwise provided for by the consolidation rules.
>
> Accounts of subsidiary undertakings having their registered offices outside the Czech Republic and keeping their books in foreign currency shall be converted into Czech crowns at the rate valid on the parent undertaking's balance sheet day.

Although the first paragraph above refers to data being reclassified, the emphasis is clearly on valuation and evaluation, that is, on the size of the actual figures themselves. Putting these paragraphs together with item (e) from the list of possible exclusion reasons suggests that differences in accounting policy are not a valid reason for non consolidation, but differences in bookkeeping systems could be.[7]

Reciprocal (cross) shareholdings are not in principle forbidden, and are to be treated depending on the intention behind their acquisition.

> In case they were acquired for a short term, with a view to resale, they are shown in the consolidated balance sheet as the item "short-term financial assets."
>
> In case they were acquired for the purpose of long-term holding, these shareholdings are shown in the consolidated balance sheet as a decrease of equity under the item "Reserves (derived from profit)" and disclosed in the notes on the accounts.

In no case, therefore, is the share capital itself reduced.

GOODWILL

One of the greatest international problems currently related to consolidation is the treatment of goodwill. A variety of ideas have been proposed over the years, including:

(a) retain it in the balance sheet, unless it has demonstrably become worthless;
(b) write it off over time to the income statement;
(c) write it off immediately to the income statement;
(d) write it off immediately to reserves (i.e., with no reduction in reported earnings).

Methods (b) and (d) have generally been the practice in Europe over recent years. The EC Directives say the following about goodwill (Article 30, Seventh Directive):

1. A separate item as defined in Article 19(1)(c) which corresponds to a positive consolidation difference shall be dealt with in accordance with the rules laid down in [the Fourth] Directive for the item "goodwill."
2. A Member State may permit a positive consolidation difference to be immediately and clearly deducted from reserves.

The rules from the Fourth Directive (EC 1978) are as follows. Articles 34.1(a) and 37.2 state the maximum amortization period for goodwill.

> Where national law authorizes the inclusion of formation expenses under "Assets," they must be written off within a maximum period of five years (Article 34.1(a)).
>
> Article 34(1)(a) shall apply to goodwill. The Member States may, however, permit companies to write goodwill off systematically over a limited period exceeding five years provided that this period does not exceed the useful economic life of the asset and is disclosed in the notes on the accounts together with the supporting reasons therefore (Article 37.2).

IAS 22 ¶42 (revised in 1993) states as follows:

> Goodwill should be amortised by recognizing it as an expense over its useful life. In amortising goodwill, the straight-line basis should be used unless another amortisation method is more appropriate in the circumstances. The amortisation period should not exceed five years unless a longer period, not exceeding twenty years from the date of acquisition, can be justified.

The Czech requirements are striking—particularly so from an Anglo-Saxon perspective. Goodwill may be treated:

(a) either by its posting in extraordinary charges or extraordinary income of the consolidated profit-and-loss account according to the nature of the difference, or
(b) by its inclusion in a separate item "Positive consolidation difference" or "Negative consolidation difference" in accordance to the nature of the difference. The consolidation difference is depreciated at 20 percent annually in extraordinary charges or income of the consolidated profit-and-loss account through the item "Offsetting the positive/negative consolidation difference." The amount of depreciation decreases directly the items "Positive consolidation difference" or "Negative consolidation difference."

The use of the word "extraordinary" in the translation should not be taken at face value. There are, of course, difficulties in defining the English-language word. In the United Kingdom, "extraordinary" under FRS 3 (ASB 1993) has a different and much narrower meaning than it did previously under SSAP 6 (ASC 1986). From a comparative international perspective differences in implication abound.

Just as importantly, the original Czech word "Mimorádných" could be translated as either "extraordinary" or "exceptional"—or "unusual" for that matter. One can surmise that the Czech term is an attempted translation from Article 29 of the Fourth Directive (EC 1978). Since EC member states have interpreted this in their own ways, it is reasonable that the Czechs should do the same. More fundamentally, how could they avoid making their own decision as to how to interpret it, as nobody can present them with a detailed agreed interpretation?

At any rate, it is clear that all goodwill, whether positive or negative, must be passed through the profit and loss account either immediately or over five years (NB: not *within* five years, but over *exactly* five years and necessarily on a straight-line basis). Immediate write-off appears not to be allowed under the revised IAS 22, though it is not excluded by the Fourth Directive (Art 34(1)(a) and Art 37(2)). In the FEE survey of European practice (FEE 1991), out of 127 published financial statements showing evidence of goodwill on consolidation, only one expensed the whole amount to income in the year in which it occurred. This approach to goodwill elimination is not only very prudent (significantly more so than Germany, for example, which allows both elimination directly to reserves and amortisation over periods exceeding five years) but it is also extremely prescriptive, apparently allowing no reference to economic considerations of benefits and useful life. It remains to be seen what policies are adopted in practice in the Czech Republic. At the time of writing, no examples are known. There are no tax effects arising from the decision on the treatment of goodwill.

The final important point relating to all this is that the book value/fair value alternative is not mentioned. By inference it is the book value method which is automatically assumed. Elsewhere the regulation states:

> A positive consolidation difference is a positive difference after the first consolidation which will be calculated as a difference between the purchase price of the shares in subsidiary undertakings and their valuation in accord with the parent undertaking's proportion which they represent of the actual equity capital and reserves of those subsidiaries without profit or loss for the financial year as at which such subsidiaries are included in the consolidation for the first time.

The phrase "the *actual* equity capital and reserves" could perhaps be interpreted either way, but we are confident that it is intended in its narrow accounting sense of "the figure" not in its broader economic sense of "the reality." Fair values are not to be used.

This definition of how to calculate the consolidation difference has other implications. I. Zelenka (1995) argues as follows:

> Consolidation difference is determined as the difference between the cost of investment and share in the equity without the profit on the last day of financial year, (in the case of CR it is 31 December) and not at the moment of acquisition.... A claim of recognition of consolidation difference on the last day of financial year is not clearly apparent from the definition in the Consolidation Measure, but it is possible to quote one of the co-authors of this Measure, who in his publication presents:
>
> The difference between the cost of shares, which subsidiary of associated company issued, and proportional part of the equity without profit of current accounting period on the day of closing the accounting books is called the difference after first consolidation (Rynes 1995).

These procedures mean that alterations to revenues, including distributable profits, between the acquisition date and the end of the year, are ignored. It therefore follows, for example, that:

> Pre-acquisition profits are not taken into account in the determination of consolidation difference. In comments to the Consolidation Measure, the solution is explained by efforts to simplify the preparation of consolidated accounts, until the consolidation will be common procedure. However, the impact of it on the information quality for users can be great, if we consider, for instance, acquisition several days before the end of the financial year and the high income of the purchased company. On the assumption of the existence of Pre-acquisition income, "goodwill" will be overvalued in the first consolidation, on the assumption of Pre-acquisition loss, "goodwill" will be undervalued (I. Zelenka 1995).

It is useful to explore these issues by means of some simple figures. The following illustration is taken in all its essentials from V. Zelenka (1995), but the terminology has been adapted and the analysis extended.

EXAMPLE: Consolidation difference after the first consolidation for the year 1993.

- "X" acquired 500 ordinary shares in "Y" (100 percent of the company) at a price of 10 Kc per share on December 31, 1990;
- Share capital of "Y" at December 31, 1990 was 1,000 Kc and Reserves of "Y" at December 31, 1990 were 2,000 Kc;
- At December 31, 1993 share capital of "Y" was 1,000 Kc, profit for the year was 400 Kc, other reserves (brought forward) were 2,600 Kc;
- Consolidated final accounts are to be drawn up by company "X" *for the first time* for the year 1993 according to the Czech Consolidation Measure;
- The useful life of the goodwill is expected to last for four years;
- It is assumed that book value equals fair value.

We summarize below five different treatments of goodwill (consolidation difference) in the consolidated final accounts of company "X" at December 31, 1993:

	Goodwill before amortization	Goodwill-Balance at 12/31/1993	Reserves	
			P & L Account	Other
1.	1,400	0	−1,400	0
2.	1,400	1,120	−280	0
3.	1,400	560	−280	−560
4.	2,000	800	−400	−800
5.	2,000	500	−500	−1,000

The five treatments are explained as follows:

1. solution according to Consolidation Measure, 100 percent amortization of consolidation difference in the year 1993;
   "goodwill" calculation based on the balances in the balance sheet at the end of the year (not at the date of acquisition, and excluding the profit for 1993):
   5,000 - 1 x (4,000 - 400) = 1,400
2. solution according to Consolidation Measure with 20 percent amortization of consolidation difference from the 1990 acquisition (first tranche of amortisation in the 1993 accounts):
   1,400 ÷ 5 = 280
   "goodwill" calculation is the same as in 1.
3. part of the consolidation difference from the years 1991 and 1992 is brought forward direct to Reserves (560) and for the year 1993 to the profit of the accounting period. Amortization would then commence retrospectively from the date of acquisition.
   "goodwill" calculation is the same as in 1.
4. solution proceeding from approach no. 3 with a difference in the amount of goodwill. The annual amortization of goodwill is
   2,000 ÷ 5 = 400
   goodwill is based on the difference between price of share acquisition and the proportion of owners' equity at the date of acquisition:
   5,000 - 1 x 3,000 = 2,000
5. goodwill is amortized over its useful life and as in approaches 3 and 4 the proportion of the goodwill for the years 1991 and 1992 is brought forward direct to Reserves (without profit). The annual amortization is
   2,000 ÷ 4 = 500.
   the amount of goodwill equals the amount in 4.

Clearly a number of other permutations are possible, and it should be remembered that the example assumes away the book value/fair value distinction. Zelenka regards the five solutions given as in ascending order of merit, and stresses that only the first two are allowed under the Czech 1993 rules. His preferences seem broadly correct, though his apparent belief in the economic validity of a given "useful life" for the consolidation difference seems suspect to more cynical Western Europeans.

In summary, therefore, the first consolidation difference arising in 1993 potentially consists of three elements, that is,

(i) differences between book values of separable net assets, and fair values.
(ii) differences caused by share and reserve movements in subsidiaries or associates from 1990-1992.
(iii) goodwill purchased.

Since the regulation makes no attempt to segregate these three elements, the possibility of arguing for and allowing different treatments for the different elements does not arise.

Disclosure of Group Accounts

With regard to disclosure of information regarding group accounts, the decree on consolidation only states that consolidated financial statements should be published in certain cases. However, it fails to prescribe in what cases and how the statements should be made available to the public. The Commercial Code similarly fails to specify what information should be disclosed. In the decree, there is no mention of the relationship between individual and group accounts, or of notes to supplement consolidated accounts. Finally, there are no sanctions for companies which fail to prepare the annual report, to publish it or to have their accounts audited (I. Zelenka 1995). The Security Act has penalties for cases when companies fail to provide information to the public. However, the act does not require the publication of consolidated accounts.

It should not therefore be a surprise that, out of 35 holding companies which are included in the Prague Stock Exchange Index, only nine actually published consolidated financial statements in 1994. In 12 cases it was not possible to recognize the status of the company from the information published by the companies (I. Zelenka 1995). There is some evidence that poor disclosure and the dangerous flexibility allowed by the consolidation regulation have affected investment decisions. According to a manager of Creditanstalt Fund, which has disposed of 23 companies so far, the fund has mainly sold three types of company: holding companies, because of concerns about whether the earnings of the subsidiaries are fairly represented; joint ventures with foreign participation, because of worries regarding the reliability of earnings due to transfer pricing; and some small companies or ones where they had only small stakes (Gray 1995).

The inadequacy of consolidated accounts is not an isolated case. According to the same study of the 50 companies included in the Prague Stock Exchange Index, many companies fail to provide other information which is normally regarded as important by investors. For example, no disclosure of directors' interest and transactions with related parties was recorded. Only 48 percent of the companies from the survey published the supervisory board report. Only 64 percent of the companies disclosed information about their ownership structure. In the annual reports, only brief information about likely future plans and research and development was given. Preparers of the financial reports seem to be preoccupied with an analysis of the past rather than plans for the future (I. Zelenka 1995).

The above examples may indicate that regulators and/or companies are not aware of the importance of financial reports to investors. Another explanation may be that, since an operating system for corporate governance is not in place, insiders are reluctant to provide information, and use this as a way to obstruct control and restructuring.[8] However, other explanations are possible. It may well be the case that both regulators and preparers are confused and that they are actually learning as they go along.

We have felt it necessary to go into certain aspects of the Czech consolidation regulations in some detail, to give a practical illustration. However, the detail must not be allowed to obscure the general point. This is that a fundamental and important piece of radical regulation has been introduced rapidly and, in some respects, rather badly, in an environment which at the time did not obviously contain either the expertise to apply it or the mechanisms necessary to enforce it. It is worth considering why this has been the case.

ACCOUNTING IN TRANSITION—SIGNALLING HYPOTHESIS

Although a new regulation was put in place, a reader who takes for granted a general understanding of the market economy ethos, independent professional accounting and auditing bodies, and an education system designed to stimulate individualism, should pause and consider the implications of previous Czech experience. In Table 1, we summarize the characteristics of recent changes in Czech accounting. The table speaks for itself, and need not be paraphrased here. The movement from columns II to IV is of course a continuum. Nevertheless column III does, we think, reasonably reflect and summarize relevant elements associated with the transitional period. The gap between desired and actual is obvious (and has been documented for some other economies in transition as well) (Schroeder 1995; Bailey 1995). A system comparable to that which has been developing in the United Kingdom, for example, for hundreds of years cannot be completely created in less than a decade. The changes in Czech accounting must be accompanied by corresponding changes in the country's economic and social structure, and these are all taking place simultaneously.

Table 1. Accounting in Transition—Case for the Czech Republic

No.	*Distinguishing Features*	*Classical Socialism*	*Czech Transitional Period*	*Developed Market Economies*
1.	Objectives of enterprises	Maximum Output, Resource constrained	Maximum profit; No bankruptcy (some enterprises still subsidized?)	Maximum profit: Demand constrained - hard budgeting
2.	Corporate control	Internal Discipline	Internal discipline; Product markets; Limited labor market discipline; Very limited capital market discipline.	Internal discipline: Product markets; Labor markets; Capital markets.
3.	Relevant information for decision making	Shortages; Risk "minimized" by planning.	Prices; Risk related to privatization and restructuring; poor disclosure	Prices; Market and specific risk; Accounting figures.
4.	Users of accounting information	Central authority; Accounting information is not publicly available.	Predominantly central authority (tax); Management accounting in embryonic stage.	Creditors, investor, managers.
5.	Ownership of accounting	Accounting is socialized.	Mostly privatized accounting	Accounting is privatized.
6.	Level (in respect to aggregation)	Macro	Micro; "Preparer friendly".	Micro, "User friendly".
7.	Accounting practices	Uniformity	Form and content of financial statements is stipulated by the Law.	Variety
8.	Regulation	Ministry of finance; Law; Accounting and taxation not separated.	Ministry of finance; Law: Accounting and taxation are separated; Weak enforcement.	Ministry of Finance/Profession.
9.	Profession	Accountants are regarded as bookkeepers.	Retraining is needed; No influential professional bodies yet; Presence of international accounting firms.	Influential professional bodies.

Source: Columns II and IV are developed from Kornai (1992).

There have been several attempts to explain the process of change and the role of accounting in transitional economies in the recent literature. Bailey (1995) observed that commercially necessary accounting changes are lagging behind legally specified changes in East European transitional economies, and suggested that accounting reforms in transitional economies are externally driven, in particular to assuage the expectations of international agencies. Following the analysis provided by Weber (1921/64), concerning the interconnection between the efficacy of accounting and the market economy, it has been proposed that actual changes in accounting should proceed in advance of the legislated changes with the maturing of the new market economies.

Krzywda and colleagues (1995a) analyzed changes in Polish accounting within a European historical context, referring to socioeconomic factors. They concluded that Central and Eastern European policymakers would be restricted in their choice of accounting principles to the models available in the economies of their Western European neighbors.

Seal and colleagues (1995) applied organizational change theory to changes in Czech accounting. Economic and political disturbances provided the impetus for changes, which are, according to the authors, of a second-order nature. The path of change was described by a colonizational, rather than by an evolutionary model. The new organization of Czech accounting is described as an unresolved excursion toward a new model.

It could also be argued that the economics of information literature provides a theoretical framework for the analysis in that changes in accounting regulation appear to have played a signalling role aiming to differentiate economic reform programs and to attract foreign investors.

ACCOUNTING REFORMS AS A SIGNALLING MECHANISM—THE CASE OF THE CZECH REPUBLIC

Signalling theory has been used in many areas of corporate finance and positive accounting theory. For example, Ross (1977) and Leland and Pyle (1977) analyzed a choice between corporate debt and equity finance as a signal of companies' quality, while Bhattacharya (1980) and Miller and Rock (1985) considered the choice of a company's dividend policy as a signal of the company's market value. Although the authors assumed different non-observable variables that determine companies' value, the introduction of information asymmetry led them to the common conclusion that the market value of the firm would depend upon the company's capital structure and dividend policy.

The signalling problem has been used as an example of market failure (nonprovision of accounting information) from those who are convinced that accounting information is a public good. The existence of an inefficient signalling market equilibrium would make a stronger case for more regulation of the provision of accounting information. However, Watts and Zimmerman (1986) argued that private costs are required to explain why signalling behavior is engaged in. They illustrated that signalling activities do not indicate market failure once private costs of contracting are taken into consideration. With a high cost of setting up and monitoring contracts, and/or when those costs are the same for the individuals and the government, signalling is rational, and there is no market failure.

The possibility that accounting reforms may have been used by East European countries in transition as a communication device has already been suggested by some authors. For example, Schroeder (1995), researching the development of Polish Financial Reporting, pointed out:

> When de facto accounting change lags behind de lege change, there is the opportunity for accounting to act as a tool of *reassurance* (emphasis added) either in the process of transition itself or in the existing system (p. 3).

Bailey (1995) in his proposition of a theoretical framework for the analysis of the nature of accounting change in the former socialist countries, made the following observation:

> However, premature (i.e., in terms of its sophistication) accounting reform may be enacted as a measure of accounting appeasement as to *assuage the expectations of international agencies* [emphasis added]. In this connection it may be remarked that, during recent years, presentations have been made at academic accounting conferences which test the credulity of the listeners with respect to the claims for swiftly implementing accounting reforms. Aspirations for, and the actuality of, the current accounting situation have become confused; political and academic considerations have merged (p. 610).

We take these observations further, and within the context of the comprehensive program of reforms in the Czech Republic, initiated during 1990 and fully adopted in January 1991, propose a signalling role of accounting reforms during the privatization phase of reforms. The stylized signalling hypothesis is presented in Table 2.

In the early 1990s, Czech society was facing a huge systemic uncertainty—in particular, uncertainty about the irreversibility of changes, and the direction of future changes (i.e., enforcement of property rights, uncertainty about privatization of the remaining state sector).[9] At the same time, the success of reform programs was contingent on foreign investments and the help of international agencies (e.g., The World Bank, The International Monetary Fund, The European Bank for Reconstruction and Development). Delay in the implementation of reforms, and the lack of foreign investments, could have jeopardized the whole program of reforms, and created internal opposition to the new policies. On the political level, Czechs clearly expressed the desire for membership in the EU. Under these circumstances, the Czech government may have had a strong incentive to inform foreign investors (both private and institutional) about their commitment to market reforms, and about the direction of future changes. In addition, internationally, the Czech Republic competes with other Central and East European countries, both on the economic and political levels. There was a need to differentiate the Czech program of market reforms from other programs. For

Table 2. Signalling Hypothesis—Stylized

Seller:	Czech Government
Product:	Program of Market Reforms
Buyer:	Foreign investors (EU); Private and institutional
Objectives:	Reduce uncertainty about market reforms by altering information asymmetry
	Differentiate from other economies in transition
	International recognition (EU membership)
Signalling Mechanism:	Changes in accounting regulation are related to the quality of market reforms.
	Incentive to engage in activities is great because it is believed that the program is of high quality;
	Real cost signalling (similar to education).

example, one can argue that there was hardly any need for the consolidation regulation in the initial phase of transition in the Czech Republic as many of the state-owned enterprises had just been broken up in order to improve competition in the home market. "Even the concept of group accounting takes on an almost politically unacceptable nuance" (Garrod and McLeay 1996, 9). However, the Czech Republic is overtly aiming at eventual membership in the European Union, and more generally at being a fully fledged participant in the world market in goods, services, and finance. Consequently, the introduction of a new comprehensive accounting legislation was a very important signal about government determination to pursue market reforms, and provide transparency for foreign investors.

Comprehensive and fast changes in accounting, and indeed in any other area, in economies in transition, were possible only by the extensive involvement of the state (the Finance Ministry in this case). The scope and depth of changes in regulation indicate a strong determination for continuation with market reforms. However, the changes are not costless (and they are not likely to be if signalling is going to be successful). The costs can be classified as direct and indirect. The direct costs are "real" costs incurred at the state and enterprise level, and they are related to enacting and enforcing legislation (state level), and implementing legislation (enterprise level). Costs of education and training have occurred at both levels. A part of this cost has been paid for by multinational financial organizations through technical assistance, especially by the World Bank. The indirect costs are political costs and the possible costs of premature changes in accounting.[10] The political costs can be measured by the gap between Klaus' free market pluralistic rhetoric and the considerable government interference.[11] The new accounting regulation in the Czech Republic has been state-dominated and implemented by the law, as was also the case with privatization and other measures from the same period (EBRD 1994; Friedman and Rapaczynski 1994). However, recent economic literature concerning the speed of transition seems to suggest that the equilibrium speed of transition is likely to be slow. This may justify measures by the government to accelerate the transition. Some of these measures (e.g., restraints of wages in the state sector, top-down privatization and restructuring) may be imposed on firms rather than chosen by them (Aghion and Blanchard 1993).

The benefits of the signalling exercise can be measured by the increasing confidence in the Czech market reform program, by the amount of foreign investments made in the Czech Republic, and by the transfer of knowledge and professional skills from foreign experts and accounting firms. It cannot be denied that a part of signalling costs has been consumed and spent on the genuine improvement of accounting. Whether the benefits from signalling offset the potential losses as a consequence of the rapid and extensive changes in accounting, influenced by the EU directives, is a question which deserves attention.

However, it is clear that in the current, post-privatization stage of transition in the Czech Republic, the focus needs to be further shifted from the preparers to the users of accounting information. The objective of financial reporting would depend on the characteristics of emerging institutions and markets. In addition, accounting regulation may well be in conflict with the needs of market participants, both domestic and foreign. What once was regarded as a positive signal for investors, namely the visible importation of intermediary practices, may soon become a negative one as they are perceived as out of tune with current consumer needs. It may well be the case that imported solutions, originally accepted uncritically, will be reconsidered and perhaps extensively altered.

Finally, the argument for the importance of signalling theory is given added force by the recent move by the International Accounting Standards Committee and the International Organization of Securities Commissions (IOSCO) to secure the acceptance of international accounting standards as the basis of financial reporting across all stock exchanges. It is planned that an agreement to this effect will be in place by the end of 1998 with the result that any company which prepares its accounts on the basis of international accounting standards will be deemed to meet the reporting requirements of any stock exchange whose regulatory authority is a member of IOSCO.

The implication of this is that the adoption by a company of international accounting standards will provide a signal to investors regarding the quality of its financial reports. One, somewhat sinister, effect of this is the suggestion that international standards are at least adequate as a world-wide model, with the result that a range of countries across the world, including both transitional and developing economies, will be encouraged to abandon the search for a reporting system which meets their own needs in preference for a model which is accepted by international capital markets as providing the required signal.

CONCLUSION AND SUGGESTIONS FOR FURTHER RESEARCH

Substantial changes in Czech accounting started in the early 1990s, as a part of the so-called velvet revolution and related market reforms. Macro and micro reforms have changed ownership structure, the objectives of enterprises, and the entire institutional setting. However, because of the dramatic scale of economic reforms, an automatic transition towards a market economy was not possible. A transitional period was inevitable. Accounting is not an exception in that respect: "You cannot necessarily change accounting rules without also changing the economic and social structures to which they relate" (von Colbe 1983). To illustrate this, we first of all, in Table 1, summarized characteristics of Czech accounting in transition. Then, in Table 2, we proposed a stylized signalling hypothesis as applied in the Czech situation. Regarding the role of accounting in transition, we classified the process of accounting change in transitional period in Table 3.

In the privatization phase (1989-1994), international (EU) accounting standards were imported, although in some cases (e.g., consolidation accounts) there was hardly any need for them. The imitation of international standards was initiated by the need for international recognition and the promotion of market reforms in the Czech Republic. This supports the argument for a signalling role of accounting during the privatization phase of market reforms in the Czech Republic.

In the second phase after 1994, changes in Czech accounting are affected by emerging financial market forces. With the emergence of financial markets, the users of accounting information have become more important. The existing accounting regulation proved to be inadequate for the specific Czech circumstances in many areas and we witnessed changes in the regulations. Consequently, EU accounting standards were challenged and critically assessed. We expect that departure from EU standards will be significant in some areas, and that market forces will further test to what extent accounting regulations comply with the new institutional setting. This is not only because of changes in the

Table 3. Accounting Location in Transition

Phases	*Role of Accounting*	*Regulation*
Privatization	Signal related to the quality of market reforms	Regulation in front of needs (anticipating changes)
	International recognition	Predominantly influenced by international standards
Post-privatization	Accounting as a tool for different interest groups? (e.g., corporate control)	Regulation behind the needs (catching up with changes)
	Information for creditors and investors	Influenced by emerging market institutions

Czech economy, but also due to changes in the moving target the Czechs are aiming at. The European Commission is investigating ways of allowing EU companies to prepare their consolidated accounts on the basis of international accounting standards, following complaints that accounts prepared on the basis of national legislation are not accepted in the main securities markets outside Europe (Financial Times 1995b).

A factor perhaps worthy of emphasis is the actual process of adopting existing foreign regulation. Many conceptual problems are involved in consolidation theory and practice. The Czech terminology is often unclear in precise meaning and the Czech regulations are themselves at times confused or unclear. This confusion and lack of clarity is not in the least surprising, and certainly not blameworthy. It is well known, after all, that even leading international accounting firms have had major difficulties with the valuation of state enterprises in the economies in transition. We would hypothesize that the fact that the book/fair value alternative has not been mentioned is due to the general confusion and problems related to asset valuation in the Czech Republic. Financial markets are in an embryonic stage and book values are inherited from the central planning period. Introduction of "fair value" would create further confusion. Examples of problems related to interpretation and adoption of fair value, extraordinary charges/income, and actual equity capital, illustrate the scope for separate research on the practical effects that different language versions of accounting standards might have.

As to the speed of the process and the sequencing of changes, there does seem to be evidence that the necessary regulations are deliberately being introduced in stages. Amendments to the 1993 measure are already planned. Such piece-meal legislation is of course likely to lead to confusion by preparers, and inconsistency of reported figures over time. However, for a transitional economy, such as the Czech Republic, it is probably a good approach, because sticking to inflexible policies which do not change with the development of internal market forces, can be dangerous. Poland provides an interesting comparison. A 1991 Polish regulation required the use of book values for consolidation purposes; in 1994 this was changed to require fair values. Legislators are facing the uncertainty of the continuing changes in the environment and often do not have a full understanding of all the issues concerned. Furthermore, it takes time before proper coordination among the regulators, such as the Security Commission, Ministry of Finance, and Professional bodies, is established.

Our analysis of the importance of the signalling role of accounting leads to a point of some significance. It has often been argued that developing countries tend to have ready-made "foreign" systems imposed upon them even though these ready-made systems were developed in different countries, for different purposes, and are thoroughly unsuitable for the needs of the developing country at the relevant point of time. An early explanation of this argument comes in Briston (1978). More recently, and in a context explicitly intended to include the East European economies in transition, Wallace and Briston (1993, 217) put the point as follows:

> The main issue is whether the objectives of the assistance-granting country (or aid-agency) and the receiving country are congruent.... The biggest problem developing countries have is that of too many foreign "experts" marketing half-baked solutions to problems that neither they nor the recipient countries understand. In seeking solutions to the national accounting infrastructure development problems of developing countries, it is imperative to understand these problems and identify their needs and priorities.

This argument is well made, and we agree with it entirely. However, the implication of the argument is often taken to be that the country granting assistance is to blame and that the foreign experts referred to by Wallace and Briston are the root cause of the problem. However, our analysis of the signalling hypothesis as applied to and illustrated by the particular example of the Czech Republic and its introduction of consolidated financial statements, suggests a different conclusion. This is that the Czech Republic wishes to import the standard techniques and practices of "developed" accounting nations as quickly as possible consistent with training and experience practicalities even though the business and finance market has no great need of such imports at this time. The problem is not merely that donor countries are anxious to transfer unsuitable and unnecessary technologies, but also that recipient countries are often anxious to receive such unsuitable and unnecessary technologies, for reasons which may be rational, but are not essentially accounting-related.

Given the seriousness and scale of the transitional process in the Czech Republic, dramatic changes in the environment and accounting have occurred. As a result, we believe there is a good case for further research into the process of accounting change and choice. Different environmental factors, and the manner by which such factors influence accounting change can be identified. For example, we expect a political dimension of the accounting change to be very important in the Czech Republic as well as in other transitional economies. With a considerable government interference and new market institutions and accounting profession, conflicting interests of different social groups may be reflected in the accounting area. For example, with economic reforms, the value of state enterprise assets has been drastically reduced compared to their book values. The Czech government may be reluctant to allow full revaluation (almost inevitably devaluation) of assets and recognition of some liabilities, because this would lead to a capital deficit on a large scale. This is related to delays in the application of bankruptcy law in respect of state enterprises. This raises the interesting speculation that the going concern convention, in its Fourth EU Directive sense, is "enacted" but not "adopted." In addition, the government seems to influence accounting regulation by favoring certain accounting techniques in order to protect tax revenues. For example, FIFO method for inventories only is allowed. With, for example 10 percent per annum inflation, FIFO is biased and will show higher taxable profits.[12] The dominant position of the Ministry of Finance in accounting regulation may reflect the government's desire to continue with control of enterprises in the areas of macroeconomic management and taxation.

We postulate that accounting reforms in the Czech Republic played a signalling role during the privatization phase, with the main objective being to reduce uncertainty regarding the market reforms and gain international recognition, in particular by EU countries. With the maturing of market mechanisms, accounting changes in the post-privatization phase are expected to be market-driven, and accounting will start performing a similar role to the role it plays in other developing countries: the production of information, a framework for information diffusion, and monitoring and contract enforcement.[13] If the extreme view is taken that accounting regulation was introduced *purely* for signalling purposes, then some of the problems of detail and implementation would not matter anyway. It is still too early to favor any of the proposed explanations for very poor disclosure in the Czech Republic and further empirical research in this area is needed. A study of differences in the choice of methods for consolidation and differences in disclosure (voluntary and involuntary) between enterprises in the Czech Republic will be helpful in answering some of the above questions.

We would also hypothesize that there is a relationship between different privatization methods and emerging financial institutions in transitional economies and the role of accounting in these countries. For example, in the countries (e.g., Poland) where insiders have played a significant role in privatization, accounting may be used as a tool in preventing outsider control and subsequent restructuring. A broader study on how different privatization methods and reforms of the banking sector have influenced changes in accounting in transitional economies will be helpful in this respect. The signalling hypothesis as applied here also needs to be considered and tested in the context of other transitional and developing economies both in Eastern Europe and elsewhere.

Consolidation and its introduction are only a microcosm of the general regulatory and attitudinal developments currently afoot both in the Czech Republic and in many other economies in transition. A larger study of this whole process, well beyond the capacity of the present authors in isolation, should be mounted while the process is still ongoing.

ACKNOWLEDGMENTS

Helpful discussions with and suggestions from Ivan Zelenka and Vladimir Zelenka, formerly and currently of Prague School of Economics, are acknowledged. The authors accept sole responsibility for the contents of this chapter.

NOTES

1. See *European Accounting Review*, vol. 4, 1995 (special issue).

2. On the importance of the speed of transition in CEEC, and its policy implications, see Aghion and Blanchard (1993).

3. In this respect, problems which CEEC countries are facing now are similar to problems in some countries in the process of decolonization. For example, Tanzania is also struggling to deal with "transitional problems" (and has been for more than 30 years).

4. For example, in Poland, the valuation of the first five privatized enterprises by specialized Western consultants has cost about 20 percent of the value of these firms (Bolton and Roland 1992, 26). For a detailed explanation of problems related to the valuation of state enterprises in Poland, see Friedman and Rapaczynski 1994, 41.

5. The program in Hungary, launched at the end of 1993, is based on ad hoc purchases of bad debts by the government, and the Loan Workout Program. In the Loan Workout Program there are two schemes. In the "quick scheme," debtors propose restructuring programs which are then evaluated by special committees consisting of creditors, social security and tax agency representatives, the enterprise owners, and various ministry officials. Alternatively, banks notify all enterprises with qualified debts and invite them to participate in the program without the owners' and ministries' involvement. The Polish program is based on bank-led financial restructuring. State-owned commercial banks have established special workout departments and have assigned the bad loans to them (Simoneti and Kawalec 1995).

6. The NH-30 Stock Index fell from 4000 (February 1994) to 1235 by the end of March 1994 (Gray 1995).

7. During exposure of an early draft of this chapter, Marek Schroeder pointed out that one might have expected, in the list of allowed exclusions, the situation where the trade or business activity of a subsidiary is dissimilar from those of the other enterprises within the group (an argument recognized, but not supported, in IAS 27 paragraph 12, (IASC 1989)). Speculating extensively, therefore, it can be suggested that exclusion (e) above is an unsuccessful attempt to allow for dissimilar activity exclusions. Schroeder points out, quite correctly, that different industries have or had different charts of accounts. So "a different chart of accounts" could be, allowing for the multi-translations involved, an attempted rendering of "a dissimilar business activity."

8. There is some evidence for this type of behavior in Russia. Friedman, Pistor, Rapaczynski (1995) have found that only 10.4 percent of voucher funds have regular access to financial data concerning their companies, and 12.5 percent of them have no access in any of their companies. As to the quality of financial information, 33 percent of funds judge it to be a "poor" reflection of the company's true financial performance.

9. This has also been observed by other authors; see Seal and colleagues (1995) for Czech Republic, Krzywda and colleagues (1995a, 1995b) for Poland, and Bailey (1995) for Eastern Europe in general.

10. Bailey (1995) expresses his concern that premature changes in accounting would be beneficial only to a small fraction of enterprises seeking a quotation on a national stock exchange in Eastern Europe. In addition a part of indirect costs may be related to the importation of an inappropriate accounting system from a developed country (Briston 1978).

11. As cited in the Financial Times Survey on Czech Republic, June 2, 1995. For more on Klaus's views on pluralism see Klaus (1992) as cited in Seal and colleagues (1995).

12. Similar evidence has been found for Poland, see Schaffer (1992).

13. As defined by Lee (1987).

REFERENCES

Aghion, P., and O. J. Blanchard. 1993. On the speed of transition in Eastern Europe. Mimeographed.

ASB (Accounting Standards Board). 1993. *Reporting Financial Performance.* (FRS3). London: ASB.

ASC (Accounting Standards Committee). 1986. *Extraordinary Items and Prior Year Adjustments.* (SSAP6). London: ASC.

Bailey, D.T. 1995. Accounting in transition in the transitional economy. *The European Accounting Review* 4 (4): 595-623.

Bhattacharya, S. 1980. Imperfect information, dividend policy and "the bird in the hand" fallacy. *Bell Journal of Economics*, Spring.

Bolton, P., and G. Roland. 1992. The economics of mass privatization: Czechoslovakia, East Germany, Hungary and Poland. *LSE Financial Markets Group Discussion Paper No. 155.*

Briston, R.J. 1978. The evolution of accounting in developing countries. *International Journal of Accounting Education and Research* 14 (1): 105-120.

Bromwich, M., and A. G. Hopwood. 1983. *Accounting Standards Setting: An International Perspective.* Pitman.

Czech Ministry of Finance. 1993. *Measures Setting Out Procedures for the Consolidation of Accounts.* Ref. no. 281/73570/93. Prague.

Czechoslovak Federal Ministry of Finance. 1990. *Decree 1990 No. 23/90.*

Czechoslovak Federal Ministry of Finance. 1991. *Draft Law of Accounting, No. 563/91.*

Czechoslovak Government. 1989. *Decree 1989 No. 236/89.*

Dewatripont, M., and E. Maskin. 1990. Credit and efficiency in centralized and decentralized economies. Mimeographed.

Dittus, P. 1994. Corporate governance in Central Europe: The role of banks. Basle: Bank for International Settlements. Mimeographed.

EC. 1978. *Fourth Directive.* EC Commission, Brussels.

EC. 1983. *Seventh Directive.* EC Commission, Brussels.

European Bank for Reconstruction and Development (EBRD). 1994. *Transition Report.* October.

FEE. 1991. *FEE European Survey of Published Accounts 1991.* London: Routledge.

Financial Times. 1995a. *Supplement: Czech Republic.* June 2.

Financial Times. 1995b. Accounting rules may be changed. November 16.

Friedman, R., K. Pistor, and A. Rapaczynski. 1995. Corporate governance in an insider-dominated economy: A report from Russia. *Economics of Transition* 3 (1).

Friedman, R., and A. Rapaczynski. 1994. *Privatization in Eastern Europe: Is the State Withering Away*? Budapest: CEU Press.

Fries, S. M. 1995. Enterprise restructuring and control in transition economies. *Economics of Transition* 3 (1).

Garrod, N., and S. McLeay 1996. *Accounting in Transition.* London: Routledge.

Gray, G. 1995. Czech Republic's invisible revolution. *Euromoney* (April).

Hayek, F. V. 1945. The use of knowledge in society. *American Economic Review* 35(4): 515-530.

Hrncir, M. 1993. Reform of the banking sector in the Czech Republic. Paper from the International Conference on Development of the Financial System in Central and Eastern Europe, October 28-30, Vienna.

IASC. 1989. *IAS 27, Consolidated Financial Statements and Accounting for Investments in Subsidiaries.* London: IASC.

IASC 1993. *IAS 22 (revised), Business Combinations.* London: IASC.

Klaus, V. 1992. Address to the Cato Institute conference on money in transition: From plan to market. (March), Washington DC, as cited in Seal et al. 1995.

Kornai, J. 1992. *The Socialist System: The Political Economy of Communism.* New York: Princeton University and Oxford University Press.

Krzywda, D., D. Bailey, and M. Schroeder. 1995a. A theory of European accounting development applied to accounting change in contemporary Poland. *The European Accounting Review* 4 (4): 625-659.

Krzywda, D., D. Bailey, and M. Schroeder. 1995b. The national role of financial accounting in the Polish transitional economy. Paper presented at the 4th EIASM Workshop on Accounting in Europe, Geneva.

Lange, O. 1936/1964. On the economic theory of socialism. *Review of Economic Studies* 4(1-2), reprinted in *On the Economic Theory of Socialism*, ed. B. E. Lippincott. New York: McGraw Hill.

Lee, C.J. 1987. Accounting infrastructure and economic development. Guest editorial to the *Journal of Accounting and Public Policy* 6(2): 75-85.

Leland, H., and D. Pyle. 1977. Informational asymmetries, financial structure, and financial intermediation. *Journal of Finance* (May): 371-388.

Miller, M. H., and K. Rock. 1985. Dividend policy under asymmetric information. *Journal of Finance* (September): 1031-1052.

Ross, S. 1977. The determination of financial structure: The incentive signalling approach. *Bell Journal of Economics* 8: 23-40.

Rynes, P. 1995. Podvojne Ucetnictvi a Ucetni Zaverka 95. Trizonia, Praha, as cited in Zelenka, V. 1995.

Schaffer, M. 1992. The enterprise sector and the emergence of the Polish fiscal crisis 1990-1991. Mimeographed.

Schroeder, M. 1995. The development of Polish financial reporting in relation to business information needs. Paper presented at the Symposium on Communism to Capitalism, London.

Schroll, R. 1995. The new accounting system in the Czech Republic. *The European Accounting Review* 4 (4): 827-833.

Seal, W., P. Sucher, and I. Zelenka. 1995. The changing organization of Czech accounting. *The European Accounting Review* 4 (4): 659-685.

Simoneti, M., and S. Kawalec (Eds.). 1995. *Bank Rehabilitation and Enterprise Restructuring.* Ljubljana: Central and Eastern European Privatization Network (C.E.E.P.N.).

United Nations (UN). 1993. *Accounting, Valuation, and Privatization.* New York: United Nations Conference of Trade and Development Program on Transitional Corporations.

von Colbe, W. B. 1983. A discussion of international issues in accounting standard setting. In *Accounting Standards Setting: An International Perspective*, eds. M. Bromwich and A. G. Hopwood, 121-126. Pitman.

Wallace, R.S.O., and R. J. Briston. 1993. Improving the accounting infrastructure in developing countries. *Research in Third World Accounting* 2: 201-224.

Watts, R. L., and J. L. Zimmerman. 1986. *Positive Accounting Theory.* NJ: Prentice-Hall.

Weber, M. 1921/1964. *The Theory of Social and Economic Organization.* New York: Free Press.

Zelenka, I. 1995. Comparison of the financial reporting practices in the U.K. and Czech Republic. Paper presented at the 18th EAA Congress, Birmingham.

Zelenka, V. 1995. Legal framework for consolidated financial statements compared with international practice. Paper presented at the 18th EAA Congress, Birmingham.

PART IV

ACCOUNTING AND BUDGETARY CONTROL IN THE MIDDLE EAST

STRATEGIES FOR ENHANCING THE ACCOUNTING PROFESSION AND PRACTICES IN BAHRAIN:
ACCOUNTING EXPERTS' PERCEPTIONS

Hasan Al-Basteki

ABSTRACT

This chapter examines accounting experts' perceptions on strategies for enhancing the accounting profession and practices in Bahrain. Fourteen possible strategies were presented to three groups of accounting experts: partners in public accounting firms operating in Bahrain, managers of accounting and finance functions in Bahraini publicly traded companies, and directors of accounting and finance departments in various governmental entities. Subjects were asked to rate the effectiveness of each strategy according to a five-point Likert-type scale. The study found that raising educational requirements for accountants at the entry level to the profession, requiring and providing continuing education for certified accountants, and strengthening the power and responsibilities of the Bahrain Accounting Society were perceived to be the most effective strategies for enhancing the accounting profession and practices in Bahrain. These findings have important implications for various groups interested in enhancing the accounting profession and practices in Bahrain.

Research in Accounting in Emerging Economies, Volume 4, pages 165-189.

ISBN: 1-55938-995-8

INTRODUCTION

Researchers have long argued that economic development and prosperity in developing countries cannot reach its full potential without the existence of a well developed accounting profession and practices in these countries. Seidler (1967, 1969) argued that the value of the accounting profession, as a positive mechanism in the formation of capital markets, national planning, price control and tax consideration in developing countries, is far greater than its value in already developed markets. Enthoven (1973) also pointed out that a sound accounting system is an essential element in the economic development of Third World countries. Similar arguments were made by AAA (1978), Chandler and Holzer (1981), Jensen and Arrington (1983), Lin and Deng (1992), Belkaoui (1994) and Radebaugh and Gray (1997). In fact, it was argued in an accounting forum, held under the auspices of the U. N. Intergovernmental Working Group of Experts for International Standards of Accounting and Reporting (ISAR) in 1993, that it would be impossible for developing nations to join the global economy without a strong accounting profession (Baliga 1993).

Bahrain has experienced huge economic growth in the last two decades.[1] The GNP jumped from US$ 83.5 millions in 1970 to US$ 3,547.8 millions in 1990, an increase of 4149% over two decades (Ministry of Finance and National Economy 1991). The number of locally formed companies had also increased substantially from less than 100 in 1960 to 2,292 firms in 1991, consisting of 30 public joint stock companies, 226 closed joint stock companies, 665 private companies with limited liability (WLL), 105 exempt companies, 1,207 partnerships, and 59 branches of foreign companies (Central Statistics Organization 1992). However, the accounting profession and practices did not develop quickly enough to match the speed of the economic growth. Bahrain still lacks a strong and active accounting society or association to monitor and promote the profession. In addition the educational requirements for accountants, at the entry level to the profession, are quite general and do not ensure the competency of those who enter the profession. There are still no mandatory requirements related to continuing professional education (CPE) for accountants practicing in Bahrain. Finally, there is still neither a code of ethics nor disciplinary measures in Bahrain for accountants in the public practice.

Many strategies were suggested in the accounting literature for enhancing the accounting profession and practices in developing countries. These strategies and their theoretical support are reviewed and discussed in detail later on in this chapter. However, one would not expect the suggested strategies to be universally applicable to all developing countries. Different developing countries are at different stages of social, legal, economic, political, and accounting developments. This study seeks to identify the strategies that are most relevant to the development of the accounting profession and practices in Bahrain. More specifically, the study examines the perceptions of "accounting experts" practicing in Bahrain on the relevance and importance to Bahrain of 14 different strategies suggested in the accounting literature as important for enhancing the accounting profession and practices in developing countries. Thus, the study will provide empirical evidence on the importance of the theoretically proposed strategies to a specific developing country.

The remainder of the chapter is divided into five sections. Section one presents information about the accounting profession, education, and practices in Bahrain. Section two provides a review of previous research that examined the status of the accounting profession in developing countries and methods for its improvement. Section three discusses the research methodology. Section four reports the findings of the study. The last section summarizes the study and presents a number of conclusions.

THE CURRENT STATE OF THE ACCOUNTING PROFESSION, EDUCATION, AND PRACTICES IN BAHRAIN

Regulation of Corporate Financial Reporting in Bahrain

The legal framework for corporate financial reporting in Bahrain is limited in scope and expressed in loose and general terms. The Bahrain Commercial Companies Law of 1975 requires that Bahraini companies prepare, for each financial year, a balance sheet and a profit and loss statement (Article 166). The Law also requires that these statements be audited by independent auditors (Article 184). The law, however, neither specifies the accounting standards which should be used in preparing companies' financial reports nor the auditing standards that should be followed by auditors in performing their audits. In fact, there are no locally agreed set of accounting standards that can be followed by companies in preparing their annual financial reports. The exception to this is locally incorporated banks where the Bahrain Monetary Agency (the central bank) requires these banks to prepare their accounts in accordance with International Accounting Standards. Also, auditors practicing in Bahrain do not have a set of local auditing standards that they can follow. In the last few years, however, most Bahraini publicly owned companies claim that they follow International Accounting Standards (IASs) issued by the International Accounting Standards Committee (IASC). In addition, international accounting firms practicing in Bahrain claim that they follow voluntarily the International Auditing Standards issued by the International Federation of Accountants (IFAC).

The Accounting Profession

Bahrain has a weak and generally inactive accounting profession. Currently, there is no professional body in Bahrain with the power to regulate the activities of the accounting profession. Accountants and auditors practicing in Bahrain did form a professional body in 1972 called the Bahrain Society of Accountants and Auditors. The society, however, has no regulatory powers. It does not have the power to license accountants and auditors or to establish auditing standards. Membership in the society is voluntary, that is, accountants practicing in Bahrain are not required to be members of the society. In the first few years of its establishment, the society's activities were limited to conducting seminars and workshops. The society was totally inactive during the period 1977 to 1984. Over the last 10 years and until now, the activity of the society has been limited to organizing a few accounting seminars and lectures.

The Ministry of Commerce and Agriculture is responsible for licensing auditors to practice in Bahrain. The Ministry maintains a "Register of Auditors." To be registered as an auditor in Bahrain, the individual has to meet the following two requirements:

(1) hold a university degree which includes accounting and auditing courses
(2) have a minimum of three years accounting or auditing experience.

The licensing regulation, however, does not require auditors to undergo any continuing professional education (CPE) after receiving their licenses.

Currently, licensed auditors practicing in Bahrain come from various countries with the majority being from India.

Accounting Education

College education in Bahrain is mainly provided by the University of Bahrain, the Arabian Gulf University, and a number of specialized colleges and training centers such as the Bahrain Institute of Banking and Finance, the College of Health Sciences, and the Bahrain Hotel and Catering Training Center. The University of Bahrain is the only institution that offers a degree in accounting in Bahrain. English is the language of instruction for business and accounting courses in the College of Business at the University of Bahrain. Curricula and textbooks adopted for these courses are similar to those adopted by universities in the United States.

LITERATURE REVIEW AND STRATEGIES EXAMINED IN THIS STUDY

Researchers addressing the question of enhancing the accounting profession and practices in developing countries have suggested a number of strategies that should be adopted by developing countries. These strategies can be classified into two main categories: (1) education-related strategies, and (2) practice-related strategies. Education-related strategies are those strategies that relate to the ways and means of improving the education and training of accountants. Practice-related strategies, on the other hand, are those related to the regulation, supervision, and organization of the accounting profession, including the setting of accounting and auditing standards and the social role of accountants. The remainder of this section provides a review of previous research with respect to each of the two categories of strategies already mentioned and discusses the strategies that will be examined in this study. However, it is important to mention here that studies on enhancing the accounting profession and practices in developing countries are extremely limited.

Education-Related Strategies

The importance of accounting education, training, and research in enhancing the accounting profession and practices in developing countries cannot be over emphasized. Scott (1970) argued that accounting education is the place to start any attempt for enhancing the accounting practices in developing countries. Similarly, Enthoven (1985, 209) stated that "underlying the existing weaknesses and the scope for improvement in developing countries' accounting systems we find educational weaknesses." The American Accounting Association (AAA) formed a committee in 1973 named "the Committee on Accounting in Developing Countries" to examine accounting practice and education problems facing developing countries. The committee concluded that many of the most important accounting practice problems are the result of causes deeply rooted in accounting education. The committee, thus, suggested that their findings provide support for the proposition that international cooperation in development of accounting education in developing nations directly help alleviate accounting education problems and, in turn, enhance the accounting practices in these countries.

One of the most important problems facing most developing countries is the lack of adequate accounting education at the college level. The AAA's (1976) Report of the Committee on Accounting in Developing Countries and the AAA's (1978) Report of the Committee on International Accounting Operations and Education, suggested three main reasons that contributed to the lack of well developed college level accounting education in developing countries. These are: (1) the lack of qualified accounting instructors at the college level, (2) the inadequacy of locally written textbooks, and (3) the limited professional development opportunities for accounting educators. The importance of upgrading accounting instructors in developing countries was also suggested by a number of researchers. Abdolmohammadi (1988) posited that one important way to enhance the accounting profession in developing countries is to upgrade and train the accounting faculty in these countries. Abdolmohammadi then developed a model for exchange of accounting faculty between the Pacific Basin countries and developed countries. The model includes programs for encouraging doctoral education and research sabbaticals between accounting educators in developing countries and their colleagues in developed countries. Similarly, based on a survey of accounting teachers in the United States with international accounting work experience in developing countries, Novin and Baker (1990) suggested that training and upgrading domestic accounting professors is an important strategy for enhancing the accounting education and profession in developing countries.

The development and availability of local accounting textbooks as a means for enhancing the accounting profession and practices in developing countries was also emphasized in the accounting literature. Tipgos (1987) argued that improving locally available accounting textbooks and training materials would allow the accounting profession in developing countries to develop. Similarly, Novin and Baker (1990) found that "developing accounting textbooks in domestic languages" is perceived by accounting teachers in the United States with international accounting work experience in developing countries as one of the important strategies for improving the accounting profession and practices in developing countries. Finally, Baliga (1993) reported that a call was made, in the 1993 accounting forum held under the auspices of the U. N. Intergovernmental Working Group of Experts for International Standards of Accounting and Reporting (ISAR), for the development of texts dedicated to the national accounting environment as an important strategy for enhancing the accounting profession and practices in developing nations.

Cooperation between accounting educators and accountants in practice has also been suggested as an important strategy for enhancing the accounting profession and practices in developing countries. The current fast changing and demanding business environment makes it essential for a dynamic partnership to be formed between accounting educators and accountants in practice. Many new accounting issues and problems are being faced by developing countries that require cooperative research efforts to solve. In addition, the profession must communicate to the academic community, the skills and knowledge necessary for practice and provide feedback on the strengths and weaknesses of accounting graduates. In turn, the academic community will incorporate the feedback, received from those in practice, to re-engineer accounting curricula. Also, cooperation in the area of teaching will help by bringing in real world problems to classrooms and thus, enhance learning and students' judgment and abilities, to deal with and solve, complex problems.

Many ways of cooperation between accounting educators and accountants in practice were suggested by researchers addressing the question of enhancing the accounting profession and practices in developing countries. Tipgos (1987) suggested the following specific strategies for cooperation between accounting educators and those in practice: (1) establish faculty internship programs, (2) have cooperative teaching arrangements between universities and the profession, and (3) develop plans to encourage coordinated between accounting faculty and outside parties. He argued that adopting these strategies would eventually enhance the accounting profession and practices in developing countries. Novin and Baker

(1990) also reported that providing practical training to accounting students during their college education and encouraging profession-university cooperation are two important strategies for enhancing the accounting profession and practices in developing countries.

Beside the strategies discussed above, Tipgos (1987) proposed a two-tiered accounting education model and called on developing nations to implement it as one of the important strategies for enhancing the accounting profession and practices in developing countries. In Tipgos' (1987) model, accounting college education should be divided into two levels. The first level is a two-to-three years of study with the objective of preparing paraprofessional or accounting technicians. The second level is a continuation of the first level, lasting for two or three years and leading to the attainment of full professional status.

Many of the strategies discussed in this section were tested with respect to Thailand. Akathaporn and colleagues (1993) investigated the perceptions of accounting educators, governmental accountants, and public accountants in Thailand on the effectiveness of using nine education-related strategies for the enhancement of accounting education and practice in Thailand. They found the following to be among the most important strategies: (1) developing accounting textbooks in domestic languages, (2) training and upgrading domestic accounting professors, (3) raising educational requirements for accountants, and (4) encouraging profession-university cooperation.

Practice-Related Strategies

In addition to education-related strategies, accounting practice and profession in developing countries can be enhanced through practice-related strategies. This includes supervising and regulating the accounting profession, standardizing practice by issuing accounting and auditing standards, and formulating programs for continuing training and education of accountants. These and other practice-related strategies are discussed below.

One of the most important strategies for enhancing the accounting profession and practices in developing countries, is to establish a strong professional accounting body and empower it to be responsible for supervising and regulating the accounting profession. Mueller (1968) was among the first to argue that a country's accounting profession plays a major role in establishing accounting practices. Enthoven (1985) noted that accounting professional institutes in developing countries tended to be fairly weak, which had a negative influence on the accounting profession and practices in these countries. He then pointed out the important role that such institutes play in setting accounting and auditing standards, designing codes of practice, running training and educational programs, giving qualification tests, doing research and exchanging information with other accounting bodies. Baliga (1993) reported that the establishment of a strong accounting profession is one of the important strategies for enhancing accounting in developing countries, that was noted by the 1993 accounting forum held under the auspices of the U. N. Intergovernmental Working Group of Experts for International Standards of Accounting and Reporting.

Another important strategy for enhancing the accounting profession and practices in developing countries is to standardize accounting and auditing practices by enforcing a set of accounting and auditing standards. These standards can be either locally developed or be adopted from standards developed elsewhere. Some researchers have argued strongly that developing countries should set their own accounting and auditing standards because accounting is a product of the social, economic, legal, and political environment in which it operates (Arpan and Radebaugh 1985; Hove 1986; Choi 1991). Considering this line of argument, Tipgos (1987) and Novin and Baker (1990) suggested that setting accounting standards and auditing standards are two of the most important strategies for enhancing the accounting profession and practices in developing countries. Other researchers, however, pointed out the many advantages for developing countries in adopting International Accounting Standards (IASs) and International Standards on Auditing (ISAs). Belkaoui (1994), for example, noted that adopting such standards would enable the profession in developing countries to emulate well-established professional standards of behavior and conduct. Choi and Mueller (1992) pointed out that these and other benefits led several developing countries to adopt IASs fully. These included countries such as Cyprus, Malawi, Oman, and Pakistan.

Enhancing the accounting profession and practices in developing countries can also be achieved by ensuring that only qualified and competent accountants enter the profession and by having in place a mechanism for continuous updating and upgrading of their knowledge and skills, to meet the challenges of a fast changing and highly competitive business environment. One way to ensure that this happens is to establish professional accounting examinations and certification procedures for accountants entering the profession (Novin and Baker 1990). Another means would be to formulate rules and coordinate professional development and continuing education programs for those certified to practice (Tipgos 1987). Also, the establishment of a code of ethics and disciplinary measures for accountants is important for maintaining the integrity of the profession and the quality of work done by accountants (Tipgos 1987).

Beside the strategies discussed above, Novin and Baker (1990) reported that accounting teachers in the United States, with international accounting work experience in developing countries, suggested the following as important strategies for enhancing the accounting profession and practices in developing countries: (1) encouraging participation of accountants in society activities, (2) using computers for processing accounting data, and (3) determining the number of accountants needed by a country.

Akathaporn and colleagues (1993) investigated the perceptions of accounting educators and governmental and public accountants in Thailand on the effectiveness of using the 12 practice-related strategies suggested by Novin and Baker

(1990) for the enhancement of accounting education and practice in Thailand. They found the following four strategies perceived to be the most important for the development of accounting practices in Thailand were:

(1) limiting public accounting to certified accountants,
(2) setting auditing standards,
(3) having professional accounting examinations and certifications, and
(4) setting accounting standards.

The Strategies Examined in This Study

The strategies for enhancing the accounting profession and practices in developing countries that were suggested in the accounting literature reviewed above can be summarized in 21 specific strategies; 8 education-related strategies and 13 practice-related strategies. However, since there were many strategies suggested in the literature and since it is possible that some of these strategies are not applicable or relevant to Bahrain, the initial list of 21 was reviewed and evaluated for its relevance and importance to Bahrain by the researcher and two faculty members from the Department of Accounting at the University of Bahrain. Seven of the 21 strategies were eliminated in this stage. The remaining 14 strategies were divided into two groups: education-related strategies (six strategies) and practice-related strategies (eight strategies). The Appendix presents the 21 strategies divided into two main parts: (1) education-related strategies, and (2) practice-related strategies. Each part was further subdivided into two categories; those strategies that were examined in this study and those strategies that were not examined in this study. For each of the 14 strategies that were examined in this study, a brief explanation of its relevance to Bahrain was provided. Similarly, justifications were provided for each of the seven strategies that were not examined in this study.

RESEARCH METHODOLOGY

The Sample of Experts

The subjects of this study were accounting experts practicing in Bahrain. Accounting experts were defined for the purpose of this study as those who meet all of the following three criteria:

(1) Education: hold a Bachelor or higher degree or have a professional accounting qualification such as Chartered Accountants (CAs), Certified Public Accountants (CPAs), Cost and Management Accountants (ACMAs), or the like
(2) Years of experience: 15 years of accounting experience or more
(3) Senior position: hold senior accounting position in his/her respective organization. Senior position is defined here to mean belonging to one of the following three groups[2]:

(a) Partners in public accounting firms practicing in Bahrain
(b) Heads or managers of accounting and finance functions in Bahraini publicly traded companies.
(c) Directors of accounting and finance departments in various governmental entities.

The above three groups are referred to hereafter as partners, private sector accountants, and public sector accountants, respectively.

It is important to mention here that there is no generally accepted definition or measure of expertise given in the accounting literature. However, accounting researchers have suggested a number of measures that can be used as surrogates for expertise. Libby (1985) suggests that domain-specific knowledge is the essential determinant of expertise and that expert knowledge is gained through many years of experience. Bonner (1990), Libby and Frederick (1990), and Ashton (1991) also pointed out that experience is an important determinant of expertise. Frederick (1991), however, argues that "expertise" is a complex concept that cannot be completely accounted for by one measure, such as number of years of experience. Based on the aforementioned literature, the three criteria for defining "accounting experts" were developed in this study.

Fourteen people from each of the above three groups were identified to form the sample for this study.[3] The fourteen partners were conveniently identified from the eight public accounting firms operating in Bahrain. The number of partners from each accounting firm ranges between one and three partners. The fourteen private sector accountants were randomly selected from a list of 33 heads or managers of accounting departments in the 33 publicly traded corporations listed in the Bahrain Stock Exchange.[4] The 33 corporations represent all the corporations listed in the Bahrain Stock Exchange as of December 31, 1994. The fourteen public sector accountants were chosen from the 14 ministries in the state of Bahrain; one from each ministry.

The Questionnaire

To assess which strategies are perceived by the accounting experts to be most effective in enhancing the accounting profession and practices in Bahrain, a two-part self-report questionnaire was constructed. Part one had five questions covering respondents' demographic characteristics. These include sex, age, years of experience, level of education, and professional qualification. The second part of the questionnaire incorporated 14 strategies which could be adopted to enhance the accounting profession and practices in Bahrain.

Respondents were instructed to rate the effectiveness of each strategy according to a five-point Likert-type scale (0 = not effective and 4 = extremely effective). Respondents were also provided with space at the end of the questionnaire to state strategies for enhancing the accounting profession and practices in Bahrain other than the 14 listed in the questionnaire.

Since it is impossible to predict how questionnaire items will be interpreted by respondents, the questionnaire was pilot tested on a small sample of subjects. This sample consisted of six people; two from each of the three groups of accounting experts defined earlier. The results and feedback of the pilot test were used to refine the questionnaire.[5]

One major problem with the use of questionnaires in research, is a possible response bias resulting from the order under which the questions are presented in the questionnaire. Dillehay and Jernigan (1970) suggested that the first question in a series has more influence than later questions causing what is commonly referred to as *primacy bias*. To mitigate the possible impact of the order of presenting the 14 strategies on subjects' responses, two sets of the questionnaires were prepared (set A and set B). Each set differed in only one aspect; the order of presenting the 14 strategies.

Procedure

Each of the three groups of accounting experts, was divided randomly into two subgroups called group A and group B. Individuals in subgroups A were mailed set A questionnaires whereas individuals in subgroups B were mailed set B questionnaires. Subjects were requested to complete and mail back, or facsimile, the completed questionnaire as soon as possible but not later than two weeks from the date received. Two telephone follow-ups were made; the first after three weeks from the initial mailing date and the second after one week from the date of the first follow-up.

Responses

Of the total 48 questionnaires mailed, 37 were returned; 13 from partners, 11 from private sector accountants, and 13 from public sector accountants. This represents an overall response rate of 77 percent. Eight of the questionnaires were excluded because the respondents do not fit the definition of "accounting expert" used in this study. Thus, the useable response rate was 60 percent.

Overall, the final sample is representative of the population as it consists of the following: 11 of the 17 partners in audit firms practicing in Bahrain (i.e., 65 percent of the population); nine of the 33 heads/managers of accounting and finance functions in Bahraini publicly traded companies (i.e., 27 percent of the population); and nine of the 14 directors of accounting and finance departments in various governmental entities (i.e., 64 percent of the population).

Nonresponse bias represents one of the serious problems in the use of mail questionnaires (Oppenheim 1966). However, in this study, nonresponse bias does not represent a problem due to the low nonresponse rate. Although it varied across the three groups of experts (19 percent for partners, 31 percent for private sector

Table 1. Demographic Information on Respondents

	Overall		Partners		Private		Public	
	No.	%	No.	%	No.	%	No.	%
SEX								
Male	29	100%	11	38%	9	31%	9	31%
AGE GROUP								
40-49	7	30%	3	27%	2	22%	2	22%
50 and over	22	62%	8	73%	7	78%	7	78%
TOTAL	29	100%	11	100%	9	100%	9	100%
EDUCATION								
B.Sc. degree	22	76%	11	100%	6	67%	5	56%
Masters degree	7	24%	0	0%	3	33%	4	44%
TOTAL	29	100%	11	100%	9	100%	9	100%
PROFESSIONAL*								
Yes	21	72%	11	100%	7	78%	3	33%
No	8	28%	0	0%	2	22%	6	67%
TOTAL	29	100%	11	100%	9	100%	9	100%

Notes: * Hold professional accounting qualification, for example, CPA, CA, ACMA, or the like.
Partners: Partners in public accounting firms practicing in Bahrain.
Private: Managers of accounting and finance functions in Bahraini publicly traded companies.
Public: Directors of accounting and finance departments in various governmental entities

accountants, and 19 percent for public sector accountants), the overall nonresponse rate was only 23 percent.

Table 1 presents demographic information of the respondents. The Table shows that all respondents were male. Twenty-two of the respondents (or 76 percent) were 50 or more years old. Of the total respondents, 22 (or 76 percent) had B.Sc. degrees and 7 (24 percent) held masters degrees. With respect to professional accounting qualification, 21 of the 29 respondents (or 72 percent) had professional qualification such as CPA, ACMA, CA, or the like.

RESULTS

The results of this study are summarized in Tables 2 through 5. Table 2 presents frequency and percentage analysis for all respondents with respect to each of the 14 strategies included in this study. Table 3, on the other hand, presents mean and standard deviation analysis for each of the 14 strategies, by group of experts. Table 4 shows the results of two nonparametric statistics that are performed, in order to test the differences in perceptions between, and among, the three groups of experts. Table 5 presents the results of Spearman rank (rho) correlation among the 14 strategies. The balance of this section is divided into two parts: part one covers the most effective strategies as perceived by the subjects of this study and part two covers the least effective strategy.

Table 2. Strategies for Enhancing the Accounting Profession and Practices in Bahrain Frequency & Percentage Analysis (All Respondents)

Strategy**	Practice/ Education		0*	1*	2*	3*	4*	Weighted Value***
1. Raising educational requirements for accountants at the entry to the profession level.	P	Freq.	0	0	0	12	17	104
		%	0%	0%	0%	41%	59%	
2. Requiring and providing continuing education for certified accountants.	P	Freq.	0	0	0	14	15	102
		%	0%	0%	0%	48%	52%	
3. Strengthening the powers and responsibilities of the Bahrain Accounting Society.	P	Freq.	0	0	2	15	12	97
		%	0%	0%	7%	52%	41%	
4. Providing practical training to accounting students during their college education.	E	Freq.	0	1	6	6	14	95
		%	0%	3%	21%	21%	55%	
5. Establish programs for cooperative teaching arrangements between the profession and the university	E	Freq.	0	0	2	18	9	94
		%	0%	0%	7%	62%	31%	
6. Establish code of ethics for accountants and disciplinary measures against violators.	P	Freq.	0	2	5	10	12	90
		%	0%	7%	17%	35%	41%	
7. Formulate plans to encourage internship for accounting educators.	E	Freq.	0	0	7	14	8	88
		%	0%	0%	24%	48%	28%	
8. Training and upgrading local accounting educators.	E	Freq.	0	0	10	9	10	87
		%	0%	0%	35%	31%	35%	
9. Draw plans to encourage coordinated research between accounting educators and practitioners	E	Freq.	0	0	17	11	1	71
		%	0%	0%	59%	38%	3%	
10. Encouraging participation of accountants in social activities.	P	Freq.	0	4	14	7	4	69
		%	0%	14%	48%	24%	14%	
11. Setting local accounting standards.	P	Freq.	3	9	7	6	4	57
		%	10%	31%	24%	21%	14%	
12. Having locally developed and supervised professional accounting examinations and certification.	P	Freq.	0	11	12	4	2	55
		%	0%	38%	41%	14%	7%	
13. Setting local auditing standards.	P	Freq.	6	7	7	6	3	51
		%	21%	24%	24%	21%	10%	
14. Developing accounting textbooks in Arabic language.	E	Freq.	10	9	5	4	1	35
		%	35%	31%	17%	14%	3%	

Notes: * The response scale; 0 (the strategy is not effective) to 4 (the strategy is extremely effective).
** Ranked in descending order by the frequency of the "extremely effective" rank..
*** Weighted Value = Σ (Frequency x Response scale).

The Most Effective Strategies

Table 2 shows that accounting experts practicing in Bahrain view the following three strategies to be the most effective for enhancing the accounting profession

Table 3. Strategies for Enhancing the Accounting Profession and Practices in Bahrain Mean and Standard Deviation Analysis (By Group of Experts)

	Strategy	*Practice/ Education*		*Overall*	*Partners*	*Private*	*Public*
1.	Raising educational requirements for accountants at the entry to the profession level.	**P**	Mean Std.	3.59 (0.50)	3.64 (0.50)	3.67 (0.50)	3.44 (0.53)
2.	Requiring and providing continuing education for certified accountants.	**P**	Mean Std.	3.52 (0.51)	3.55 (0.52)	3.56 (0.53)	3.44 (0.53)
3.	Strengthening the powers and responsibilities of the Bahrain Accounting Society.	**P**	Mean Std.	3.28 (0.80)	3.18 (0.87)	3.44 (0.53)	3.22 (0.97)
4.	Providing practical training to accounting students during their college education.	**E**	Mean Std.	3.28 (0.92)	3.27 (0.79)	3.33 (0.87)	3.22 (1.20)
5.	Establish programs for cooperative teaching arrangements between the profession and the university.	**E**	Mean Std.	3.24 (0.58)	3.18 (0.60)	3.22 (0.67)	3.33 (0.50)
6.	Establish code of ethics for accountants and disciplinary measures against violators.	**P**	Mean Std.	3.10 (0.94)	3.64 (0.50)	3.56 (0.53)	2.00 (0.71)
7.	Formulate plans to encourage internship for accounting educators.	**E**	Mean Std.	3.03 (0.73)	3.09 (0.90)	2.89 (0.78)	3.11 (0.78)
8.	Training and upgrading local accounting educators.	**E**	Mean Std.	3.00 (0.85)	3.09 (0.83)	2.89 (0.93)	3.00 (0.87)
9.	Draw plans to encourage coordinated research between accounting educators and practitioners.	**E**	Mean Std.	2.45 (0.57)	2.55 (0.69)	2.44 (0.53)	2.23 (0.50)
10.	Encouraging participation of accountants in social activities.	**P**	Mean Std.	2.38 (0.90)	2.45 (1.04)	2.33 (0.87)	2.33 (0.87)
11.	Setting local accounting standards.	**P**	Mean Std.	1.97 (1.24)	0.73 (0.47)	2.56 (1.13)	2.89 (0.60)
12.	Having locally developed and supervised professional accounting examinations and certification.	**P**	Mean Std.	1.90 (0.90)	1.45 (0.52)	2.11 (1.05)	2.22 (0.97)
13.	Setting local auditing standards.	**P**	Mean Std.	1.76 (1.30)	0.45 (0.52)	1.89 (0.60)	3.22 (0.67)
14.	Developing accounting textbooks in Arabic.	**E**	Mean Std.	1.21 (1.18)	0.82 (0.40)	1.00 (1.22)	1.89 (1.54)

Notes: * Ranked in a descending order by overall mean.
** The response scale is 0 to 4 (not effective to extremely effective).

Table 4. Difference in the Perceptions of the Three Groups of Accounting Experts

Strategy	Practice/ Education	P-Value: The Three Groups	Partners & Private	Partners & Public	Private & Public
1. Raising educational requirements for accountants at the entry to the profession level.	**P**	0.588	0.890	0.403	0.357
2. Requiring and providing continuing education for certified accountants.	**P**	0.874	0.961	0.661	0.647
3. Strengthening the powers and responsibilities of the Bahrain Accounting Society.	**P**	0.861	0.574	0.800	0.804
4. Providing practical training to accounting students during their college education.	**E**	0.948	0.804	0.769	0.960
5. Establish programs for cooperative teaching arrangements between the profession and the university.	**E**	0.869	0.860	0.586	0.758
6. Establish code of ethics for accountants and disciplinary measures against violators.	**P**	0.000*	0.721	0.000*	0.001*
7. Training and upgrading local accounting educators.	**E**	0.868	0.600	0.809	0.778
8. Formulate plans to encourage internship for accounting educators.	**E**	0.773	0.531	0.934	0.539
9. Draw plans to encourage coordinated research between accounting educators and practitioners.	**E**	0.789	0.829	0.508	0.638
10. Encouraging participation of accountants in social activities.	**P**	0.945	0.778	0.778	1.000
11. Setting local accounting standards.	**P**	0.000*	0.000*	0.000*	0.351
12. Having locally developed and supervised professional accounting examinations and certification.	**P**	0.128	0.141	0.052	0.781
13. Setting local auditing standards.	**P**	0.000*	0.000*	0.000*	0.002*
14. Developing accounting textbooks in Arabic.	**E**	0.248	0.967	0.114	0.173

Notes: * Indicates that significant differences between the two groups or among the three groups exist at the $p \leq 0.05$ level.

and practices in Bahrain: (1) raising the educational requirements for accountants at the entry the profession level, (2) requiring and providing continuous education to practicing accountants, and (3) strengthening the powers and responsibilities of the Bahrain Accounting Society. Seventeen of the 29 (59 percent) accounting experts view "raising the educational requirements for accountants at the entry level to the profession" as an extremely effective strategy and twelve experts (41 percent) think it is a very effective strategy. Similarly, all respondents think that "requiring and providing continuous education for practicing accountants" is extremely effective (52 percent of the subjects) or very effective (48 percent of the subjects) strategy in enhancing the accounting profession and practices in Bahrain. Finally, 27 of the 29 (or 93 percent) accounting experts who responded perceive "strengthening the powers and responsibilities of the Bahrain Accounting Society" to be either extremely or very effective strategy in enhancing the profession in Bahrain.

The findings are not surprising, considering the current state of the accounting profession in Bahrain. As discussed in section one of this chapter, the educational requirement to register as an auditor in Bahrain is a "university degree which includes accounting and auditing courses." This requirement is quite general, flexible and open to interpretation and subjective judgment. It can lead to the entrance of unqualified and incompetent accountants into the profession. Thus, the call by accounting experts to raise "educational requirements for accountants at the entry level to the profession" is justified. In addition, there is no mandatory Continuing Professional Education (CPE) program for accountants practicing in Bahrain. CPE programs have an important role in maintaining and updating the technical knowledge of accountants which in turn would enhance the accounting profession and practices. Thus, it is expected that "requiring and providing continuing education for certified accountants" be viewed as an effective strategy. Finally, unlike many developed countries, Bahrain lacks a professional accounting body responsible for organizing and promoting the profession. The Bahrain Accounting Society has no power over its members. Membership is voluntary and the society is more of a social rather than professional body. As such, the call by the accounting experts for strengthening the powers and responsibilities of the society as an effective strategy for enhancing the accounting profession in Bahrain is not surprising.

No statistically significant correlation (at $p \leq 0.05$) exists between two of the three strategies that were perceived to be most effective and the other strategies examined in this study (see Table 5).[6] These two strategies are: (1) raising the educational requirements for accountants at the entry level to the profession strategy and (2) requiring and providing continuous education to practicing accountants' strategy. This suggests that the above strategies are viewed by the "accounting experts" who participated in this study, to be independent of each other. However, a statistically significant negative correlation exists between the "strengthening the powers and responsibilities of the Bahrain Accounting Society" strategy and "establishing programs for cooperative teaching arrangements between the profession and the University" strategy. Thus, the "experts" believe

Table 5. Correlation Among the Strategies

	S1	S2	S3	S4	S5	S6	S7	S8	S9	S10	S11	S12	S13	S14
S1. Establish code of ethics for accountants and disciplinary measures against violators.	1	−0.19	−.25	.13	−.29	.10	−.40*	−.65*	.09	−.09	.20	.20	−.15	−.24
S2. Requiring and providing continuing education for certified accountants.	−.19	1	.05	.08	−.04	.05	.09	−.02	−.25	.14	−.29	.08	−.13	.07
S3. Establish programs for cooperative teaching arrangements between the profession and the university.	−.25	.05	1	.00	−.09	−.02	−.04	.18	−.26	−.23	−.39*	−.54*	−.13	.14
S4. Training and upgrading local accounting educators.	.14	.08	.00	1	.75*	0.81*	−.20	.00	−.17	−.66*	0.05	.05	.36	−.78*
S5. Having locally developed and supervised professional accounting examination and certification.	−.03	−.04	−.09	.75*	1	.77*	.14	.28	−.18	−.67*	.14	.24	.49*	−.78*
S6. Formulate plans to encourage internship for accounting educators.	.10	.05	−.02	.81*	.77*	1	−.24	.01	−.25	−.72*	.04	.37	.81*	-.02
S7. Setting local accounting standards.	−.40*	.09	−.04	−.2	.14	−.24	1	.64*	−.25	.07	−.08	.08	.20	.14
S8. Setting local auditing standards.	−.65*	−.02	.18	.00	.28	.01	.64*	1	−.10	−.23	−.13	−.07	.29	−.00
S9. Raising educational requirements for accountants at the entry to the profession level.	.09	−.25	−.26	−.17	−.18	−.25	−.25	−.10	1	.17	.12	.30	−.09	.18
S10. Draw plans to encourage coordinated research between accounting educators and practitioners.	−.09	.14	−.23	−.66*	−.67*	−.72*	.07	−.23	.17	1	.07	.11	−.51*	.64*
S11. Encouraging participation of accountants in social activities.	.20	−.29	−.39*	.05	.14	.03	−.08	−.13	.12	.07	1	.05	−.08	−.26
S12. Strengthening the powers and responsibilities of the Bahrain Accounting Society.	.20	.08	−.54*	.05	.24	.04	.08	−.07	.30	.11	.05	1	.13	−.25
S13. Developing accounting textbooks in Arabic.	−.15	−.13	−.13	.36	.49*	.37	.20	.29	−.09	−.51*	−.08	.13	1	−.25
S14. Providing practical training to accounting students during their college education.	−.24	.07	.14	−.78*	−.78*	−.81*	.14	.00	.18	.64*	−.26	−.25	−.25	1

Note: * Statistically significant at $p \leq 0.05$.

that by strengthening the powers and responsibilities of the Bahrain Accounting Society, the importance of establishing programs for cooperative teaching arrangements between the profession and the University diminishes.

Each of the three groups of accounting experts (partners, private sector accountants, and public sector accountants) ranks the following two strategies among the three most effective in enhancing the accounting profession and practices in Bahrain: (1) raising the educational requirements for accountants at the entry level to the profession, and (2) requiring and providing continuous education to practicing accountants. However, they disagree with respect to the strategy that should be ranked third. Partners and private sector accountants view the establishment of a code of ethics for accountants and disciplinary measures against violators as the third most effective strategy. Public sector accountants, on the other hand, perceive the establishment of a program for cooperative teaching arrangements between the profession and the university to be the third most effective strategy.

To systematically assess whether significant differences exist between the three groups of accounting experts with respect to each of the fourteen strategies, two nonparametric tests were conducted: Mann-Whitney U test and Kruskal-Wallis ANOVA by ranks.[7] Mann-Whitney U test, which is the most powerful and sensitive nonparametric alternative to the t test for independent samples (Siegel and Castellan 1988), was selected in order to test for whether significant differences exist between each of the following three pairs of accounting experts: (1) partners and private sector accountants, (2) partners and public sector accountants, and (3) private sector accountants and public sector accountants. Kruskal-Wallis ANOVA by ranks was selected in order to assess whether significant differences exist between the three groups of accounting experts. The results of the two nonparametric tests are presented in Table 4.

Kruskal-Wallis ANOVA by ranks test shows that, at the conventional level of $p \leq 0.05$, no significant differences exist among partners, private sector accountants and public sector accountants with respect to any of the three strategies that were perceived to be most effective. Also, no statistically significant differences exist between any two groups of experts. Thus, one can conclude that there is general agreement among all respondents over the three most effective strategies for enhancing the accounting profession in Bahrain stated earlier; which are (1) raising the educational requirements for accountants at the entry level to the profession, (2) requiring and providing continuous education to practicing accountants, and (3) strengthening the powers and responsibilities of the Bahrain Accounting Society.

The Least Effective Strategies

Of the 14 strategies presented in the questionnaire, the following four strategies were perceived to be the least effective: (1) developing accounting textbooks in Arabic, (2) setting local auditing standards, (3) developing local accounting examinations and certification, and (4) setting local accounting standards. The overall mean for each of the above strategies was below 2 in a scale from 0 to 4.

These findings are not surprising. Bahrain views itself as an international financial and service center. It has a large number of international financial institutions and other service companies. In addition, the "Big Six" international accounting firms are present in Bahrain, with a market share that exceeds 95 percent. Furthermore, local (i.e., Bahraini national) accountants make up only 15 percent or less of all accountants practicing in Bahrain.[8] Finally, English is the dominant communication language used by Bahraini companies for local communication. English is also the language of instruction (teaching) in the College of Business at the University of Bahrain.[9] In such an environment, it is not surprising to find that accounting experts view "developing accounting textbooks in Arabic," "setting local accounting standards," "setting local auditing standards," and "having locally developed and supervised professional accounting examinations and certification" as strategies that have little or no effectiveness.

Positive and statistically significant correlation exists between "developing accounting textbooks in Arabic" strategy and "having locally developed and supervised professional accounting examinations and certification" strategy. Similarly, positive statistically significant correlation exists between "setting local accounting standards" strategy and "setting local auditing standards" strategy. Thus, the above pairs of strategies are viewed by the accounting experts to be dependent.

Some differences do exist between the three groups of experts in ranking the least effective strategies (see Table 3). Partners rank "setting local auditing standards" to be the least effective strategy. This is followed by "setting local accounting standards" strategy and "developing accounting textbooks in Arabic" strategy, respectively. Private sector accountants, on the other hand, rank the three least effective strategies in the following order: (1) developing accounting textbooks in Arabic, (2) setting local auditing standards, and (3) developing local accounting examinations and certification. For public sector accountants, "developing accounting textbooks in Arabic" is also the least effective strategy. This is followed by "establishing a code of ethics for accountants and disciplinary measures against violators" strategy and "developing local accounting examinations and certification" strategy, respectively.

Kruskal-Wallis ANOVA by ranks test shows that, at the conventional level of $p \leq 0.05$, significant differences exist among partners, private sector accountants, and public sector accountants with respect to two of the four strategies that perceived to be least effective (see Table 4). These strategies are: (1) the setting of local accounting standards, and (2) the setting of local auditing standards. Thus, disagreements do exist between the three groups of experts with respect to two of the above strategies. Further analysis using Mann-Whitney U tests of differences between pairs of two groups of accounting experts, shows that the perceptions of partners, private sector accountants, and public sector accountants are significantly different from each other with respect to "setting of local accounting standards" strategy. The results of Mann-Whitney U tests also suggest that the perceptions of partners are significantly different from those of public sector accountants and private sector accountants with respect to the effectiveness of "setting of local accounting standards" strategy. Partners feel that "setting of local accounting standards" is an unimportant strategy for enhancing the accounting profession and practices in Bahrain. Public sector accountants and private sector accountants, on the other hand, have more positive feelings about the effectiveness of this strategy.

SUMMARY AND CONCLUSIONS

This chapter has provided evidence on the perception of three groups of accounting experts regarding 14 strategies for enhancing the accounting profession and practices in Bahrain. The overall results indicate that "raising the educational requirements for accountants at the entry level to the profession" is perceived to be the most effective strategy. This is followed by "requiring and providing continuous education to practicing accountants" strategy. The third most effective strategy, as perceived by the experts, is "strengthening the powers and responsibilities of the Bahrain Accounting Society." No statistically significant differences exist between the three groups of experts (partners, private sector accountants, and public sector accountants) with respect to any of these three strategies.

The findings of this study have important implications for the accounting profession and practices in Bahrain. They provide a guide for government officials, accounting educators, and practicing accountants who face the challenge of enhancing the accounting profession and practices in Bahrain. By highlighting the most effective strategies for enhancing the accounting profession and practices in Bahrain, a working plan can be drawn and implemented. The findings of this study have also shown that strategies for enhancing the accounting profession and practices in developing countries that are suggested in the accounting literature are not uniformly applicable to all developing countries. For example, it has been suggested by accounting researchers that developing accounting textbooks in local languages, setting local accounting and auditing standards, and developing local accounting examinations and certification are important strategies for enhancing the accounting profession and practices in developing countries. However, this was found not to be the case in Bahrain. Thus, each country has its own views on how to enhance its accounting profession and practices based on its local conditions and environment.

An important limitation in this study is that it is based on a list of predetermined strategies that might not be conclusive. Perhaps there might be some other strategies that were not examined in this study. However, it is worth mentioning that the questionnaire used in this study included, as well as the list of the predetermined strategies, an open ended question requesting subjects to state any other strategies they believe are important for enhancing the accounting profession and practices in Bahrain. No suggestions were made of any additional strategies.

A fruitful extension of this study would be to examine possible alternatives for the implementations of the strategies that are perceived to be most effective and to study possible problems or difficulties associated with these implementations. Researchers may also examine the generality of some of the findings of this study to other developing countries.

APPENDIX

The Relevance of the Strategies Enhancing the Accounting Profession and Practice in Bahrain

EDUCATION-RELATED STRATEGIES:

A. Strategies Examined in This Study

	The Strategy	*Justification*
1.	Providing practical training to accounting students during their college education.	Employers in Bahrain always claim that accounting graduates in Bahrain are not competent because they lack practical knowledge and training. Boosting their competence can thus be achieved through well structured and supervised practical training programs.
2.	Establish programs for cooperative teaching arrangements between the profession and the university.	No such programs exist now. Cooperative teaching programs are expected to enrich students knowledge and experience through real-world issues and cases. Such programs are also expected to encourage professional accountants and academics to work together toward improving the accounting profession and practice in Bahrain.
3.	Draw plans to encourage coordinated research between accounting educators and practitioners.	No such plans exist now. Coordinated research should help solve many of the problems that face the accounting profession and practice in Bahrain and thus lead to their improvement.
4.	Formulate plans to encourage internship for accounting educators.	No such plans exist now. Through internship, accounting educators would have first-hand experience about the accounting practices in Bahrain. This would, in turn, enrich both their teaching and research and lead to enhancing the accounting profession and practice in Bahrain.
5.	Training and upgrading local accounting educators.	There is no system in place for ensuring that adequate training is provided for accounting educators in Bahrain. For example, Accounting Faculty in the University of Bahrain are not subject to any formal requirements for attending conferences or publishing to keep their jobs. As a result, on average Faculty members attend less than one conference per year.
6.	Developing accounting textbooks in Arabic.	One might argue that the English language is an obstacle that discourage Bahrainis from studying accounting and entering the profession. Thus, developing accounting textbooks in Arabic would have a positive impact on the accounting profession and practices in Bahrain.

(*continued*)

Appendix (Continued)

The Strategy	*Justification*
B. Strategies Not Examined in This Study	
1. Implement a two-tiered education system in accounting.	The University of Bahrain is already implementing a two-tiered one track system where all students do the Associated Accounting Diploma first and only those with good grades are allowed to continue for degree in accounting.
2. Developing a faculty exchange program between developing and developed nations.	Although this is an important strategy, it is premature for Bahrain at this stage because the number of local accounting faculty is limited. In 1994, there was only one Bahraini accounting faculty in the Department of Accounting at the University of Bahrain.
PRACTICE-RELATED STRATEGIES:	
A. Strategies Examined in This Study	
1. Raising educational requirements for accountants at the entry to the profession level.	The current educational requirement is to "hold a university degree which includes accounting and auditing courses." This is quite general and does not ensure the competency of people who enter the profession.
2. Requiring and providing continuing professional education (CPE) for certified accountants.	Currently, there are no CPE requirements for accountants practicing in Bahrain. Thus, no mechanism exists to ensure that professional accountants in Bahrain are up-to-date with current technical knowledge applicable to their work area.
3. Strengthening the powers and responsibilities of the Bahrain Accounting Society.	The Bahrain Accounting Society is not playing the usual role that is expected from a professional accounting body. One important reason for this is that the Society lacks the power and the professional supervision over accountants practicing in Bahrain.
4. Establish a code of ethics for accountants and disciplinary measures against violators.	There is neither a code of ethics nor disciplinary measures in Bahrain for accountants in public practice. It is essential that ethical requirements be established for accountants in Bahrain to ensure the highest quality of performance. This in turn will enhance the accounting profession and practice in Bahrain.
5. Encouraging participation of accountants in social activities.	Participation of accountants in Bahrain in social activities is quite limited. Being more involved in social activities is expected to enhance the image of accountants in Bahrain and boost their role in the society. This in turn should reflect positively on the profession in Bahrain.
6. Setting local accounting standards.	Currently, there are no locally issued accounting standards that should be followed by companies in Bahrain. Some companies claim that they implement International Accounting Standards. Others, claim that they use generally accepted accounting principles. However, no definition of "generally accepted accounting principles" is provided.
7. Having locally developed and supervised professional accounting examinations and certification.	Accountants in Bahrain are not required to pass uniform local examinations and be certified in order to practice. Thus, no quality control mechanism exists to ensure that only competent people can enter the profession.

(*continued*)

Appendix (Continued)

	The Strategy	*Justification*
8.	Setting local auditing standards.	Currently, there are no locally issued auditing standards that should be followed by auditors practicing in Bahrain. Some auditors claim that they follow International Auditing Standards. Others, claim that they use generally accepted auditing practice. However, no definition of these practices is provided.
B.	Strategies Not Examined in This Study	
1.	Using computers for processing accounting data.	Currently, computers are widely used in processing accounting information in various organizations in Bahrain. In addition, the use of computers in any given organization is determined by the outcome of a cost-benefit analysis specifically performed for this purpose.
2.	Writing accounting standards into law.	The important issue here is to standardize the practice by having a set of generally accepted accounting standards in the country. Whether these standards are written into law or enforced by other means is of secondary importance. In fact, writing accounting standards into law makes them less flexible for amendments and changes which are necessary in today's fast moving and changing business environment.
3.	Determining number of accountants needed by a country.	This strategy assumes that a shortage exists in the number of accountants needed in developing countries. This is not the case in Bahrain because Bahrain has a large number of expatriate accountants working on a limited period contract basis.
4.	Adopting International Accounting Standards (IASs)	IASs are widely used in Bahrain. Banks operating in Bahrain are currently required to prepare their financial reports in compliance with IASs. Many other companies in Bahrain also use IASs on a voluntary basis.
5.	Adopting International Standards of Auditing (ISAs)	Audit firms practicing in Bahrain claim that they are currently following the ISAs issued by IFAC.

NOTES

1. Bahrain is an island nation located in the Arabian Gulf. It is about 15 miles from the east coast of Saudi Arabia.
2. A possible fourth group of accounting experts can be university accounting teachers. However, this group was not considered in this study because a sufficient number of subjects in this group who are sufficiently aware of local accounting profession and practices are not available.
3. Number of subjects in each group was limited to 14 because it is difficult to identify more than 14 people with respect to one group of accounting experts: public sector accountants. The researcher was able to identify only 14 directors of accounting and finance departments in various governmental entities.
4. Bahrain Stock Exchange is the only stock exchange in the country.
5. A copy of the final form of the questionnaire is available from the author upon request.
6. The correlation analysis is based on Spearman Rank (rho) correlation.

7. Nonparametric, rather than parametric, tests were selected because the size of the sample in this study is small.

8. Speech presented by Sh. Ahmed Bin Saqar Al-Khalifa (under-secretary, Ministry of Labor and Social Affairs) in a conference organized by AAT (UK) in Bahrain in January 1996.

9. College of Business at the University of Bahrain is the only school in the country that offers a B.Sc. Degree in accounting.

REFERENCES

Abdolmohammadi, M. J. 1988. A model for educational exchange of accounting faculty between the Pacific Basin countries and advanced world institutions. *Proceedings of the Fifth Pan Pacific Conference,* 515-517. Singapore.

Akathaporn, P., A. M. Novin, and M. J. Abdolmohammadi. 1993. Accounting education and practice in Thailand: Perceived problems and effectiveness of enhancement strategies. *The International Journal of Accounting* 28: 259-272.

American Accounting Association (AAA). 1978. *Accounting Education and the Third World.* A report by the Committee on International Operations and Education, Sarasota, FL.

American Accounting Association (AAA). 1976. Committee on Accounting in Developing Countries report. *The Accounting Review*, Supplement to 51: 198-212.

Arpan, J., and L. Radebaugh. 1985. *International and Multinational Enterprises.* Boston and New York: Warren Gorham and Lamont.

Ashton, R.H. 1991. Experience and error frequency knowledge on potential determinants of audit expertise. *The Accounting Review* 66 (2): 218-239.

Baliga, W. 1993. Lagging state of third-world accounting focus of U.N. forum. *Journal of Accountancy* 175 (6): 15-16.

Belkaoui, A. R. 1994. *International and Multinational Accounting.* Chicago, IL: The Dryden Press.

Bonner, S. E. 1990. Experience effects in auditing: The role of task-specific knowledge. *The Accounting Review* 65 (1): 72-92.

Central Statistics Organization—Directorate of Statistics. 1992. *Statistical Abstract 1991.* Manama, State of Bahrain.

Chandler, J., and H. Holzer. 1981. The need for systems education in developing countries. In *Accounting Education in Economic Development Management,* ed. A. Enthoven. Amsterdam: North-Holland.

Choi, F. D. 1991. *Handbook of International Accounting.* New York: John Wiley & Sons, Inc.

Choi, F. D., and G. G. Mueller. 1992. *International Accounting.* Englewood Cliffs, NJ: Prentice-Hall.

Dillehay, R. and L. Jernigan. 1970. The biased questionnaire as an instrument of opinion change. *Journal of Personality and Social Psychology*: 651-664.

Enthoven, A. J. 1973. *Accounting and Economic Development Policy.* New York: Elsevier.

Enthoven, A. J. 1985. Accounting in developing countries. In *Comparative International Accounting* (2nd ed.), eds. C. Nobes and R. Parker. New York: Philip Allan.

Frederick, D. M. 1991. Auditors representation and retrieval of internal control knowledge. *The Accounting Review* 66 (2): 240-258.

Hove, M. R. 1986. Accounting practices in developing countries: Colonialism's legacy of inappropriate technologies. *The International Journal of Accounting, Education, and Research* 22 (1): 81-100.

Jensen, R. E., and C. E. Arrington. 1983. Accounting education: Turning wrongs into rights in the 1980s. *Journal of Accounting Education* 1 (1): 5-18.

Libby, R. 1985. Availability and the generation of hypotheses in analytical review. *Journal of Accounting Research* 23 (2): 648-667.

Libby, R., and D. M. Frederick. 1990. Expertise and the ability to explain audit findings. *Journal of Accounting Research* 28 (2): 348-367.

Lin, Z., and S. Deng. 1992. Educating accounting in China: Current experiences and future prospects. *The International Journal of Accounting* 27: 144-177.

Ministry of Finance and National Economy. 1991. *30 Years of Economic and Social Development in the State of Bahrain.* Manama, Bahrain: Ministry of Finance and National Economy.

Mueller, G. G. 1968. Accounting principles generally accepted in the United States versus those generally accepted elsewhere. *The International Journal of Accounting* 3 (2): 91-103.

Novin, A. M., and J. Baker. 1990. Enhancing the accounting education and the accounting profession in developing countries. *Foreign Trade Review* (October-December): 247-257.

Oppenheim, A. N. 1966. *Questionnaire Design and Attitude Measurement.* New York: Basic Books Inc.

Radebaugh, S. J., and S. J. Gray. 1997. *International Accounting and Multinational Enterprises* (4th ed.). New York: John Wiley & Sons.

Seidler, L. J. 1967. International accounting—The ultimate theory course. *The Accounting Review* 42 (4): 775-781.

Seidler, L. J. 1969. Nationalism and the international transfer of accounting skills. *The International Journal of Accounting Education and Research* 5 (1): 33-45.

Siegel, S., and N. Castellan, Jr. 1988. *Nonparametric Statistics for the Behavior Science* (2nd ed.). New York: McGraw Hill.

Scott, G. M. 1970. *Accounting in Developing Countries.* University of Washington, Graduate School of Business Administration.

Tipgos, M. A. 1987. A comprehensive model for improving accounting education in developing countries. *Advances in International Accounting* 1: 383-404.

AN EXAMINATION OF THE RELATIONSHIPS AMONG BUDGET PARTICIPATION, INFORMATION ASYMMETRY, BUDGET EMPHASIS, BUDGET ATTITUDES, AND BUDGETARY SLACK:

EVIDENCE BASED ON A CASE STUDY FROM BAHRAIN

P. L. Joshi

ABSTRACT

This chapter reports the results of a study that used multivariate statistical techniques to examine the relationships between budgetary slack and budgetary variables: participation, information asymmetry, budget emphasis, and budget attitudes, based on a case study of a large-sized company located in the State of Bahrain.

Research in Accounting in Emerging Economies, Volume 4, pages 191-210.

ISBN: 1-55938-995-8

Through questionnaire responses from 43 managers a multiple regression model was developed to test the interaction hypothesis. The regression model explained about 67 percent of the variation in budgetary slack and the regression function was found to be statistically significant. The findings indicate that when information asymmetry, budget participation, and budget emphasis are high (low), and budget attitude is positive (negative), budgetary slack will be low (high). In other words, the findings suggest that budgetary slack is lowest when all the independent variables are high and vice versa. A salient feature of the findings is its confirmation that human nature is unchanging across time and space. Echoes from the literature from other environments over the past four decades support this conclusion.

INTRODUCTION

Budgetary control systems and their related procedures involve a number of psychological and behavioral implications for managers in budget planning, execution and control. Horngren and Sundem (1993, 237) argue that "too often, top management and its accountants are overly concerned with the mechanics of budgets, ignoring the fact that effectiveness of any budgeting system depends directly on whether the managers and employees understand and accept the budget." To gain an insight into the behavioral aspects of budgeting, current empirical research has provided some valuable information as to how behavioral factors influence the actual performance of managers in their workplace, for example, impact of excessive budget pressure, the creation of interdepartmental conflicts, the interactive effects of participation and motivation, performance evaluation, creation of budgetary slack, attitudes, and so forth. Among these behavioral issues, the role of participation and the creation of budgetary slack in a participative environment are more relevant because a crucial problem in budget administration is acceptance of budgets by employees. Additionally, Parker (1979) states that participation can offer the facilitation of information exchange in response to uncertainty. If participation releases more information to budget planners, then the uncertainty surrounding their projections will diminish and their plans will be based more upon informed, rational judgments and less upon guesswork. In the light of these, current literature on budgeting appears to lend support to the notion that the contemporary budget process is gradually becoming more participatory. In this regard, Mann (1989) observes that companies frequently include middle and lower level managers in establishing performance goals as well as other aspects of the budget, either because they are most familiar with the operations being budgeted, or because top management wants to obtain motivational benefits from their participation.

Researchers have studied the relationships between participation and budgetary slack, information asymmetry and budgetary slack, budget emphasis in performance evaluation and budgetary slack. In addition, the literature provides some linkages between budgetary slack, participation, information asymmetry and budget emphasis (e.g., Penno 1984; Baiman and Lewis 1989; Dunk 1993). However, there is a lack of attention on the part of the researchers to the study of the role of budget attitudes on budgetary slack. At the same time, most of the studies related to budgetary variables have been conducted, taking data from western and Asia-Pacific countries. Very little evidence is available on budgetary behaviors in utilizing data from Middle Eastern countries. Therefore, the present study makes an attempt to fill this gap in knowledge by studying budgeting and participation in a large-sized company in Bahrain.

The Role of Budget Attitudes

Apart from the participation of subordinates, budget emphasis and information asymmetry, the role of attitudes of subordinates toward budgets may directly or indirectly contribute to the reduction or increase in slack. Prior research has paid little attention to this issue. Oppenheim (1966) defines an attitude as "a state of readiness, a tendency to act or react in a certain manner when confronted with certain stimuli." Baron and Byrne (1984) state that attitudes are a relatively lasting cluster of feelings, beliefs, and behavior tendencies directed toward specific persons, ideas, objects, or groups. Attitudes are reinforced by beliefs and often attract strong feelings that will lead to particular forms of behavior (Katz and Stotland 1959). In other words, as a result of experience, attitudes are viewed as stable dispositions to behave toward objects in a certain way. For example, when managers come to know that management will cut their budgets, they may start developing a definite framework of attitude towards budgets by creating budgetary slack. Kenis's (1979) findings, for example, suggest that managers react positively and relatively strongly to increased clarity of budget goals and that this may also improve budget-related attitudes. Most of the task (goal-setting) studies confirm the positive effects of goal clarity on attitudes and performance (e.g., Latham and Yukl 1975; Steers 1976). It is to be noted that some attitudes go much deeper than others and touch upon one's fundamental philosophy of life, while others are relatively superficial (Oppenheim 1966). Costello and Zalkind (1963, 260) explain that attitudes are learned and the sources of attitudes come from societal influence, major group membership, the family, education, peer groups and prior work experience.

Collins and colleagues (1987) examine the pattern of game play as well as leadership styles and role stress to determine whether these factors are correlated with subordinates' attitudes towards achieving their targets. The study reports that budgetary game patterns are found to be significantly associated with managers' attitude towards achieving their budgets, particularly when considered in the context of their superiors' leadership styles and amount of role stress. Milani (1975) found that attitudes of subordinates towards their job, company, and performance are not significantly associated.

Kenis (1979) suggests that budgetary goal characteristics may play an important role in improving the attitudes of managers towards budgets, while an improperly applied budget can lead to dysfunctional behavior and negative attitudes among managers. Hence, it may be argued that positive attitudes of managers towards budgeting may help in building a somewhat more realistic budget, and the degree of budgetary slack can be reduced. A negative attitude, on the other hand, may lead to the withdrawal of employees' support and cooperation in the budgetary process, subtle attempts to beat the system, and as such, it may lead to the creation of a higher level of budgetary slack. Managers may also play budgets as a game, for example, the end-of-year "spend-it or lose-it" game, the "build-a-kingdom" game, and so on.

Thus, the objective of this chapter is to report on the results of an examination of the relationships among several indicators of budget behavior namely; budgetary slack, participation, information asymmetry, budget emphasis, and budget attitudes. The rest of the chapter is organized as follows. The next section provides a detailed literature review on the subject and derives therefrom the formulation of hypotheses. Then the background, including the description of the budgetary procedures adopted by the company that provides the context of this case study, is discussed. This section also explains the method of selection of respondents. The chapter then explains how the research variables are operationalized in the study. Results are then analyzed and discussed. The conclusions include the limitations of the study.

REVIEW OF LITERATURE

Participation and Budgetary Slack

Argyris (1952) concludes that the greatest contributions from budgetary activities would occur if subordinates were allowed to participate in the activities of budget creation. Other authors have suggested that participation in setting budgetary goals encourages managers to identify with the goals, accept them more fully, and work more toward their achievement (e.g., Becker and Green 1962; Wallace 1966; Hanson 1966; Dunbar 1971). Participation reduces information asymmetry and brings about a greater commitment by the lower level managers to meet the budget. In contrast, it is also said (e.g., Stedry 1967) that participation may not work in all situations because the encouragement of lower and middle level managers to participate in the creation of budgets may have negative effects. Often, managers use their influence to arrive at a goal which is less demanding and can use participation to build slack into the budgets by overestimating costs and underestimating revenues. While some slack may be desirable because it acts as a lubricant for the managers, excessive slack is clearly detrimental to the organization. In this regard, Emmanuel and Otley (1985) state that participation is really a "double-edged sword" as it can give rise to relevant targets being set, but may lead to the creation of budgetary slack. Empirical evidence from the United States of America, the United Kingdom, and other countries provides ample support to the notion that participation in the budget-setting process is usually used as a means to build slack by the subordinate managers into their expected standard of performance. Williamson (1964) provides evidence of early attempts by managers to influence the budget-setting process and obtain budget slack. Cyert and March (1963) opine that budgetary slack arises unintentionally in the bargaining process and is a natural result of the participation process. Schiff and Lewin (1970) in their definitional analysis, and casual evidence provided by Kamin and Ronen (1981), suggest that managers behave as if they are building slack when they are allowed to participate in the budgeting process. In fact, Lowe and Shaw (1968) provide evidence through field research that participation leads to the creation of high slack in the process of sales forecasting.

Additionally, other studies examine whether budgetary slack is a likely result in all participatory environments. Lukka (1988)[1] points out that if there is a high degree of participation in the budget-setting process, this may provide managers with an opportunity to directly contribute to the creation of high slack. On the contrary, Onsi (1973), Cammann (1976), and Merchant (1985) provide evidence that participation may lead to a reduction in slack due to possible communication between managers. In this situation, subordinates feel less compelled to create slack. Besides, there is also evidence that managers operating in a tough environment may bias their estimates in the opposite direction, and set themselves budgets that are unlikely to be achieved (e.g., Otley 1978).

Information Asymmetry and Budgetary Slack

Empirical studies also suggest that the degree of information asymmetry is related to the tendency to encourage participation and the presence of budgetary slack. Subordinates possessing private information which is more than that of their superior is an example of information asymmetry (Dunk 1993). Magee (1980) and Baiman (1982) point out that when subordinates participate in the budget-setting process, it gives superiors an opportunity to gain access to local (private) information which may be incorporated into the standards or budgets against which their performance may be evaluated. Christensen (1982), Pope (1984) and Young (1985) find that subordinates may withhold or misrepresent some of the valuable information in order to create slack. Apparently, it is evident that a subordinate's private information may have the potential to improve the decisions within the organization. However, as Christensen (1982) notes, when participation occurs between the better informed subordinates and less informed superiors, and the subordinates' information is used as a basis for establishing performance targets, the subordinate has the opportunity to cheat. Thus, while participation of subordinates may give superiors access to private information, information asymmetry may still create slack.

Interaction of Participation, Information Asymmetry, Budget Emphasis and Budgetary Slack

Chow and colleagues (1988) and Waller (1988) provide evidence that when budget emphasis is high and coupled with a low degree of information asymmetry, subordinate managers may have the incentive to create slack. But they may not be able to succeed in taking advantage of slack because management may have other methods of detecting it. On the other hand, Baiman and Lewis (1989) argue that if budget emphasis and information asymmetry are both high, then subordinate managers are most likely to go for a negotiated slack budget. Recent evidence is provided by Dunk (1993) on the impact of budget emphasis and information asymmetry on the relationship between budgetary slack and participation. Dunk's study is based on cross-sectional data collected from Australian firms. His study concludes that whether budgetary slack is a likely outcome in all the participative budgets is a matter of conjecture. His study provides little support for the view that high participation may result in increased slack when the other two predictors namely, budget emphasis, and information asymmetry are high. Participation may induce subordinates to create slack. However, participation alone may not be sufficient. Accordingly, his study found that slack is low when participation, information asymmetry and budget emphasis are all high.

Thus, the preceding review of literature on budgetary slack and the related variables suggests that there are three stages of evolution of thoughts since 1960 which are summarized in Table 1.

Table 1. Summary of Literature Review on Budgetary Slack

1.	First stage of evolution of thought: High participation leads to the creation of budgetary slack (e.g., Williamson 1964; Cyert and March 1963; Lowe and Shaw 1968; Schiff and Levin 1970; Kamin and Ronen 1981; Lukka 1988, and even Emmanuel and Otley 1985).
2.	Second stage of evolution of thought: High participation leads to a reduction in budgetary slack (e.g., Onsi 1973; Cammann 1976; Merchant 1985).
3.	Third stage of evolution of thought: Participation alone is not sufficient to create slack; information asymmetry and budget emphasis through interaction with participation may also contribute in generating slack (e.g., Magee 1980; Baiman 1982; Pope 1984; Young 1985; Waller 1988; Baiman and Lewis 1989; Chow et al. 1988: Dunk 1993).

Hypothesis

Since the main concern of this study is to examine relationships and joint effects of budget participation, information asymmetry, budget emphasis and budget attitudes on budgetary slack, then, the following hypothesis is formulated as a basis for this study:

H0: It is predicted that there are no relationships among budgetary slack, information asymmetry, budget participation, budget emphasis and budget attitudes that affect the budgetary slack.

THE COMPANY'S BACKGROUND AND SELECTION OF RESPONDENTS

Dunk (1993) suggests that cross-sectional survey methods may not be sufficient for the investigation of budgetary slack and that case studies may assist in providing additional information on the circumstances in which slack may occur. Therefore, chief executives of three large-sized companies in Bahrain were contacted to conduct this study. Two of them refused to participate in the study, and the remaining company, namely BATELCO, a multi-product telecommunication company was selected as a case study for the present study. The company's annual sales turnover in 1995 was over US$220 million with an employee strength of 2,100. The three large-sized companies were targeted because they were well established and reputable. While it may be argued that a one-company sample may not generate a generalizable set of results, the company which participated in this study is an established one that has reached a stable state where significant changes are unlikely to occur in the future. Also, by studying only one company, the effects of differing corporate tradition will be neutralized as all the managers questioned come from the same company. In addition, such a company will have clearly defined areas of responsibility for managers. However, no restrictions were imposed on the areas of responsibility from which managers could be selected by the researcher.

The company has more than 300 well-defined cost centers. The management control systems are well established and BATELCO has planning and budgetary processes which start at the operational levels. At BATELCO, every department prepares its own budget. Budgetary guidelines and assumptions are decided by all the divisions together. The accounting department coordinates all the other departments in order to prepare an overall budget for the organization. This department also follows up on the budgets on a monthly basis.

The budgetary process begins in the month of July with the preparation of a timetable for the budget for the following year. By the end of September, the final budget is submitted in a consolidated form to the Executive Committee for approval. The company prepares a long-range three-year plan which is revised every year. Each department gives data and information on economic and other environmental variables, key performance indicators, and so forth, in a prescribed format to the accounting department. Data gathered pertain to increases in number of employees; materials usage; material prices and price changes; contractors and other services; insurance requirements; changes in personnel policies that may affect the budget and administration's expectations with regard to policies. Upon completion of the above stages, the company prepares capital, expense, and revenue budgets. Departmental budgets are reviewed by a committee consisting of divisional managers and the general manager of the company.

The company has a 12-grade salary structure. After discussions with the general and divisional managers, it was decided to select grade two, three and four categories of managers because of their deeper understanding of budgetary systems in the company and their involvement in the budgeting exercise. Finally, a total of 47 middle and senior managers responsible for budget preparation were selected from this company.

The research method involved two separate phases: first, a questionnaire was administered to all 47 managers through inter-company mail handled by the personnel department of the company; and second, unstructured, post-hoc interviews were conducted with two divisional managers as well as with 10 managers who were selected randomly. This was undertaken in order to validate the findings of this study and to extract additional information on budgetary slack.

A total of 46 questionnaires were returned, three of which were finally eliminated from the analysis because they did not meet the criteria for information asymmetry (i.e., superiors had more information than the subordinates). Therefore, the responses of 43 managers (91.5 percent response rate) are analyzed in this study. Out of 43 managers, nine (20.9 percent) are expatriates (six British and three Indians). The remaining 34 managers are Bahraini. The respondents' mean age is 41 years and their average length of experience with the company is 12.5 years.

MEASUREMENT OF RESEARCH VARIABLES

To test the hypothesis, procedures for measuring budgetary slack, participation, information asymmetry, budget emphasis, and budget attitudes were drawn from the literature. The measurement of each variable included in the present study is discussed below.

Budgetary Slack

It can be described as a deliberately created difference between honest budget estimates and submitted budget estimates which are padded (Young 1985).

Merchant (1985), Lukka (1988), and Dunk (1993) give a similar definition of slack which is defined as "the express incorporation of budget amounts that are easier to attain."[2]

Budgetary slack is measured with six questions (see Appendix B) developed by Dunk (1993). The items are measured on a seven-point Likert scale, (1) indicating strongly agree and (7) strongly disagree. Dunk reported a Cronbach alpha of 0.681, whereas in this study, the value of Cronbach alpha is 0.755. A factor analysis of this variable reveals that all the items are single factor loaded which accounts for 47.3 percent of total variance.

In order to verify whether the managers were providing correct information on budgetary slack, they were asked two questions. For example, the manager was asked how much slack in terms of percentage he or she incorporated into his or her budget. If the answer was, say 10 percent, then the manager was asked how realistic his or her budgeted amount was. If the answer was, say 85 percent, then the manager was told that in fact he or she incorporated 15 percent slack and not 10 percent. The manager was then given a chance to revise his or her statements.

About 80 percent of managers were willing to state explicitly that they bargain for slack. The managers cited five prime reasons for creating slack:

(i) as a result of pressure from top management to attain budget targets so that profits grow consistently;
(ii) as a hedge against uncertainty;
(iii) as there is no prioritization of all activities, top management often resort to arbitrary cuts in their budgets;
(iv) they feel that it is too time-consuming and bothersome to request revisions in the budget in their company when unexpected conditions arise, and
(v) they doubt management flexibility.

The controller also gave three ways of creating slack in the company:

(i) tendency of management to approve expenditures unwisely towards the end of the period;
(ii) including discretionary special projects, and
(iii) discretionary increase in personnel requirements.

In addition, one of the divisional managers commented that higher degree of slack occurs more frequently in capital expenditure budgets compared to operating budgets. He suggested that as slack cannot be controlled completely, perhaps it may be minimized through (1) the investigation of both positive and negative variances, (2) assuring lower management that subsequent budget allowances will not be affected by past budget excess, and (3) through the introduction of revised budgets to take care of changes after the original budget had been approved.

Budget Participation

It is used to describe the extent to which a subordinate is allowed to select his own course of action (Strauss 1963). In participation, a budget is developed through a process of joint decision making by superiors and subordinates.[3] Milani's (1975) six-item (see Appendix A) measure, used previously in studies of this type, is employed to assess the subordinates' degree of participation in the budgeting process. Earlier analysis performed by Brownell (1982) provides adequate confirmation of the single factor structure of Milani's measure. Therefore, only Milani's measure is used in the analysis. Respondents used a seven-point Likert scale to produce their perceptions of the element of participation. The Cronbach alpha is 0.740. A factor analysis reveals that all the items are single factor loaded which explains 44.3 percent of total variance.

Information Asymmetry

Subordinates often acquire private information in the process of discharging their delegated duties. Young (1985) states that an information asymmetry exists whenever information is known to the subordinates but not to their superiors. This variable is measured by using a six-item (see Appendix A) measure developed by Dunk. Each variable is measured on a point scale of 1 to 7, so that a response recording scale 1 for an item indicates that the superior has more information than his or her subordinates. Whereas, a record of 7 on that item implies that the subordinate manager has more information than his superiors. A subordinate manager had to score more than 24 points on the scale for there to be any information asymmetry. A score of 1 to 3 means that the superiors had more information and a score of 5 to 7 indicates that the subordinate had more information. A score of 4 indicates that both of them had about the same quality of information. Therefore, respondents had to score more than 24 points as there were six questions relating to information asymmetry. A score of 24 indicates a zero level of information asymmetry as per the assumptions made in this study. This type of assumption is also made in other studies, for example, Dunk (1993). Only in the case of three respondents was the score less than 24, which indicated that the information difference was in favor of the superiors. These three cases were dropped from the analysis. The Cronbach alpha is 0.601 and a factor analysis indicates that all six items are single factor loaded which accounts for about 36.0 percent of total variance.

Budget Emphasis

This variable is defined as the superiors' evaluation styles in meeting budget targets and is used to evaluate the performance of subordinates (Hopwood 1972). An eight-item (see Appendix B) measure developed by Hopwood (1972) and subsequently used by other researchers (e.g., Otley 1978; Brownell 1982, 1985; Dunk

1993) is used, with some changes in the style of administration and wording (e.g., "How well I achieve my budget targets" "How efficiently I manage my costs." Whereas Hopwood's original instrument was "meeting the budget"; "concern with costs"). To address budget emphasis, the eight-item measure was used by Hopwood to determine the styles of evaluation by the presence or absence of the item in "meeting the budget" and "concern with cost." Only the item "meeting the budget" is considered as an indicator of budget emphasis. This item is measured on a Likert scale of 1 to 7 in this study.

Budget Attitudes

This variable is defined as subordinates' feelings, disposition and/or feelings about the budget-setting process (Milani 1975). It is measured with nine questions (see Appendix B) developed by Collins (1978) and subsequently used by Collins and colleagues (1987). The items are anchored on a seven-point Likert scale by (1) strongly disagree and (7) strongly agree. Subordinates are considered to have a positive attitude if they strive to meet or exceed their budgets, or even induce other subordinates to achieve their budgets. A negative attitude is considered to be developed when they withhold support of the budget or do not induce other subordinates to achieve their budgets. A factor analysis of the budget attitude measures indicated that one item, namely, "I often receive recognition for achieving budget goals" did not load on the factor at 0.35 level,[4] which was the criterion for item inclusion; therefore, this item was dropped from the instrument. The remaining eight items are single factor loaded which accounts for 40.4 percent of total variance. The Cronbach alpha is 0.75 for the eight item measures. Descriptive

Table 2. Descriptive Statistics for Budget Participation, Budget Emphasis, Budget Attitudes, Information Asymmetry, and Budgetary Slack

Variable	*n*	*Mean*	*Std. Dev.*	*Actual Min*	*Range Max*
Budgetary slack	43	23.41	6.06	12 (6)	36 (42)
Information asymmetry	43	31.72	4.09	25 (6)	40 (42)
Budget participation	43	29.44	5.16	11 (6)	38 (42)
Budget emphasis	43	4.93	1.53	2 (1)	7 (7)
Budget attitudes	43	40.18	8.08	21 (8)	53 (5)

Note: Figures in parentheses show theoretical (minimum and maximum) ranges.

Table 3. Reliability Test (Cronbach Alpha)

Variables	*No. of items*	*Cronbach Alpha*
Budgetary slack	6	0.755
Information asymmetry	6	0.601
Budget participation	6	0.740
Budget emphasis	1	NA
Budget attitudes	8	0.750

Note: Results computed on the STATISTICA software package.

statistics and the values for Cronbach alpha for each variable are presented in Tables 2 and 3 respectively.

RESULTS AND DISCUSSION

The following regression model was used to test the interaction hypothesis:

$$\begin{aligned} BS = {} & b_0 + b_1 IA + b_2 BP + b_3 BE + b_4 BA + b_5 IAxBP + b_6 IAxBE \\ & + b_7 IAxBA + b_8 BPxBE + b_9 BPxBA + b_{10} BExBA + b_{11} IAxBPxBE \\ & + b_{12} IAxBPxBA + b_{13} IAxBExBA + b_{14} BPxBExBA \\ & + b_{15} IAxBPxBAxBE + e \end{aligned}$$

where: *BS* = budgetary slack
IA = information asymmetry
BP = budget participation
BE = budget emphasis
BA = budget attitudes.

In the regression analysis, budgetary slack is taken as the dependent variable. Four independent variables, namely, budget participation, budget emphasis, information asymmetry, and budget attitudes are regressed on the dependent variable. Table 4 reports the coefficients of correlations between pairs of these variables. The low coefficients suggest that there is no risk of multicollinearity if these variables were introduced into a regression analysis. Table 5 shows that the interactive variable (b_{15}) is found to be statistically significant at $p = < 0.008$ and that the model as a whole explains about 67 percent of the variations in budgetary slack ($p < 0.001$). In other words, the results indicate that when information asymmetry, budget participation, and budget emphasis are high (low), and budget attitude is positive (negative), budgetary slack will be low (high). Therefore, the analysis rejects the null hypothesis. The overall regression function is found to be significant at $p < 0.001$ level as indicated by the F-ratio (value = 3.582). The variables that prove to be significant are information asymmetry

Table 4. Correlation Among Independent Variable

	Information asymmetry	*Budget participation*	*Budget emphasis*	*Budget attitude*
Information asymmetry	1.000			
Budget participation	–0.015	1.000		
Budget emphasis	0.091	0.165	1.000	
Budget attitudes	0.014	0.140	0.136	1.000

(b_1) ($t = 3.148$; $p < 0.01$), budget participation (b_2) ($t = -3.065$; $p < 0.01$), budget emphasis (b_3) ($t = 2.853$; $p < 0.01$), and budget attitudes ($t = 2.99$; $p < 0.01$). When the nationality of the respondents (a proxy for culture variables; 0 for Bahraini and 1 for non-Bahraini) is incorporated in the regression equation as a dummy variable, however, no significant effect is observed in the results. Therefore, the results are not reported here.

Thus, the results provide evidence in support of the utility of participative budgeting, but fail to support the view that when participation, information asymmetry, and budget emphasis are high and budget attitude is positive, budgetary slack will be high. In other words, the findings suggest that budgetary slack is lowest when all the independent variables are high and vice versa. The findings seem to be in line with the findings of Onsi (1973), Merchant (1985), and Dunk (1993).

To justify these findings, the basic logic dictates that the greater the ignorance or information gap between superiors and subordinates, the greater the slack may be. Since a manager does not like to be described as under-performing, s/he has to protect him/herself from blame by building more slack into the budget. When information asymmetry and participation are low (in practice, participation more often tends to be pseudo participation), the manager may prepare a budget based on guesswork, gut feeling, or past experience and overestimate budget requirements, and thus budgeting may be imbued with the game spirit. Besides, management quite often keep informal pressure or pressure through budgets on their employees. To overcome the negative impact of such work-related pressure, managers often introduce organizational slack into the system (Hofstede 1967).

A salient aspect of the findings from this study is its confirmation that human nature is unchanging across time and space. Echoes from the literature in the past four decades support this conclusion. For example, Abruzzi (1956) concluded that the budget centers "cheat" and "distort" their production record in order to make the record reflect what they believe would result in their own benefit. Similarly, Jasinski (1956) provided evidence which suggests that budget centers fudge records to serve their interest. Additionally, the budget review process at a high level may lack rigor because of time pressures. The review process is usually broad based because it takes a macro view of the budget estimates. In this regard, Anthony and colleagues (1985) rightly state that "lack of definite policies

Table 5. Results of Hypothesis Test

Variables	*Coefficient*	*Value**	*t-test*	*p-value*
Intercept	b_0	–520.67 (224.32)	–2.319	0.020
Information asymmetry	b_1	13.07 (4.15)	3.148	0.003
Budget participation	b_2	–111.08 (36.23)	–3.065	0.004
Budget emphasis	b_3	97.56 (34.19)	2.853	0.008
Budget attitudes	b_4	33.73 (11.24)	2.990	0.005
Information asymmetry × Budget participation	b_5	277.93 (90.07)	3.085	0.004
Information asymmetry × budget emphasis	b_6	–232.18 (82.56)	–2.812	0.009
Information asymmetry × Budget attitudes	b_7	–74.70 (20.46)	–3.650	0.001
Budget participation × Budget emphasis	b_8	25.13 (14.27)	1.760	0.089
Budget participation × Budget attitudes	b_9	577.52 (154.02)	3.749	0.000
Budget emphasis × Budget attitudes	b_{10}	–631.66 (172.31)	–3.665	0.001
Information asymmetry × Budget participation × Budget emphasis	b_{11}	–2.36 (1.59)	–1.478	0.150
Information asymmetry × Budget participation × Budget attitudes	b_{12}	–302.77 (72.14)	-4.196	0.000
Information asymmetry × Budget emphasis × Budget attitudes	b_{13}	220.60 (63.71)	3.462	0.001
Budget participation × Budget emphasis × Budget attitudes	b_{14}	174.03 (72.51)	2.400	0.023
Information asymmetry × Budget participation × Budget emphasis × Budget attitudes	b_{15}	–39.32 (13.83)	–2.843	0.008

Notes: R-square = 0.665; n = 43; F = 3.582; df = (15, 27) ($p < 0.01$).
* Figures in parentheses show standard errors.

regarding budgets, and failure by higher level management to take sufficient time to evaluate budgetary requests often cause 'padding' to occur. It can be said that budget padding problems exist because of insufficient attention to policy-making, communication, the budget approval process and ineffective leadership."

CONCLUSIONS AND LIMITATIONS OF THE STUDY

The results of the present case study show that there is some bond of association between budgetary slack, budget participation, budget emphasis, information asymmetry and budget attitudes. The overall relationship is found to be negative and statistically significant, and the interaction model explains about 67 percent of the variations in budgetary slack.

The findings of this study, however, should be considered in the light of their limitations. The scope of the study is limited by its sample size, measures of budget attitudes, weak measure of information asymmetry, organizational level, and industrial coverage. Only middle and senior managers are covered. Perhaps the results may have been different if managers from other organizations and other levels of management had been included in the sample. The Likert-type attitude measurements used may also have produced some response bias. Further, as results are obtained from data derived from a case study, such results may not be extended to other sectors of that population. Another limitation of the study is that statistical inference is derived from one company and in one budget period. Perhaps results would have been different were the analyzed data to be drawn from several budget periods. Therefore, further investigation may be required to study the circumstances in which budgetary slack may occur by incorporating corporate culture, managerial roles (classified by line and staff functions), and multiple budget periods in the analysis.

APPENDIX A

Results of Factor Analysis

	Question	*Factor Loading*
Budgetary Slack:	v1	0.773
	v2	0.662
	v3	0.706
	v4	0.763
	v5	0.588
	v6	0.591
Eigen value: 2.841% of variance explained: 47.3 %		

(continued)

Appendix A (Continued)

	Question	Factor Loading
Information Asymmetry:	v1	0.622
	v2	0.360
	v3	0.680
	v4	0.571
	v5	0.420
	v6	0.789
Eigen value: 2.147% of variance explained: 35.8%		
Budget Participation:	v1	0.767
	v2	0.797
	v3	0.734
	v4	0.416
	v5	0.728
	v6	0.538
Eigen value: 2.658% of variance explained: 44.3%		
Budget Attitudes:	v1	0.822
	v2	0.640
	v3	0.367
	v4	0.673
	v5	0.752
	v6	0.396
	v7	0.709
	v8	0.698
Eigen value: 3.229% of variance explained: 40.4 %		

APPENDIX B

List of Questions Included in the Study

BUDGETARY SLACK:

1. Standards set in the budget include high productivity in my area of responsibility (V1).
2. Budgets fixed for my area of responsibility are safely attainable (V2).
3. I have to carefully monitor costs in my area of responsibility because of budgetary constraints (V3).
4. Budgets for my area of responsibility are not particularly demanding (V4).
5. Budgetary targets have not caused me to be particularly concerned with improving efficiency in my area of responsibility (V5).
6. Targets incorporated in the budgets are difficult to reach (V6).

(continued)

Appendix B (Continued)

INFORMATION ASYMMETRY:

1. In comparison with your superior, who is in possession of better information regarding the activities undertaken in your area of responsibility? (V1).
2. In comparison with your superior, who is more familiar with the input-output relationships inherent in the internal operations of your area of responsibility? (V2).
3. In comparison with your superior, who is more certain of the performance potential of your area of responsibility? (V3).
4. In comparison with your superior, who is more familiar technically with your area of responsibility? (V4).
5. In comparison with your superior who is better able to assess the potential impact on your activities of factors external to your area of responsibility? (V5).
6. In comparison with your superior, who has better understanding of what can be achieved in your area of responsibility? (V6).

BUDGET PARTICIPATION:

1. The portion of the budget you are involved in setting (V1).
2. The kind of reasoning provided to the budget manager by the superior when budget is revised (V2).
3. The frequency of budget related discussions initiated by the budget manager (V3).
4. The amount of influence the budget manager felt he had on the final budget (V4).
5. The importance of the budget manager's contribution to the budget (V5).
6. The frequency of budget related discussions initiated by the budget manager's superiors when budgets are being revised (V6).

BUDGET EMPHASIS:

1. How well I get along with my boss (V1).
2. The effort I put into my job (V2).
3. How well I achieve my budget targets (meeting the budget) (V3).
4. My concern with quality (V4).
5. How efficiently I manage my costs in the budget period (concern with costs) (V5).
6. My attitude towards my work and company (V6).
7. My ability to handle employees (V7).
8. My co-operation with my colleagues (V8).

(continued)

Appendix B (Continued)

BUDGETARY ATTITUDES:	
1.	I frequently make a sincere personal effort to achieve my budgetary objectives (V1).
2.	I never get what I want in my budget (V2).
3.	My boss believes budgeting is very important (V3).
4.	I frequently allow erroneous or incompatible data to be put into the budgetary process even though this may hamper budget administration (V4).
5.	My budget requests are often approved (V5).
6.	I often exceed my approved budget objectives (V6).
7.	I frequently feel a personal sense of failure when budget objectives are not met (V7).
8.	I frequently withhold my full support of the budget (V8).
9.	I often receive recognition for achieving budget goals (V9).

ACKNOWLEDGMENTS

The author is extremely grateful to two anonymous referees for their comments and suggestions for improving this chapter. Special thanks are due to Professor R.S.O. Wallace for his thought-provoking comments and for providing editorial assistance for this chapter. Thanks are due to Dr. Peterson, University of Bahrain, for his comments on the earlier draft of this chapter. However, for any error, I own the responsibility. An earlier version of this chapter was presented at the 18th Annual Congress of the European Accounting Association held in Birmingham in 1995.

NOTES

1. Lukka (1988) gives a list of factors, such as individual goals, reward structure, organizational norms, and uncertainty, which may influence the building of slack. Welsch and colleagues (1988) state that slack often results from a logically circular phenomenon.
2. Managers build slack into the budget because the budget may be typically cut in the higher level review and budgets are cut because slack is created (see Welsch et al., 56).
3. This is consistent with agency theory. Agency theory models a situation in which a principal (superior) delegates decision making authority to an agent (subordinate) who receives a reward in return for performing some activity on behalf of the principal.
4. Evidence is there that researchers have even considered a 0.30 factor loading as the cut off point for the selection of variables in factor analysis (see Onsi 1973).

REFERENCES

Abruzzi, A. 1956. Theory of work management. *Management Science* 2 (2): 114-130.

Anthony, R. N., G. A. Welsch, and J. S. Reece. 1985. *Fundamentals of Management Accounting*. Homewood, IL: Irwin.

Argyris, C. 1952. *The Impact of Budgets on People*. New York: Controllership Foundation Inc.

Baiman, S. 1982. Agency research in management accounting: A survey. *Journal of Accounting Literature* 1: 154-213.

Baiman, S., and B. Lewis. 1989. An experimental testing of the behavioural equivalence of strategically equivalent employment contracts. *Journal of Accounting Research* 27 (1): 1-20.

Baron, R. A., and D. Byrne. 1984. *Social psychology: Understanding human interaction* (4th ed.). Boston: Allyn and Bacon.

Becker, S., and D. Green. 1962. Budgeting and human behavior. *The Journal of Business* 35 (3): 392-402.

Brownell, P. 1982. The role of accounting data in performance evaluation, budgetary participation, and organizational effectiveness. *Journal of Accounting Research* 20 (2): 12-27.

Becker, S., and D. Green. 1985. Budgetary systems and the control of functionally differentiated organizational activities. *Journal of Accounting Research* 23 (2): 502-512.

Cammann, C. 1976. Effects of the use of control systems. *Accounting, Organizations and Society* 1 (4): 301-313.

Chow, C. W., J. C. Cooper and W. S. Waller. 1988. Participative budgeting: Effects of truth inducing pay scheme and information asymmetry on slack and performance. *The Accounting Review* 63 (1): 111-122.

Christensen, J. 1982. The determination of performance standards and participation. *Journal of Accounting Research* 20 (2): 589-603.

Collins, F. 1978. The interaction of budget characteristics and personality variables with budgetary response attitudes. *The Accounting Review* 55 (2): 324-325.

Collins F., P. Munter, and D. W. Finn. 1987. The budgeting games people play. *The Accounting Review* 62 (1): 29-49.

Costello, T. W., and S. S. Zalkind. 1963. *Psychology in Administration*. Englewood Cliffs, NJ: Prentice-Hall.

Cyert R. M., and J. G. March. 1963. *The Behavioural Theory of the Firm*. Englewood Cliffs, NJ.: Prentice-Hall Inc.

Dunbar, R. L. M. 1971. Budgeting for control. *Administrative Science Quarterly* (March): 88-96.

Dunk, A. S. 1993. The effect of budget emphasis and information asymmetry on the relation between budgetary participation and slack. *The Accounting Review* 68 (2): 400-410.

Emmanuel, C., and D. T. Otley. 1985. *Accounting for Management Control*. London: Van Nostrand Reinhold.

Hanson, E. I. 1966. The budgetary control function. *The Accounting Review* 41 (2): 239-243.

Hofstede, G. H. 1967. *The game of budgetary control*. Netherlands: Koninklijke Van Corcum and Comp. N.V. Assen.

Hopwood, A. G. 1972. An empirical study of the role of accounting data in performance evaluation. *Journal of Accounting Research* 10 (Supplement): 156-182.

Horngren, C. T., and G. L. Sundem. 1993. *Introduction to Management Accounting*. Englewood Cliffs, NJ: Prentice-Hall Inc.

Jasinski, F. 1956. Use and misuse of efficiency controls. *Harvard Business Review* (July-August).

Kamin, J. Y., and J. Ronen. 1981. Effects of budgetary control on management sciences: Some empirical evidence. *Decision Sciences*: 471-485.

Katz, D., and E. Stotland. 1959. A preliminary statement to a theory of attitude structure and change. In *Psychology: A Study of Science*. Vol. 3: *Formulations of the Person and the Social Context*, ed. S. Koch. New York: McGraw Hill Inc.

Kenis, I. 1979. Effects of budgetary goal characteristics on managerial attitudes and performance. *The Accounting Review* 54 (4): 707-721.

Latham, G. P., and G. A. Yukl. 1975. A review of research on the application of goal setting in organizations. *Academy of Management Journal* (December): 824-845.

Lowe, E. A., and R. W. Shaw. 1968. An analysis of managerial biasing: Evidence from a company's budgeting process. *The Journal of Management Studies* 5 (3): 304-315.

Lukka, K. 1988. Budgetary biasing in organization: Theoretical framework and empirical evidence. *Accounting, Organizations and Society* 13 (3): 281-301.

Mann, G. J. 1989. Reducing the budget slack. *Journal of Accountancy* (August): 116-120.

Merchant, K. A. 1985. Budgeting and propensity to create budgetary slack. *Accounting, Organizations, and Society* 10 (2): 201-210.

Magee, R. P. 1980. Equilibria in budget participation. *Journal of Accounting Research*, 18 (2): 551-573.

Milani, K. 1975. Relationship of participation in budget setting to industrial supervisor performance and attitudes. *The Accounting Review* 50 (2): 274-284.

Onsi, M. 1973. Factor analysis of behavioral variables affecting budgetary slack. *The Accounting Review* 48 (3): 535-548.

Oppenheim, A. N. 1966. *Questionnaire Design and Attitude Measurement.* Great Britain: Gover Publishing Company.

Otley, D. T. 1978. Budget use and managerial performance. *Journal of Accounting Research* 16 (1): 122-149.

Parker, L. D. 1979. Participation in budget planning: The prospects surveyed. *Accounting & Business Research* 9 (34): 123-137.

Penno, M. 1984. Asymmetry of pre-decision information and managerial accounting. *Journal of Accounting Research* 22 (1): 177-191.

Pope, P. F. 1984. Information asymmetries in participative budgeting: A bargaining approach. *Journal of Business Finance & Accounting* 11 (1): 41-59.

Schiff, M., and A. Y. Lewin. 1970. Where traditional budgeting fails. *Financial Executive* 36 (5): 50-62.

Stedry, A. C. 1967. *Budget Control and Cost Behaviour.* New York: Markham Publishing Company.

Steers, R. M. 1976. Task-goal attributes, achievement, and supervisory performance. *Organization Behaviour and Human Performance* (June): 392-403.

Strauss, G. 1963. Some notes on power equalization, and supervisory performance. *Organization Behaviour and Human Performance* (June): 392-403.

Wallace, M. E. 1966. Behavioural consideration in budgeting. *Management Accounting* (August): 3-8.

Waller, W. S. 1988. Slack in participating budgeting: The joint effect of a truth inducing pay scheme and risk preferences. *Accounting, Organizations, and Society* 13 (1): 87-98.

Welsch, G. A., R. N. Hilton, and P. N. Gordon. 1988. *Budgeting: Profit Planning and Control.* Englewood Cliffs, NJ: Prentice-Hall Inc.

Williamson, O. E. 1964. *The Economics of Discretionary Behavior: Managerial Objectives in a Theory of the Firm.* Englewood Cliffs, NJ: Prentice-Hall Inc.

Young, S. M. 1985. Participating budgeting: The effects of risk aversion and asymmetric information on budgetary slack. *Journal of Accounting Research* 23 (2): 29-42.

THE DISTRIBUTION OF FINANCIAL RATIOS OF SAUDI ARABIAN COMPANIES

J. S. Al-Rumaihi, D. M. Power, and C. D. Sinclair

ABSTRACT

This study examines the distribution of accounting ratios for 37 Saudi Arabian companies over a four-year period from 1990 to 1993. Specifically, the distributions of four profitability ratios, three efficiency ratios, two liquidity ratios, and one gearing and one stock market ratio are analyzed. The results indicate that the distributions of these ratios are not normal. After trimming outlier observations and transforming the data, however, approximate normality is achieved. Accounting ratio data for Saudi firms may therefore need to be adjusted before being analyzed using statistical techniques which assume that variables are normally distributed.

Research in Accounting in Emerging Economies, Volume 4, pages 211-225.

ISBN: 1-55938-995-8

INTRODUCTION

Financial ratios have been used in a variety of contexts to evaluate published accounting information since the late 1980s.[1] Some of these contexts include audit risk assessment, bankruptcy prediction (Altman 1968), bond rating (Pinches and Mingo 1973), commercial credit scoring (Kaplan and Urwitz 1979) and security analysis (O'Connor 1973). The use of financial ratios to appraise the performance and financial status of a firm is based on a number of assumptions.[2] One of the more important of these assumptions is that the cross-sectional distribution of the ratios is known, and it is this assumption which is subjected to critical scrutiny in this chapter.

Understanding the nature of the cross-sectional distribution of financial ratios is important for the following reasons.[3] First, knowledge of the particular distribution of a ratio may help to identify an appropriate benchmark against which to judge a firm's performance; if the ratio is normally distributed, then the industry mean may be a suitable measure of comparison, but if it is not normally distributed, then the median may be a more appropriate figure. Second, outlying values of a particular ratio can be identified and their distorting effect on any statistical analysis can be mitigated once the distribution of the ratio is known. Third, knowledge of the distribution can influence the choice of statistical techniques to be employed when analyzing financial ratios; for example, statistical analysis of ratios using ordinary least squares regression to examine the relationship between a ratio and a variable of interest requires that the ratios be normally distributed and if this assumption is invalid, the inferences drawn from the analysis may be inappropriate. Finally, Buckmaster and Siniga (1990, 149) argue that understanding a particular ratio's distribution will help in the selection of a suitable procedure to transform the distribution from one shape into another if the original distribution is inappropriate to the statistical test being considered (see also Bougan and Drury 1980).

The purpose of this chapter is to examine the distribution characteristics of 11 financial ratios for a sample of Saudi Joint Stock Companies. To date, a lot of research has been undertaken into the distribution of accounting ratios of companies in developed markets such as the United Kingdom and the United States. However, very little is known about the distribution of these ratios for companies in less-developed countries such as Saudi Arabia. The findings of this study should therefore be important to both practitioners and academics. This study should help Saudi analysts to evaluate the financial performance of a particular company by enabling them to compare the magnitude of a particular ratio with the distribution of this ratio for that whole economy. Also, this study is timely in that it should aid the growing number of researchers who are beginning to undertake academic studies involving accounting data from Saudi companies to establish the appropriate method of analysis to use.

The remainder of this chapter is divided into four sections. The next section summarizes the findings of previous research. The third section describes the data used in the study. The fourth section outlines the statistical tests which were conducted and discusses the results. The final section presents the conclusions.

THE FINDINGS OF PREVIOUS RESEARCH

Research into the distribution of financial ratios goes back several decades and was carried out primarily in the United States. For example, Horrigan (1965) was one of the first to analyze the cross-sectional distribution of a large number of financial ratios in a systematic fashion; he examined the distribution of 17 ratios for 50 companies for the period 1948 to 1957. His main conclusion was that the financial ratios for his sample tended to be approximately normally distributed but were frequently positively skewed. He suggested that this result was due to the fact that "most of these ratios have an effective lower limit of zero but an indefinite upper limit" (559). In a follow-up U. S. study, O'Connor (1973) investigated the cross-sectional distributions of 10 ratios for a larger sample of 127 U.S. companies over a more recent period—January 1950 to March 1966—and found that there was widespread skewness in the ratios' distributions. However, in spite of this skewness, he reported that the nature of the distributions tend to be approximately symmetrical.

In one of the most comprehensive analyses in this area to date, Deakin (1976) examined the cross-sectional distributions of 11 ratios for all U.S. manufacturing companies listed on the COMPUSTAT data file for the period 1955-1973. He found that the distributions of the ratios deviated significantly from the normal distribution except for the total debt/total asset ratio. However, the skewness in the ratios' distributions could be reduced by applying square root or log-normal transformations to the data.[4]

Bird and McHugh (1977) extended Deakin's analysis by focusing on the distribution of ratios within an industry. Specifically, they examined the distribution of five ratios for 68 companies in three industries for the years 1967, 1969 and 1971: the food sector, the electricity sector and the housing sector. They utilized the Shapiro-Wilk (1965) test for normality and concluded that "the financial leverage and efficiency ratios were generally normally distributed in all industries but the quick asset and asset structure ratios were generally not normally distributed at the [5 percent] significance level."

Frecka and Hopwood (1983) were two of the first scholars to investigate the impact of outliers[5] on the cross-sectional distribution of 11 financial ratios of U.S. firms for the period 1950-1979; they analyzed the ratios which were examined in Deakin's study. The size of their sample varied over the time period covered and ranged from 346 firms in 1950 to 1,243 firms in 1978. The main conclusion of their study was that the skewed ratio distributions which Deakin had highlighted were due to the existence of outliers. Furthermore, using a square root transformation to adjust the raw data, normality or approximate normality could be attained except for the cash flow/total debt ratio.

The impact of outliers on the distribution of the 11 ratios used in Deakin's 1976 study was investigated more recently by So (1987). He used data for the period from 1970 to 1979. The results of his study extended the conclusion of Frecka and Hopwood. According to his analysis, there were a number of factors,[6] in addition to the existence of outliers, which caused the distribution to be nonnormal; removing the outliers did not necessarily imply that a normal distribution would be achieved for all the ratios examined in his study.

Recent research into the distribution of accounting ratios has employed more sophisticated testing procedures. For example, Buckmaster and Siniga (1990) investigated distributional forms for 41 ratios of large industrial firms based on two systems of frequency curves suggested by Pearson and Johnson.[7] The data were collected from the quarterly industrial COMPUSTAT tapes for the period 1969-1978. In addition to investigating whether or not the distributions of ratios were normal, they also determined the actual shape of the distributions. Their findings supported the earlier research which had shown that ratios were not normally distributed; they reported that the majority of the distributions analyzed in their study took the form of the J-shape.[8] In addition, most of the distribution forms tended to be stable over time.

Throughout the 1980s and 1990s, and increasing number of studies have analyzed data from countries other than the United States. Whittington (1980), Bougan and Drury (1980), and Sudarsanam and Taffler (1995)[9] have examined the distributions of financial ratios for U. K. firms, while Martikainen and colleagues (1995) have analyzed Finnish data.[10] The findings of these non-U. S. studies have generally supported the findings of their U. S. counterparts. Accounting ratios tend to be positively skewed and need to be transformed before they approximate a normal distribution.

DATA, STATISTICAL TESTS, AND CALCULATIONS

The financial ratio data used in this study were obtained from the Market Report data base which is constructed by the Dowlog Technology Company.[11] This data base includes a wide range of accounting information for 62 Saudi joint stock companies beginning in 1987. However, this study does not use data for the whole of this time period because only a small number of companies were initially included in the dataset. The data in this study cover the four-year period from 1990 to 1993. Only a subset of the total sample of companies in the data base are considered in this investigation. Electricity companies were eliminated from the study on the ground that information for these firms was not complete; a large number of the accounting ratios for companies in this sector could not be calculated because certain information was not included in their annual financial statements. In addition, all 11 banks were excluded from the study because a unique set of ratios with features which are quite different from those of other industries tend to be calculated for the institutions in this sector. The final sample included 37 firms which represents 60 percent of the quoted firms in Saudi Arabia.[12,13] These firms are spread across the four main sectors represented in the Saudi economy: data for seven agricultural companies, seven cement companies, 12 manufacturing companies and 11 service sector firms were analyzed. The findings of this study should therefore not be attributable to the distribution of ratios in any one sector but rather have economy-wide generalizability.

The distributions of 11 ratios are examined for the sample of firms in this study.[14] Four measures of profitability were analyzed: the gross profit margin (GPM), the net profit margin (NPM), return on equity (ROE) and return on total assets (RTA). Three measures of efficiency were also considered: the cost of goods sold/sales ratio (COG), the total expenses/sales ratio (TES) and the asset turnover ratio (ATR). Two measures of liquidity were calculated; the current ratio (CUR) and the current assets/total liabilities ratio (CTL). Finally, one leverage measure—the total liabilities/total equity ratio (LEV)—and one stock market ratio—the price/earnings ratio (P/E)—were estimated. Obviously, other ratios could have been calculated from the financial statement information but the 11 ratios selected have the virtues of (i) spanning different aspects of firm performance, (ii) being used in practice, and (iii) facilitating comparison with other studies from developed countries which have analyzed these measures. These ratios are widely used to assess various aspects of company performance; they tend to be calculated by investors when analyzing financial statements to determine whether or not they should purchase or retain shares in a company. They are also calculated by bankers and other creditors in evaluating the risks of their loans to local firms. Finally, these ratios are increasingly being estimated by academics who wish to examine company performance and possibly relate this performance to stock market share price and trading volume activity (Al-Bogami 1996).

SAMPLE STATISTICS

A number of descriptive statistics were calculated for each ratio and are displayed in Table 1. In particular, the mean (MEAN), the standard deviation (STDEV), the minimum (MIN) and maximum (MAX) values were estimated for all ratios. Measures of skewness (SKEW) and kurtosis (KURT) were also calculated; the former measure indicates whether the shape of the distribution is symmetrical while the latter statistic tests whether the number of extreme obervations of the ratio differs from what one would expect if the values of the ratio were normally distributed.

Table 1. Descriptive Statistics for the Ratios of the Sample Firms

RATIO	*N*	*MEAN*	*STDEV*	*MIN*	*MAX*	*SKEW*	*KURT*
GPM	112	28.429	29.125	−116.499	100.000	−0.735	6.147
						(0.228)	(0.453)
COG	100	74.666	18.305	45.767	155.690	1.293	3.650
						(0.241)	(0.467)
TES	104	17.001	22.319	0.140	215.355	7.147	61.687
						(0.237)	(0.469)
P/E	132	21.241	56.658	−319.398	353.155	−0.441	20.741
						(0.211)	(0.419)
CUR	148	6.428	16.864	0.449	146.099	7.135	54.325
						(0.199)	(0.396)
CTL	148	5.488	13.978	0.446	117.141	6.903	51.008
						(0.199)	(0.396)
LEV	148	0.376	0.350	0.008	1.661	1.557	2.453
						(0.199)	(0.396)
NPM	112	17.035	33.276	−127.565	104.680	−1.268	5.407
						(0.228)	(0.453)
ATR	112	0.357	0.273	0.010	1.191	1.205	0.936
						(0.228)	(0.453)
ROE	144	8.004	10.101	−29.982	35.692	−0.469	2.229
						(0.202)	(0.401)
ROA	144	5.933	7.668	−21.789	24.805	−0.408	1.736
						(0.202)	(0.401)

Note: See Appendix for definitions of ratios.

Four main points emerge from an analysis of this table. First, there is a wide range of values reported in the table. The mean company in the sample appears to be profitable, highly liquid, financed primarily by equity and trades at a fairly high P/E multiple in the stock market. A comparison of these descriptive results with the summary statistics reported in Bougan and Drury (1980) suggests that the Saudi companies examined in this study have (i) a higher net profit margin and current ratio and (ii) a lower leverage than their U.K. counterparts. For example, the mean net profit margin of the Saudi companies in this sample was 17 percent, compared with 8.9 percent for the U.K. firms, while the average leverage of the Saudi firms at 35.6 percent was almost half the value reported for the typical U.K. company. As one would expect, larger U.K. companies with relatively easy access to short-term funding if required, are able to operate with a much lower safety level of liquidity, and service a much higher level of debt.[15] Second, there seems to be a great deal of volatility in the ratios of the sample firms since the standard deviation values are relatively large.[16] This is especially true for the price/earnings ratio, the current ratio, the current asset/total liability ratio and the net profit margin ratio, where the standard deviation is more than twice the value of the mean. This high degree of variability is confirmed by an analysis of the minimum and maximum values; the gap between these two figures is extremely large for several of the ratios analyzed. Third, the ratios examined in this study do not appear to be normally distributed—a finding which is similar to the results obtained in the vast majority of investigations using data from developed countries (e.g., Deakin 1976). Seven of the 11 ratios do not have any negative values. Also, the skewness and kurtosis statistics are all significant at the 5 percent level, indicating that the distributions of these ratios are not symmetrical and tend to have an unusually high proportion of extreme values. Finally, five of the ratios were positively skewed while six were negatively skewed.[17] Of the five ratios which were positively skewed, four related to measures of profitability and the fifth related to the price/earnings ratio. The leverage, efficiency and liquidity ratios were all negatively skewed; they had a large tail of small or negative values. This finding conflicts with the results from the majority of the U.S. and U.K. literature which suggests that most accounting ratios are positively skewed (e.g., Bird and McHugh 1977).

A FORMAL TEST OF NORMALITY

The NSCORES test (Filliben 1975) was used to investigate whether each ratio was normally distributed. This test is essentially equivalent to the Shapiro-Wilk (1965) test, and is based on the straightness of a quantile-quantile plot; this graph plots the ordered values of the ratio against the expected values of the order statistics for a sample of the same number of observations from the standard normal distribution. The test therefore compares the actual distribution with a normal distribution for a series with the same mean and an identical number of observations. A straight line plot is consistent with the view that the ratio is normally distributed. The straightness of the plot is typically assessed, using correlation analysis. Consequently, normality is rejected if the correlation between the actual and expected series falls below the critical value. The results of this test for the complete set of values of each ratio are shown in Table 2.

The findings in this table confirm the earlier results from analyzing the descriptive statistics; the hypotheses that the ratios are normally distributed are rejected. In each instance, the actual correlation is less than the critical value of the correlation at the 5 percent level. There is a good deal of variation in the correlation values reported, however. In seven instances, the values are greater than 0.91 while in the remaining four instances the values are less than 0.76. For the total expenses/sales ratio, price/earnings ratio, current ratio and current assets/total liabilities ratio therefore, the evidence from this NSCORES test suggests that their distributions differ quite markedly form the normal distribu-

Table 2. NSCORES Tests for Normality: Applied to the Complete Samples

Ratio	*N*	*Correlation*	*Critical Value*	*Decision*
GPM	112	0.930	0.987	R
COG	100	0.952	0.987	R
TES	104	0.628	0.987	R
P/E	132	0.753	0.988	R
CUR	148	0.551	0.989	R
CTL	148	0.524	0.989	R
LEV	148	0.913	0.989	R
NPM	112	0.932	0.987	R
ATR	112	0.943	0.987	R
ROE	144	0.975	0.988	R
ROA	144	0.977	0.988	R

Notes: This table reports the results of an NSCORES test which investigates whether a ratio is normally distributed. The test estimates the correlation between the ordered values of the ratio and the expected values of the order statistics for a sample of the same number of observations from the standard normal distribution. Normality is rejected if the correlation falls below the CRITICAL VALUE of the correlation at the 5 percent level. The final column reports on whether the null hypothesis that the ratio has a normal distribution is accepted (A) or rejected (R).

tion. For the other seven ratios, however, the correlations are relatively high and the rejection of the hypothesis that the ratios are normally distributed may be due to a small number of extreme observations.

To test this proposition, some of the extreme observations were trimmed, that is, they were not removed from the data, but their values were only used in arriving at the rank orders of the observations and not in calculating the correlation coefficient.[18] Due to the relatively small number of observations included in the study, the number of outliers trimmed was limited to a maximum of twelve for each ratio. Table 3 shows the results of the NSCORES tests after these outliers were trimmed.

An inspection of the results in Table 3 reveals that all the correlations improved once the data were trimmed and the extreme values removed.[19] Some of the improvements were dramatic. For example, the correlation for the total expenses/sales ratio increased from 0.628 to 0.991—a rise of over 57 percent—while the correlation for the current ratio increased from 0.551 to 0.894—a rise of over 62 percent. However, the hypotheses that the ratios for this sample of Saudi firms are individually normally distributed are accepted for only four ratios: gross profit margin, cost of goods sold/sales, total expenses/sales and return on equity. For the other seven ratios the correlations are still below their critical values and normality must be rejected.

Table 3. NSCORES Tests for Normality: With Certain Observations Trimmed

Ratio	*N*	*Number Trimmed*	*Correlation*	*Critical Value*	*Decision*
GPM	112	12	0.950	0.987	R
COG	100	5	0.982	0.987	R
TES	104	12	0.985	0.987	R
P/E	132	12	0.856	0.988	R
CUR	148	6	0.895	0.989	R
CTL	148	11	0.891	0.989	R
LEV	148	12	0.920	0.989	R
NPM	112	12	0.951	0.987	R
ATR	112	9	0.948	0.987	R
ROE	144	9	0.979	0.988	R
ROA	144	12	0.985	0.988	R

Notes: This table reports the results of an NSCORES test which investigates whether a ratio is normally distributed. The test estimates the correlation between the ordered values of the ration and the expected values of the order statistics for a sample of the same number of observations from the standard normal distribution. Normality is rejected if the correlation falls below the CRITICAL VALUE of the correlation at the 5 percent level. Trimmed values were ignored in the calculation of the correlation, but not in the caluculation of the NSCORES values. The final column reports on whether the null hypothesis that the ratio has a normal distribution is accepted (A) or rejected (R).

ADJUSTMENTS TO ACHIEVE NORMALITY

In the academic literature which has examined this topic using financial data from developed countries, an alternative approach is sometimes adopted to obtain a normal distribution; the data are transformed by applying a particular transformation to the ratio observations which adjusts the shape of the distribution of the underlying series (e.g., Foster 1986; Deakin 1976; Barnes 1982). The most commonly used transformation is the natural logarithm:

$$y_i = log_e (x_i) \tag{1}$$

where x_i is the actual value of the ratio, log_e is the natural logarithm and y_i is the transformed value of the ratio. This transformation can readily be applied to ratios whose values are all positive. However, for the ratios which have some negative values, it is necessary to add a suitable constant (a) to each observation before applying the log transformation:

$$y_i = log_e (x_i + a) \tag{2}$$

Another frequently used transformation is the square root:

$$y_i = \sqrt{x_i} \tag{3}$$

This transformation can also be applied to ratios whose values are all positive and has the benefit of making ratios more normally distributed when the distribution of their values is positively skewed.

The inverse cotangent (equation 4 below) is less frequently used but is a particularly appropriate transformation to apply to ratios such as the price/earnings ratio for two reasons. First, the reciprocal element of the transformation removes the discontinuity encountered in the price/earnings ratio when the earnings figure changes from a very small positive to a very small negative value. Second, the inverse tangent component of the transformation straightens the normal quantile-quantile plot of this ratio increasing the possibility that the adjusted series will be normally distributed.

$$y_i = arctan(1/x_i) \tag{4}$$

Table 4 displays the results of the test of these NSCORES after the best (in the sense of maximizing the correlation) of these transformations was performed and once certain of the observations were trimmed.

A comparison of Table 3 and Table 4 indicates that a substantial improvement occurred in the correlations and thus in the normality of the distributions of some of the ratios after using the log normal transformation. The improvement is especially pronounced for the current ratio, the current assets/total liabilities ratio and the debt/equity ratio, and is relatively modest but important for the return on total assets ratio and the net profit margin. All five of these ratios appear to be log-normally distributed since the log normal transformation yields correlations for the NSCORES test which are no longer below their critical values. Moreover, the number of observations that have been trimmed has gone down for each of these five ratios. The result of applying the square root transformation to the asset turnover ratio is to increase the correlation with the corresponding NSCORES values to 0.991, which is comfortably above the critical value of 0.987, and hence we conclude that the transformed values do follow the normal distribution. The inverse cotangent transformation also normalizes the price/earnings ratio, achieving a particularly high correlation of 0.995. Again, the number of trimmed values has decreased in both instances.

For each of the 11 ratios considered in this study, the hypothesis that either the observations themselves or transformed versions thereof are normally distributed is accepted, albeit subject to a procedure of trimming up to 12 observations from the total. The evidence for Saudi Arabian firms is similar to the U.S. findings of Deakin (1976). He reported that the log-normal transformation was particularly appropriate for the current asset/current liability ratio and return on total assets ratio while the square root transformation made the leverage ratio more normally distributed; for example, the hypothesis that the return on total assets ratio was

Table 4. NSCORES Tests for Normality Applied to Transformed Ratios: With Certain Observations Trimmed

Ratio	*N*	*Number Trimmed*	*Transformation*	*Correlation*	*Critical Value*	*Decision*
GPM	112	12	NONE	0.996	0.987	A
COG	100	5	NONE	0.988	0.987	A
TES	104	12	NONE	0.991	0.987	A
P/E	132	8	ARCTAN (1/X)	0.995	0.988	A
CUR	148	3	LOG_e (X)	0.992	0.989	A
CTL	148	3	LOG_e (X)	0.992	0.989	A
LEV	148	4	LOG_e (X)	0.992	0.989	A
NPM	112	8	LOG_e (X+100)	0.990	0.987	A
ATR	112	0	SQUARE ROOT (X)	0.991	0.987	A
ROE	144	9	NONE	0.990	0.988	A
ROA	144	11	LOG_e (X+22)	0.994	0.988	A

Notes: This table reports the results of an NSCORES test which investigates whether the new variable that results from applying a transformation to a ratio is normally distributed. The transformation, if any, applied to each ratio is shown in column 4. The test estimates the correlation between the ordered values of the ratio and the expected values of the order statistics for a sample of the same number of observations from the standard normal distribution. Normality is rejected if the correlation falls below the CRITICAL VALUE of the correlation at the 5 percent level. Trimmed values were ignored in the calculation of the correlation, but not in the calculation of the NSCORES values. The final column reports on whether the null hypothesis that the ratio has a normal distribution is accepted (A) or rejected (R).

normally distributed was rejected in only one of the 19 years examined in Deakin's study after the log-normal transformation was undertaken. The evidence is slightly different from the results of Ezzamel and colleagues (1987) where they discovered that the leverage and working capital ratios were normally distributed without any transformation for the sample of U.K. firms in their analysis. However, this U.K. study primarily examined data for two industries (the Retail Food and the Metals sectors) neither of which is considered in our investigation of Saudi firms.[20]

SUMMARY AND CONCLUSIONS

This study examined the cross-sectional distribution of eleven financial ratios for a sample of Joint Stock Companies which operate in Saudi Arabia. Based on the raw data, our results indicate that the distribution of financial accounting ratios exhibit major departures from normality. Two aspects of this non-normality were considered: first, the effect of trimming outlying observations was investigated and, second, the impact of applying one of three transformations to the original data was examined. After trimming the outliers, our results indicated that seven of the ratios were still not normally distributed. The log-normal transformation imposed normality on five of these seven ratios. The square root transformation was very effective in obtaining normality for one of the remaining ratios. The remaining ratio, the price/earnings ratio became normally distributed when subjected to the arctan transformation.

In arriving at the conclusions to this investigation, a number of limitations should be borne in mind. First, the sample size was not as large as that used in similar studies of developed countries. Second, unlike Bird and McHugh (1977), no industry analysis of the ratio distributions was undertaken; again, the sample size did not allow such an analysis to take place. Third, the accounts of the sample companies were not scrutinized to determine whether similar accounting policies were followed.

Nevertheless, despite these limitations, the study represents a valuable attempt to increase our understanding of the distribution of financial ratios in Saudi Arabia and offers useful insights into subsequent investigations which use such ratios in their analyses.

APPENDIX

Ratio Definitions

Ratio	*Code*	*Ratio Calculation*
Gross Profit Margin	GPM	Gross Profit/Sales (%)
Cost of Goods/Sales Ratio	COG	Cost of Goods/Sales (%)
Total Expenses/Sales Ratio	TES	Total Expenses/Sales (%)
Price/Earnings Ratio	P/E	Market Price/Earnings per Share
Current Ratio	CUR	Current Assets/Current Liabilities
Current Assets/Total Liabilities	CTL	Current Assets/Total Liabilities
Leverage	LEV	Total Liabilities/Total Equity
Net Profit Margin	NPM	Net Profit/Sales (%)
Asset Turnover Ratio	ATR	Sales/Total Assets (%)
Return on Equity	ROE	Net Profit/Total Equity (%)
Return on Total Assets	ROA	Net Profit/Total Assets (%)

NOTES

1. For a useful summary of the historical development of financial ratios see Dev (1976).
2. A detailed list of these assumptions is provided in Lev (1974), Whittington (1980), Foster (1986) and Lev and Sunder (1979) and includes assumptions about the relationship between the

numerator and denominator, the availability of data and the comparability of financial statement information across companies and over time.

3. Horrigan (1965, 559) stated that "the most fundamental and perhaps most important question about the statistical nature of financial ratios concerns the types of distributions they exhibit."

4. Deakin (1976) was not able to provide specific guidelines to determine when a particular transformation would be helpful.

5. Outliers are very large or very small observations that seem inconsistent with the remainder of the data (Foster 1986). However, the decision as to whether an observation is an outlier tends to be subjective on the part of the decision maker (Barnett and Lewis 1978).

6. Some of these factors include (i) the violation of the assumption that the numerator and denominator are strictly proportional (e.g., Barnes 1982; Whittington 1980) and (ii) the occurrence of unusual economic activities during the period covered by the study.

7. These systems are based on the work in Pearson (1948), Johnson (1949) and Elderton and Johnson (1969).

8. For more detail about the classification of ratios according to the shape of their distribution and the implications of any classifications see Buckmaster and Siniga (1990).

9. Sudarsanam and Taffler (1995) concentrate on the assumption that the ratio numerator has a strict proportionate relationship with the ratio denominator. They find that for the majority of the 24 ratios considered, the actual relationship between the two components of the ratio appears to be log-linear. On the basis of this finding, they conclude that "the evidence ... suggests that [ratios] may be log-normally distributed" (58).

10. This is one of the few studies to examine the distribution of financial ratios for a less-developed country. It examined the distributions of 10 financial ratios for 34 firms over the period 1974-1987. Their results suggest that ratios are not normally distributed, this was especially true for both the leverage and current ratio in every single year. In order to achieve normality, they utilized two techniques. For those ratios which had a lower limit of zero, the square root transformation was used. For others, outliers were trimmed from either the right-hand or left-hand side of the distribution based on the results from the skewness tests.

11. This is a private company located in Riyadh which supplies accounting information from joint stock companies operating in the Kingdom of Saudi Arabia to local investors.

12. A total number of 60 companies were listed on the Saudi stock market in 1991 at the start of this study. This number had increased to 68 by the end of 1994, however, data for these new listings were not available. According to a recent survey reported in Al-Bogami, the shares of many of the companies excluded from our analysis are not actually traded on the Saudi stock market because the government owns a substantial proportion of their equities.

13. The total sample was 37 firms but not all the financial ratios could be calculated for this sample. Therefore, the actual sample for each ratio varies from a low of 25 to a high of 37 firms.

14. The definitions of the ratios analyzed in this chapter are presented in the Appendix.

15. The leverage estimated by Bougen and Drury, however, was calculated in a slightly different fashion from the ratio analyzed in this study which may account for some of the difference.

16. For example, in Bougen and Drury's analysis, standard deviations for the net profit margin and the current ratio were only 5.4 percent and 0.6 percent respectively compared to 33.3 percent and 16.9 percent for the Saudi companies in this analysis. Obviously, there was a greater degree of variability in the financial performance of the sample companies in this study.

17. The number of negatively skewed ratios varied across the four years covered in this study. Only two of the 11 ratios were negatively skewed in 1990 and 1991, while three of the ratios were negatively skewed in 1992 and 1993. In general, the return on equity and return on assets ratios were negatively skewed in the two earlier years while the profit margin ratios were negatively skewed in the two later years.

18. This process is equivalent to trimming each observation to the value of the corresponding quantile, a normal distribution with the same mean and variance as the ratio in question.

19. Not surprisingly, trimming outliers reduced the kurtosis statistics for all 11 ratios; the kurtosis for two of the ratios —the total expenses/sales and return on assets ratio—became statistically insignificant. However, some of the skewness statistics increased in size and remained statistically significant.

20. Although not reported in this chapter, the analysis was also performed for each of the four sectors (agriculture, chemicals, manufacturing, and service industries) and a number of interesting results were observed. First, in the majority (45/48) of cases either the raw ratio or some transformation of this data was normally distributed; in three instances for the service sector (price/earnings ratio, the return on equity ratio and the return on assets ratio), the hypothesis that the data were normally distributed was convincingly rejected at the conventional 5 percent level of significance. Second, a similar amount of data trimming was required for the different ratios although the number of observations which had to be trimmed varied from one ratio to another, in particular, a relatively small fraction of data points were deleted for the gross profit margin and the return on assets ratio. Finally, it is worth noting that the number of observations in certain sectors was small and a larger sample of companies across a longer time span might have yielded other results.

REFERENCES

Al-Bogami, S.A.S. 1996. An examination of the usefulness of interim financial statements to investors in the Saudi stock market. Doctoral dissertation, University of Dundee.

Altman, E. 1968. Discriminant analysis and the prediction of corporate bankruptcy. *Journal of Finance* 23(4):589-609.

Barnes, P. 1982. Methodological implications of nonnormally distributed financial ratios. *Journal of Business Finance and Accounting* 9(1): 51-62.

Barnett, V., and T. Lewis. 1978. *Outliers in Statistical Data.* New York: Wiley and Sons.

Bird, R.G., and A.J. McHugh. 1977. Financial ratios—An empirical study. *Journal of Business Finance and Accounting* 4(1): 29-45.

Bougan, P.D., and J.D. Drury. 1980. UK statistical distributions of financial ratios. *Journal of Business Finance and Accounting* 7(1): 39-47.

Buckmaster, D., and E. Siniga. 1990. Distribution forms of accounting ratios: Pearson's and Johnson's taxonomies. *Journal of Economic and Social Measurements* 16: 149-160.

Deakin, E.B. 1976. Distribution of financial accounting ratios: Some empirical evidence. *The Accounting Review* 51(1): 90-96.

Dev, S. 1976. Ratio analysis and the prediction of company failure. In *Debits, Credits, Finance, and Profits,* eds. H. Edey and B. Yamey. London: Sweet and Maxwell.

Elderton, W.P., and N.L. Johnson. 1969. *Systems of Frequency Curves.* London: Cambridge University Press.

Ezzamel, M., C. Mar-Molinero, and A. Beecher. 1987. On the distributional properties of financial ratios. *Journal of Business Finance and Accounting* 14(4): 463-481.

Filliben, J.J. 1975. The probability plot correlation coefficient test for normality. *Technometrics* 17: 111-117.

Foster, G. 1986. *Financial Statement Analysis.* Englewood Cliffs, NJ: Prentice-Hall.

Frecka, T.J., and W.S. Hopwood. 1983. The effects of outliers on the cross-sectional distributional properties of financial ratios. *The Accounting Review* 58(1): 115-128.

Horrigan, J.O. 1965. Some empirical bases of financial ratio analysis. *The Accounting Review* 40(3): 558-568.

Johnson, N.L. 1949. Systems of frequency curves generated by methods of translation. *Biometrika* 36: 149-176.

Kaplan, R.S., and G. Urwitz. 1979. Statistical models of bond ratings: A methodological enquiry. *Journal of Business* 52(2): 231-262.

Lev, B. 1974. *Financial Statement Analysis: A New Approach*. NJ.: Prentice-Hall.

Lev, B., and S. Sunder. 1979. Methodological issues in the use of financial ratios. *Journal of Accounting and Economics* 1: 187-210.

Martikainen, T. 1992. Time-series distribution properties of financial ratios: Empirical evidence from Finnish listed firms. *European Journal of Operational Research* 77(3): 344-355.

Martikainen, T., J. Perttunen, P. Yli-Olli, and A. Gunasekaran. 1995. Financial ratios distribution irregularities—Implications for ratio classification. *European Journal of Operational Research* 80(1): 34-44.

O'Connor, M.C. 1973. On the usefulness of financial ratios to investors in common stock. *The Accounting Review* 48(2): 339-352.

Pearson, E.S. 1948. Contributions to the mathematical theory of evolution II: Skew variations in homogeneous materials. In *Karl Pearson's Early Statistical Papers,* ed. Pearson. London: Cambridge University Press.

Pinches, G.E., and K.A. Mingo. 1973. A multivariate analysis of industrial bond ratings. *Journal of Finance* 28(1): 1-18.

Shapiro, S.S., and M.B. Wilk. 1965. An analysis of variance test for normality (complete samples). *Biometrika* 52: 591-611.

So, J.C. 1987. Some empirical evidence on the outliers and the non-normal distribution of financial ratios. *Journal of Business Finance and Accounting* 14(4): 483-496.

Sudarsanam, P.S., and R.J. Taffler. 1995. Financial ratio proportionality and inter-temporal stability: An empirical analysis. *Journal of Banking and Finance* 19: 45-60.

Whittington, G. 1980. Some basic properties of accounting ratios. *Journal of Business Finance and Accounting* 7(2): 219-232.

EXTERNAL REPORTING IN LESS DEVELOPED COUNTRIES WITH MODERATELY SOPHISTICATED CAPITAL MARKETS:

A STUDY OF USER NEEDS AND INFORMATION PROVISION IN JORDAN

Mohammad Abu-Nassar and Brian A. Rutherford

ABSTRACT

This study explores the adequacy of information provision in a less developed country with a moderately sophisticated capital market. User groups surveyed are individual shareholders, institutional shareholders, bank loan officers, academics, and stockbrokers. In addition, preparers' perceptions of user needs are explored.The user groups had similar overall information needs although a number of significant differences at the level of individual items and pairings of groups are identified, a finding which casts some light on earlier studies of developed countries which have yielded conflicting results. Less consensus between users and preparers is found.

Research in Accounting in Emerging Economies, Volume 4, pages 227-246.

ISBN: 1-55938-995-8

The overall level of disclosure is found to be poor and highly variable although positive correlations are found between disclosure of individual items and perceptions of user needs; this relationship is weaker when users' own perceptions are studied than when preparers' perceptions of users' needs are studied.

INTRODUCTION

A number of studies of the adequacy of information provision in relation to the expressed needs of users have been carried out (see, for example, Chandra 1974; Firth 1978; McNally et al. 1982) but these have focused largely on developed countries with sophisticated capital markets (though see Wallace 1988a, 1988b). The purpose of this study is to explore the issues involved in the context of a less developed country with a moderately sophisticated capital market.

THE FINANCIAL REPORTING ENVIRONMENT

Jordan is a small, moderately prosperous open economy with a free capital market and a parliamentary system of government. Industry is dominated by the service sector, with mining and manufacturing contributing only some 17 percent to GDP. The country's stock market (the Amman Financial Market) commenced operation in 1978 with quotations covering 57 companies; this number rose to 120 in 1988 but has since fallen slightly as a result of merger activity (see Civelek and El-Khouri 1991).

The legal and regulatory framework for financial reporting in Jordan is very limited in scope and is expressed in loose and general terms. The Companies Law 1989 requires that companies prepare an annual report, including a profit and loss account and balance sheet with comparative figures, a statement of changes in financial position[1] and explanatory notes. The accounts must give an "honest and fair" view and be audited. There are no further requirements concerning the form and content of the financial statements beyond a requirement that companies should maintain proper accounting records in accordance with generally accepted accounting principles, which are not themselves defined by law.

Jordanian tax law requires that all deductions claimed for tax purposes should correspond to sums appearing in the financial statements. Since 1985 depreciation rates for tax purposes have been specified by law and only the straight-line method can be used. Other deductions must be calculated in accordance with generally accepted accounting principles, but, again, these are not defined.

The accounting profession in Jordan has recently been formally established but has yet to issue local statements of accounting practice. It has recommended adoption of International Accounting Standards, with effect from January 1990, but in the absence of any legal power or effective disciplinary mechanism, the use of these standards is likely to come about slowly and in a limited way. The Amman Financial Market has so far issued no requirements relating to the content of company annual accounts.

RESEARCH DESIGN: USERS' NEEDS

This study surveys five main groups of external users of corporate annual reports in Jordan: individual shareholders, institutional shareholders, bank loan officers, academics, and stockbrokers. Preparers of accounting information are represented by financial directors of all companies listed on the Amman Financial Market.

In order to develop a list of items of information potentially of use to readers of financial statements, the relevant literature, including previous empirical studies, was reviewed. This study focuses on items found to be of importance in previous studies and on items of relevance in the context of the companies included in the study of information provision reported later in the paper. A substantial selection of items actually disclosed by Jordanian companies was included so that respondents would be familiar with the items and thus be better able to evaluate their importance (see Stanga 1980) and because it is easier to extend disclosure by starting with items acceptable to companies (see Belkaoui 1979). A pilot test was carried out. After these steps had been taken, the final list contained 81 information items.

Respondents were asked to determine the degree of importance of each information item for their decision-making purposes using a five-point scale from 1 (of no importance) to 5. Respondents were reminded that disclosing more information may involve additional costs for companies and asked to take this into account. They were asked to reply on the basis of the decisions for which they were responsible with reference to public companies; for example, bank loan officers were asked to evaluate the relative importance of each item within the framework of lending decisions to a public company listed on the

Table 1. Samples and Response Rates

Survey Group	*Number Surveyed*	*Number of Usable Responses*	*Response Rate*
1. Individual Shareholders	200	76	38.00
2. Institutional Shareholders	100	44	44.00
3. Bank Loan Officers	100	61	61.00
4. Stockbrokers	27	20	74.07
5. Academics	36	23	63.89
Total	463	224	48.38
6. Preparers	112	83	74.11

Table 2. Summary of the Importance of Information Items as Perceived by User Groups

No.	Item	*Individuals*	*Institutions*	*Stockbrokers*	*Banks*	*Academics*
1.	Breakdown of tangible and intangible assets	3.57	3.82	3.60	3.93	3.96
2.	Original cost and accumulated depreciation for tangible fixed assets	3.80	4.05	3.65	3.90	4.13
3.	Depreciation rates or useful lives of assets	3.20	3.84	3.40	3.85	3.30
4.	Capital expenditure for the past year	3.86	3.84	3.45	3.84	3.74
5.	Current resale value of fixed assets	3.76	3.52	3.55	3.62	3.52
6.	Gross and disaggregated value of current assets	3.61	4.02	3.50	4.26	4.04
7.	Current resale value of finished goods inventory	3.79	3.82	3.40	3.93	3.52
8.	Current market value of quoted investments	3.79	3.98	3.60	3.75	4.09
9.	Information relating to investments (e.g., names, percentage ownership)	3.54	3.73	3.95	3.54	3.57
10.	Aged analysis of debtors	3.53	3.68	3.65	3.90	3.17
11.	Security status of debentures	3.74	3.66	3.70	3.93	3.09
12.	Information relating to subsidiaries (e.g., names, addresses, percentage ownership)	3.57	3.89	3.95	3.77	3.78
13.	Gross and disaggregated value of current liabilities	3.38	3.95	3.40	4.11	3.83
14.	Schedule of interest and principal due on long-term debt	3.74	3.95	3.60	4.13	4.00
15.	Breakdown of borrowings (e.g., lending institution, date of maturity, security)	3.26	3.55	3.40	4.20	3.65
16.	Number and amount of authorized and issued shares	3.54	3.96	3.25	3.61	3.83
17.	Number and type of ordinary shareholders (e.g., institutions, individuals)	3.11	3.07	2.85	2.82	3.39
18.	Information on contingent liabilities	3.66	4.25	3.95	3.85	3.91
19.	Gross and disaggregated amount of shareholders' equity	3.67	4.18	3.80	4.15	3.91
20.	Equity interest owned by management	3.66	3.73	3.15	3.57	3.78
21.	Number of shares owned by directors	3.66	3.77	3.25	3.57	3.91
22.	Number of shares owned by foreign parties	3.30	3.48	3.05	3.26	3.57
23.	Foreign assets and liabilities	3.63	3.98	3.10	3.93	3.91
24.	Information relating to post balance sheet events	3.88	4.39	4.10	3.98	4.13
25.	Nature and amount/effects of all major accounting changes during the past year	3.32	4.04	3.55	3.67	4.13

26.	Sales revenue	3.92	4.14	3.90	4.43	4.52
27.	Breakdown of expenses into fixed and variable components	3.50	3.45	3.70	4.02	3.48
28.	Amount and breakdown of expenses	3.37	3.36	3.30	3.84	3.48
29.	Overall financing cost	3.41	3.36	3.55	3.79	3.52
30.	Expenditure on human resources (eg. training, welfare facilities)	3.11	3.02	3.15	3.23	3.13
31.	Analysis of sales revenue and earnings attributable to foreign operations	3.74	3.84	3.90	4.03	3.78
32.	Breakdown of earnings by source	3.68	4.00	3.95	4.10	3.91
33.	Period's depreciation on tangible assets	3.22	3.16	3.15	3.62	3.43
34.	Information about research and development expenditures for the past year	3.09	3.16	3.30	3.43	3.57
35.	Expenditure on advertising and publicity for the past year	3.03	3.00	2.95	3.11	3.39
36.	Breakdown of sales revenue by major product line, class of customer and geographical location	2.96	3.39	3.20	3.64	3.48
37.	Breakdown of earnings by major product line, class of customer and geographical location	3.04	3.36	3.10	3.41	3.57
38.	Amount of each subsidiary's earnings and parent's share	3.43	3.95	3.80	3.43	3.74
39.	Extraordinary gains and losses	3.71	3.93	3.90	3.67	4.09
40.	Description of marketing network for finished goods	3.00	3.02	2.85	3.52	2.87
41.	Discussion of the impact of inflation on the financial results	3.37	3.50	3.75	3.46	3.74
42.	Basis of accounting	3.07	3.77	3.30	3.52	4.09
43.	Revenue recognition method	3.58	3.93	3.70	3.77	3.74
44.	Depreciation methods	2.97	3.41	3.25	3.36	3.83
45.	Currency translation method	3.33	3.86	3.55	3.59	3.96
46.	Accounting treatment of foreign exchange gains and losses	3.36	3.95	3.65	3.44	3.65
47.	Method used to determine the cost of inventories (e.g., LIFO, FIFO)	3.37	3.50	3.45	3.80	3.96
48.	Basis used to determine the carrying amount of inventories (e.g., lower of cost or market)	3.45	3.91	3.60	3.92	4.04
49.	Statement of source and application of funds	3.53	4.05	3.65	4.10	4.22
50.	Statement of value added	3.05	3.20	3.20	3.08	3.13
51.	Inflation adjusted accounts as supplementary statements	3.46	3.45	3.55	3.48	3.65
52.	Statement of foreign currency transactions	3.24	3.23	3.25	3.10	3.39
53.	Rate of return required on projects	3.26	3.07	3.35	3.02	3.00

(continued)

Table 2 (Continued)

No.	Item	Individuals	Institutions	Stockbrokers	Banks	Academics
54.	Statement of company objectives	3.58	3.91	3.55	3.72	3.43
55.	Statement of dividend policy	3.84	4.07	3.70	3.54	3.74
56.	Auditors' report	3.67	4.14	3.90	4.08	4.13
57.	Discussion of results with reasons for changes	3.64	4.09	3.75	4.18	3.78
58.	Discussion of competitive position of the company	3.63	3.80	3.75	4.05	3.57
59.	Discussion of new product development	3.57	3.55	3.65	3.64	3.65
60.	Discussion of financial strength of the company	4.24	4.59	4.40	4.39	4.09
61.	Share of market in major product/service areas	3.82	3.80	3.90	4.13	3.74
62.	Physical level of output and capacity utilization	3.75	3.93	3.95	4.11	3.65
63.	Forecast of following year's profits	3.84	3.64	3.90	3.80	3.57
64.	Expected future growth in earning per share	3.75	3.64	3.80	3.39	3.61
65.	Expected future growth in sales	3.74	3.80	3.95	4.00	3.65
66.	Discussion of major factors likely to influence following year's results	3.78	3.84	3.90	3.97	3.52
67.	Future economic outlook for the company	3.76	3.95	3.85	4.02	3.35
68.	Future economic outlook for the industry	3.84	3.95	3.75	4.00	3.43
69.	Planned expenditure on R&D for the following year	3.14	3.25	3.25	2.95	3.09
70.	Planned advertising and publicity expenditure for the following year	2.82	3.18	2.95	2.80	2.96
71.	Cash flow projections for the following one to five years	3.12	3.02	3.40	3.61	3.39
72.	Budgeted capital expenditure for the following year	3.20	3.45	3.35	3.70	3.39
73.	Names of senior management, lines of authority and remuneration	3.47	3.77	3.40	3.46	2.96
74.	Comparative balance sheets for the past five to ten years	3.17	3.20	3.75	3.70	3.48
75.	Comparative profit and loss accounts for the past five to ten years	3.17	3.27	3.55	3.72	3.57
76.	Summary of net sales for at least the most recent five years	3.14	3.39	3.65	3.89	3.61
77.	Historical summary of price range of ordinary shares	3.20	3.36	3.10	3.20	3.57
78.	Description of major products/services produced by the company	3.30	3.50	3.00	3.30	2.96
79.	Indication of employee morale (e.g. labor turnover, strikes and absenteeism)	3.01	3.32	2.65	3.25	2.83
80.	Brief narrative history of the company	2.99	3.02	2.85	3.33	2.65
81.	Information on corporate social responsibility (eg. attitude of the firm, expenditures)	2.83	2.91	2.80	2.57	3.09

Amman Financial Market. Financial directors of companies were asked to make their judgments for each item as preparers having regard to the information needs of external users generally.

A questionnaire containing the list of information items was distributed to the five user groups. Since the total population of two of the groups, stockbrokers and academics, is relatively small in Jordan the questionnaire was sent to every member of these two groups. The bank loan officers were selected at random from each of the major banks and finance institutions in Jordan. The institutional shareholders were also selected at random from the 1991 Jordanian Companies Guide. In the case of the individual shareholders, the survey was confined to those who had satisfied a certain minimum level of usage and understanding of corporate annual reports, as disclosed in a further section of the questionnaire.[2] Table 1 summarizes the composition of the samples and the response rates for each of the groups surveyed. The response rates of 48 percent for users and 74 percent for preparers are adequate when compared with other studies. However, to examine whether the results of the study might be affected by significant non-response bias, Oppenheim's method (see Oppenheim 1966) was applied to individual shareholders and to preparers. The first and last 20 percent of responses from each of the two groups were identified and significant differences between the mean values for early and late responses were tested statistically using the Mann-Whitney U test for each of the items of information. Only two information items within the individual shareholder group and seven information items within the preparer group were found to show differences at a significance level of 0.05. It was thus concluded that the results of the study were not affected by material nonresponse bias.

RESEARCH DESIGN: INFORMATION PROVISION

This study examines voluntary disclosures made in 1990 by the 96 companies listed on the Amman Financial Market (out of a total of 112) for which financial statements could be obtained without undue delay. A company was awarded the appropriate score for items published in its annual report and a score of zero for items applicable to the company but not disclosed. Whether the item was applicable to the company in question was determined on the basis of scrutiny by the researchers and information sought from preparers. In some cases, items of information can be disclosed in varying degrees of detail, for example the breakdown of sales revenue by major product line, class of customer and geographical location. Some previous studies have used the number of words and numbers contained in a disclosure to assign the disclosure score for this type of information, for example Robbins and Austin (1986). While it offers an objective measurement, this approach was not considered an effective way of capturing the degree of disclosure involved (see Marston and Shrives 1991) and, following studies by, for example, Choi (1973) and Buzby (1974b), judgment was used to award scores for this type of information.

PERCEIVED IMPORTANCE OF INFORMATION ITEMS

The findings of the survey of users and preparers are summarized in Tables 2 and 3. Table 2 gives the mean value for each item for each user group while Table 3 gives the mean value for users as a whole and for preparers and indicates the difference between the two means. The mean for users as a whole is arrived at by giving each group equal weight.

Table 2 reveals how the different groups of users perceived the relative importance of the various items of information. For example, the most important item for bank loan officers making a lending decision was sales revenue, followed by a discussion of the financial strength of the company, while they considered information about corporate social responsibility and planned advertising and publicity expenditure to be the least important items on the list.

All five groups of users placed great importance on sales revenue, a discussion of the financial strength of the company, the auditors' report and information relating to post balance sheet events. Preparers ranked as the most important of the external users' needs, the statement of sources and application of funds, the auditors' report, a discussion of the financial strengths of the company and gross and disaggregated amounts of shareholders' equity; only the second and third of these were in fact in the list of items ranked most important by users.

In general, a large number of items were considered by users to be important or very important; of the 405 mean scores computed (81 items and 5 groups), 252 were at the level of 3.5 or above.

Users placed a low value on information relating to disclosure of forecasts and budgetary projections (items numbered 69, 70, 71 and 72). This, initially perhaps surprising, result is consistent with studies in the United States (Buzby 1974b; Chandra 1975; Benjamin and Stanga 1977) and in the United Kingdom (Firth 1978). It is likely that the result is attributable to lack of confidence by users in the reliability of the information that would be provided (Firth 1978) although it is also true that users are less familiar with this kind of information in practice.

Table 3 reveals that preparers' perceptions of user needs place less overall importance on items than do users themselves. User groups considered 53 of the 81 items more important than did preparers. This finding is consistent with a study undertaken by Courtis (1992), who examined the findings of 11 studies concerned with disclosure in corporate annual reports and established that financial analysts consistently place more importance on information items than do preparers. Although preparers were asked to evaluate the importance of each item on the basis of their perceptions of the needs of external users, the costs of preparing and publishing the information as well as competitive disadvantages may nonetheless

Table 3. Summary of the Importance of Information Items as Perceived by Users and Preparers of Corporate Annual Reports

No.	*Item*	*Users*	*Prep.*	*Diff.*
1.	Breakdown of tangible and intangible assets	3.77	3.70	+.07
2.	Original cost and accumulated depreciation for tangible fixed assets	3.91	3.96	−.05
3.	Depreciation rates or useful lives of assets	3.60	3.76	−.16
4.	Capital expenditure for the past year	3.74	3.59	+.15
5.	Current resale value of fixed assets	3.56	3.05	+.51
6.	Gross and disaggregated value of current assets	3.89	4.04	−.15
7.	Current resale value of finished goods inventory	3.69	3.72	−.03
8.	Current market value of quoted investments	3.84	4.00	−.16
9.	Information relating to investments (e.g. names, percentage ownership)	3.66	3.67	−.01
10.	Aged analysis of debtors	3.59	3.26	+.33
11.	Security status of debentures	3.62	3.26	+.36
12.	Information relating to subsidiaries (e.g. names, addresses, percentage ownership)	3.79	3.76	+.03
13.	Gross and disaggregated value of current liabilities	3.74	3.70	+.04
14.	Schedule of interest and principal due on long-term debt	3.92	3.87	+.05
15.	Breakdown of borrowings (e.g. lending institution, date of maturity, security)	3.61	3.63	−.02
16.	Number and amount of authorized and issued shares	3.64	3.91	−.27
17.	Number and type of ordinary shareholders (e.g. institutions, individuals)	3.05	2.99	+.06
18.	Information on contingent liabilities	3.92	3.99	−.07
19.	Gross and disaggregated amount of shareholders' equity	3.94	4.10	−.16
20.	Equity interest owned by management	3.58	3.16	+.42
21.	Number of shares owned by directors	3.63	3.34	+.29
22.	Number of shares owned by foreign parties	3.33	3.09	+.24
23.	Foreign assets and liabilities	3.71	3.52	+.19
24.	Information relating to post balance sheet events	4.10	3.89	+.21
25.	Nature and amount/effects of all major accounting changes made during the past year	3.74	3.74	.00
26.	Sales revenue	4.18	4.02	+.16
27.	Breakdown of expenses into fixed and variable components	3.63	3.23	+.40
28.	Amount and breakdown of expenses	3.47	3.55	−.08
29.	Overall financing cost	3.53	3.46	+.07
30.	Expenditure on human resources (eg. training, welfare facilities)	3.13	3.14	−.01
31.	Analysis of sales revenue and earnings attributable to foreign operations	3.86	3.77	+.09
32.	Breakdown of earnings by source	3.93	3.87	+.06
33.	Period's depreciation on tangible assets	3.32	3.63	−.31
34.	Information about research and development expenditures for the past year	3.31	3.14	+.17

(*continued*)

Table 3 (Continued)

No.	*Item*	*Users*	*Prep.*	*Diff.*
35.	Expenditure on advertising and publicity for the past year	3.10	2.93	+.17
36.	Breakdown of sales revenue by major product line, class of customer and geographical location	3.33	3.17	+.16
37.	Breakdown of earnings by major product line, class of customer and geographical location	3.30	3.03	+.27
38.	Amount of each subsidiary's earnings and parent's share	3.67	3.91	−.24
39.	Extraordinary gains and losses	3.86	3.70	+.16
40.	Description of marketing network for finished goods	3.05	2.83	+.22
41.	Discussion of the impact of inflation on the financial results	3.56	3.38	+.18
42.	Basis of accounting	3.55	3.92	−.37
43.	Revenue recognition method	3.74	3.82	−.08
44.	Depreciation methods	3.36	3.82	−.46
45.	Currency translation method	3.66	3.72	−.06
46.	Accounting treatment of foreign exchange gains and losses	3.61	3.75	−.14
47.	Method used to determine the cost of inventories (e.g., LIFO, FIFO)	3.62	4.00	−.38
48.	Basis used to determine the carrying amount of inventories (e.g., lower of cost or market)	3.78	4.04	−.26
49.	Statement of source and application of funds	3.91	4.13	−.22
50.	Statement of value added	3.13	2.77	+.36
51.	Inflation adjusted accounts as supplementary statements	3.52	2.95	+.57
52.	Statement of foreign currency transactions	3.24	2.78	+.46
53.	Rate of return required on projects	3.14	2.57	+.57
54.	Statement of company objectives	3.64	3.75	−.11
55.	Statement of dividend policy	3.78	3.77	+.01
56.	Auditors' report	4.04	4.12	−.08
57.	Discussion of results with reasons for changes	3.89	3.75	+.14
58.	Discussion of competitive position of the company	3.76	3.34	+.42
59.	Discussion of new product development	3.61	3.53	+.08
60.	Discussion of financial strength of the company	4.34	4.10	+.24
61.	Share of market in major product/service areas	3.88	3.13	+.75
62.	Physical level of output and capacity utilization	3.88	3.26	+.62
63.	Forecast of following year's profits	3.75	3.27	+.48
64.	Expected future growth in earning per share	3.65	2.99	+.66
65.	Expected future growth in sales	3.83	3.45	+.38
66.	Discussion of major factors likely to influence following year's results	3.80	3.41	+.39
67.	Future economic outlook for the company	3.79	3.50	+.29
68.	Future economic outlook for the industry	3.80	3.42	+.38
69.	Planned expenditure on R&D for the following year	3.14	2.79	+.35
70.	Planned advertising and publicity expenditure for the following year	2.94	2.59	+.35
71.	Cash flow projections for the following one to five years	3.31	2.77	+.54

(continued)

Table 3 (Continued)

No.	Item	Users	Prep.	Diff.
72.	Budgeted capital expenditure for the following year	3.42	2.98	+.44
73.	Names of senior management, lines of authority and remuneration	3.41	3.20	+.21
74.	Comparative balance sheets for the past five to ten years	3.46	2.84	+.62
75.	Comparative profit and loss accounts for the past five to ten years	3.46	2.80	+.66
76.	Summary of net sales for at least the most recent five years	3.54	3.06	+.48
77.	Historical summary of price range of ordinary shares	3.28	2.72	+.56
78.	Description of major products/services produced by the company	3.21	3.28	−.07
79.	Indication of employee morale (e.g. labor turnover, strikes and absenteeism)	3.01	2.81	+.20
80.	Brief narrative history of the company	2.97	3.04	−.07
81.	Information on corporate social responsibility (eg. attitude of the firm, expenditures)	2.84	3.08	−.24

have influenced their judgment (Firth 1979a). Interestingly, preparers, like users, attach a low value to forward-looking information.

THE DEGREE OF CONSENSUS BETWEEN DIFFERENT GROUPS

It is sometimes suggested that, although different groups of users have a common interest in a company's affairs, they may have different information needs. Olson (1977), for example, argues that, "obviously, various groups have a stake in financial reporting, and their expectations differ. These expectations, in fact, are so diverse that I believe financial reporting should not attempt to satisfy them all" (68). Empirical support for this position was provided by Benjamin and Stanga (1977), who investigated the expressed information needs of commercial bank loan officers making loan decisions and professional financial analysts making security investment recommendations. Significant differences were found for 51 of the 79 items of information included in their study.

By contrast, Firth (1978), who questioned financial directors, auditors, financial analysts and bank loan officers in the United Kingdom, found that financial analysts and bank loan officers were in substantial agreement regarding the importance of 81 percent of the 75 items of information included in his study and McCaslin and Stanga (1986) found only 7 of 30 items showed significant differences between analysts and bankers in judgments of the relevance of the items in question.

These studies examined only a very limited range of groups (predominantly bank loan officers and financial analysts) and reached inconsistent conclusions. The current study examined five user groups at three levels. At the first level, an attempt was made to examine the extent to which there were significant differences among all the five groups of users for all the 81 items of information in aggregate. At the second level, the significant differences among the five groups of users in their perceptions of each of the 81 items of information were tested. Finally, the study examined whether there were significant differences between all possible pairs of user groups for each of the 81 items.

In order to establish whether there were significant differences between the groups for all items in aggregate the Kruskal-Wallis H Test was employed. A chi-square value of 6.5383 was obtained and, since this is lower than the level necessary to reject the null hypothesis (9.4877), it was concluded that the five groups of users have similar overall information needs.[3]

Moving to the second level of the analysis, for each of the 81 information items the null hypotheses that there were no significant differences among the five groups of users concerning the perceived importance of the item was tested using the Kruskal-Wallis one-way analysis of variance test. Although the earlier general analysis indicated that there were no significant differences among the users in their overall information needs, at this level, the null hypothesis was rejected for 29 out of the 81 information items included on the list.[4]

The Mann-Whitney U test was used for the third level of investigation, examining whether there was a significant difference between pairings of user groups. There was a significant difference for only one pairing, individual shareholders and bank loan officers.[5] In general, then, this study indicates that a high degree of consensus exists among user groups but identifies some areas of significant difference.

The analysis set out above was extended to include preparers as a further group. At the first level, significant differences between groups were detected using the Kruskal-Wallis H test, which yielded a chi-square value of 11.8399 against a critical value of 11.0705. Testing at the level of individual items identified 41 items out of 81 for which differences were significant. When pairings of groups were investigated, it was found that preparers showed significant differences with only one group of users, individual shareholders.[6] This result is somewhat surprising since it is often suggested that the investor group is considered by companies to be one of their most important target groups of users. It would appear, however, that the degree of consensus between preparers and users of accounting information regarding the perceived importance of information is only moderate. This may come about because communication between preparers and users is ineffective (Chandra 1974), because there is a time lag between the development of user needs and the response of preparers (McNally et al. 1982), or because preparers are reluctant to experiment with new ideas and approaches (Chandra 1974). In addition, preparers may be influenced by the costs and competitive disadvantage of providing more information (Firth 1978).

A number of studies of the degree of consensus between parties to the reporting process have been carried out in the context of developed countries. They have generally identified significant differences between preparers, users and auditors (see, for example, Chandra 1974; Chandra and Greenball 1977; Firth 1978; McKinnon 1984), although at least one study (Belkaoui 1979, relating to Canada) has found a high degree of consensus. The present study indicates the degree of consensus in a developing country but also suggests that lack of consensus between users, broadly defined, and preparers may be attributable to differences between preparers and particular groups of users.

ADEQUACY OF DISCLOSURE LEVELS

Adequacy of disclosure was measured using both weighted and unweighted approaches. The unweighted approach gives a score of one for all disclosure and hence assumes that all items of information are equally important to users. The disclosure index is the ratio of number of items disclosed to the total number of items that the company could disclose. This approach has been used by Chow and Wong-Boren (1987), Cooke (1989a, 1989b, 1992) and Spero (1979).

Under the weighted approach, the relative importance of information items to users is taken into account in measuring the level of disclosure. This approach has been used by, for example, Buzby (1974b), Cerf (1961), Firth (1979a, 1979b, 1980, 1984), Kahl and Belkaoui (1981), and Singhvi and Desai (1971). To measure the level of disclosure under this approach in the current study, the relative importance of each of the 81 information items as measured in the survey undertaken for this study was used, employing overall weights obtained by giving each group of users equal weight. The disclosure index was obtained by dividing the score for the amount of information published in the annual report by the maximum score available for information applicable to that company.

Buzby (1974a, 45) pointed out that, "if the disclosure of information is to be effective, it must be timely," yet this principle has been largely ignored in previous studies. Given the importance of timeliness, it could be misleading to evaluate the quality of disclosure by companies ignoring the fact that companies release their annual reports at different intervals after the date of the financial statements. In the current study a third approach was used to reflect both the weights employed in the second approach and the importance of timeliness.

To estimate the weight to be attached to the timeliness factor for evaluation purpose, the five groups of users surveyed in the current study were asked to indicate the importance to them of the timeliness of reports relative to the information contained in such reports. The implied assumption here was that the percentage attached to the timeliness factor would determine the extent to which users prefer to have the annual report earlier at the expense of getting less information. Buzby (1974a), in his investigation of the nature of adequate disclosure, pointed out that

Table 4. The Importance of Timeliness of Reports to Users Relative to the Information in Reports

Survey Group	%
1. Academics	20.65
2. Bank Loan Officers	17.30
3. Individual Shareholders	17.11
4. Institutional Shareholders	15.46
5. Stockbrokers	13.25
Mean	16.75

"an implicit assumption in timely disclosure is that the speed with which information is disclosed is balanced against the necessary levels of accuracy and completeness" (45).

The importance of timeliness relative to the information contained in reports, for each of the five groups of users in the study, is summarized in Table 4. The overall mean of 16.75 percent was divided by 90 days, the maximum time allowed for filing under Jordanian company law, and each company was awarded points on the basis of the number of days between its financial year-end and the date of release of its annual report, with higher scores for earlier release. The disclosure score for each company was then calculated combining this score with the weights derived above scaled to 83.25 percent (i.e., 100-16.75).

The Kruskal-Wallis test was used to establish whether there were any significant differences between the results of the three approaches. The result showed that there was no significant difference between the three approaches ($p = 0.3736$; chi-square = 1.9693). This was confirmed by the Spearman test of the extent of correlation between the scores awarded to companies by the three approaches.[7] This result was unsurprising since the weights given to the 81 information items were in general very bunched: 74 items had weights ranging between 3.01 and 3.94, so that the weighted and unweighted approaches are likely to yield similar results, and the relatively low importance given to the timeliness factor means that incorporating timeliness will result in little change.

Because the results of the three approaches are broadly similar, the level of disclosure by Jordanian companies will be discussed here by reference to the weighted-timeliness approach only.[8] The overall level of disclosure by Jordanian companies seems to be very poor. An overall mean score of 37.70 percent was obtained for the 96 companies in the survey: companies in Jordan appear to disclose only about one third of what might be expected in order to provide users with the information they perceive themselves as needing. An important implication of this inadequate disclosure is that large security price fluctuations in the stock market are likely to occur (see Singhvi and Desai 1971).

The extent of disclosure varied widely within the sample: scores achieved ranged from 17.08 percent to 60.72 percent with a standard deviation of 8.87

Table 5. Ranking of Information Items in Order of Actual Disclosure by Companies

No.	Item	No.	% of Cos	% of App Cos
1.	Gross and disaggregated value of current liabilities	96	100.00	100.00
2.	Gross and disaggregated amount of shareholders' equity	96	100.00	100.00
3.	Auditors' report	96	100.00	100.00
4.	Sales revenue amount	96	100.00	100.00
5.	Gross and disaggregated value of current assets	93	96.88	96.88
6.	Discussion of results with reasons for changes	90	93.75	93.75
7.	Breakdown of tangible and intangible assets	90	93.75	93.75
8.	Number and amount of authorized and issued shares	89	92.71	92.71
9.	Overall financing cost	87	90.63	92.55
10.	Depreciation methods	88	91.67	91.67
11.	Period's depreciation on tangible assets	87	90.63	90.63
12.	Original cost and accumulated depreciation for tangible fixed assets	86	89.58	89.58
13.	Statement of source and application of funds	85	88.54	88.54
14.	Brief narrative history of the company	83	86.46	86.46
15.	Statement of company objectives	81	84.38	84.38
16.	Description of major products/services produced by the company	81	84.38	84.83
17.	The basis used to determine the carrying amount of inventories (e.g. lower of cost or market)	48	80.00	80.00
18.	Capital expenditures for the past year	75	78.13	78.13
19.	Depreciation rates or useful lives of assets	74	77.08	77.08
20.	Amount and breakdown of expenses	73	76.04	76.04
21.	Breakdown of earnings by source	63	65.63	67.02
22.	Expenditure on advertising and publicity for the past year	63	65.63	65.63
23.	Extraordinary gains and losses	59	61.46	62.11
24.	Method used to determine the cost of inventories (e.g. LIFO, FIFO)	37	38.54	61.67
25.	Information on contingent liabilities	59	61.46	61.46
26.	Currency translation method	55	57.29	61.11
27.	Discussion of financial strength of the company	55	57.29	57.29
28.	Breakdown of borrowings (e.g. lending institution, date of maturity, security)	49	51.04	56.98
29.	Information relating to investments (e.g. names, percentage ownership)	49	51.04	53.85
30.	Accounting treatment of foreign exchange gains and losses	45	46.88	50.00
31.	Schedule of interest and principal due on long-term debt	40	41.67	46.51
32.	Summary of net sales for at least the most recent five years	43	44.79	44.79
33.	Description of marketing network for finished goods	41	42.71	42.71
34.	Current market value of quoted investments	35	36.46	38.46

(continued)

Table 5 (Continued)

No.	Item	No.	% of Cos	% of App Cos
35.	Revenue recognition method	36	37.50	37.50
36.	Future economic outlook of the company	33	34.38	34.38
37.	Breakdown of sales revenue by major product line, class of customer and geographical location	33	34.38	34.38
38.	Expenditure on human resources (e.g., training, welfare facilities)	31	32.29	32.29
39.	Basis of accounting	29	30.21	30.21
40.	Discussion of new product development	28	29.17	30.11
41.	Discussion of competitive position of the company	27	28.13	28.13
42.	Discussion of the major factors likely to influence following year's results	23	23.96	23.96
43.	Analysis of sales revenue and earnings attributable to foreign operations	18	18.75	23.08
44.	Expected future growth in sales	20	20.83	20.83
45.	Future economic outlook for the industry	19	19.79	19.79
46.	Discussion of the impact of inflation on the financial results	18	18.75	18.75
47.	Foreign assets and liabilities	16	16.67	18.60
48.	Information about research and development expenditures for the past year	16	16.67	17.98
49.	Information relating to subsidiaries (e.g., names, addresses, percentage ownership)	11	11.46	15.07
50.	Measure of physical level of output and capacity utilization	9	9.38	14.06
51.	Breakdown of earnings by major product line, class of customer and geographical location	11	11.46	11.98
52.	Nature and amount/effects of all major accounting changes made during the past year	9	9.38	9.38
53.	Information relating to post balance sheet events	8	8.33	8.42
54.	Indication of employee morale(e.g. labor turnover, strikes and absenteeism)	8	8.33	8.33
55.	Statement of foreign currency transactions	6	6.25	6.52
56.	Forecast of following year's profits	6	6.25	6.25
57.	Information on corporate social responsibility (e.g., attitude of the firm, expenditures)	6	6.25	6.25
58.	Amount of each subsidiary's earnings and parent's share	4	4.17	6.06
59.	Number and type of ordinary shareholders (e.g. institutions, individuals)	5	5.21	5.21
60.	Share of market in major product/service areas	5	5.21	5.21
61.	Number of shares owned by foreign parties	3	3.13	3.16
62.	Comparative balance sheets for the past five to ten years	3	3.11	3.11
63.	Current resale value of finished goods inventory	1	1.04	2.50
64.	Budgeted capital expenditures for the following year	2	2.08	2.08
65.	Security status of debentures	1	1.04	1.04
66.	Expected future growth in earning per share	1	1.04	1.04
67.	Cash flow projections for the following one to five years	1	1.04	1.04
68.	Comparative profit and loss accounts for the past five to ten years	1	1.04	1.04
69.	Historical summary of price range of ordinary shares	1	1.04	1.04

Note: None of the remaining information items were disclosed by any company.

percent. This means that the highest scoring company disclosed more than three times as much information as that scoring lowest. Differences in the extent of disclosure between companies are likely to cause lack of comparability between financial statements (Buzby 1974a). It should be noted that the vast majority of the 81 information items exceeded minimum legal requirements so that companies disclosed these items voluntarily, though one reason for companies to disclose more than the minimum specified in the legislation might be the legal requirement to give an "honest and fair view" of the true financial standing of the company.

THE PATTERN OF DISCLOSURE AND USER NEEDS

Table 5 shows the information items ranked by frequency of disclosure. It indicates the number of times disclosure was made, the percentage of companies making the disclosure and the percentage of companies to which the item was relevant making the disclosure. The average score for the 81 items was 37.7 percent with a very high standard deviation of 35.7. The first four items in the ranking were disclosed by all companies and the following 26 items by at least 50 percent of companies. At the other extreme, no company disclosed the lowest-ranking 12 items.

The relationship between frequency of disclosure and user needs was explored using the Spearman Correlation test. For preparers' perceptions of users' needs, a correlation coefficient of 0.6494 (significant at $p = 0.0001$) was found. This means that Jordanian companies appear to consider their estimation of the importance of information items to users in making their disclosure decisions. A rather less strong but nonetheless significant positive correlation coefficient of 0.384 (significant at $p = 0.0001$) was found between frequency of disclosure and user needs as expressed by all users in aggregate,[9] that is companies do tend to disclose those items of information judged by users to be relatively important. The relationship was also tested separately for individual user groups and significant positive relationships emerged for academics ($r = 0.4194$), bank loan officers ($r = 0.4192$) and institutional shareholders ($r = 0.4002$). By contrast, no significant relationships were found between disclosure and the importance of information as perceived by individual shareholders or stockbrokers. It is possible that the information these two groups consider themselves to need is regarded by preparers as too costly to produce or potentially damaging to the competitive position of the company. Another possible cause might be that individual shareholders are thought by preparers to be unlikely to be able to understand the information they perceive themselves to need; it seems unlikely that this explanation could extend to stockbrokers.

CONCLUSIONS

This study explored the adequacy of information provision, judged from the perspectives of users and preparers, in a less developed country with a moderately sophisticated capital market, Jordan. In indicating the information they needed, users assessed as important a high proportion of the items about which they were asked while, as in developed countries, placing a low value on future-oriented disclosures. Although preparers were asked to assess items from the point of view of users, they in fact tended to give items less importance than users themselves, a finding also consistent with studies of developed countries.

The five users groups investigated, individual shareholders, institutional shareholders, bank loan officers, academics and stockbrokers, had similar overall information needs although differences between groups in relation to individual items were established for about one third of the items covered and a significant overall difference emerged in respect to one pair of groups, individual shareholders and bank loan officers. This picture of a high degree of consensus within which some significant differences can be detected helps to elucidate previous studies of developed countries which have yielded apparently conflicting results. Substantially less consensus was found between users and preparers and, in particular, it was found that the perceptions of preparers and individual investors differed markedly.

Judged by the expressed needs of users, the overall level of disclosure by Jordanian companies was found to be poor, with on average only approximately one third of the information perceived by users as necessary to satisfy their needs being disclosed in practice. The degree of disclosure was highly variable between companies as was the level of disclosure between individual items. There was a significant positive correlation between level of disclosure of items and perceptions of need, the relationship being stronger in the case of preparers' perceptions than users'.

NOTES

1. The requirement to publish a statement of changes in financial position is implicit in the stipulations applying to audit.
2. Administered in connection with a further empirical study. A discussion paper setting out the results of this study is available from the second named author.
3. Further information about the statistical results can be obtained from the first named author.
4. The items were numbers 6, 11, 13-15, 19, 23, 25-27, 33, 36, 40, 42, 44, 45, 48, 49, 56-58, 71, 72, 74-76, 79, and 80. Further information is available from the first named author.
5. $p = 0.0222$; $Z = -2.2869$.
6. $p = 0.0029$; $Z = -2.9742$.
7. Full results are available from the first named author.
8. Full scores under all three approaches are available from the first named author.
9. See the previous section for a description of the basis of aggregation of user needs.

REFERENCES

Belkaoui, A. 1979. Is there a consensus on disclosure? *CA Magazine* (May), 44-46.

Benjamin, J. J., and K. G. Stanga. 1977. Differences in disclosure needs of major users of financial statements. *Accounting and Business Research* 7 (27): 187-192.

Buzby, S.L. 1974a. The nature of adequate disclosure. *Journal of Accountancy* (April): 38-47.

Buzby, S.L. 1974b. Selected items of information and their disclosure in annual reports. *The Accounting Review* 49 (3): 423-435.

Cerf, A. 1961. *Corporate Reporting and Investment Decisions.* Berkeley, CA: University of California.

Chandra, G. 1974. A study of the consensus on disclosure among public accountants and security analysts. *The Accounting Review* 49 (4): 733-742.

Chandra, G. 1975. Information needs of security analysts. *The Journal of Accountancy* (December): 65-70.

Chandra, G., and N. Greenball. 1977. Management reluctance to disclose: An empirical study. *Abacus* (December): 141-154.

Choi, F.D.S. 1973. Financial disclosure and entry to the European capital market. *Journal of Accounting Research* 11 (2): 159-175.

Chow, C.W., and A. Wong-Boren. 1987. Voluntary financial disclosure by Mexican corporations. *The Accounting Review* 62 (3): 533-541.

Civelek, M., and R. El-Khouri. 1991. Stock price volatility and macroeconomic variables: Evidence from Amman stock market. *Abhath Al-Yarmouk* 7: 9-27.

Cooke, T.E. 1989a. Disclosure in the corporate annual reports of Swedish companies. *Accounting and Business Research* (Spring): 113-124.

Cooke, T.E. 1989b. Voluntary corporate disclosure by Swedish companies. *Journal of International Financial Management and Accounting* 1: 171-195.

Cooke, T.E. 1992. The impact of size, stock market listing and industry type on disclosure in the annual reports of Japanese listed corporations. *Accounting and Business Research* 22: 229-237.

Courtis, J.K. 1992. The reliability of perceptions-based annual report disclosure studies. *Accounting and Business Research* 23 (89): 31-45.

Firth, M. 1978. A study of the consensus of the perceived importance of disclosure of individual items in corporate annual reports. *The International Journal of Accounting Education and Research* 14 (1): 57-70.

Firth, M. 1979a. The disclosure of information by companies. *Omega* 7 (2): 129-135.

Firth, M. 1979b. The impact of size, stock market listing and auditors on voluntary disclosure in corporate annual reports. *Accounting and Business Research* 9 (33): 273-280.

Firth, M. 1980. Raising finance and firms' corporate reporting policies. *Abacus* 16 (2): 100-115.

Firth, M. 1984. The extent of voluntary disclosure in corporate annual reports and its association with security risk measures. *Applied Economics*: 269-277.

Kahl, A., and A. Belkaoui. 1981. Bank annual reports disclosure adequacy internationally. *Accounting and Business Research* 11 (44): 189-196.

Marston, C. L., and P. J. Shrives. 1991. The use of disclosure indices in accounting research: A review article. *British Accounting Review* 23: 195-210.

McCaslin, T. E., and K. G. Stanga. 1986. Similarities in measurement needs of equity investors and creditors. *Accounting and Business Research* 16 (47): 151-156.

McKinnon, S. M. 1984. A cost-benefit study of disclosure requirements for multinational corporations. *Journal of Business Finance and Accounting* (Winter): 451-468.

McNally, G. M., L. H. Eng, and C. R. Hasseldine. 1982. Corporate financial reporting in New Zealand: An analysis of user preferences, corporate characteristics and disclosure practices for discretionary information. *Accounting and Business Research* 12 (46): 11-20.

Olson, W. E. 1977. Financial reporting: Fact or fiction? *Journal of Accountancy* (July): 68-71.

Oppenheim, P. 1966. *Questionnaire Design and Attitude Measurement.* London: Heinemann.

Robbins, W., and K. Austin. 1986. Disclosure quality in governmental financial reports: An assessment of the appropriateness of a compound measure. *Journal of Accounting Research* 24 (2): 412-421.

Singhvi, S. S., and H. B. Desai. 1971. An empirical analysis of the quality of corporate financial disclosure. *The Accounting Review* 46 (1): 129-138.

Spero, L. L. 1979. The extent and causes of voluntary disclosure of financial information in three European capital markets: An exploratory study. Doctoral dissertation, Harvard University Graduate School of Business.

Stanga, K. G. 1980. The relationship between relevance and reliability: Some empirical results. *Accounting and Business Research* 10 (38): 29-38.

Wallace, R. S. O. 1988a. Corporate financial reporting in Nigeria. *Accounting and Business Research* 18 (69): 352-362.

Wallace, R. S. O. 1988b. Intranational and international consensus on the importance of items in financial reports: A Nigerian case study. *British Accounting Review* 20 (3): 223-265.

COMPANIES' VOLUNTARY DISCLOSURE BEHAVIOR WHEN RAISING EQUITY CAPITAL:

A CASE STUDY OF JORDAN

Roger Buckland, Mishiel Suwaidan, and Lydia Thomson

ABSTRACT

This chapter examines the relationship between voluntary disclosure behavior of companies and the raising of capital on financial markets, in the context of a developing country (Jordan), where the regulation of disclosure, both legally and by the accounting profession, is weak. The methodology compares disclosure in annual reports for pairs of companies, matched in time and by size and industry, and differentiated by a capital-raising event. It reports a small but statistically significant increase in disclosure in capital-raising companies. The additional items disclosed are identified as concentrated in the categories of income statement, financial history, and ratio information. However, the authors conclude that in developing countries the free market pressures toward disclosure provided by the need to raise capital are unlikely to replace the need for a strong regulatory framework to ensure full and consistent disclosure.

Research in Accounting in Emerging Economies, Volume 4, pages 247-266.

ISBN: 1-55938-995-8

INTRODUCTION

The voluntary disclosure of information by companies contributes to knowledge about their past and present performance and informs expectations about their future. There have been many studies of the factors influencing the willingness to disclose information, both for individual items and for some overall measure or index of disclosure.[1] Among the major individual factors identified are company size and industry classification. A third influence that has been identified as associated with increased disclosure is the firm's need for capital. For example, Choi (1973a, 1973b) argued that increased disclosure reduces the amount of uncertainty associated with the present and future affairs of the company and thus will tend to lower a company's cost of capital. A similar argument was made by Mueller and colleagues (1987, 68): "[S]ecrecy is self-defeating. Failure to make reasonable disclosure in response to user needs can severely limit the pool of funds available to a corporation. Potential providers of capital, when kept in the dark, will simply put their money elsewhere." The theoretical justification for relating the availability of funds to the level of voluntary disclosure attained by a company can be seen in the context of agency theory. In an environment in which there is asymmetry of information between agents, shareholders and bondholders, the disclosure of additional information is viewed as an attempt by the agent to alleviate adverse selection and moral hazard problems in order to facilitate new capital financing (Ruland et al. 1990). Since shareholders and bondholders are risk averse, any additional information disclosed which reduces their perceived risk will be rewarded by a lower required rate of return (Choi and Levich 1990).

Previous studies of disclosure have found that companies with shares listed on a financial market exhibit increased levels of disclosure, whether because of the listing requirements, or as a way of reducing the cost of capital (see, for example, Wallace et al. 1994). However, this study focuses on a different question, whether a listed company is stimulated to further disclosure by the need to raise further capital. Empirical studies in developed economies have confirmed that the event of raising capital is associated with an increase in voluntary disclosure (Choi 1973a; Firth 1980). However, as yet the issues have not been addressed in the context of a developing country. Here stock markets are likely to be relatively new and unsophisticated. Funds for investment may be limited, or alternatively, there may be a shortage of investment vehicles for the available funds. The imperfections of these markets may mean that increased information flows are less important in the raising of finance. On the other hand, the motivation for increased disclosure may well be stronger than in the context of a developed country, as the extent of existing disclosure is likely to be low in the absence of a strong regulatory framework, such as that provided by sophisticated company legislation or a well-established accountancy profession. If this is so, voluntary disclosure could play a vital role in providing information to the market, and, in turn, the stimulation of such disclosure by the need to raise capital could be a significant agent of change in accounting practice.

To examine these issues, the present study explores the extent to which companies listed on the Jordanian stock exchange (the Amman Financial Market, or AFM), altered their disclosure practices around the time they raised additional equity capital in the market, during the period 1980-1992. In the remainder of the paper we first sketch in the necessary background to financial reporting in Jordan, and the development of the AFM. The following sections develop the research methodology, which matches a sample of capital-raising companies with a second, control group which did not raise capital. We then present the research results, which indicate a significant positive relationship between the raising of capital and increased voluntary disclosure. Examination of the additional items disclosed shows that they are particularly relevant to the users of company accounts. We conclude by discussing the implications of such a stimulus to disclosure in the evolution of accounting practice in a developing country with a recently introduced stock market.

THE JORDANIAN CONTEXT

The Amman Financial Market

The establishment of the AFM, the only stock exchange in the country, was a major step in developing the financial sector in Jordan to enable it to realize a better utilization of available financial resources. It was set up in 1976 as a government agency, but with legal, financial and administrative independence from government, through the Amman Financial Market Law 1976, no. 31. Trading started on January 1, 1978.

As pointed out by Civelek and El-Khouri (1991, 11), the market is small and thin. It began with 57 listed companies, increasing to 148 companies by 1995. In 1992 market capitalization was JD 2270.6 million, and trading volume JD 878.7 million, in the context of an economy with a GDP of JD 3493 million.[2] Companies are officially grouped into four sectors: banking and finance (contributing 42.7 percent of total capitalization in 1994); insurance (2.4 percent); services (6.8 percent); and industrial (i.e., manufacturing, 48.1 percent).

Reporting Requirements

There are two major sources of regulation of corporate financial reporting in Jordan: the Companies Acts of 1964 and 1989, and the AFM Laws of 1976.[3] The Companies Act 1964 requires the board of directors of every limited shareholding company to prepare and publish an audited balance sheet and a profit and loss account, with "a sufficient exposition" of the major items of revenues and expenses.

There were no other specific disclosure requirements. The 1989 Act recognized the large economic growth that had taken place in the country, and the establishment of the AFM. It requires a balance sheet and profit and loss account, with comparative figures, which show "the true results," and which are prepared in accordance with generally accepted accounting principles (GAAP). However, GAAP are not further defined in the act, and no formats are provided for the two statements.

The second source of regulation for listed companies are the AFM rules. The 1976 Act required companies "to supply information considered necessary by the market ... in particular the balance sheet and final accounts for the preceding year, signed by a licensed auditor," but made no further mention of specific disclosures, or standards to which the accounts should conform.

In developed countries, in the absence of comprehensive legal regulation of disclosure, standards of reporting can be set and enforced by the accounting profession. In Jordan, although a requirement for audited accounts was present in the Companies Act 1964, the accounting profession was weak and loosely regulated until the Auditing Law of 1985. This set up examination and licensing requirements for auditors, and provided for the establishment of the first professional association, the JACPA. Although the JACPA has not issued any national standards or defined GAAP, it issued in 1989 a directive recommending that its members should consider international accounting standards (IAS) as local GAAP. However, according to Matter (1995) the lack of legislation means that compliance with such standards by auditors and companies is questionable. There was also only limited influence from the international accounting firms: in the study period, none of the "Big Six" had branches in the country, although four local firms had professional cooperation arrangements with international firms.

In summary, it is clear that in the majority of the period covered by this study (1980-1992), there was little detailed regulation, either legal or professional, of what should be disclosed by Jordanian companies. This creates uncertainty as to what constitutes mandatory and voluntary disclosure as companies can exercise considerable discretion over their reporting policies. This paper therefore takes a broad view of voluntary disclosure (like El-Essa 1991), defining it in terms of those items of information which are neither specified in the Companies Act nor in the AFM Laws. A similarly broad definition had been adopted by Firth (1979) in studying voluntary disclosure in the United Kingdom, Cooke (1989b) in Sweden, and Raffournier (1995) in Switzerland.

METHODOLOGY

Channels for Disclosure

The objective of the study is to compare changes in disclosure by companies raising capital on the AFM with companies that did not raise capital. There are a number of possible vehicles for the disclosure of financial information. Where capital is raised, one important information channel might be the share prospectus the contents of which are prescribed by AFM regulations. The prospectus is composed of 14 sections requiring information about the company and the securities being offered. Historical information is stressed in that a company must provide financial statements, including a statement of changes in financial position, for three years, and information on the movements of the company's share price over the past two years. In addition, the prospectus should include the names of shareholders whose ownership exceeds 10 percent of the company's share capital, and information about the application of the offer proceeds, a description of the company's activities, its future plans, and its capital structure.

However, the issue of the prospectus is a one off event, offering no possibility of examining voluntary disclosure over a period of time, and as noncapital-raising companies do not issue prospectuses, a matched-pairs design cannot be used. Thus we chose to examine disclosure in the annual accounts, which are one of the major channels for providing information about a company to the market, particularly in a developing country where other sources of information are sparse. Previous studies of Jordan indicated that user groups, including investors, considered annual reports as the most important source of information for decision making (Solas and Bakay 1989; Abu-Nassar and Rutherford 1996). The disclosure of information in the prospectus may have no influence on disclosure in the annual accounts. Alternatively, it is possible that disclosure in the annual report is stimulated by the information required for the prospectus, as this is now available without further cost. Moreover, disclosure in the year of issue may lead to disclosure in future years to maintain consistency of reporting.

Sample Selection

Both newly established companies raising capital for the first time through a public offering of shares and established companies increasing their capital by an additional issue could have been included in the study. However, due to problems of obtaining information on disclosure practices before the capital-raising event for newly established companies, the study is therefore limited to established companies. As shown in Table 1, the number of such existing companies raising capital on the AFM is small. It was thus necessary to draw data over a long time period, defined by the start of trading on the AFM in 1978 and the last published annual reports available at the commencement of the study, 1992. The population of capital-raising companies in this period was 46.

There is evidence (for example, Barrett 1977) that levels of disclosure increase through time, and this is likely to be particularly relevant in the context of a developing country where initial disclosure is low. To allow for this, the research design used pairs of companies, matched in time, where one company raised capital, and one served as a control. A five-year window was chosen, starting three

Table 1. Companies Making Public Offerings of Shares on the AFM, 1980-1991

Year	*Listed Companies**	*Capital-Raising Companies***	*Sample Companies*
1980	71	10	3
1981	72	4	2
1982	93	12	6
1983	106	4	3
1984	116	1	1
1985	116	3	2
1986	114	3	3
1987	114	4	3
1988	115	1	1
1989	114	1	1
1990	109	1	1
1991	109	2	2
Total		46	28

Notes: * Source: AFM monthly statistical bulletin, No. 9, 1993c.
** Source: Several issues of AFM annual reports.

years ($t-3$) before the capital-raising event (t) to one year after ($t+1$). Previous research has shown that this observation period is sufficient to capture any changes in disclosure (Choi 1973a; Firth 1980). Firth (1980) argued that it is unlikely that a capital-raising company will start changing its disclosure policies three years in advance of its financing plans.

The requirement for annual reports for three years prior to, and one year after, the raising of capital, reduced the number of companies to 28, representing 60 percent of the total number of companies raising equity capital in Jordan during the period 1980-1991.

In selecting control companies, the first matching criterion used was company size, which has been found in several studies to be an important factor influencing the level of disclosure (for example, Cooke 1993; Raffournier 1995). While it is less clear that size will affect the *change* in disclosure through time, as far as possible companies were matched by size, measured by total assets.[4] While every attempt was made to satisfy the size criterion, in a few cases it was not possible to have a pair within plus or minus 20 percent difference in total assets, due to the limitation of the number of companies listed on the AFM. In such cases, the strategy adopted was to select a control with the closest total assets to that of the capital-raising company. Correlation of total assets for the capital-raising group and the control group gave a coefficient of 0.80, showing the overall level of matching.[5]

Industry grouping has also been found to influence the level of disclosure, and it is possible that there may be industry-wide trends in disclosure through time (Belkaoui and Kahl 1978). To control for this, a second matching criterion of

Table 2. Sample Companies by Industry Type

Industry Type	*Number of Companies*
Banks & Financial Companies	5
Insurance Companies	4
Service Companies	2
Manufacturing Companies	17
Total	28

industry category, as defined by the AFM, was used. Within the industrial sector, companies were further matched on the basis of the main reported line of business, where this was possible. However, precise matching by activity was secondary to matching by company size, due both to the limited number of companies listed on the AFM and to the limited number of companies that could be grouped under a similar line of business. Further, company size has been shown to be more important in influencing disclosure than industry type (for example, Choi 1973a). Table 2 illustrates the distribution of the sample of companies according to the industry classification, and Appendix A provides a listing of the companies selected for the study, with information about their size, their industry class, and the time window for observation of disclosure.

The sample selection adopted thus controls as far as possible for time period, size, and industry. The experimental design should randomize the influence of other variables that might affect disclosure, such as the auditors used. Thus, it is reasonable to assume that a significant change in disclosure over the five-year window for a capital-raising company compared to that of its control can be attributed to the event of raising capital.

Measurement of Disclosure

In order to make comparisons between the capital issuing group and the control group, a method of measuring the degree of disclosure must be chosen. Previous studies have compiled a list of items that might be presented in corporate annual reports and have measured disclosure against this list. To select a set of financial and non-financial items whose disclosure may be relevant for investment decision-making and which may be voluntarily disclosed by Jordanian companies, an extensive review of the disclosure literature was undertaken. This includes the work of Cerf (1961), Singhvi and Desai (1971), Choi (1973a), Buzby (1974), Stanga (1976), Barrett (1977), Firth (1979), Kahl and Belkaoui (1981), Firer and Meth (1986), Chow and Wong-Boren (1987), Wallace (1988), Cooke (1989a, 1991), Williams and Graves (1994), and Hossain and colleagues (1994). The items identified from this literature review were screened for their use in more than one study. In addition, a review of a pilot sample of annual reports issued by

AFM-listed Jordanian companies was conducted in order to identify items that were voluntarily disclosed. A final list of 75 items of information was drawn up, categorized into seven types: general information, balance sheet information, income statement and other statements information, projections and future information, financial history information, ratios and other statistics, and market-based information (Appendix B gives details of the individual items).

Having identified the list of items, the simplest way of measuring disclosure is to count the number of these disclosed in a specific company's annual report. However, not all items in the list will be applicable to all companies, for example, companies in the service sector are unlikely to have high levels of inventories and so disclosure of the inventory breakdown will not be applicable to them. One can adjust for this by constructing an index, measured as the percentage of items disclosed of those relevant to that company. A further possible refinement in measuring disclosure is to weight the items in the index, where the weights are usually based on the relative importance of selected items of information, as perceived by user groups such as financial analysts. Following Buzby (1974), this scheme has been used by several researchers (for example, Stanga 1976; Kahl and Belkaoui 1981; Firth 1979; Firer and Meth 1986; Malone et al. 1993). However, while some items should carry more weight than others (for example disclosure of a statement of changes in financial position when compared to the number of employees), specific weights are difficult to establish. This is particularly so when considered retrospectively across extended periods of time. Further, weighted and unweighted index approaches have been found to give very similar results empirically, especially where the disclosure index is composed of a large number of items (Firth 1979; Chow and Wong-Boren 1987; Cooke 1989b).

For the present study we therefore considered and tested two disclosure measures: first, the number of items disclosed, and, second, an unweighted disclosure index, constructed as the percentage of items disclosed of those relevant to that company. The matching by industry used in the experimental design will promote commensurability of the two measures, as many of the applicability problems are greater for comparisons across industry groups.

RESULTS

The major research hypothesis tested is stated below:

H1: The increase in disclosure across the five-year window around the capital-raising event is greater in the capital-raising companies than in the control group.

All the tests and analyses described below were carried out for both disclosure measures, the number of items disclosed and the disclosure index. The

Table 3. Number of Items Disclosed by Capital-Raising and Control Companies

	Capital-Raising Group			*Control Group*			*Difference*
Sample Pair	Xi_{t-3}	Xi_{t+1}	$Xi_{t+1} - Xi_{t-3}$	Yi_{t-3}	Yi_{t+1}	$Yi_{t+1} - Yi_{t-3}$	$(Xi_{t+1} - Xi_{t-3})$ - $(Yi_{t+1} - Yi_{t-3})$
1	22	23	1	16	15	−1	2
2	17	19	2	19	22	3	−1
3	20	32	12	20	17	−3	15
4	13	23	10	29	28	−1	11
5	25	27	2	24	25	1	1
6	14	17	3	19	20	1	2
7	5	19	14	17	12	−5	19
8	16	17	1	14	17	3	−2
9	24	28	4	25	31	6	−2
10	24	30	6	27	26	−1	7
11	17	20	3	21	19	−2	5
12	19	27	8	18	29	11	−3
13	17	23	6	20	17	−3	9
14	20	21	1	16	23	7	−6
15	15	16	1	14	17	3	−2
16	20	14	−6	15	11	−4	−2
17	13	16	3	20	19	−1	4
18	18	20	2	16	15	−1	3
19	17	25	8	25	31	6	2
20	17	18	1	10	15	5	−4
21	20	16	−4	18	14	−4	0
22	18	30	12	18	21	3	9
23	15	22	7	16	13	−3	10
24	18	31	13	23	30	7	6
25	41	45	4	31	40	9	−5
26	9	19	10	15	25	10	0
27	27	29	2	27	27	0	2
28	22	36	14	30	27	−3	17
Mean	18.68	23.68	5.00	20.11	21.64	1.54	3.46

two measures were found to be very highly correlated, and the analyses carried out led to identical conclusions. To simplify the exposition, we therefore restrict the reporting of the results to those concerning the number of items disclosed.

Table 3 shows, for each pair of companies, the number of items disclosed three years before the capital-raising event and one year after. On average the capital-raising group disclosed 18.68 items at time (t–3), compared to 20.11 for the control group. Over the five year period to time (t+1) the capital-raising group increased their average disclosure by 5.00 items to 23.68, while the control group also increased average disclosure, but by only 1.54 items, to 21.64. The net increase for the capital-raising group over the control group is thus 3.46 items.

As discussed above, the total number of potential items identified for measurement of disclosure was 75. Table 3 therefore indicates that average levels of disclosure are around 25 percent. However, the sample comprises observations of disclosure over a period of more than ten years, and for companies across a range of sectors. Thus too much weight should not be attached to the actual level of disclosure, except to comment that even in the companies with the highest level of disclosure there is plenty of room for increases. What is more significant is the comparison of disclosure for each pair of companies. If the raising of additional capital promotes disclosure, the matching used in the research design should ensure that prior to the capital-raising event there is little difference in disclosure, while subsequently disclosure should be greater for the capital-raising company than for the control. This allows us to restate our main hypothesis H1 as a number of subsidiary hypotheses. Formally, if Xi refers to disclosure for the ith capital-raising company, and Yi to disclosure for its control, the following hypotheses can be tested:

H2: $Xi_{t-3} - Yi_{t-3} = 0$

H3: $Xi_{t+1} - Yi_{t+1} > 0$

A stronger test allows for the fact that disclosure levels before the capital-raising event may be different and tests whether the net increase in disclosure is positive, by formally testing the hypothesis:

H4: $(Xi_{t+1} - Xi_{t-3}) - (Yi_{t+1} - Yi_{t-3}) > 0$

These hypotheses can be tested parametrically using the paired sample t-test. However, if the distribution of the underlying population variables from which the samples are drawn does not meet the normality assumptions necessary for the application of parametric tests, the nonparametric Wilcoxon signed ranks test should be applied (see Siegel 1956, 75-83).

Table 4 shows that the results for the parametric and nonparametric tests are very similar. In both cases, there is no significant difference in the amount of disclosure between the capital-raising group and the control group at t–3, but at t+1 the capital-raising group discloses significantly more information (at better than the 5 percent level) than the control group. Both tests also support H4, that the net increase in disclosure is positive, at even higher significance levels of around 1 percent. Thus the major research hypothesis H1 is strongly supported: the increase in disclosure across the five-year window around the capital-raising event is greater in the capital-raising companies than in the control group.

However, some caveats must be made to these findings. Firstly, although significantly greater than zero, the average extra amount of information

Table 4. Tests of Differences in Disclosure Between the Capital Raising and Control Groups

Panel a: Parametric Tests, Paired Sample T-Tests

Hypothesis		*Mean*	*SD*	*SE of Mean*	*t-value*	*P value*[*]
H2	$X_{t-3} - Y_{t-3}$	−1.43	5.73	1.08	−1.12	0.272
H3	$X_{t+1} - Y_{t+1}$	2.04	5.24	0.99	2.06	0.025
H4	$(X_{t+1} - Y_{t+1}) - (X_{t-3} - Y_{t-3})$	3.46	6.60	1.250	2.78	0.005

Panel b: Non-parametric tests, Wilcoxon Signed Rank Test

Hypothesis		*N*	*N for Test*	*Wilcoxon Statistic*	*P value*[*]	*Estimated Median*
H2	$X_{t-3} - Y_{t-3}$	28	25	119.0	.247	−1.0
H3	$X_{t+1} - Y_{t+1}$	28	27	261.0	.043	2.0
H4	$(X_{t+1} - Y_{t+1}) - (X_{t-3} - Y_{t-3})$	28	26	265.5	.012	3.0

Panel c: Regression Analysis

Dependent Variable	*Predictor*	*Coefficient*	*Standard Deviation*	*t-ratio*	*P value*	*R-sq adj*
$(X_{t+1} - Y_{t+1}) - (X_{t-3} - Y_{t-3})$	Constant	2.40	1.00	2.40	.024	.397
	$X_{t-3} - Y_{t-3}$	−0.75	0.17	−4.33	.000	

Note: [*] Prob. values are calculated for a 2-tailed test for H2, and for 1-tailed tests for H3 and H4.

provided is small, averaging around 3.5 items from the disclosure list of 75, an increase of around 20 percent on the around 20 items already being disclosed. Secondly, although the mean difference between the capital-raising and control groups at *t*-3 is not significantly different from zero (Table 4), examination of Table 3 shows that this conceals a wide range of both positive and negative differences. These initial differences may be random, or due to imperfect experimental design. For example, because of the limited number of companies on the AFM, matching for size may be inexact. However, while the correlation between the size difference and the initial disclosure difference is positive, it is low ($r = 0.3$) and not significantly different from zero. Further, as discussed above, while size has been shown to affect the level of disclosure, there is no evidence that it would affect changes in disclosure across the five-year window. However, the initial differences may reflect one company lagging behind the disclosure "ethos" for a particular sector. In this case, there may be a tendency for it to increase disclosure through time towards the group norm. Table 3 shows that the net increase in disclosure does seems to show positive values where disclosure in the capital-raising group at t–3 (X_{t-3}) is less than for the control group (Y_{t-3}), and vice versa. This suggests that there is some "catch-up" effect, which may be influencing the results. To allow for this, the net difference in disclosure $[(X_{t+1} - Y_{t+1}) - (X_{t-3} - Y_{t-3})]$ was regressed against the initial difference in disclosure ($X_{t-3} - Y_{t-3}$) (see Table

Table 5. Mean of Items Disclosed by Type of Information

Information Type	*Items*	*Average Items Disclosed*						
		Capital-Raising Group			*Control Group*			*Difference*
		X_{t-3}	X_{t+1}	$X_{t+1} - X_{t-3}$	Y_{t-3}	Y_{t+1}	$Y_{t+1} - Y_{t-3}$	$(X_{t+1} - X_{t-3}) - (Y_{t+1} - Y_{t-3})$
General Information	17	4.43	5.25	.82	4.86	5.43	0.57	0.25
Balance Sheet	15	5.98	6.80	.82	5.86	6.29	0.43	0.39
Income statement	14	4.32	6.18	1.86	4.82	5.46	0.64	1.21
Projections & Future	9	1.21	1.25	0.04	1.10	.96	−0.14	0.18
Financial History	7	1.36	2.18	0.82	1.60	1.71	0.11	0.71
Ratios & Statistics	10	1.39	1.96	0.57	1.75	1.61	−0.14	0.71
Market-Based	3	0.00	0.07	0.07	0.04	0.11	0.07	0.00
Total	75	18.7	23.7	5.0	20.1	21.6	1.5	3.5

4c). The significant negative coefficient reported on the initial difference in disclosure tends to support the catch-up effect. However, the constant term implies a net increase in disclosure for the capital-raising group over the control group of 2.4 items, after controlling for the catch-up effect; and the coefficient is statistically significant at the 2.5 percent level. Thus H1 is again upheld.

The initial analysis reported above showed that the capital-raising event was associated with an average net increase in disclosure of 3.46 items, or 97 items across the 28 pairs of companies. Further investigation was undertaken to identify the causes of the increase. The overall increase in disclosure is made up of disclosure of new items of information by the capital-raising companies (84 items), and by the continued disclosure by the capital-raising companies, when items are dropped from the reports of the control group (13 items). Statistical analysis using paired sample *t*-tests shows insignificant difference in behaviour between the capital-raising and control groups in the dropping of items (a one-tailed probability of 78 percent), but significantly more new items are disclosed by the capital-raising than the control group (a one-tailed probability value of 0.3 percent). Thus the event of capital-raising does seem to be associated with a change in behavior, and a positive decision to provide more information in the annual reports of capital-raising companies.

The next stage of the analysis was to identify what types of new information were being provided. Table 5 shows average disclosure for each of seven categories (as defined in Appendix B). While there is a positive increase in disclosure in all categories, Table 5 clearly shows that the main increases in disclosure come in the Income Statement (an average net increase of 1.21 items), in Financial History (0.71) and in Ratios and Statistics (0.71). Table 6 summarizes the results of statistical tests on the categorized data, confirming that the

Table 6. Paired Sample Tests of Differences in Disclosure Between the Capital-Raising and Control Groups, by Type of Information

Hypothesis		*Parametric Test t-test Prob. value**	*Non-parametric test Wilcoxon Signed Ranks Prob. value**
	General Information		
H2	$X_{t-3} - Y_{t-3}$	.167	.108
H3	$X_{t+1} - Y_{t+1}$	.330	.293
H4	$(X_{t+1} - Y_{t+1}) - (X_{t-3} - Y_{t-3})$	.294	.300
	Balance Sheet		
H2	$X_{t-3} - Y_{t-3}$	.461	.477
H3	$X_{t+1} - Y_{t+1}$	.102	.152
H4	$(X_{t+1} - Y_{t+1}) - (X_{t-3} - Y_{t-3})$	.135	.259
	Income Statement		
H2	$X_{t-3} - Y_{t-3}$	.142	.126
H3	$X_{t+1} - Y_{t+1}$	.032	.034
H4	$(X_{t+1} - Y_{t+1}) - (X_{t-3} - Y_{t-3})$	.003	.004
	Projections & Future Information		
H2	$X_{t-3} - Y_{t-3}$	.299	.302
H3	$X_{t+1} - Y_{t+1}$	.059	.068
H4	$(X_{t+1} - Y_{t+1}) - (X_{t-3} - Y_{t-3})$	.259	.257
	Financial History		
H2	$X_{t-3} - Y_{t-3}$	.211	.211
H3	$X_{t+1} - Y_{t+1}$	.071	.055
H4	$(X_{t+1} - Y_{t+1}) - (X_{t-3} - Y_{t-3})$	.024	.028
	Ratios & Other Statistics		
H2	$X_{t-3} - Y_{t-3}$	.120	.133
H3	$X_{t+1} - Y_{t+1}$	.062	.082
H4	$(X_{t+1} - Y_{t+1}) - (X_{t-3} - Y_{t-3})$	.013	.026
	Market Based Information		
H2	$X_{t-3} - Y_{t-3}$	.163	.158
H3	$X_{t+1} - Y_{t+1}$	.335	.342
H4	$(X_{t+1} - Y_{t+1}) - (X_{t-3} - Y_{t-3})$	.500	.500
	All information		
H2	$X_{t-3} - Y_{t-3}$	.272	.247
H3	$X_{t+1} - Y_{t+1}$	.025	.043
H4	$(X_{t+1} - Y_{t+1}) - (X_{t-3} - Y_{t-3})$	.005	.012

Note: * Prob. values are calculated for a 2-tailed test for H2, and for 1-tailed tests for H3 and H4.

categories showing significant increases in disclosure are the Income Statement, Financial History, and Ratios and Statistics.

Examination of the disaggregated data for these three categories gives some indication of the individual items for which net disclosure increased most. These are found to be:

Income Statement:

a statement of changes in financial position (8 companies);

breakdown of sales revenues (6);

breakdown of operating expenses (5);

expenditure on publicity and advertising (5).

Financial History:

sales for the past 3-5 years (6);

sales for the past 6-10 years (5);

other financial data for the past 3-5 years (5).

Ratios and Other Statistics:

expenditure on human resources (6).

In the other categories, the only items where there was a net disclosure increase of five or more companies were: information on the impact of inflation (5), list of marketable securities (9), and capital expenditure for the past year (7).

DISCUSSION AND CONCLUSIONS

As described above, the context for this study was a developing country, which had only recently established a financial market, and where there was very little regulation of the disclosure of information, either legal or professional. The design of the study, using pairs of companies matched in time, and for size and industry, isolates the impact of capital-raising on the disclosure of information in the main financial document, the annual report. We have reported above results that support the main hypothesis, that for Jordanian companies over the period 1980-1992 the event of raising capital is associated with significant increased disclosure. Moreover, these results are robust for two measures of disclosure (the increase in the number of items disclosed, or the increase in an unweighted disclosure index) and for both parametric and nonparametric tests. However, the amount of additional disclosure is small, raising the low initial level on average only by around 20 percent. Further, there is little consistency across the sample in the additional items disclosed, the most frequent items applying to only around a third of companies.

The types of additional information disclosed were seen to be concentrated in three categories, income statement information, financial history, and ratios and other statistics. Some of these items seem to be stimulated by the publication of the prospectus, with its requirement for a statement of changes in financial position, and emphasis on the provision of historical information. Arguably, prospectus publication has made such items available to capital-raising firms for disclosure at minimal cost. The disclosure of other information required by the prospectus, such as share price movements, has not increased.

It is interesting to appraise the usefulness of the additional information disclosed to the users of the accounts, focussing on investors and potential investors and their decisions to buy, hold, or sell shares. A possible framework is provided by the U.K. Accounting Standard Board's (ASB's) definition in the Draft Statement of Principles (1995) that the objective of financial statements is "to provide information about the financial position, performance and financial adaptability of an enterprise, that is useful...for making economic decisions" (para. 1.1), and that these decisions involve "predicting cash flows and assessing financial adaptability" (para. 1.9). As shown above, one of the most common items of additional information is a statement of changes in financial position (equivalent to a cash flow statement), which has a direct relevance to predicting future cash flows. Disclosure of the history of sales, and of other financial data also improves the forecasting of future performance, as it might be argued does also the disclosure of the breakdown of operating expenses. Other current expenditure which will impact on future performance includes capital expenditure and spending on human resources (for training, and so on), and advertising.[6] Information on the marketable securities held can also be considered to aid predictions of current and future liquidity. Thus it does seem that what additional information is disclosed is well tailored to the needs of existing or prospective shareholders in determining whether to invest in a company.

In conclusion, we have shown that in this case of a developing country, the need to raise capital on a financial market does provide some stimulus to the disclosure of information, and the additional information disclosed is likely to be useful to investors. However, the extent of additional disclosure is limited, and items disclosed are not consistent across companies. Thus the need to raise capital has not acted in Jordan as a powerful engine of change in disclosure practices. It is therefore unlikely that in similar developing countries the existence of a stock market, and the disclosure behavior of capital-raising companies, will reduce the need for a strong regulatory regime as the means to ensure full and consistent disclosure.

APPENDIX A

Capital-Raising Companies and Their Control

Pair	Capital-Raising Group	Year of Raise	T. Assets ('000)	Control Group	T. Assets ('000)	Period Covered
	Banks					
1	Jordan National Bank	1982	111258	Jordan Kuwait Bank	86476	1979-83
2	Cairo Amman Bank	1985	129266	Arab Bank for Invest.	100146	1982-86
3	Bank of Jordan	1986	126541	Jordan Gulf Bank	109210	1983-87
4	Jordan Islamic Bank	1986	161661	Housing Bank	427072	1984-87
5	Amman Bank for Invest.	1991	89021	Business Bank	94027	1988-92
	Insurance					
6	Jordan French Insurance	1981	3761	Jordan Insurance	7558	1978-82
7	Jerusalem Insurance	1982	2353	Middle East Insurance	2055	1979-83
8	Yarmouk Ins & Reins	1984	1747	Jordan Gulf Insurance	1958	1981-85
9	Arabian Seas Insurance	1990	3300	United Insurance	3393	1987-91
	Service					
10	Arab International	1987	9824	Jordan Hotels & Tour	9128	1984-88
11	Irbid District Elect	1983	14571	Jordan Electricity	44263	1980-84
	Manufacturing					
12	Cement Factories	1980	53580	Phosphate Mines	73072	1978-81
13	Petroleum Refinery	1980	105548	Arab Potash	100547	1978-81
14	Jor Pipes Manufacture	1980	3608	Paper & Cardboard	2965	1978-81
15	Jordan Tanning	1981	2436	Chemical Detergent	1991	1978-82
16	Arab Inv & Inter Trade	1982	5563	Jordan Worsted Mills	5231	1979-83
17	Dar Al-Dawa	1982	2898	Jordan Beer Factories	1811	1979-83
18	Arab Pharma Manufac	1982	15732	Jordan Tobacco	11101	1978-83
19	Jor Spinning & Weavi	1982	4978	Ceramic Industries	3977	1979-83
20	Woolen Industries	1983	862	Printing & Packaging	700	1980-84
21	Rafia Industries	1983	756	Paper Converting	1476	1980-84
22	Indu Comm & Agricult	1985	9094	National Steel Indust.	8338	1982-86
23	National Industries	1986	4726	Jordan Wood Indust.	3379	1983-87
24	Inter Petro-Chemical	1987	8532	Jordan Glass Fact.	14283	1984-88
25	Phosphate Mines	1987	178792	Arab Potash	130674	1984-88
26	Cable & Wire Manufac	1988	6097	Sulpho Chemicals	7699	1985-89
27	Dar Al-Dawa	1989	9000	Arab Aluminium	8079	1986-90
28	Arab Centre for Phar	1991	6988	General Investment	4122	1988-92

APPENDIX B

Items and Categories in the Measures of Disclosure

General Information

1. List of directors.
2. Information on senior executives.
3. General outlook of the economy.
4. Discussion of major industry trends.
5. Date of incorporation.
6. Statement of the company's objectives.
7. Narrative history of the company.
8. Description of principal plants.
9. Description of marketing network for finished goods/services.
10. Summary of major products (services) produced.
11. Information on corporate social responsibility.
12. Contribution to the country.
13. Multiple language presentation.
14. General information on the impact of inflation on the company.
15. Information on the competitive position of the company.
16. Discussion of research and development activities.
17. Discussion of accounting policies underlying the preparation of financial statements.

Balance Sheet

18. Disclosure of market value of marketable securities.
19. List of marketable securities.
20. Inventory flow method used (Fifo, Lifo, and so on).
21. Basis of inventory valuation (cost, replacement costs, and so on).
22. Breakdown of inventories into raw material, work in process, and finished goods.
23. Market value of inventory.
24. Disclosure of original costs of fixed assets and accumulated depreciation.
25. Breakdown of fixed assets into land, building, equipment, and so on.
26. Market value of fixed assets.
27. Capital expenditure for the past year.
28. Breakdown of current liabilities.
29. Schedule of interest and principal due on long-term debts in future years.
30. Disclosure of commitments, contingencies, etc.
31. Allowance for doubtful accounts.
32. Breakdown of assets by product lines, customer classes or geographic allocations.

Income Statement and Other Statements

33. Breakdown of sales (revenues) by major product lines, customer classes or geographical locations.
34. Breakdown of net income by major product lines, customer classes or geographical locations.
35. Breakdown of other sources of revenues.
36. Method used in revenue recognition.
37. Cost of goods sold.
38. Method used for the depreciation of fixed assets.
39. Foreign currency translation method.
40. Accounting treatment of foreign exchange gains and losses.

(continued)

Appendix B (Continued)

Income Statement and Other Statements

41. Amount expended on advertising and publicity.
42. Breakdown of expenses into Fixed and variable.
43. Discussion of the company' results for the past year and reasons for change.
44. Statement of changes in financial position.
45. Price-level adjusted statements as supplementary information.
46. Breakdown of operating expenses.

Projections and Future Information

47. New products (services) development.
48. Factors influencing future business: technological, political, and economic.
49. Forecast earnings per share for next year.
50. Information on sales (revenues) for next year.
51. Forecast cash flow for the next year.
52. Capital expenditure for the next year.
53. Research and development expenditure for the next year.
54. Management discussion of future policies and objectives.
55. Post-balance sheet events.

Financial History

56. Balance sheet for the past three years
57. Income statement for the past three years.
58. Comparative statement of changes in financial position.
59. Sales (revenue) for the past 3-5 years.
60. Sales (revenue) for the past 6-10 years.
61. Net income for the past 3-5 years.
62. Other financial data for the past 3-5 years.

Ratios and other statistics

63. Growth rate in earnings.
64. Return on capital employed.
65. Interest coverage.
66. Current ratio.
67. Other ratios (e.g., debt/equity, debt/total assets, and so on).
68. The company's market share of major products/services.
69. Measure of physical level of output and rate of utilization.
70. Rate of return required by the company on its projects.
71. Number of employees.
72. Expenditure on human resources (e.g., training, developing, and so on).

Market-based Information

73. Price range of the company's share for the past few years.
74. Earnings per share.
75. Largest shareholders and size of holdings.

NOTES

1. See, for example, the work of Cerf (1961), Singhvi and Desai (1971), Choi (1973a), Buzby (1974), Stanga (1976), Barrett (1977), Firth (1979), Kahl and Belkaoui (1981), Firer and Meth (1986), Chow and Wong-Boren (1987), Wallace (1988), Cooke (1989a, 1991), Williams and Graves (1994), and Hossain and colleagues (1994).

2. In 1992 the exchange rate was JD 1.00 to UK £0.831, or US $1.47.

3. A further possible influence is the Income Tax Law of 1985, which includes directives on such matters as the calculation of depreciation, and the treatment of bad debts. However, while affecting the accounting methods used, there is no requirement for the disclosure of information in company reports.

4. Other possible measures of size are market capitalization and turnover. The three size measures are correlated at around 0.8, and in a parallel study (Suwaidan 1997) of the company characteristics affecting the level of disclosure in Jordanian companies, size measured by assets, turnover and market capitalization gave very similar results.

5. The Spearman rank correlation coefficient was 0.97.

6. It is interesting to note that expenditure on staff training and on advertising are exactly the type of "revenue investment," that is, expenses largely incurred for the benefit of future periods, which the ASB proposed that companies should disclose in FRED 1 (ASB 1991). The proposal was not carried through to the final standard (FRS3, ASB 1992), though elements of the thinking on revenue investment can be traced in the non-mandatory "Operating and Financial Review" (ASB 1993).

REFERENCES

Abu-Nassar, M., and B. A. Rutherford. 1996. External users of financial reports in less developed countries: The case of Jordan. *British Accounting Review* 28 (1): 73-87.

ASB. 1991. Financial Reporting Exposure Draft 1. *The Structure of Financial Statements—Reporting of Financial Performance*. London: Accounting Standards Board.

ASB. 1992. Financial Reporting Standard 3. *Reporting Financial Performance*. London: Accounting Standards Board.

ASB. 1993. *Operating and Financial Review*. London: Accounting Standards Board.

ASB. 1995. Exposure Draft. *Statement of Principles for Financial Reporting*. London: Accounting Standards Board.

Barrett, M. E. 1977. The extent of disclosure in annual reports of large companies in seven countries. *International Journal of Accounting Education and Research* 12 (2): 1-25.

Belkaoui, A., and A. Kahl. 1978. *Corporate Financial Disclosure in Canada*. Research Monograph No. 1, Canadian Certified General Accounting Association, Vancouver, Canada.

Buzby, S. L. 1974. Selected items of disclosure and their disclosure in annual reports. *The Accounting Review* 49 (3): 423-435.

Cerf, A. R. 1961. Corporate reporting and investment decisions. Unpublished doctoral thesis, University of California at Berkeley.

Choi, F. D. S. 1973a. Financial disclosure and entry to the European capital market. *Journal of Accounting Research* 11 (2): 159-175.

Choi, F. D. S. 1973b. Financial disclosure in relation to a firm's capital costs.*Accounting and Business Research* 3 (12): 282-292.

Choi, F. D. S., and R. M. Levich. 1990. *The Capital Market Effects of International Accounting Diversity*. Homewood, IL: Irwin.

Chow, C. W., and A. Wong-Boren. 1987. Voluntary financial disclosure by Mexican companies. *The Accounting Review* 63 (2): 533-541.

Civelek, M., and R. El-Khouri. 1991. Stock price volatility and macroeconomic variables: Evidence from Amman stock exchange. *Abhath Al-Yarmouk* 7 (3): 9-27.

Cooke, T. E. 1989a. Disclosure in corporate annual reports of Swedish companies. *Accounting and Business Research* 19 (74): 113-124.

Cooke, T. E. 1989b. Voluntary corporate disclosure by Swedish companies. *Journal of International Financial Management and Accounting* 2 (Summer): 171-195.

Cooke, T. E. 1991. An assessment of voluntary disclosure in the annual reports of Japanese corporations. *International Journal of Accounting Education and Research* 26 (3): 174-189.

Cooke, T. E. 1993. Disclosure in Japanese corporate annual reports. *Journal of Business Finance and Accounting* 20 (4): 521-535.

El-Essa, Y. A. 1991. The importance of accounting information and its availability in published annual reports for investors in AFM. *Mu'tah Journal for Research and Studies* 6 (2): 385-413.

Firer, C., and G. Meth. 1986. Information disclosure in annual reports in South Africa. *Omega* 14 (5): 373-382.

Firth, M. 1979. The disclosure of information by companies. *Omega* 7 (2): 129-135.

Firth, M. 1980. Raising capital and firms' corporate reporting policies. *Abacus* 16 (2): 100-115.

Hossain, M., T. M. Tan, and M. Adams. 1994. Voluntary disclosure in an emerging capital market: Some empirical evidence from companies listed on the Kuala Lumpur stock exchange. *The International Journal of Accounting* 29 (4): 334-351.

Kahl, A., and A. Belkaoui. 1981. Bank annual report disclosure adequacy internationally. *Accounting and Business Research* 11 (43): 189-196.

Malone, D., C. Fries, and T. Jones. 1993. An empirical investigation of the extent of disclosure in the oil and gas industry. *Journal of Accounting, Auditing and Finance* 8 (3): 249-273.

Matter, M. 1995. Accounting profession in Jordan: Current reality and future prospects. *Banks in Jordan* 14 (5): 20-27.

Mueller, G., H. Gernon, and G. Meek. 1987. *Accounting: An International Perspective*. Homewood, IL: Irwin.

Raffournier, B. 1995. The determinants of voluntary financial disclosure by Swiss listed companies. *European Accounting Review* 4 (2): 261-280.

Ruland, W., S. Tung, and N. George. 1990. Factors associated with the disclosure of managers' forecasts. *The Accounting Review* 66 (3): 710-721.

Siegel, S. 1956. *Nonparametric Statistics for Behavioural Sciences*. New York: McGraw-Hill.

Singhvi, S. S., and H. Desai. 1971. An empirical analysis of the quality of corporate financial disclosure. *The Accounting Review* 46 (1): 129-138.

Solas, C., and V. H. Bakay. 1989. The information needs of investors in unregulated capital markets: The Middle East capital markets as a case study. Paper presented at the First Conference in Accounting and Finance, December 10-12, Yarmouk University, Jordan.

Stanga, K. 1976. Disclosure in published annual reports. *Financial Management* 5 (4): 42-52.

Suwaidan, M. S. 1997. Voluntary disclosure of accounting information: The case of Jordan. Unpublished doctoral thesis, University of Aberdeen, Scotland.

Wallace, R. S. O. 1988. Intranational and international consensus on the importance of disclosure items in financial reports: A Nigerian case study. *British Accounting Review* 20 (2): 223-265.

Wallace, R. S. O., K. Naser, and A. Mora. 1994. The relationship between the comprehensiveness of corporate annual reports and firm characteristics in Spain. *Accounting and Business Research* 25 (97): 41-53.

Williams, J. R., and O. F. Graves. 1994. Corporate financial disclosure, company characteristics and environmental factors: A study of 13 countries. Paper presented to the 17th Annual Congress of the European Accounting Association, April.

PART V

ACCOUNTING EDUCATION AND FINANCIAL REPORTING IN SOUTHERN AFRICA

ACCOUNTING EDUCATION CHANGE: A CASE STUDY OF TANZANIA

David Alexander, Richard J. Briston, and R. S. Olusegun Wallace

ABSTRACT

This chapter looks at Tanzania as a case study of the regulatory and, particularly, educational problems of the development of accounting in the African context. The chapter outlines the background and then discusses the local professional body and professional examination system in some detail. Significant difficulties become apparent, and possible solutions are considered, but the difficulties of achieving a genuine local context without adequate local resources remain a major problem.

INTRODUCTION

In a chapter in *Research in Third World Accounting*, Volume 1, Briston and Wallace (1990), describing accounting education and corporate disclosure regulations in Tanzania, emphasized the individuality of developments in that country arising from the country's socialism and substantial independence from IMF influence.

Research in Accounting in Emerging Economies, Volume 4, pages 269-287.

ISBN: 1-55938-995-8

More recently, the situation in Tanzania has changed drastically in a number of respects. State socialism is being replaced by privatization and the accounting education system has been redesigned. What has not significantly changed, however, is the shortage of resources. This chapter provides an update of the position in terms of the objectives and achievements of accounting education in Tanzania, the local perceptions of the changes in the role of accounting needed to service the different economic and political environment now anticipated, and of the considerable difficulties which lie ahead. We embed this update of the Tanzanian situation in an exploration of key issues of principle, and our final section discusses and appraises an array of possible solutions available to assist Tanzania and the many other countries whose needs and problems are not dissimilar.

SOCIAL AND ECONOMIC ENVIRONMENT OF TANZANIA

The early background can be given by quoting from the Briston and Wallace paper (except that the present tense where used must now be changed to the past tense), as follows:

> Tanzania ... placed emphasis on promoting national unity and self-reliance as pre-requisites to economic development. She encouraged communal schemes and rallying activities, with a higher concern for the involvement of her people than for material profit. She pursued policies of popular mobilization, such as the nationalization of foreign assets and speedy indigenization with little regard to the conventional requirements of efficiency and economic development. Given the overwhelming influence which her first President, Julius Nyerere, had over her people between 1964 and 1984, it is no exaggeration to suggest that Tanzania was directed by one man over this period. Nyerere offered a radical leadership which went to the root of a problem or situation and followed its development until a solution was achieved. Even if that solution meant sudden changes and untried measures, he would single-mindedly pursue that logically determined course without yielding to the experience of others or the argument of precedent.

Beneath the façade of radical leadership and visible socialism is the stark reality of abject poverty. In the last 20 years or so Tanzania, like most African countries, has been severely and adversely affected by a chronic shortage of foreign exchange. The economies, and in many cases, the social fabric, have been devastated by drought, war and famine, high costs of imported fuel and high interest rates on foreign debt. Much of the broad scenario is encapsulated by the following extract from the *Tanzania Daily News* of June 14, 1994:

> Africa's maternal mortality is put at 700 per 100,000 live births and is the highest in the world. Life expectancy, at 51 years, is still the lowest in the world while undernourishment moved from 101 million in 1961-90 to 168 million in 1988-91 and may double by the year 2010.
>
> The continent's social challenge also involves bringing under control the rapid population and urbanization growth which has given rise to the many jobless and unemployed who are often ready participants in civil strife and unrest. Such unrest, coupled with the problems of ethnic imbalances, social injustice and corruption, have created serious problems of governance.

As at the end of 1996, evidence of the legacy of state socialism abounds in two quite different respects. The first is that the most significant organizations in the country are state-owned. The second level of this legacy is behavioral, in that modern corporate leaders, used to receiving instructions in the past from state functionaries, now lack initiative and self-reliance, and this attitude has influenced local accounting thought and practice in all its manifestations.

It is against this background that a policy of gradual privatization and movement toward a capitalist economy is being attempted. As evidence of this policy, the Prime Minister was quoted in the *Tanzania Daily News* of June 16, 1994, confirming the policy of privatization and a Capital Markets Act was passed by Parliament at the end of 1993, designed to lead to the creation of a stock exchange in the capital, Dar-es-Salaam.

There can be no doubt that the new personalities who took over the running of the country following the retirement of President Nyerere in 1984 influenced these changes. However, the collapse of the communist system in Europe, firstly outside the USSR and finally in the USSR itself at the end of the 1980s, and the resultant rapid shifts in economic philosophy toward capitalism and private investment in these former socialist countries was a further factor, if only because aid, both financial and managerial, from these countries disappeared as soon as the socialist role model ceased to dominate.

The Role of Accounting

The claimed role of accounting in a broadly capitalist economy is well-known. The IASC states (IASC 1996, ¶ 12) "The objective of financial statements is to provide information about the financial position, performance and changes in financial position of an enterprise that is useful to a wide range of users in making economic decisions."

The IASC Framework document suggests that these users can be grouped and considered as follows: investors, employees, lenders, suppliers and other trade creditors, customers, governments and their agencies, and, last but hopefully not least, the public. The document goes on to say (¶ 10):

> While all of the information needs of these users cannot be met by financial statements, there are needs which are common to all users. As investors are providers of risk capital to the enterprise, the provision of financial statements that meet their needs will also meet most of the needs of other users that financial statements can satisfy.

This last sentence would certainly earn a fail mark on any course in logic or philosophy, but the view is widely followed in practice. Accepting, however, that the needs of different users are likely to be different, at least in relative if not in absolute terms, it is clear that different national environments (cultural, political, and economic) are likely to lead to different accounting practices. Indeed accounting (as opposed to bookkeeping) is very much a social science. It therefore reflects the biases and norms, sometimes long term, sometimes transitory, of the societies in which it is embedded.

It is very important to remember that this "standard" exposition omits altogether any reference to the needs of management. Management are the people who have to take decisions, both day-to-day and strategic, about how the scarce resources within their control are to be used. They need information that will enable them to predict the likely outcomes of alternative courses of action. As part of this process, they will need feedback on the results of their previous decisions in order to extend successful aspects of the decisions, and to adapt and improve the unsuccessful aspects.

It can be persuasively suggested that in countries or economies without a sophisticated finance market, the relative importance of management information and management accounting becomes all the greater. The most important point is the final words of paragraph 12 of the IASC Framework, already quoted. Accounting information needs to be useful "in making economic decisions."

All this contrasts very sharply with the practices and attitudes which had developed under communism as practiced in Eastern Europe. As a formal measured and carefully worded statement, consider the following, written in the context of Poland but of general application (Bailey et al. 1990):

> After World War II, and with the creation of a centrally planned economy, there occurred a radical change in the function of accounting. By using the Soviet economy as a model accounting was transformed into a tool at the disposal of the central authorities for exercising an administrative surveillance over the activities of the nationalized enterprises in order to achieve the production goals in the national economic plans.
>
> The transformation of accounting at that time was achieved through the introduction of a standardized accountancy system which was compulsorily imposed upon enterprises, outside their individual control. Responsibility for the operation of the standardized accountancy system rested upon the Ministry of Finance, which was responsible for the design of the system and for the issue of the regulations governing accounting practices and procedures. The Ministry of Finance assumed responsibility for the content of educational programs in accounting although the educational institutions themselves were controlled by the educational ministries. The Accounting Association, recreated in a new form in 1956, also came under the Ministry of Finance.
>
> Accounting was transformed into a primarily clerical task for the classification and accumulation of data through accounting records for the purpose of the completion of periodical accounting and statistical returns for submission to superior authorities. The accounting task was thus confined to the creation of a record of accomplished activities in terms of historic cost.
>
> Accounting data was not used for the evaluation of enterprise performance and was not a significant consideration in the determination of investment strategies. An increasingly irrational pricing structure caused accounting to become decreasingly suitable for either purpose.

> Accounting therefore regressed to bookkeeping. De-skilling through the standardization of practices and procedures caused it to become an unattractive occupation with comparatively low social status.

Change

Much of Africa, and Tanzania represents a good illustration, is faced with all the problems implicit in the earlier discussion. There is acute scarcity of resources and of experience, and the experience and institutional framework which do exist are significantly influenced by the ethos of state control. Accounting has not been seen as focused on decision-making. What educational implications arise from this unsatisfactory situation?

Accountancy and accounting education throughout the world are in a state of flux, if not of crisis. In the United States, for example, the Accounting Education Change Commission (AECC) was set up in the late 1980s. Its report "Objectives of Education for Accountants" (AECC, 1990) included the following paragraphs:

> *Desired Capabilities*
>
> Accounting programs should prepare students to *become* professional accountants, not to *be* professional accountants at the time of entry to the profession. At the time of entry, graduates cannot be expected to have the range of knowledge and skills of experienced professional accountants. To attain and maintain the status of a professional accountant requires continual learning. Therefore, pre-entry education should lay the base on which life-long learning can be built. In other words, graduates should be taught how to learn. The base on which life-long learning is built has three components: skills, knowledge, and professional orientation.
>
> *Courses and Course Content*
>
> The overriding objective in developing course content should be to create a base upon which continued learning can be built. Professional accounting education has four components: general education, general business education, general accounting education, and specialized accounting education. The components can be addressed in a variety of ways. No one model of accounting education will be appropriate for all colleges and universities. Nevertheless, some minimum coverage of all four areas, including integration of the areas, should be part of the education of every accountant.
>
> *Instructional Methods*
>
> The overriding objective of accounting programs should be to teach students to learn on their own. Therefore, accounting programs should not focus primarily on preparation for professional examinations. Students should be taught the skills and strategies that help them learn more effectively and how to use these effective learning strategies to continue to learn throughout their lifetimes.

What this extract fails to include is explicit emphasis on the attitude change needed by the accounting practitioner—on the need to engender a more positive approach to risk-taking and the giving of creative advice. So, what are the real needs for accounting skills development and education in the African context? An excellent general insight into this area is given by a quotation from a report to a working group of the United Nations Economic and Social Council (United Nations 1993a):

> The educational needs of accountants are driven by their role and responsibilities. These are a function of the degree of country development and the particular economic environment. For one of the most interesting items in the questionnaire it was asked whether the needs for accounting education in developing countries were different from those in developed countries. The responses indicated that in general, accountants in developing countries need basic skills in order to control and manage state enterprises, collect taxes, monitor transitional corporations (particularly in the area of control of transfer pricing), deal with inflation and foreign exchange fluctuations and help run small businesses. Accountants in developed countries need more advanced skills to deal with complex financial markets and transactions, give financial advice to investors and help chief executive officers make both short-and long-term management decisions.
>
> Some accountants, particularly in the newly industrializing countries, are being caught in the middle, as is shown in one national response where the respondents noted that the major forces shaping the role of accountants in their country were the growing trend of globalization of business activities, the rise in importance of the service sector of their economy, the increasing diversity and complexity of financial arrangements, the ever-growing importance of information technology, rising public expectations and changing consumer needs.

This illustrates neatly but precisely the dilemma in which Tanzania and other similar countries find themselves. There is in a real sense a need to move in two directions at once, or, perhaps to put the point better, at two speeds at the same time.

A parallel report to the same working group (United Nations 1993b) reviews the state of accounting education. The first part of the "summary" included therein contains a stark message:

> The present report is concerned explicitly with the current state of accounting education. It constitutes a global view based on responses to a questionnaire sent to all member Governments. As such, it provides a unique opportunity to draw conclusions from a large sample (83 questionnaires returned), across many countries (62), and thereby enhances the state of knowledge of global accounting and auditing education. The average profile of the accounting education system that emerges from the data reveals a technically oriented curriculum taught by underpaid (and frequently inadequately prepared) faculty, who sometimes use irrelevant teaching material.

The Tanzanian Illustration

This section explores the Tanzanian situation in some detail, emphasizing developments regarding the professional body and the examination system and its implications.

The accounting profession is effectively under the complete control of the National Board of Accountants and Auditors (NBAA), created in 1972 by the

Auditors and Accountants (Registration) Act. There is also a professional body, the Tanzania Association of Accountants (TAA). This was established in 1983, its formation being supported and sponsored by the NBAA. However it is the NBAA which has complete and sole control of many of the issues which are normally regarded as coming within the responsibilities of a professional body, such as examinations, qualifications, and code of conduct.

The NBAA is charged under the 1972 Act as follows (NBAA 1992):

> to among other things, promote and provide opportunities, and facilities for the study of, and training in Accountancy, Auditing and Allied subjects. The Board is also charged with the responsibility of conducting examinations in Accountancy, Auditing and Allied subjects, and granting relevant certificates and diplomas.
>
> While Accountancy training in the country is done by various training institutions including private firms, the conduct of professional accountancy examinations is wholly a preserve of the NBAA.

The running of NBAA on a day-to-day basis is the responsibility of the Registrar, who acts as chief executive. There is a Governing Board, which meets about four times per year, and a number of Committees of the Board. In keeping with the political philosophy of the 1970s and 1980s described in Briston and Wallace (1990), the Registrar is formally responsible directly to the Minister of Finance, and NBAA is itself a "parastatal" organization. Originally the Governing Board consisted entirely of government nominees, but now much of the membership of the Board is appointed by a ballot of TAA members.

The essential attitude underlying accounting developments since national independence has been precisely the same, that is, independence and a determination that Tanzanian accounting will make its own decisions and develop in its own way. This does not mean that history has been rapidly overturned. For example the ruling Company Law as at June 1994 was the 1932 Companies Ordinance (as amended). This is basically the U.K. Companies Act of 1929. Paragraph 134 (1) (b) requires the auditor's report to state "whether, in their opinion, the balance sheet referred to in the report is properly drawn up so as to exhibit a true and correct view of the state of the company's affairs according to the best of their information and the explanations given to them, and as shown by the books of the company" (NBAA 1990).

Equally, the spirit of independence does not mean that foreign influences have been rejected. Briston and Wallace (1990) show how the first Tanzanian accounting standard, TSSAPI on accounting procedures and the maintenance of accounting records, is based heavily on the Swedish Accounting Act of 1976 (though with references to reindeer-breeding omitted!). The point here is that, in the context of the 1970s, Tanzania needed information and regulation concerning the techniques of basic recordkeeping which Anglo-Saxon countries (but not, for example, Francophone countries or the former communist bloc) have traditionally taken for granted and not requiring central specification or regulation. The NBAA therefore looked elsewhere and made its own choice of the most relevant model to adapt for local needs.

The reverse side of the coin is that Tanzania has had the sense to recognize that the blanket adoption of some imported regulatory and professional framework designed for a different political, cultural and economic environment (e.g., from the United Kingdom or the United States), or designed for no particular national environment but certainly crucially influenced by broadly defined Anglo-Saxon capitalist norms (IASC), would clearly be irrational and ineffective. The contents of TSSAP 1, 2, and 3 are fully covered in Briston and Wallace (1990). There have been no further significant developments since 1990, and the TSSAPs are not further considered here.

The other obvious manifestation of this spirit of independence as regards the thrust of this paper is in the whole area of accounting education. The NBAA is always willing to receive suggestion and advice (one of the present authors visited Tanzania in June 1994 on a consultancy sponsored jointly by the British Council and NBAA), and, as discussed later, it is in need of significant external financial support. But throughout it has maintained its formal independence from overseas influences. Although NBAA received help from Sweden and Canada when it was created in 1975, there have been no on-going agreements with other professional accounting bodies or other national governments, and no sharing of syllabus or examination papers.

The original examination structure created by the NBAA in 1975 is discussed in Briston and Wallace (1990), where it is described as a three-tier model: technician, semi-professional, and professional. NBAA (1992) actually describes this structure as a four-tier scheme: BBC (Basic Book-keeping Certificate), NABOCE (National Book-Keeping Certificate), NAD (National Accountancy Diploma), and CPA (Certified Public Accountant).

Table 1. Technician (ATEC) Examinations Structure

Technician Level I	
T.01	Bookkeeping and Accounts I
T.02	Elements of Business Mathematics and Statistics
T.03	Commercial Knowledge and Office Practice
T.04	Communication Skills
Technician Level II	
T.05	Bookkeeping and Accounts II (including Elements of Auditing)
T.06	Elements of Costing and Materials Management
T.07	Political Economy
T.08A	Cooperative Principles and Accounting
T.08B	Government Accounting and Financial Procedures

Source: NBAA (1992, 25-52).

Table 2. Professional (CPA) Examinations Structure

Professional Level	
P.01	Financial Accounting I
P.02	Economics
P.03	Business Mathematics and Statistics
P.04	Business Law
Professional Level II	
P.05	Cost Accounting
P.06	Auditing I
P.07	Data Processing and Management Information Systems
P.08	Taxation I
Professional Level III	
P.09	Financial Accounting II
P.10	Quantitative Techniques
P.11	Taxation II
P.12	Business Administration and Management
Professional Level IV	
P.13	Financial Accounting III
P.14	Management Accounting
P.15	Auditing and Investigation
P.16	Financial Management

Source: NBAA (1992, 53-117).

With effect from the May 1991 examination sitting, this structure was completely redesigned as a two-tier model, consisting of ATEC (Accounting Technician) and CPA. ATEC consists of eight papers in two levels as shown in Table 1 and CPA consists of 16 papers in four levels as shown in Table 2.

The NBAA *Students Handbook* (NBAA 1992) contains a detailed syllabus for each paper (and a brief statement of aims), together with a suggested reading list. Analysis of this material and of Tables 1 and 2 suggests the following points:

- Syllabuses are wide-ranging and, in the context of the preparation date (circa 1990), reasonably up-to-date as regards content.
- Reading lists are variable and somewhat haphazard. They reflect a lack of awareness of current literature, probably due to a shortage of both relevant local material and of money to buy imported texts. As an example, the reading list for the final Financial Accounting paper (paper P.13) is shown in Table 3. The emphasis on U.K. texts, not all of which are of obvious relevance, is all too clear.
- The Students Handbook makes no attempt at specification in terms of student skills and abilities. There seems to have been no influence from, for example Bloom's hierarchical taxonomy (Bloom 1956), the Behavioural Objectives movement or the recent preoccupation with competence-based

qualifications (see e.g., the special edition of *Accounting Education* on Competencies, Vol. 4, No. 1 [1995]).

- The coverage reflects the broad economic and political assumptions of the time and context in which the syllabus was proposed, that is, state socialism and a preponderance of "parastatals."

ACCOUNTING EDUCATION AND EXAMINATIONS IN TANZANIA

Accounting education and training is available full-time from several institutions which set their own examinations, and part-time from a number of training institutions which provide tuition aimed at NBAA's own external national examinations. Three of the full-time courses are granted exemptions up to and including the whole of professional level II (NBAA 1992). These courses are at the University of Dar-es-Salaam, the Institute of Development Management, and the Institute of Financial Management. Before NBAA's own examinations each student is "required to attend a full-time review class of at least eight weeks immediately before writing the examination."

In 1961 Tanzania had no professionally qualified accountants (Briston and Wallace 1990). In the period from May 1975 to May 1994, a total of 39 examination

Table 3. Reading List for Financial Accounting III (Paper P.13)

as per Reading List for Paper P.09—Financial Accounting III, Professional Level II, plus the following:	
NBAA	Study Guide for Advanced Accounting—*Accounting for Bankruptcy, Receiverships and Compulsory Liquidation of Companies* by A. T. Benedict.
IASC	International Accounting Standards
BPP Publishing Ltd. (UK)	Executorship, Trusts and Accounts (Manual for ACCA Level 2).
	Insolvency (Manual for ACCA Level 2)
	Advanced Financial Accounting (Manual for ACCA Level 3)
Allen & Unwin	*Accounting under Inflationary Conditions* by P. Kirkman
Pitman	*Accounting Case Problems* by Coy & Keers
H.F.L.	*Spicer & Pegler's Executorship Law and Accounts* by K. S. Carmichael
MacDonald & Evans	*The Law Relating to Bankruptcy, Liquidations and Receivership* by C. A. Sales

Note: The above list is not necessarily exhaustive.
Range of international accounting journals—relevant articles and topic issues.

Source: NBAA (1992, 104-105).

sessions, NBAA has produced a total of 647 CPAs (NBAA 1994a), together, of course, with larger numbers of lower level qualifications, and students still in the pipeline. By January 1, 1994, there were also 136 U.K.-qualified accountants working in Tanzania (20 Chartered, 100 Certified, 13 Management, and 3 Public Finance) (CAJIC 1994).

One of the most laudable activities of NBAA is the publication, after every semi-annual examination session, of an extremely detailed Examiners' Report. This not only gives detailed comments paper by paper and question by question on difficulties and weaknesses experienced by candidates, but also provides a variety of statistics which other professional accounting bodies would do well to emulate.

Tables 4 to 8 are extracted from the Examiners' Report on the May 1994 session. Table 4 shows candidate numbers for the previous six sessions. Table 5 gives, as an example of a detailed results analysis, the breakdown for the final prequalification examination (Professional Level IV) and Table 6, again by way of illustration, shows the array of results for P.13, one of the papers included in the overall results of Table 5. Finally Table 7 takes the figures quoted in Table 5 and analyzes the results by the institutions which had prepared the candidates, and Table 8 provides an analysis of the Table 5 data in terms of the various study and examination/qualification routes by which candidates had arrived at the Level IV stage.

Readers will find much of interest from a detailed consideration of these tables. One of the major points is that an enormous effort is being made to create a structure and process which is dealing with generally small numbers (see Table 4). Secondly, it is clear from Table 5 that results are often poor or worse. (The

Table 4. Statistical Analysis of NBAA Examinations Candidature

EXAMINATIONS	*ATEC I*	*ATEC II*	*PROF I*	*PROF II*	*PROF III*	*PROF IV*	*NAD II*	*NAD I&II*	*CPA I*	*CPA II*	*TOTAL*
34th Session Nov. 1991	486	336	89	173	–	–	86	125	182	295	1772
35th Session May 1992	523	597	205	238	390	–	–	–	–	–	1963
36th Session Nov. 1992	408	620	232	220	406	56	–	–	–	–	1941
37th Session May 1993	396	583	242	165	422	96	–	–	–	–	1904
38th Session Nov. 1993	267	547	290	162	383	118	–	–	–	–	1767
39th Session May 1994	346	561	291	133	381	181	–	–	–	–	1893

Source: NBAA (1994a, 4).

Table 5. NBAA Examinations—Professional Level IV Results, May 1994

	TOTALS		*PASSES*		*REFERRALS*		*RE-REFERRALS*		*FAILURES*	
Type of Candidates	*No.*	*%*	*No.*	*%*	*No.*	*%*	*No.*	*%*	*No.*	*%*
Sat for the first time	108	63.9	4	25.0	20	74.1	–	–	84	82.4
Referred at Previous Exams	23	13.6	9	56.3	–	–	14	58.3	0	0.0
RE-referred at Previous Exams	13	7.7	3	18.7	–	–	10	41.7	0	0.0
Failures from Previous Exams	25	14.8	0	0.0	7	25.9	–	–	18	17.6
TOTAL	169	100.0	16	100.0	27	100.0	24	100.0	102	100.0

Source: NBAA (1994a, 16)

Table 6. NBAA Paper P.13 (Financial Accounting III), Analysis of Candidates' Performance at the May 1994 Examinations, Classification of Marks

	0-19	*20-39*	*40-59*	*60-79*	*80-100*	*Total*
Number of Candidates	10	100	25	–	–	135
Percentage	7.4	74.1	18.5	–	–	100

Note: The pass mark is 40 percent.
Source: NBAA (1994a, 61).

average pass rate for all six levels taken together in May 1994 was 30.8 percent; the pass rate for Professional Level IV in November 1993 was 12.0 percent). Two likely implications arise from this, namely that standards expected in the examinations are strictly maintained and that the average level of candidate preparation is poor, relative to those standards. The authors' own contacts and experience suggest that both these implications are valid.

Perhaps the most interesting point about Tables 6, 7, and 8 is that they are published at all. In the case of Tables 7 and 8 given here, the numbers involved are so small (particularly the numbers of successful students) that it seems difficult to achieve a meaningful interpretation. However, it must be remembered that tables equivalent to 7 and 8 are published separately for each of the 6 levels, and all are published regularly twice each year. Over time, therefore, and given some local knowledge, much can be deduced from this published information, and NBAA should be congratulated on their transparency.

The NBAA is rightly determined that its qualification should receive, and justify, a status fully commensurate with professional accounting bodies across the world. As it states (in bold type) (NBAA, 1994a):

Table 7. NBAA Professional Level IV Examinations, May 1994 Results Analyzed by Institutions

	Institutions											
	IAA		*CORE*		*PT IFM*		*PRIVATE*		*PT-MOSHI*		*TOTAL*	
Type of Candidates	*No.*	*%*	*No.*	*%*	*No.*	*%*	*No.*	*%*	*No.*	*%*	*No.*	*%*
Entries	45	102	22	110	36	109	77	108	1	100	181	107
Absentees	1	2	2	10	3	9	6	8	0	0	12	7
Candidate who sat	44	100	20	100	33	100	71	100	1	100	169	100
Passes	4	9	1	5	0	0	11	15	0	0	16	9
Referrals	11	25	7	35	6	18	3	4	0	0	27	16
Re-Referrals	0	0	1	5	2	6	21	30	0	0	24	14
Failures	29	66	11	55	25	76	36	51	1	100	102	60
TOTAL	44	100	20	100	33	100	71	100	1	100	169	100

Source: NBAA (1994a, 81).

Table 8. NBAA Professional Level IV—Results of May 1994 Examinations, Analyzed by Prior Qualifications of Candidates

CANDIDATES		*Qualifications of Candidates Prior to Professional Level IV Examinations*											
TYPE	*No.*	*PROF II/ PROF III*		*ADCA (IDM) /PROF III*		*B.Com./ PROF III*		*ADA (IFM)/ PROF III*		*ADA NSTI/ PROF III*		*CPA I/II/ PROF III*	
	(x)	*f*	*xf*	*f*	*xf*	*f*	*xf*	*f*	*xf*	*f*	*xf*	*f*	*xf*
PASSES	= 3	5	15	2	6	3	9	1	3	0	0	5	15
REFERRALS	= 2	11	22	11	22	9	18	5	10	0	0	15	30
FAILURES	= 1	30	30	17	17	13	13	6	6	4	4	32	32
TOTAL		46	67	30	45	25	40	12	19	4	4	52	77
S = (Σxf)/(Σf)		S= 67/46 = 1.45		S = 45/30 = 1.50		S = 40/25 = 1.60		S = 19/12 = 1.58		S = 4/4 = 1.00		S = 77/52 = 1.48	
POSITION		5th		2nd		1st		2nd		6th		4th	

Source: NBAA (1994a, 86).

> We would like to re-emphasize to the NBAA professionals that they are expected to be professionally competent enough to be able to hold on their own as their counterparts of other reputed professional bodies abroad.

The board, and its registrar, are actively seeking advice and support as to what is necessary to fulfil this aim. In terms of the final qualification exam papers, that is, Professional Level IV, the current position could perhaps be described as variable. This can be illustrated by the following two questions, taken from the May 1994 Level IV papers (NBAA, 1994b), the first from P.13 (financial accounting) and the second from P.15 (auditing and investigation) (see Appendix).

The first of these questions is in effect a piece of low-level bookwork. The wording suggests that it is based directly on the *Corporate Report* (ASSC 1975). No analysis or application is required, and the material should be covered in any foundation course in accounting (though not in bookkeeping). This question is not testing final qualification stage ability.

The second question however is a different matter. It is up-to-date, both as to the date of the quotation and as to the topic itself. It is international in scope. It is open-ended and potentially contentious, and seeks analysis, argument, and opinion from candidates. It is all the more impressive (and demanding) when placed in the context of what is still a largely state-controlled and parastatal-dominated economy.

In order to discuss possible remedies in Tanzania and their implications for other African countries (and, indeed, for developing nations generally), it will be helpful to deepen the analysis of the characteristics of accounting thought and practice in Tanzania as they are now, and to compare this situation with what is perhaps needed. Only when we have analyzed what needs to happen to accounting and to accountants can we rationally suggest the education, training, and resource impacts necessary to achieve these reforms.

The effect that widespread state centralization and control of the economy has on the internal reality and external perception of accounting and accountants is now becoming more widely understood, because of experiences in Eastern Europe and the former USSR (see, for example, the chapters on Eastern Europe in Alexander and Archer 1998). Accounting, as the earlier quotation from Bailey and colleagues (1990) argued, generally degenerated to mere bookkeeping and the filling in of forms, for since decisions were not taken by management but by state officials, and those decisions were not taken on economic grounds, accounting ceased to have any decision-making connotations. In parallel with this decline in importance came a decline in the status of accountants.

Not surprisingly, 30 years of state socialism in Tanzania have gone some way toward creating a similar position. As was suggested to one of the authors in private conversation in Tanzania in June 1994, when you have a state-owned monopoly operating under government-imposed fixed price controls, management is neither difficult nor risky. Accounting is probably even less so—it is not possible to provide the wrong information for decision-making purposes when no economic decisions are being taken.

Understandably, the accounting profession in Tanzania, which has been created entirely within this same 30-year period (by an NBAA created through the Ministry of Finance), reflects this background and role. Accounting has generally been perceived as a subservient reporting function "just dealing with the figures." The examination system for NBAA naturally developed a tendency to reflect this, with a concentration on technical manipulation and learning and this, in turn, naturally tended to lead to a teaching and learning regime directed toward the same ends.

A picture emerges, therefore, of a self-perpetuating spiral. Accounting activity is not dynamic and exciting in reality or perception. Accounting qualification examinations and courses leading thereto become less dynamic and exciting. Tutors, and the students who become future practitioners, tutors and examiners, similarly become less dynamic and exciting.

It is to the great credit of NBAA that it is both well aware of the problems, and determined to act positively to break out of this situation. The freer capitalist economy which Tanzania clearly intends to create requires a different breed of accountants. This is not merely a function of putting new areas such as portfolio theory or management theory into the syllabus, although that is undoubtedly necessary. More important, it is a question of engendering new attitudes, abilities, and skills. Management and decision-making in a dynamic capital market-based economy involves subjective analysis and risky decision-making—as does external investment in business organizations. Accounting and the accountant are an essential part of this information flow and decision-making process.

The Problems Summarized

It would be very easy simply to put the difficulties down to lack of resources. But this would be too vague to be helpful, and we attempt to specify the problems under three heads.

The first problem is a scarcity of the skills necessary for syllabus and examination development. The existence of this problem is clearly shown by our earlier exposition, both in the specific case of Tanzania and in the general case of developing countries.

The second problem is the lack of training facilities, of all kinds. Interviews with representatives of three of the leading Tanzanian training institutions in the summer of 1994 (Dar-es-Salaam School of Accountancy, DSA; Institute of Development Management, IDM; Institute of Finance Management, IFM) produced a clear picture of leaders who knew broadly what needed to be done but had little expectation of being able to do it. For example from 1987-1990 DSA benefited from a World Bank project, under which lecturers from the school were sent away both to learn the necessary skills to produce teaching manuals and to actually produce such manuals. The project was of fixed duration and did not achieve self-perpetuation; the manuals produced had never been updated since. The NBAA reference library, in June 1994, had not received a single acquisition since 1992.

The third problem, well illustrated in the case of Tanzania by the tables already referred to, is the lack of a critical mass of students and examinees. Small numbers provide insufficient fees to finance an effective and developing examination system and provide too small a market to justify the commercial production of texts and learning materials. This gives in a sense another twist to the vicious circle argument suggested earlier in the paper. What can be done to deal with these problems and to alleviate the circle of inadequacy?

Possible Solutions

As is so often the case, it is relatively easy to pose the problem, but far more difficult to identify a feasible solution. Among those which might be considered are the following:

(a) *Internal development.* Unfortunately it is now almost impossible for a nation to avoid outside influences in its search for an appropriate accounting system, for however primitive its level of economic development, it is still likely to be affected in its choice of accounting priorities by external pressures exercised through multinational companies, international accounting firms, overseas professional bodies, and so forth. The Anglo-Saxon system is so well-established and so remunerative for accountants who operate within it that it is inevitably the first choice in most developing capitalist economies, particularly those which have a professional accounting body, however rudimentary.

(b) *The adoption of an overseas model.* This is a feasible, though expensive and inappropriate approach. Given the popularity of Anglo-Saxon accounting, a country could adopt either the U.S. or the U.K. model. Of these two, the easier to transfer is the U.K. model because two of the main U.K. professional accounting bodies allow students to study and sit their examinations locally. Although this is much cheaper than funding study overseas for intending accountants, it does have damaging side effects. Not only are there still significant costs in the form of membership and examination fees and the purchase of textbooks, but there is also pressure upon local educational institutions to offer courses related to the examinations of U.K. professional bodies rather than to local needs and practice. Furthermore, the U.K. system is intended to meet the information needs of stock market participants rather than those of decision-makers in a developing economy, and is thus likely to prove dysfunctional.

(c) *The establishment of a regional model.* This has been attempted in several areas including Southern Africa and the Arabian Gulf. The main barriers to this solution are cultural, political, language, and economic differences between the countries concerned, which might make it difficult to achieve either a generally acceptable solution at all or one which is relevant to the problems of all of the individual countries. Another problem is that regional solutions, in the same way as single country remedies, tend to concentrate upon the harmonization of external financial reporting rather than upon the broader attributes of an accounting system in its fullest sense. Finally, in many regions there is one country which is more highly developed and which thus seeks to impose its own practices upon the others in the group.

(d) *The establishment of an international model.* It might have been expected that the International Accounting Standards Committee would have been helpful in the establishment of a relevant model which would assist developing nations, given that one of the objectives of its five year plan adopted in 1990 was "to ensure that International Accounting Standards meet the financial reporting needs of developing and newly industrialized countries and encourage the implementation of those Standards" (Cairns 1995, 10). Such standards, if prepared with that objective in mind, would at least be relevant to developing countries even if they placed an exaggerated emphasis upon the role of external financial reporting within an overall accounting system. However, a further objective adopted at the same time was "to develop International Accounting Standards that meet the need for truly international standards of accounting and disclosure by capital markets and the international business community and which are acceptable for use in the financial statements of all issuers of equity and debt securities." These two objectives are unlikely to be compatible, given that the information needs of host governments in monitoring the activities of multinationals is unlikely to coincide with either the information needs of international capital markets or the range of information that multinationals are likely to be prepared to publish (see Briston 1984). The subsequent consolidation of the links between IASC and IOSCO (the International Organization of Securities Commissions) suggests that the second objective will have priority over the first and that the needs of developing countries will be secondary to those of IOSCO members.

One ray of hope, if we must accept a limited definition of accounting, is the recent decision of the ACCA to adopt IASC standards as the basis of its examinations. This will have the advantage of making the syllabuses much more relevant for overseas students and may relax the pressure upon local colleges to teach purely U.K. material. The problems of relevance and cost will, however, persist, in that the ACCA has a developed nation emphasis in its definition of accounting, and the costs of student membership, textbooks, tuition, and so on, will remain high. If the ACCA really wishes to make a significant contribution to the enhancement of accounting in poorer nations it might consider charging differential subscriptions and fees (say at marginal cost) in respect to those nations.

It is thus evident that there is no simple solution to the problem of accounting development and, indeed, little agreement as to what constitutes accounting in that context. Ultimately it would appear that nations should be encouraged to identify their own information needs for the purpose of economic management.

Tanzania has endeavored to adopt this policy but, as this paper has demonstrated, it is virtually impossible to achieve relevant accounting development without suffering contamination from international influences.

APPENDIX

Sample Questions from May 1994 Professional Level IV Examinations

Following the massive changes taking place in the economy, and in the light of the introduction of Capital as well as Stock Exchange Markets, the accountancy profession is supposed to work out better financial reporting standards. To assist the government in the regulations of the publication of accounting information and also to take care of the interests of user groups, some kinds of *Corporate Reporting Guidelines* should be issued by the NBAA.

REQUIRED:

(i) List seven categories of user groups who might be identified in the guidelines.

(7 marks)

(ii) State and briefly explain ten desirable characteristics of good financial accounting reports.

(10 marks)

(Total = 17 marks)

"The world over, the accountancy profession is faced with severe criticism basically because the expectation of the users is not compatible with what accountants deliver. Other professionals like lawyers and economists are taking advantage of the *Expectations Gap*. Lawyers are minting money from the auditing firms. Managements are losing credibility when the survival of their enterprises are at stake, and at the same time, the auditing firms are losing integrity" (*The Accountant*, 6 (2) July-December 1993: 14).

DISCUSS on the writer's remarks, citing as far as possible relevant texts.

(20 marks)

REFERENCES

Accounting Education. 1995. Special issue on Competencies 4 (1). London: Chapman & Hall.

AECC. 1990. *Objectives of Education for Accountants.* Accounting Education for Change Commission, USA.

Alexander, D., and S. Archer. 1998. *The European Accounting Guide.* New York: Harcourt Brace.

ASSC. 1975. *The Corporate Report.* London: Accounting Standards Steering Committee.

Bailey, D. T., et al. 1990. *Accountancy Development in Poland.* London: British Council.

Bloom, B. 1956. *Taxonomy of Educational Objectives: Handbook 1—The Cognitive Domain*. London: Longmans.

Briston, R. J. 1984. Accounting standards and host country control of multinationals. *British Accounting Review* 16 (1): 12-26.

Briston, R. J., and R. S. O. Wallace. 1990. Accounting education and corporate disclosure regulation in Tanzania. *Research in Third World Accounting* 1: 281-299.

Cairns, D. 1995. *A Guide to Applying International Accounting Standards*. London: Accountancy Books.

CAJIC. 1994. Private correspondence with the authors by the Chartered Accountants Joint International Committee, London.

Gleim, I. 1994. *CPA Exam: A Comprehensive Analysis Manual*. USA: Gleim Publications.

IASC. 1996. *Framework for the Preparation and Presentation of Financial Statements*. London: International Accounting Standards (IASC).

NBAA. 1990. *Companies Ordinance (CAP.212)*. Reproduced by NBAA, Dar-es-Salaam.

NBAA. 1992. *The National Accounting Examination Scheme, Students Handbook*. Dar-es-Salaam: National Board of Accountants and Auditors.

NBAA. 1994a. *Examiners' Report—The 39th Examination Session*. Dar-es-Salaam: National Board of Accountants and Auditors.

NBAA. 1994b. *Certified Public Accountant Examination, Professional Level IV May 1994*. Dar-es-Salaam: National Board of Accountants and Auditors.

UNIDO. 1993. *Workshop on Privatization Policy, Strategy and Practice in the Context of the Least Developed Countries in Africa*. Report ref. PPD.256 (SPEC) dated November 26, 1993. USA: United Nations Industrial Development Organization.

United Nations. 1993a. *Report of the Secretary General to the Intergovernmental Working Group of Experts on International Standards of Accounting and Reporting*. Ref. E/C.10/AC.3/1993/3. USA: United Nations Economic and Social Council.

United Nations. 1993b. *Report of the Secretary General to the Intergovernmental Working Group of Experts on International Standards of Accounting and Reporting*. Ref. E/C.10/AC.3/1993/2. USA: United Nations Economic and Social Council.

NONCOMPLIANCE WITH CORPORATE ANNUAL REPORT DISCLOSURE REQUIREMENTS IN ZIMBABWE

Stephen Owusu-Ansah

ABSTRACT

This chapter reports on some aspects of the results of an empirical investigation into the degree of corporate compliance with mandatory disclosure requirements in Zimbabwe. A disclosure instrument, consisting of 214 mandated information items from three regulatory sources in Zimbabwe, was employed to derive an index of the disclosure in the annual report and accounts of 49 nonfinancial listed companies in Zimbabwe. The analyses of the less-than-perfect indexes awarded to sample annual reports suggest significant departures from disclosure requirements in Zimbabwe. There were several instances where the sample companies failed completely to disclose some required applicable information items.

Research in Accounting in Emerging Economies, Volume 4, pages 289-305.

ISBN: 1-55938-995-8

INTRODUCTION

The objective of this chapter is to report on the results of a study that empirically assessed the degree of compliance with annual report mandatory disclosure requirements in Zimbabwe. The results indicate that mandated information disclosure in annual reports of the sample companies falls short of the regulatory minima. The results provide evidence in support of the conclusions in prior studies that listed companies in emerging economies publish annual reports that do not adequately comply with statutory and regulatory disclosure requirements (Wallace 1988; Tai et al. 1990; Ahmed and Nicholls 1994; Owusu-Ansah 1998).

The role of accounting information in any economy cannot be over-emphasized. Efficient resource allocation among competing interests in any economy is aided by accounting information. Although different economic systems may attach different levels of importance to the accounting function, there is no case where the need for accounting information has been nonexistent. Recognizing this fact has led many countries to require public companies to fully disclose a set of pre-determined information items that are considered important for investment decision-making purposes in their annual reports. The existence of an elaborate disclosure regulatory regime in any economy does not, however, guarantee corporate compliance with the requirements. Hence, several prior studies have investigated the quality of information disclosed in corporate annual reports (e.g., Cerf 1961; Singhvi and Desai 1971). Of particular relevance to the present study are those studies that have investigated the degree of compliance with disclosure requirements by companies in emerging economies (Marston 1986; Wallace 1988; Tai et al. 1990; Ahmed and Nicholls 1994; Solas 1994). The external validity of the findings of these studies is limited as countries are distinctly unique in terms of social, cultural, religious, political, and economic settings—factors which invariably affect the nature and the extent of information disclosed in corporate annual reports (Al-Hashim and Arpan 1992).

In addition, Ahmed and Nicholls (1994) have argued that while there are considerable incentives for voluntary disclosure in emerging economies, there are also reasons for not complying with mandatory disclosure requirements. This study, therefore, seeks to provide a further insight into, and to enhance the current knowledge on the degree of compliance of annual report disclosures with statutory and regulatory requirements of listed companies in an emerging economy—Zimbabwe.

Zimbabwe offers a particularly appropriate context for the study for several reasons. First, it has the second oldest (after Johannesburg) equity stock market in Africa, and yet little is known about it. The Zimbabwe Stock Exchange (ZSE), then known as Rhodesian Stock Exchange, was established in 1945. Moreover, it is the third largest equity market in Africa (after Johannesburg and Egypt) in terms of total market capitalization. Its total market capitalization was US$4,827 million as of September 1996 (International Finance Corporation 1998). Finally, because the ZSE is a constituent market of the International Finance Corporation's Global and Investible Indices, and also given the fact that investment in international portfolios helps to reduce systematic risk, foreign investors may be interested in the information disclosure practices of the listed companies in Zimbabwe in an attempt to diversify their investment portfolios to that market.

The rest of the chapter consists of four major sections. The first section briefly describes the legal and institutional frameworks that influence financial accounting and reporting in the private-sector in Zimbabwe. The second section describes how the sample companies were selected. It also presents the conceptual and operational definitions of mandatory disclosure and describes the details of the data analyses. The third section reports on the outcome of these analyses. The concluding remarks and limitations of the research design are contained in the fourth section.

FINANCIAL REPORTING ENVIRONMENT IN ZIMBABWE

Zimbabwe was a self-governing British colony of Rhodesia until November 1965 when it unilaterally declared independence. Zimbabwe is a landlocked country with a total area of 390,580 square kilometers. Its total population was 11 million in mid-1995; the bulk of which is formed by two major Bantu-speaking ethnic groups: the Mashona, constituting at least 70 percent, and the Ndebele (Matabele), who constitute about 15 percent of the total. The country also has small minorities of Europeans, Asians, and persons of mixed race. Zimbabwe has one of the most diversified economies of any African country. Mining, and to a lesser extent, agriculture are the main important sectors, but manufacturing is also well developed. The country's GNP per capita in 1995 was US$540.

Due to the historical and economic links between the United Kingdom and Zimbabwe, the legal and institutional framework for corporate financial accounting and reporting of the latter is a replica of the former. The financial reporting practices of companies registered in Zimbabwe are primarily regulated by the 1952 Companies Act (Chapter 190 of the laws of Zimbabwe). The Zimbabwean Companies Act, which was modeled on the United Kingdom's 1948 Companies Act, consolidates and amends earlier laws relating to the constitution, registration, management, administration, and liquidation of companies. The primary concern of the Zimbabwean Companies Act is to protect existing and potential investors and creditors of registered companies. The Act, therefore, requires companies registered in Zimbabwe to maintain accounting records, publish annual accounts, and have them audited by an independent auditor. The annual accounts must give a *true and fair view* of the state of the company's affairs.

The accountancy profession in Zimbabwe evolved along the British tradition of self-regulation. The Institute of Chartered Accountants of Zimbabwe (ICAZ) is the main professional body regulating the practice of accounting and auditing in the country. It was established in January 1918 by Ordinance 14 of 1917. It is, however, regulated today by the Accountants Act (Chapter 215). The ICAZ is primarily responsible for the establishment and publication of financial accounting standards, and the supervision of their application throughout the country. In 1976, the ICAZ adopted International Accounting Standards (IASs) as the national standard for Zimbabwe in an attempt to improve financial accounting and reporting in the country, as the accounting requirements of the Companies Act were limited both in coverage and in detail. The adopted IASs had no legal backing until May 1996.[1]

The ICAZ also monitors and enforces compliance with disclosure requirements in Zimbabwe. Every year, it samples 25 annual reports and accounts of public companies in Zimbabwe: (i) to ascertain the extent to which the 25 companies have complied with the adopted IASs, and (ii) to encourage compliance with the IASs in the future. The ICAZ's responsibility for monitoring and enforcing compliance with the Zimbabwean reporting regulations covers the IASs, the Zimbabwean Companies Act, and the stock exchange listing rules. Unfortunately, the ICAZ has neither legal nor regulatory power to administer any sanctions against any company for noncompliance with disclosure requirements.

In addition to the reporting requirements of the Companies Act and the pronouncements of the ICAZ (which are predominantly the adopted IASs), ZSE-listed public companies are obliged to conform to the ZSE's continuous periodic reporting system. Thus, ZSE-listed companies are to report any relevant, material information necessary to enable present and potential investors to appraise their financial performance and position, to avoid the establishment of false market in their listed securities.

RESEARCH DESIGN AND METHODOLOGY

Sampling Method

A ZSE-listed company was selected for inclusion in the sample if it fulfilled the following criteria: (i) it is a nonfinancial company, as financial companies are exempted from complying with some of the accounting requirements of the Companies Act; and (ii) its equity shares have been traded on the ZSE for at least a year so that a fair assessment of the impact of the reporting requirements of the ZSE can be made. Forty-nine companies qualified for inclusion in the final sample. They represent about 86 percent of the entire nonfinancial companies listed on the ZSE. Although the sample is entirely selected from the population of public listed companies, it is truly representative of nonfinancial companies registered in Zimbabwe. Therefore, the financial reporting and disclosure practices of the sample companies can provide a basis for generalization about the Zimbabwe corporate reporting profile.

Measuring Annual Report Mandatory Disclosure

Disclosure is the communication of economic information whether financial or nonfinancial, quantitative or otherwise of a company's "financial position and performance, and financial adaptability" (Accounting Standards Board 1994). Disclosure of an item is mandatory if the item, when applicable, is expected to be disclosed in the annual reports of companies under a disclosure regulatory regime. Disclosure by a company of any item that is not mandated by law and/or by a relevant national self-regulatory body is voluntary. In this study, the disclosure of applicable mandated information items is the minimum standard of disclosure that regulatory bodies in Zimbabwe expect of listed companies. Mandatory disclosure items in this study consist of all information items required, under the Companies Act, the adopted IASs, and the ZSE listing rules, to be disclosed in corporate annual reports by ZSE-listed companies.[2]

To measure mandatory disclosure, I used a scoring template to derive an index of mandatory disclosure that: (i) quantifies both financial and nonfinancial disclosures; and (ii) is applied with reasonable consistency to all the annual reports of the companies in the sample. The template is similar in procedure to the one used by Wallace and colleagues (1994) and Wallace and Naser (1995).[3] An information item was scored one (1) when disclosed or zero (0) when not disclosed. Thus, each information item was given equal weight in the index. Although this procedure is questionable as it ignores the relative importance of each of the information items to users of corporate annual reports, it is preferred to the differential, but subjective weighting system (i.e., derived from the preferences of individual users), for the following reasons. First, it obviates the necessity of attaching judgmental ratings to the information items. Slovic (1969), Slovic and colleagues (1972), and Ashton (1974) have demonstrated that individuals (even experts) have poor insight into their own judgment process. In simple terms, the equal weighting procedure avoids the subjective judgment inherent in the differential weighting system. Second, it permits a neutral assessment of disclosure devoid of perceptual influences of a particular annual report user group. This study does not focus on the information needs of any particular annual report user group.

Besides the above reasons, the differential weighting system has several limitations including the following:

1. There is a lack of general consensus as to the relative importance of each information item within a particular study. This is evidenced by the use of mean values of questionnaire responses of a particular information item as a measure of its relative importance (Cerf 1961; Singhvi and Desai 1971; Buzby 1975).
2. There is no general consensus on the relative importance of different information items among different samples of questionnaire respondents in different studies (see Dhaliwal 1980, 388; Owusu-Ansah 1998, 207-209).

3. The relative importance of disclosure items is dynamic and not static as they depend on prevailing economic conditions (Dhaliwal 1980, 388; Owusu-Ansah 1998, 208-209).
4. Responses of any particular user group of corporate annual report will be hypothetical. Thus, respondents suffer no real economic consequences of their rating, and as such may not fully reflect the actual use of each information item (Libby 1981, 40-43).
5. Several prior studies suggest that the results of the equal weighting procedure are not too different from those of the differential weighting (Spero 1979; Zarzeski 1996).[4]

Handling of Inapplicable Information Items and Accumulation of Scores

A methodological problem with the index technique concerns whether undisclosed information was inapplicable to a sample company or not. Of course, it is difficult for an outsider (a researcher) to know whether a mandated information item is applicable and material, and therefore, should have either been disclosed or circumstances surrounding its nondisclosure reported, but have not. In determining whether or not the absence of a mandated information item from an annual report is a case of nondisclosure (noncompliance), several measures were taken.

1. Current figures of each information item were compared with those of the previous year as presented in the annual reports of the sample companies. Public companies in Zimbabwe are required by law to show comparative figures for each information item in their annual reports. For example, a dash in front of a particular disclosure item under the column showing current year's figures (i.e., 1994 in this study) suggests inapplicability of that item to a sample company in that reporting period. The same interpretation can be made of a dash under a column showing the previous year's figures (i.e., 1993 in this study). In some cases, 1995 annual reports of the sample companies were used to cross-check items' applicability as the 1995 annual report and accounts will also present the comparative 1994 figures for each element of the financial statements.
2. A suggestion by Cooke (1989) that the whole annual report of each sample company should be read first was implemented. The reading of the entire annual report before scoring it enabled me to form an opinion on whether an undisclosed item was, in fact, inapplicable to a sample company.
3. On *a priori* assumption, the applicability of some information items to every company in the sample was established. For instance, all the companies own inventories of one kind or another, hence the method adopted in valuing the inventories is expected to be disclosed. Thus, the applicability of information item (such as inventories valuation method) to a company in the sample was easily established.

Another problem of the index technique that arises after the scoring of the annual reports is that certain mandated information items may not be applicable to *all* the sample companies. This makes any comparison of scores among the sample companies unrealistic as there is no common basis for such comparison. Babbie (1994, 172) considers this inapplicability of certain information items to some sample companies a special case of missing data problem. He outlines several possible approaches of controlling this missing data problem. Although two of the approaches are relevant to disclosure studies, only one was used in this study.[5] In controlling the inapplicability problem of certain information items, a *relative* index was created. Thus, each sample company's disclosure practices were evaluated on the basis of the relationship between what it disclosed in its annual report and what it was expected to disclose. The relative index procedure was used for several reasons. First, it is appropriate when constructing an index out of disclosure items that do not apply equally to all the sample companies. Second, as pointed out by Moore and Buzby (1972), it is conceptually superior when considering the level of disclosure of companies with differing industrial backgrounds which is true of this study. Finally, several prior studies have used the relative index procedure to circumvent the missing data problem (Buzby 1975; Wallace 1988; Ahmed and Nicholls 1994; Inchausti 1997). This relative mandatory disclosure score (*MDS*) was derived for each sample company by using the following formula:

$$MDS_{ij} = \sum_{i=1}^{n_j} d_{ij} \div \sum_{i=1}^{m_j} d_{ij} \qquad (1)$$

Where,

d_{ij} = disclosure value of i item of information required of j sample company. It is one if it is disclosed or zero if it is not disclosed.

m_j = the number of mandated information items applicable to, and are expected to be disclosed by the j sample company, where $m_j = 214$.

n_j = the number of mandated information items applicable to the j sample company actually disclosed by that company.

Testing the Validity and Reliability of the Measuring Instrument

Following recommendations in the methodological literature, the measuring instrument was tested for its content validity and reliability before it was applied against the annual reports of the sample companies to obtain their disclosure compliance levels. These testing procedures are discussed next.

A content validity is concerned with the extent to which an instrument provides an adequate coverage of a subject matter (Emory 1976). In the context of this study, a content validity would require the disclosure measuring instrument to "include an adequate and representative set of *information* items that would tap the concept *of mandatory disclosure*" (Sekaran 1992, 171, emphasis added). To validate the measuring instrument, four independent external auditors of the companies in the sample were randomly selected and their opinions on the relevance of the disclosure items in the measuring instrument in the light of the regulatory regime were sought. The measuring instrument was revised, based on the responses received from senior partners of two of the audit firms contacted. For example, a disclosure item on foreign borrowings which carries a maximum possible score of 23 was included in the index following the responses from these auditors. Also, a number of sub-items under the IASC's disclosure items were eliminated because they were suggested to be irrelevant to the socio-economic conditions in Zimbabwe. The instrument that was finally applied against the annual reports of the sample companies consists of 30 disclosure items, disaggregated into 214 information items.

In contrast, a measuring instrument is reliable if it provides consistent results (Carmines and Zeller 1979; Babbie 1994). In the context of this study, the measuring instrument would be reliable if it generates consistent measures of the mandatory disclosure practices of the sample companies when used on different occasions or by different people. It is essential that a reliability test is done in disclosure studies as several factors may mitigate against the scoring process, and as a consequence, affect the reliability of the disclosure scores. These factors include fatigue effects, memory effects, and the emotional state of the researcher during the time the sample annual reports were being scored.

To test the reliability of the instrument used in this study, annual reports of 12 companies in the sample (representing about 25 percent of the total sample size) were randomly drawn, and were given to an independent person to score.[6] The results of the correlation test which are presented in Table 1 suggest that the

Table 1. Reliability Analysis: Results of Pearson Product-Moment Correlation ($N = 12$)

	Independent Evaluator's Scores		
Type of disclosure score	*Maximum Score*	*Actual Score*	*Relative Score (MDS)*
The Investigator's Scores:			
Maximum possible score	0.835*	0.576*	–0.340
Actual score	0.681*	0.674*	0.125
Relative score (MDS)	–0.032	0.338	0.728*

Note: * Two-tail test significant at 0.01 level.

scores obtained by the independent scorer and those of the present investigator are in substantial agreement; indicating minimal subjectivity in scoring the mandatory disclosures in the annual reports of the sample companies.

EMPIRICAL RESULTS AND DISCUSSION

As evidenced in Table 2, there is great variability in the extent by which the sample companies have complied with the disclosure requirements. About 63 percent of the companies in the sample disclosed between 70 and 81 percent of what were required of them under the disclosure regulatory regime. While only about 14 percent of the sample companies disclosed between 80 and 90 percent (the highest being 85 percent) of the applicable mandated information items, about 22 percent disclosed between 60 and 71 of what were expected of them. The sample companies scored neither below 61 percent nor above 89 percent.

A plausible explanation for the differing levels of mandatory disclosure by the sample companies is their differing individual circumstances. For example, some companies may choose to do nothing, either because they are already in compliance (i.e., they were disclosing the information voluntarily before the introduction of the regulation) or because compliance will be too costly. In addition, some companies may make major investments to meet the new requirements, while others may make only a modest effort to comply.

To determine whether or not the sample companies publish annual reports that comply with the disclosure requirements, an item-by-item comparison between actual disclosure and the disclosure requirements was undertaken.[7] Table 3 presents the results of this comparative analysis. The figures under the column titled "Applicable disclosure" represent the number of companies which, on the basis of their annual reports, were expected under the regulatory regime to comply with a particular disclosure item. These disclosure items could be complied with at varying levels of completeness (or fullness). As a result, those sample companies

Table 2. Summary Statistics of Mandatory Disclosure Scores of Sample Companies ($N = 49$)

Mandatory Disclosure Score (%)	*No. of Companies*	*Percentage of Sample*
90 and above	0	0.00
Between 80 and 89	7	14.29
Between 70 and 79	31	63.26
Between 60 and 69	11	22.45
Less than 60	0	0.00
Total	49	100.00

Table 3. Item-by-Item Comparison of Actual Disclosure and Mandatory Disclosure Requirements (Ranking in Parentheses)

Sources of Requirements/ Mandory Items (Sub-Items not Shown)	*Characteristics of Mandatory Disclosure by Sample Companies*						
	Applicability of Disclosure Items			*Not Disclosing*		*Disclosing all Applicable Items*	
	Not Applicable	*Applicable* No.	*Applicable* %	No.	%	No.	%
Companies Act							
1. Signing and publishing accounts (s. 123)	0	49	100	1	2	48	98 (2)
2. Directors' report (s. 124)	0	49	100	42	86	7	14 (21)
3. Profit and loss and balance sheet provisions (7th Sch. [i])	0	49	100	33	67	16	33 (16)
4. Holding companies (7th Sch. [ii])	46	3	100	3	100*	0	0 (23)
ZSE Listing Rules							
5. Employees' share schemes (¶ 7[iv])	31	18	100	1	6	17	94(4)
6. Directors' shareholding [¶ 9[i])	0	49	100	32	65	17	35(15)
7. Borrowing powers (¶ 9[ii])	0	49	100	8	16	41	84(7)
8. Additional requirements - IAS21 and IAS23	25	24	100	24	100*	0	0(23)
Adopted IASs							
9. Inventories (IAS 2)	0	49	100	2	4	47	96(3)
10. Depreciation (IAS 4)	0	49	100	4	8	45	92(5)
11. Disclosure of general information (IAS 5)	0	49	100	14	29	35	71(10)
12. Cash flow statement (IAS 7)	0	49	100	7	14	42	86(6)
13. Unusual items, prior period items and changes in accounting policies (IAS 8)	2	47	100	2	4	45	96(3)
14. Research and development (IAS 9)	41	8	100	2	25	6	75(9)
15. Contingencies and events occurring after balance sheet date (IAS 10)	5	44	100	35	80	9	20(20)

(*continued*)

Table 3 (Continued)

Sources of Requirements/ Mandory Items (Sub-Items not Shown)	Characteristics of Mandatory Disclosure by Sample Companies						
	Applicability of Disclosure Items			Not Disclosing		Disclosing all Applicable Items	
	Not Applicable	Applicable No.	Applicable %	No.	%	No.	%
16. Construction contract (IAS 11)	45	4	100	2	50	2	50(11)
17. Taxes on income (IAS 12)	0	49	100	35	71	14	29(17)
18. Segmental reporting (IAS 14)	2	47	100	47	100*	0	0(23)
19. Property, plant and equipment (IAS 16)	1	48	100	48	100*	0	0(23)
20. Leases (IAS 17)	45	4	100	4	100*	0	0(23)
21. Revenue recognition (IAS 18)	0	49	100	0	0	49	100(1)**
22. Retirement benefit costs (IAS 19)	0	49	100	8	16	41	84(7)
23. Foreign currency transactions (IAS 21)	3	46	100	36	78	10	22(19)
24. Business combination (IAS 22)	42	7	100	5	71	2	29(17)
25. Borrowing costs (IAS 23)	7	42	100	26	62	16	38(12)
26. Related party transactions (IAS 24)	2	47	100	30	64	17	36(14)
27. Investments (IAS 23)	18	31	100	24	77	7	23(18)
28. Retirement benefit plans (IAS 26)	0	49	100	47	96	2	4(22)
29. Consolidated financial statements and investments in subsidiaries (IAS 27)	8	41	100	10	24	31	76(8)
30. Investments in associates (IAS 28)	30	19	100	12	63	7	37(13)
Overall Mean			100		52.6		47.4

Notes: * = Denotes a complete failure to comply with the disclosure requirements.
** = Denotes a full compliance with disclosure requirements.

required to comply with a particular requirement were classified into two: (i) those not complying with *all* the sub-items (the column titled "Not disclosing"), and (ii) those complying with *all* the sub-items (the column titled "Disclosing all applicable items"). Several conclusions can be drawn from Table 3.

First, certain disclosure items such as those of IAS 18, *Revenue Recognition*, *Signing and Publishing Accounts (Section 123 of the Companies Act)*, IAS 2, *Inventories*, and *Employees Share Schemes (Paragraph 7[iv] of the ZSE Listing Rules)* were disclosed overwhelmingly by the sample companies. The high compliance with these disclosure requirements, ranked first to fourth, respectively (see figures in parentheses in the last column of Table 3), might be due to the fact that they refer to nonproprietary information items, and therefore, the sample companies perceive no competitive disadvantage from fully disclosing them in their annual reports.

Second, five significant disclosure items, ranked 23rd in Table 3, were surprisingly not disclosed by any of the sample companies. For example, all 48 sample companies that were expected to comply did not fully comply with the requirements under IAS 16, *Properties, Plant and Equipment*. Similarly, the observed segmental reporting was far below the regulatory minima stated in IAS 14, *Segmental Reporting*. About 45 percent of the sample companies were well diversified in terms of both business activity and market (Owusu-Ansah 1998). But this feature was not matched by a corresponding disclosure which adequately covers the different segments of their operations. Users of corporate financial reports, especially investors, require adequate information on the asset base of a company, and the rates of growth, profitability and risk of the different segments of its operations to evaluate its risk-return profile. Furthermore, in spite of the country's tight foreign exchange control policy, none of the 24 sample companies, expected under the regulatory regime (*Additional Requirement for Foreign Borrowings* under IAS 21 and IAS 23) to fully disclose the required information, did so.

Third, there is an apparent weakness in compliance with the pronouncements of the ICAZ (the adopted IASs). This finding is not surprising because there was no legal requirement that companies should comply with IASs. Public companies in Zimbabwe, until May 1996, were complying with IASs on a voluntary basis. Perhaps, this explains why the ICAZ places more emphasis on its enforcement and monitoring efforts on compliance with the adopted IASs than on compliance with the requirements under the Companies Act and the stock exchange listing rules.

Finally, the overall compliance level is very low (47.4 percent). Thus, as shown in Table 3, the overall mean noncompliance rate is 52.6 percent. This ranges from a high noncompliance level of 100 percent on some items to a low of 2 percent on some other items. There are five instances where the sample companies completely failed (100 percent noncompliance) to disclose the applicable information required of them under the regulatory regime. This evidence of noncompliance with statutory and regulatory disclosure requirements is very alarming, if compared with the 22 percent noncompliance rate reported by Tai and colleages (1990) for Hong Kong companies.

Low levels of disclosure compliance have also been found in emerging economies such as Nigeria (Wallace 1988), Hong Kong (Tai et al. 1990), Bangladesh (Ahmed and Nicholls 1994), and Jordan (Solas 1994). It must be pointed out, however, that low compliance with statutory and regulatory disclosure requirements is not uniquely an emerging economy phenomenon. Frost and Pownall (1994, 76) did also find substantial noncompliance with annual and interim reporting rules in the United Kingdom and the United States.

In spite of the findings of this study, disclosure of several information items that were not required under the regulatory regime was observed. They range from information items in statements of value added to social and environmental disclosure. For possible reasons why a company will make a voluntary disclosure, see Choi 1973; Ronen and Livnat 1981; Meek and Gray 1989; Skinner 1994.

The evidence presented in this chapter suggests that the mechanism used by the ICAZ to enforce and monitor corporate compliance with disclosure requirements is inadequate. It also suggests that the mechanism for self-regulation of the accountancy profession in Zimbabwe needs to be re-evaluated. The members of the ICAZ are the external auditors of the sample companies and have certified that these deficient (i.e., noncompliant) financial statements presented true and fair views of the financial operations and positions of these companies. Accounts that do not comply with accounting requirements cannot present a true and fair view of business operations as expected by the standard-setting organization, because as in the United States, there is no true and fair view over-ride in Zimbabwe, as there is in the United Kingdom.

CONCLUSIONS AND LIMITATIONS OF THE STUDY

This chapter has reported on the results of an archival study of the degree of compliance with mandatory disclosure requirements in Zimbabwe by nonfinancial ZSE-listed companies. The results indicate that the sample companies published annual reports that inadequately complied with the disclosure regulatory minima. These results suggest that the mechanism for monitoring and enforcing corporate mandatory disclosure requirements in Zimbabwe is not stringent.

The results should, however, be interpreted in the light of the following limitations. First, the study suffers from "the more disclosure the better" syndrome. The study did not consider problems of information overload that can result from large volume of disclosure. Although there is no evidence to suggest the existence of the problem of information overload in emerging economies, it is contended here that this problem may be more acute in emerging economies than in developed economies, as greater proportion of users of corporate annual reports in the former economies is unsophisticated (Jagetia and Nwadike 1983). It has also been demonstrated analytically in the literature on information economics, however, that more information is not necessarily better (Hirshleifer 1971; Baiman 1975).

Second, the study investigated a pre-determined checklist of information items deemed to be important to users of corporate annual reports in Zimbabwe by the country's standard-setters. The preferences of standard-setters may not coincide with those of users. An attitudinal survey of users may reveal a different set of information items that is preferred by them.

Third, for methodological reasons, the study is based on the assumption that each information item is equally important to an average user of corporate annual reports. Thus, a disclosed mandated information item was scored one (1), and zero (0) for a nondisclosure. In real life, some information items may have higher value to users of corporate annual reports than others. The information items should have been weighted to reflect their relative importance to the users.

Finally, the study is limited to only information required to be disclosed in corporate annual reports. Corporate specific information items useful to investors are also required to be disclosed in other media such as corporate interim reports and prospectuses. Although the annual report is only one medium by which companies communicate with the public, it is a good proxy for other media such as proxy statements, interim reports and prospectuses for the release of corporate financial information (Lang and Lundholm 1993, 258). Also, the study focused on annual report disclosure because it was noted to be the major source of official company-specific financial information in Zimbabwe (Oppong 1993). In spite of these limitations, the findings of this study are consistent with the existing literature (Wallace 1988; Tai et al. 1990; Ahmed and Nicholls 1994).

To increase the degree of corporate compliance with disclosure requirements, the ICAZ should strengthen its monitoring and enforcement mechanisms and improve its continuous professional education program for its members.

ACKNOWLEDGMENTS

This chapter draws on an aspect of my doctoral thesis submitted to Middlesex University, England. I am indebted to my supervisor, Professor R. S. Olusegun Wallace, for his support, useful suggestions and encouragement in writing this chapter. I acknowledge the useful comments of Professor Donal McKillop and Dr. Peter Oyelere on earlier drafts of the thesis. I am grateful for the financial assistance provided by the Wincott Foundation, England, for data collection in Zimbabwe, and the logistic support of King Fahd University of Petroleum and Minerals, Saudi Arabia. The usual disclaimer applies; all remaining errors are mine.

NOTES

1. They are now codified and are contained in Companies (Financial Statements) Regulations, 1996 (Chapter 190 [Statutory Instrument No. 62]).

2. Since this study focuses on mandatory disclosure, a score earned by a sample company on the index is interpreted as its disclosure requirements' compliance level.

3. A copy of the measuring instrument is available on request from the author. The measuring instrument consists of all information items mandated to be disclosed in corporate annual reports under the regulatory regime that was operational in Zimbabwe in 1994 (i.e., the Companies Act, the

adopted IASs and the listing rules of the ZSE). A disclosure item is defined as "each separately stated requirement to disclose a number and/or piece of information" in any of the three regulatory sources (Barth and Murphy 1994, 2).

4. In one study, it was proven that the equal weighting system is superior to the differential weighting system (Einhorn and Hogarth 1975). Wallace and Naser (1995) have, however, stated that a cautious approach should be taken in advancing the argument of equivalence of results of the two scoring systems. On the basis of a simple test conducted by Wallace and Naser, they concluded that the equivalence of the results of the two systems reported in those cited studies do not always hold.

5. The alternate procedure relevant to disclosure studies, but not used in this study, involves the exclusion of the inapplicable information items from the index and the subsequent analysis based on the index. Wallace and colleagues (1999) used a variant of this approach. The exclusion of items approach is appropriate if relatively few disclosure items are inapplicable to the sample companies. A potential problem with this approach is that the exclusion of the inapplicable items can bias the representativeness of the findings of the study (Babbie 1994). Similarly, the inclusion of the items can also influence the nature of the results. In short, the findings of the study may not reflect the true mandatory disclosure practices of the sample companies.

6. The independent scorer is a United Kingdom qualified certified accountant with several years of post qualification experience in both public practice and academia.

7. This procedure is to identify those disclosure items and regulatory sources that were complied with, and those that were not complied with, so that policymakers in Zimbabwe can take corrective actions. For the sake of the item-by-item comparative analysis, two extreme standpoints were taken. Thus, while recognizing that partial compliance (i.e., when a sample company discloses some of the applicable required information items) is better than noncompliance, partial compliance was considered noncompliance. Companies who *partially* complied with applicable mandated items and those who *did not comply* with the applicable mandated items were grouped into one category (under the title "Not Disclosing" in Table 3), and then compared with those companies that complied with *all* the applicable mandated items (see the last two columns of Table 3). The approach adopted in this study differs from that of Solas (1994). In Solas (1994), there were three categories of compliance levels: "noncompliance" which refers to compliance within the range of 0-10 percent of applicable items; "partial compliance" which refers to disclosure of 11-60 percent of applicable items; and "satisfactory compliance" which refers to disclosure of 61 percent and over of applicable items.

REFERENCES

Accounting Standards Board. 1994. *Statements of Principles*. London: Accounting Standards Board.

Ahmed, K., and D. Nicholls. 1994. The impact of non-financial company characteristics on mandatory disclosure compliance in developing countries: The case of Bangladesh. *The International Journal of Accounting* 29 (1): 62-77.

Al-Hashim, D., and J. Arpan. 1992. *International Dimension of Accounting* (3rd ed.). Boston: PWS-Kent Publishing Co.

Ashton, R. H. 1974. The predictive-ability criterion and user prediction models. *The Accounting Review* 49 (4): 719-732.

Babbie, E. R. 1994. *The Practice of Social Research* (7th ed.). Belmont, CA: Wadsworth Publishing.

Baiman, S. 1975. The evaluation and choice of internal information systems within a multiperson world. *Journal of Accounting Research* 13 (1): 1-15.

Barth, M. E., and C. M. Murphy. 1994. Required financial statement disclosures: Purposes, subject, number and trends. *Accounting Horizons* 8 (4): 1-22.

Buzby, S. L. 1975. Company size, listed versus unlisted stocks and the extent of financial disclosure. *Journal of Accounting Research* 13 (1): 16-37.

Carmines, E. G., and R. A. Zeller. 1979. *Reliability and Validity Assessment*. Beverly Hills, CA: Sage Publications.

Cerf, R. A. 1961. *Corporate Reporting and Investment Decisions*. Berkeley, CA: The University of California Press.

Choi, F. D. S. 1973. Financial disclosure and entry to the European capital market. *Journal of Accounting Research* 11 (2): 159-175.

Cooke, T. E. 1989. Disclosure in the corporate annual reports of Swedish companies. *Accounting and Business Research* 19 (74): 113-124.

Dhaliwal, D. S. 1980. Improving the quality of corporate financial disclosure. *Accounting and Business Research* 10 (40): 385-391.

Einhorn, H. J., and R. M. Hogarth. 1975. Unit weighting schemes for decision making. *Organizational Behavior and Human Performance* 13 (2): 171-192.

Emory, C. W. 1976. *Business Research Methods*. Homewood, IL: Richard D. Irwin.

Frost, C. A., and G. Pownall. 1994. Accounting disclosure practices in the United States and the United Kingdom. *Journal of Accounting Research* 32 (1): 75-102.

Hirshleifer, J. 1971. The private and social value of information and the reward of incentive activity. *The American Economic Review* 61 (4): 561-574.

Inchausti, B. G. 1997. The influence of company characteristics and accounting regulation on information disclosed by Spanish firms. *The European Accounting Review* 6 (1): 45-68.

International Finance Corporation. 1998. *Emerging Markets Factbook 1997*. Washington, DC: International Finance Corporation.

Jagetia, L. C., and E. C. Nwadike. 1983. Accounting systems in developing nations: The Nigerian experience. *The International Journal of Accounting Education and Research* 18 (2): 69-81.

Lang, M. H., and R. J. Lundholm. 1993. Cross-sectional determinants of analysts ratings of corporate disclosure. *Journal of Accounting Research* 31 (2): 246-271.

Libby, R. 1981. *Accounting and Human Information Processing: Theory and Application*. Englewood Cliffs, NJ: Prentice-Hall.

Marston, C. L. 1986. *Financial Reporting in India*. London: Croom Helm.

Meek, G. K., and S. J. Gray. 1989. Globalisation of stock markets and foreign listing requirements: Voluntary disclosures by continental European companies listed on the London Stock Exchange. *Journal of International Business Studies* 20 (2): 315-336.

Moore, M. L., and S. L. Buzby. 1972. The quality of corporate financial disclosure: A comment. *The Accounting Review* 47 (3): 581-584.

Oppong, A. 1993. Price-earnings research and the emerging capital markets: The case of Zimbabwe. *The International Journal of Accounting* 28 (1): 71-77.

Owusu-Ansah, S. 1998. The adequacy of corporate mandatory disclosure practices on emerging markets: A case study of the Zimbabwe Stock Exchange. Unpublished doctoral thesis, Middlesex University, England.

Ronen, J., and J. Livnat. 1981. Incentives for segment reporting. *Journal of Accounting Research* 19 (2): 459-481.

Sekaran, U. 1992. *Research Methods for Business: A Skill Building Approach* (2nd ed.). New York: John Wiley & Sons.

Singhvi, S. S., and H. B. Desai. 1971. An empirical analysis of the quality of corporate financial disclosure. *The Accounting Review* 46 (1): 621-632.

Skinner, D. J. 1994. Why firms voluntarily disclose bad news? *Journal of Accounting Research* 32 (1): 38-60.

Slovic, P. 1969. Analyzing the expert judge: A descriptive study of a stockbroker's decision processes. *Journal of Applied Psychology* 53 (4): 255-263.

Slovic, P., D. Fleissner, and W. S. Bauman. 1972. Analyzing the use of information in investment decision making. *Journal of Business* 45 (3): 283-301.

Solas, C. 1994. Financial reporting practice in Jordan: An empirical test. *Advances in International Accounting* 7: 43-60.

Spero, L. L. 1979. The extent and causes of voluntary disclosure of financial information in three European capital markets: An exploratory study. Unpublished doctoral thesis, Harvard University Graduate School of Business.

Tai, B. Y. K., P. K. Au-Yeung, M. C. M. Kwok, and L. C. W. Lau. 1990. Non-compliance with disclosure requirements in financial statements: The case of Hong Kong companies. *The International Journal of Accounting* 25 (2): 99-112.

Wallace, R. S. O. 1988. Corporate financial reporting in Nigeria. *Accounting and Business Research* 18 (72): 352-362.

Wallace, R. S. O., M. S. I. Choudhury, and A. Adhikari. 1999. Cash flow reporting in the United Kingdom: Some characteristics and firm-specific determinants. *The International Journal of Accounting* 34 (4): forthcoming.

Wallace, R. S. O., and K. Naser. 1995. Firm-specific determinants of the comprehensiveness of mandatory disclosure in the corporate annual reports of firms listed on the stock exchange of Hong Kong. *Journal of Accounting and Public Policy* 14 (4): 311-368.

Wallace, R. S. O., K. Naser, and A. Mora. 1994. The relationship between the comprehensiveness of corporate annual reports and firm characteristics in Spain. *Accounting and Business Research* 25 (97): 41-53.

Zarzeski, M. T. 1996. Spontaneous harmonization effects of culture and market forces on accounting disclosure practices. *Accounting Horizons* 10 (1): 18-37.